Communicating

A Social and Career Focus

Fifth Edition

Communicating

A Social and Career Focus

Fifth Edition

Roy M. Berko
Towson State University and
Lorain County Community College

Andrew D. Wolvin
University of Maryland
College Park and University College

Darlyn R. Wolvin
Prince George's Community College

Houghton Mifflin Company   Boston   Toronto

Dallas   Geneva, Illinois   Palo Alto   Princeton, New Jersey

Illustrations by Devera Ehrenberg.

Cover: *The Snail*, by Henri Matisse
        Tate Gallery, London/Art Resource, N.Y.

Printed in the U.S.A.

Library of Congress Catalog Card Number: 91-72005

ISBN: 0-395-59324-7

ABCDEFGH-D-9987654321

Contents

Preface

Perhaps never before in contemporary American history have we been so aware of the serious need for effective communication to address the problems facing our society. A social theorist identified this need for communicative interaction by stating, "Imperialist arrogance abroad, a collapse of the U.S. budget, racial polarization, and social disintegration at home have characterized this nation. These four ills are gnawing at the American society from the inside. They all have a common origin: The absence of true dialogue."[1] That dialogue encompasses both speaking and listening, and these are the major topics of this text.

What is This Book About?

We have begun each edition of *Communicating* by asserting the importance of communication and by indicating our firm belief that the communication skills of speaking and listening are essential to everyone's career and social success. This conviction has strengthened with each succeeding edition. Educational trends and research findings suggest that communication skills are essential for effective professional and social functioning. The Carnegie Foundation report on the undergraduate curriculum stresses, "To succeed in college, undergraduates should be able to write and speak with clarity and to read and listen with comprehension."[2] Moreover, businesses and industries, feeling that many of their employees do not possess these skills, spend large sums of money to teach their employees to communicate more proficiently.

This fifth edition retains the social and career focus of our previous writings. We have continued to combine theory with instruction on how to develop specific skills to help the reader communicate effectively.

The Structure of the Book

This text is built on a three-part framework. Part One, "Foundations of Communication," introduces basic theoretical concepts, including an overview of the communication process as well as verbal and nonverbal transactions, critical thinking, ethics, and listening.

[1] Francois de Vargbas, "Why It Is Necessary to Have Dialogue Today," *The University Reporter*, 1 (January 1991), p. 35.
[2] Ernest L. Boyer, *College: The Undergraduate Experience in America* (New York: Harper & Row, 1987), p. 73.

Part Two, "Personal Communication," covers intrapersonal and interpersonal communication. Personal relationships, communication apprehension, the interview, and small-group functions—among other topics—are discussed.

Part Three, "Public Communication," focuses on planning, developing, structuring, and presenting successful informative and persuasive briefings and speeches.

What is New in This Edition?

As always in planning a revision, we relied heavily on the astute advice and detailed reviews of instructors and students who have used past editions of *Communicating*. We also took the opportunity to update the text to address the latest curriculum and professional developments in the field of speech communication. As a result, we're confident that the following changes make this, the Fifth Edition of *Communicating*, the strongest yet:

- To reflect the growing diversity of the workplace and the classroom, the Fifth Edition contains more examples and discussion of cultural and ethnic diversity.
- Critical thinking and ethics—increasingly important topics—are given broader coverage throughout the Fifth Edition.
- Former Chapters 5 and 6 on language theory have been combined into a single chapter, increasing the focus on the practical over the theoretical aspects of language. The new Chapter 5, "The Foundations of Verbal Language," includes expanded discussion of male-female communication.
- A list of Learning Outcomes has been added at the beginning of each chapter to help students identify and master important material.

Other new or expanded topics in the Fifth Edition include informative speaking, interviewing, communication in organizations, decision making in groups, and communication in the service industry.

Acknowledgments

We wish to thank

Michelle Kost, University of Maryland–College Park, for her research assistance.

Dr. Charles Buckalew, Lorain County Community College, for his insightful advice on the subjects of ethics and logic.

Helen Shepard, Lorain County Community College, for her expert analysis of the section on Hispanic dialect.

The Reverend Ralph Hammond, for his evaluation of the material on Black English.

Eunice Berko, for her editorial assistance.

Those students and faculty at Prince George's Community College, University of Maryland–College Park, Lorain County Community College, and Towson State University, who have given us constructive suggestions on further refining the book.

We are indebted to our professional colleagues who read and critiqued the manuscript through its development.

Robert F. Edmunds, Marshall University
Lionel Grady, Southern Utah State College
Bruce C. McKinney, University of North Carolina at Wilmington
Harvey Pitman, Boise State University
William C. Schutzius, College of Mount Saint Joseph
Mark C. Setlow, Mesa Community College
Roynda Bowen Storey, Richland College
Chérie C. White, Muskingum Area Technical College

And so . . .

We hope that this book will have an impact on you, our reader—that this edition of *Communicating* will help you become more aware of the communication process and sensitive to its effect on you and others. We hope that you will be alerted to your responsibility, not only as a sender of messages, but also as a receiver—to become an analytical listener. Finally, we hope this book helps you to appreciate the role communication plays in all our lives and to seek improvement of your communication skills to assist you throughout your career and social life.

R. M. B.

A. D. W.

D. R. W.

Communicating

A Social and Career Focus

Fifth Edition

PART ONE

Foundations of Communication

1 Communication in Social and Career Settings

Chapter Outline

Learning
Outcomes

After reading this chapter you should be able to:

Identify the importance of communication in your personal and professional life

Illustrate the role of communication throughout the stages of life

State the effects of communication on couples, on families, and across cultures

Relate the effects of mass media on communication

Identify the functions of internal and external communication in business

Identify the role of communication in the health care, service, industry, education, law enforcement, and technical fields.

*D*uring our waking hours, we are constantly communicating in a variety of ways and settings, both sending and receiving messages. As adults we spend as much as 42 percent of our total verbal communication time as listeners and 40 percent of our overall communication time as speakers. Only 15 percent of our communication time is spent reading, and 11 percent is spent writing.[1]

Because we spend so much time in oral communication, effective communication skills are vital to all of us. Indeed, you are probably enrolled in this communication course to improve your communication skills and to become a more knowledgeable communicator. Employers look for employees who are effective communicators, and most successful people in our society have strong communication skills. In a popular autobiography the head of the Chrysler Corporation stressed that communication skills—both speaking and listening—are important to successfully motivate people.[2] Courses in speech communication can help you gain these skills.

During any given day, you may talk to your friends, listen to members of your family, receive correspondence, observe and react to the gestures and facial expressions of others, and even carry on conversations with yourself. You—like all people—are a communicating being. "Communication is the way relationships are created, maintained, and destroyed."[3] Every day we depend on our abilities to speak, listen, write, read, think, and interpret nonverbal messages. Without these abilities, we would lose much of what makes us human. As you begin your study of human communication, use the following definitions to establish a framework for understanding this complex process.

Communication Defined

Human communication is a conscious or unconscious, intentional or unintentional process in which feelings and ideas are expressed in verbal and nonverbal messages. This process can be accidental (having no intent), expressive (resulting from the emotional state of the person), or rhetorical (resulting from specific goals of the communicator).[4] Human communication occurs on intrapersonal, interpersonal, and public levels. Such communication is dynamic, continuous, irreversible, interactive, and contextual.[5]

Intrapersonal communication takes place within the person. It encompasses such activities as thought processing, personal decision making, and determination of self-concept. **Interpersonal communication** refers to communication in which the participants exchange feelings and ideas. Forms of interpersonal communication include conversations, interviews, and small-group discussions. **Public communication** is characterized by a speaker sending a message to an audience. Public communication may be direct, such as a face-to-face message delivered by a speaker to an audience, or indirect, such as a message relayed through radio or television.

Human communication is *dynamic* because the process is constantly in a state of change. As the attitudes, expectations, feelings, and emotions

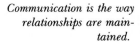

Communication is the way relationships are maintained.

of persons who are communicating change, the nature of their communication does so as well.

Communication is *continuous* because it never stops. Whether asleep or awake, we are each processing ideas and information through our dreams, thoughts, and expressions. Our brains remain active; we are communicating.

Communication is *irreversible*. Once we send a message, we cannot undo it. Once we make a slip of the tongue, give a meaningful glance, or make an emotional outburst, we cannot erase it. Our apologies or denials cannot eradicate what has taken place.

Communication is *interactive*. We are constantly in contact with other people and with ourselves. Other people react to our speech and actions, and we react to our own speech and actions and then react to those reactions. Thus a cycle of action and reaction becomes the basis for our communication.

This highly complex process of communication is *contextual* because it is very much a part of our entire human experience. The complexity of communication dictates that we develop the awareness and the skills necessary to function effectively as communicators. In our careers and in our personal lives we participate in this human process.

Communication in Social Settings

The social communication in which we participate parallels the stages we go through in life. Understanding how people communicate in each stage can help us strengthen communication within our families, with people in different cultures, and with other people in our own society. In addition, we can strengthen our communication skills by understanding the profound effect the mass media has on our communication. It is helpful, then, to consider the impact of the stages of life on the development of our communication patterns.

Communication and the Stages of Life

We pass through various stages in our lives. "During the passages, how we feel about our way of living will undergo subtle changes."[6] These changes are reflected in both our intrapersonal communication and interpersonal communication. Because most of you have passed through childhood and your early teenage years, the communication influences on your current life stages—the late teens and beyond—are the basis for this analysis.

The Late Teens and the Trying Twenties

After about the age of eighteen, most Americans begin to pull up roots and leave home to go to college, enter the world of work, or start a family. Whichever path we choose, new environments, activities, and

Starting down the Road of Life.

people bring new communication situations to which we must adjust. This is a period in which we test our beliefs. We are drawn to fads, look to our contemporaries instead of our parents for approval and emotional support, and zero in on the task of bridging the passage from one stage to another. "The task of our passage is to locate ourselves in a peer group role, a sex role, or an anticipated occupation, an ideology or world view."[7] We must also learn to use communication to help us in the passage.

Later, as we enter the trying twenties, we ask ourselves, Where do we go from here? Although it may not seem so at the time, this period of life is considerably more stable than the teenage years that preceded it and some of the periods that will follow it. During this stage, our major efforts focus on preparing for our life's work, finding a mate (if that is part of our plan), and building the life we have chosen. Usually we follow the pattern that is traditional for those who have been brought up in a religious, economic, and cultural environment similar to ours. If that pattern is to go to college, get a job, and marry, then this is what we are most likely to do. The trying twenties also offers us a chance to experiment with various roles, to explore different ways of living, and to continue to experiment in the most effective way to use communication to aid in the passage.

While traveling the path through the twenties, we are constantly being placed in positions that force us to either use communication skills or suffer from our lack of them. Thus the more prepared we are to cope with the communication requirements of college, employment interviews, jobs, and one-to-one relationships, the more likely we are to have a positive experience during this stage of life.

The Catch-30s

The thirties bring us to a point in life that is summarized by the word *should*. At this age, we often feel hemmed in and restricted—a feeling that can lead to personal conflict because we may have difficulty accepting the need for change or convincing ourselves that the patterns we have chosen can and must be altered. But we may also try to seek out new careers and change the life we made during our twenties. Either the feeling of restriction or the search for change may result in interpersonal conflicts with spouses, children, and employers. We may attack these people when, in fact, the conflict results not from anything they have done but from our own frustrated desire to alter our lives. Because we feel "stuck" with remnants of past decisions and actions—career, family, or even home—we may unwittingly take out our resentment on others.

One common response during the thirties is to strike out on a new road and engage in new activities. The unmarried often search out mates; women with young children may return to school or get jobs; couples may separate and divorce; people may change careers.

Again, those who cope well with the stress of the Catch-30s usually have a clear understanding of themselves and possess the communication skills to deal with the questions that confront them *and* the answers to those questions—how to make changes, which people to confront, how to discuss issues rather than fight about them, and how to be assertive.

The Midlife Years

Midlife, the period between the ages of forty and fifty-five, may be tougher than adolescence; it may, as one observer wrote, be "a time of great anguish."[8] The crisis that occurs during this period results from many sources: unclear female and male sexual roles, which are one result of the feminist movement and the new openness of the homosexual community; the emphasis our society places on youth; uncertainty about jobs; impending old age; and questions about the purpose of the life we have lived and the life we have left to live. Handled poorly, the midlife crisis can lead to such disastrous consequences as alcoholism, drug abuse, a broken family, financial troubles, mental disorders, and even suicide.[9] Increasingly, caring for aging parents has become one of

Continuing along the Road of Life.

the pressures of the midlife years. Because of medical advances, people are living longer, and as a result families often include the elderly. Couples who find themselves with children still at home and with older parents who need assistance may be living the life of the "sandwich generation." They are caught between the pressures of balancing all of these needs and maintaining careers and personal lives.

Sometime between the ages of forty and fifty-five, each of us experiences a **marker event.**[10] This is an incident that leads us to realize that we are no longer young, that we are vulnerable to failure and even to death. The incident may occur when our last child leaves home, when we are passed over for a promotion, when a close friend dies, or when, even though everything in our careers and lives seems to be accomplished, we are still not satisfied.

During this period of life, we come to recognize that we are not perfect, not ideal. But we must look at both the positive and negative sides. What have we accomplished? What have we still not done? If we approach this time creatively, we keep our options open, leave ourselves room to explore. The alternative is a destructive approach: drowning our troubles in booze, throwing everything—job, marriage, family—away, or burning ourselves out.[11]

Those people who are able to cope effectively with this time of life seem to have developed a clear understanding of themselves through good use of communication skills, effective listening techniques, and a positive self-image. They are able to talk out their problems with those who have supported them in the past (such as spouses or best friends). Rather than bottling up their frustrations, they decide when and to whom they can turn for support and assistance. From these people we can see that the ability to communicate effectively with self and others is essential to the successful weathering of the middle years.

And Beyond   The U.S. Bureau of the Census has estimated that there are almost 32 million people aged sixty-five years or older in America.[12] This represents a continuing, significant increase in the percentage of older persons in our population.

During our middle years and beyond, we may well have the most influence on others. Our communication skills should come into full play as we recognize that, despite our culture's apparent stress on youth, most of the people with the real power in American society are older than forty. Indeed, the average age of those in the upper echelons of business is fifty-four; in addition, people beyond the age of forty control most of this nation's wealth.

Because older Americans often live apart from their children, they can be plagued by loneliness and emotional insecurity. At a time when personal support is most needed, the best source of that support—the family—may be far away. But even if the aged are near their families, their emotional and physical dependence on their children sometimes creates a role reversal that makes communication more difficult.

Transitional Effects on Communication   As our roles in both family relationships and career positions change throughout these stages of life, our communication patterns also change. Where once we debated how to bring up the children, we now wonder what to do with retirement income. In many instances, when children leave home, couples revert to the communication patterns they used before they had children. Some individuals move to different areas of the country and have to forge new bonds and make new friends. Communication becomes the basis for developing these new relationships.

Those who adjust smoothly to such transitions as retirement, the death of a spouse, and relationships with new friends and colleagues are those who have a positive self-image and who are able to communicate effectively with themselves and with others.

Couple Communication   One area of communication that is profoundly affected by life's stages is couple communication. Couples in an intimate relationship must develop a bond of trust if they are to communicate openly with each other about their thoughts, desires, and feelings. The development of such a relationship involves considerable risk because a person does not know how far he or she can go in revealing desires and feelings and still receive support from a partner. And as the relationship necessarily evolves through life's stages, the risks in the relationship change, too.

Maintaining an intimate relationship requires continued adaptation and effective communication. People grow and change, and their relationships must do so as well. One of the major concerns of those who oppose marrying at an early age is that the couple has not had a chance to taste life as a whole and that one partner may grow in educational background and work experience, thereby leaving the other behind. In addition, the physical and emotional conditions that exist at the time of marriage do not remain the same. The cheerleader and the captain of the football team who get married right after graduation from high school may find that their "young love" undergoes a transformation when they have children, lose their physical attractiveness, or face financial worries. Unless these partners have some basis for growing together and have established communication patterns that allow for that growth, serious troubles can result.

Indeed, much of the success of a marriage or any intimate relationship may stem from having, and keeping open, channels of communication through which changing desires and feelings can be honestly expressed. Organizations such as Marriage Encounter have developed workshops and seminars to help couples develop healthy communication channels in their relationships and emphasize that effective communication is the key to a healthy relationship.

The number of divorces and separations at all ages of life and stages of marriage attests to the fact that traditional marriage patterns cannot be viewed as permanent.[13] In addition, the development of greater social awareness of and acceptance of nontraditional lifestyles—relationships between men and women of widely varying ages, homosexual relationships, and unmarried women bearing children—has led some to reassess just what makes up healthy couple communication. Whatever the nature of an intimate relationship, to handle the stresses and conflicts that arise over changing roles, responsibilities, and needs, a couple has to have strong communication skills.

Family Communication   The relationship between the partners in a couple changes with the addition of children—the partners are no longer just a couple; now they are part of a family group. Although some traditional marriage counselors suggest that having children can bring a couple closer together, the additional emotional, physical, and material responsibilities for children may in fact strain the relationship. For this reason, specialists in family communication recommend that couples recognize these strains and talk openly about them before deciding to have children.[14]

Family members should express their feelings directly and confront their problems head on.

Although the family unit is still considered the social standard in the United States, only about 7 percent of America's population fit the traditional family profile of mother, father, and children, with the father as the sole breadwinner. A modern family may consist of a single parent (male or female) with children, a two-career couple with or without children, a female breadwinner with child and househusband, a blended family of children from previous marriages, or a homosexual couple with or without children.[15] Each of these configurations requires special communication skills.

The creation of a family with children brings about a new and different unit of communication as parents and children become increasingly dependent on each other for assistance and emotional support. We are born into a family, we grow up within a family, we mature and become separate from a family, we create a new family by using information and behavior learned from the original family, and when we die, we diminish a family. Families surround us and contribute to our destiny.[16]

Numerous books on child-parent relationships stress the importance of good communication in family relationships. One writer urges family members to express their feelings directly and confront their problems head-on. He also stresses the importance of identifying who "owns" what problems so that parents do not transfer their problems to their children or vice versa.[17] Another offers practical skills for improving the verbal messages that parents send to their children by stressing the need for attention to verbal and nonverbal messages in the home to enhance the family's communication patterns.[18]

A major problem facing many families is the breakdown of the extended family unit. The members of the **nuclear family** (mother, father, and children) in past generations were often surrounded by the **extended family** (grandparents, aunts, uncles, and cousins). Now, because of the increased mobility of American life, people often cannot turn to a family member when they need help. As a result, sources outside the family—friends, social service agencies, institutions, psychologists, ministers—become important means of family support. But if these sources of support cannot communicate effectively, family problems may remain unresolved and may continue to be frustrating.

A further difficulty for many families today is that elusive commodity—time. When both parents work and their children are in school (or working themselves in after-school jobs), there is little time for communication within the family. Although an emphasis on "quality," rather than "quantity," time may offer some comfort to working parents, the realities of time pressures cannot be ignored. School children may face hours of after-school homework as well as nonacademic activities, and scheduling an entire family's activities can become a logistical nightmare. Time to communicate can be precious and may require some priority in a family's busy schedule.

The maintenance of effective family communication requires adaptation to the needs and expectations of all family members. The differing ages of the family members may also affect family communication, but too often the label *generation gap* is used to hide the realities of a "communication gap." An effort should be made to understand the varied communication needs of all members of the family, from the youngest to the oldest. Family life is an endless series of small events, periodic conflicts, and sudden crises that call for responses. Knowing something about the communication channels within the family can assist family members in strengthening their communication with one another. According to family communication specialists, a family system that is unexamined by its members usually has more communication problems than one that is not.[19]

The responsive family consists of individuals who effectively use communication skills to maintain a healthy family unit. The communication skills of coping, respecting self and others, and recognizing the consequences of communication on all members of the family can be used productively to strengthen family ties.

Intercultural Communication   Communication skills require further modification when used outside the context of familiar family and local community environments. The expansion of businesses around the world and the ability to travel far

Organizations and individuals need an understanding of intercultural communication.

and wide bring many of us into contact with people from other cultures. The interconnectedness of the economies and cultures of the world has given rise to a new "world view." Theorists who have tracked such changes describe the world view this way:

> The cold war ended in the last years of the 1980's, and the arms race has been slowed, perhaps even halted. The postwar period of nationalism and ideological cold war is over, and a new era of globalization has begun. The arts are flourishing worldwide. There is an international call to environmentalism. Communist countries experiment with democracy and market mechanisms. Among nations, the desire for economic cooperation is stronger than the urge for military adventure with its huge human and financial costs.[20]

The demands placed on the communication skills of all of us as a result of this shift have led to an emphasis on **intercultural communication**—communication between one culture and another. Edward T. Hall, the prominent anthropologist whose work is at the forefront of our understanding of intercultural communication, argued that "we don't need more missiles and H-bombs nearly so much as we need more specific knowledge of ourselves as participants in culture."[21] This knowledge centers on communication patterns within and across cultures.

Intercultural communication requires a thorough understanding of a particular culture and its communication patterns. To function effectively in China, for instance, an American diplomat should be familiar with Chinese language and culture and know what adaptations are necessary to communicate, both verbally and nonverbally, with the Chinese. In addition, the U.S. forces that were sent to the Persian Gulf in response to Iraq's 1990 invasion of Kuwait quickly discovered "they were not in the U.S. anymore." In compliance with Muslim customs, troops were denied access to alcoholic beverages and were required to limit their display of religious emblems and ceremonies. Indeed, George Bush and Saddam Hussein reflected two completely different cultures in their communication styles and messages.

Another crucial factor in intercultural communication is the recognition that "what people need most when they go overseas is to understand themselves better as Americans—because when they go they will carry with them all the 'cultural baggage' they have accumulated during their lifetimes."[22] These lifetime experiences form the basis from which we deal with and understand ourselves and others.

Intercultural communication is also important to us in other ways. The number of immigrants who continue to enter the United States increases our daily contact with different cultural patterns. As a student, you may find yourself in classrooms with students from around the world as well as from around the country. Even if you do not, each evening television brings other cultures into your living room. Or you may be brought into contact with different cultures through relatives born overseas or influenced by parents or grandparents who were.

Intercultural communication skills are also important in the world of work. Consultants to foreign business travelers suggest using the group's cultural patterns to aid communication. Stressing that "it is easier to communicate with foreigners by doing it their way," the authors of *Going International* recommend that "wherever you go, you must watch how the local people who are respected get information from one another and how they try to get it from you."[23] This communication strategy can be useful whether you find yourself communicating with people from China, Hawaii, New York City, or rural Nebraska.

As the world grows smaller, our opportunity to interact with people from many different cultures grows. Here in the United States, major metropolitan areas are facing the impact of populations consisting of many varied ethnic and racial groups. Some school systems have faced the challenge by offering bilingual educational opportunities to children from families where English is not the native language, and entire communities have had the opportunity to adapt to different cultural patterns and practices.

This multidimensional understanding of culture even extends to the workplace. Managers today are recognizing that they can accomplish their organization's goals more successfully if they understand their organization's culture. Most observers of business environments agree that communication is the key to building and maintaining strong cultures in organizations.[24]

Whether in the corporation or in the international neighborhood, culture and communication are closely linked. International students often note that one of their first impressions of Americans is that we keep considerable distance between us when we talk. (In contrast, in many other parts of the world people stand closer together when they converse.) Many foreign students at first think that this distance indicates that Americans are cold and aloof. After awhile, however, most international students realize that this is just an American communication pattern, that we are not particularly comfortable at close ranges, and that we are not displaying aloofness.

From all these examples, we can see that the effective intercultural communicator possesses an understanding of the behaviors and patterns of other cultures *and* of his or her own culture. The latter helps the communicator to recognize that one culture's approach to the world may not be the only, or even the best, one. Although we all have our own ethnocentric view of the world, we must set aside this view if we are to establish communication bonds with persons from other cultures. Such a challenge is difficult but essential in building skill in intercultural communication.

The Effects of the Mass Media on Social Communication

The development of our communication skills is influenced by many forces, among them the mass media. In fact, researchers reported that "between the ages of 6 and 18 the average child spends 15,000 to 16,000 hours in front of a television set. The same child spends about 13,000 hours in school."[25] It is estimated that 98 percent of American homes have one color television set, while 65 percent have two or more sets.[26]

This wide exposure to the mass media has many effects on Americans. Research on the effects of television indicates that the more time children spend watching television, the worse they do on achievement tests. Other findings indicate that television molds the intelligence and character of youths far more than most formal schooling does. Incredibly, in the first twenty years of an American's life, he or she usually views almost one million television commercials, which makes commercials the most influential source for the nation's youths. In addition, because of the structure of television programs, with beginnings, middles, and endings in prescribed time segments, some critics fear that children view television as a quick fix and come to believe that all problems can be taken care of in a short thirty- or sixty-minute time frame.[27] This can breed in children an expectation that their real needs can, and should, be satisfied quickly. When that does not happen, the resulting frustration may lead to a need to mask reality through such escapes as drugs or alcohol.

In addition to influencing how we see ourselves, the mass media shape our views of the world and our social relationships. This is particularly true in regard to television: since 1963, television has led all other media as the source for news in the United States.[28] Through the media, especially television, we are bombarded with stereotypes about youth, old age, sex and sex appeal, relationships, the use of leisure time, and basic needs. The influence of these messages can be seen in the changing attitudes since television began to reach millions of homes. For example, one common American belief is summed up by the catch phrase "I deserve the best." Commercials have told us again and again that this attitude is right and proper and that we can be the best by buying the correct product (whether it be a hair color, a cola drink, or a car). This expectation may be carried over into the world of work, where an employee feels that he or she deserves high wages and benefits regardless of the quality of the work done. And it may also be carried over into the schools, where a student feels entitled to high grades even with minimal efforts.

When considering the influences of the mass media, we should remember that commercial television programs are primarily designed to entertain. To get a show on the air, producers must secure sponsors that are willing to pay an exorbitant amount of money to air their commercials.[29] Because airtime is so expensive, programming must be approached cautiously so as to avoid alienating any segments of the audience and at the same time to convince viewers to purchase the sponsor's products. Consequently, shows are frequently written to appeal to the masses or to avoid offending any potential product users rather than to serve a true educational purpose.

Another belief shaped by the media is our attitude toward violence. Research that has assessed the impact of violence depicted on television has shown how it may alter our view of the world. According to one study, "Violence on television leads viewers to perceive the real world as more dangerous than it really is, which must also influence the way people behave."[30] Some people have even become afraid to leave their homes because they fear that the real world holds the same all-encompassing violence as the TV world does.

Nevertheless, despite these problems, some television programming does deal with significant social issues. Programs have gone beyond entertainment to deal with such topics as sexual abuse, alcoholism, acquired immune deficiency syndrome (AIDS), and child abuse. The media have given instant reports on breaking news stories, thereby allowing viewers to experience firsthand the strife of war, the plight of developing nations, the dismantling of communist regimes, successes and disasters in space exploration, and weather around the world.

Television also serves an important role as adviser, alerting people to present and future problems. The perils of an atomic attack, political conflicts in other countries, analyses of presidential debates and campaigns, and national health tests have all become a regular part of television programming. Shows such as "Sesame Street" continue to help young children learn such concepts as numbers, the alphabet, American Sign Language, and Spanish.

One media educator has suggested that as television viewers, we can best deal with the influences of the medium by learning to watch programs critically. For example, we should recognize that (1) each part of a program is planned for effect, (2) the number of cameras and their angles can affect what is conveyed, (3) the message is secondary to production choices for "good" pictures to make for "good" television, (4) the editing process can create the message, (5) television almost always requires the use of the sensational, violent, or bizarre, (6) television requires constant technical manipulation to maintain viewer attention, and (7) broadcast television is a business.[31] Being aware of these factors can assist us in using television rather than letting it use us.

Communication in Career Settings

We communicate not only in social settings but also in career settings. Consequently, our relationships with others also depend on effective communication in the workplace. We normally succeed in a career through good work and through communication of that work to supervisors, peers, and subordinates. Although persons involved in such fields as health, public service, engineering, and education require particularly effective means of sending and receiving messages, people in all careers depend on communication tools as the basis for success.

Communication in Business

Managers have come to recognize the increasingly vital role of communication in the functioning of any government, business, or industrial organization and the need for communication training. One management consultant, in summarizing the significance of communication, said, "Failure to make your point quickly and effectively can result in millions of dollars of lost business. Communication failure not only can destroy the chances for a successful sale, it can severely limit the career advancement of otherwise highly qualified persons."[32] A study of Master of Business Administration graduates revealed that skill in "oral persuasiveness" ranks as the most important skill in business.[33] Yet another study indicated that engineers need extensive communication skills in their work.[34]

Effective management *is* effective communication. It has been suggested that the new task of the manager "involves communication and collaboration across functions, across divisions, and across companies whose activities and resources overlap."[35] Nevertheless, most organizations still need work on their communication. A survey of chief executive officers disclosed that 97 percent of the company executives believed that personally communicating with employees had a positive impact on job satisfaction, and 79 percent felt that personal communication benefited the bottom line of company profits, yet only 22 percent of the respondents actually engaged in personal communication on a daily or weekly basis.[36] This study led one communication executive to conclude that "effective one-to-one communication skills will be a key component of a manager's job description, and the training of managers in a basic communication skills will become commonplace."[37]

A successful corporation depends not only on individual communicators but also on effective communication throughout the organization. Analysts have found that corporate excellence consists of eight characteristics. One of these, "management by wandering around," is the communication strategy of listening and responding to workers, customers, suppliers, and the organization's publics (specialized subgroups or a larger national or international population). Effective management requires that managers be in touch with all segments of an organization, and the only way to be in touch is through effective communication.[38]

As people get in touch in government and business, they find communication necessary at different levels. People in organizations must communicate both internally (with people inside the organization) and externally (with people and organizations outside the company).

The new emphasis on the team approach to production has brought about new communication formats between management and workers. (Photo courtesy Saturn Corporation)

**Internal
Communication**

If you are a member of an organization, you communicate at various levels for different purposes. Initially, you may communicate for the purpose of securing a position with the organization. This step requires enough skill in interviewing to convince the personnel officer to hire you. Once you are employed, your communication goals shift; you become concerned with developing and maintaining effective relationships with your coworkers, your supervisor, and your subordinates. Much of the success of these relationships depends on effective communication. Communication can help you to adapt to your changing roles and fulfill the expectations others have for you in the organization.

Organizations often develop formal channels of communication to facilitate their internal workings. Frequently, an organization will establish these channels through formal flow charts (Figure 1.1) and informal procedures (Figure 1.2) that specify what member of a company is responsible to what other persons for communicating ideas and information. Communication analysts recognize, however, that informal channels of communication are as important as—if not more important than—formal channels to the actual functioning of an organization.[39]

For many years, the standard operational procedure for most American businesses was a **top-down process** of communication in which the orders were sent from the chief officer (often the president or the chairperson of the board) to individuals who ranked lower on the corporate chain of command. An order from the president to the vice president, for instance, might then have been passed down to the supervisor, then to the foreman, and finally to the worker who actually had to carry out the task.

The nature of work and the type of communication used in the work environment have changed, however. American workers are asking to participate more in the communication process in most organizations. Thus the **bottom-up process,** based on the concept that change and initiative within an organization should come from those closest to the problem, has given a new emphasis to the team approach. This process has resulted in new communication formats for interaction among management and workers. Those employees who are closest to the product being produced or the service being provided now have opportunities to participate more fully in the decision-making process. They are able to suggest alterations and improvements that can aid in the development of better products and services.[40]

One example of the bottom-up communication process is the system of **quality circles,** by which a group of workers can come together to analyze a work-oriented problem and determine solutions for resolving it. The group then communicates its recommendations to upper management for processing and implementation. This format provides a systematic, official means for communicating decisions upward in an organization. Many American corporations have borrowed quality circle

Figure 1.1

*Formal Communication
Channels Within the
Formal Organization*
(From *Contemporary Management Concepts* by Bernard
Deitzer, Karl Shillif, and Michael Jucius. Grid Publishing, Inc., Columbus, Ohio,
1979, p. 183, by permission
of John Wiley and Sons,
Inc.)

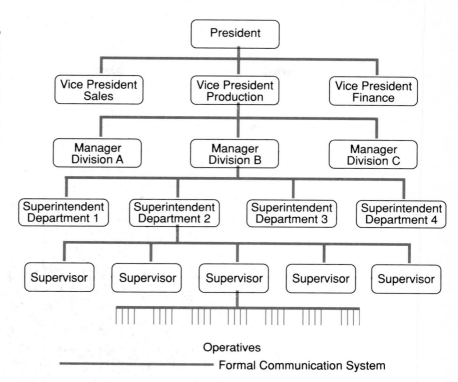

techniques from Japanese quality of work life management strategies, which are based on a high level of worker participation in the decision-making process.

The bottom-up communication process has had a significant impact in organizations. Corporations that use quality circles, suggestion boxes, improvement teams, participative goal setting, and other such strategies have discovered that turning to employees can help cut expenses, increase revenues, and develop new lines of business. As one expert in business communication indicates, "Line employees know what the problems are, and they are frequently in a position to develop innovative solutions. And employees who are asked to participate in a company's decision-making process tend to be more motivated and more productive than when they are 'just doing their job.' "[41]

Advanced technology has had a profound impact on internal communication in today's organizations. The computer is now standard office equipment. As a result, people at all levels in organizations frequently interact more directly with computer screens than with other people. Organizations have developed elaborate electronic mail systems enabling employees to send instant messages to each other, even to remote sites around the world. Telephone technology likewise has developed to a

Figure 1.2

Typical Informal Communication Channels
(From *Contemporary Management Concepts* by Bernard Deitzer, Karl Shillif, and Michael Jucius. Grid Publishing, Inc., Columbus, Ohio, 1979, p. 183, by permission of John Wiley and Sons, Inc.)

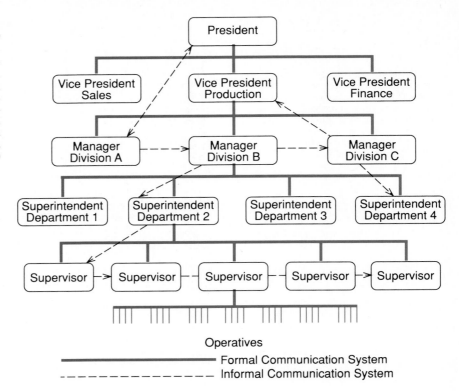

Operatives

━━━━━━━━━━━━━━ Formal Communication System
────────────── Informal Communication System

high level of sophistication so that voice mail and other features offer such options as teleconferences, voice memos, message answering machines, and computerized dialing.

All of these advances are designed to improve the flow of information so that an organization's communication process can be efficient and effective, and once the glitches are worked out, these technologies can improve the process of communication. The frustration, however, comes with technological breakdowns. In New York, for instance, an AT&T cable that could handle one hundred thousand telephone calls at once was severed, leaving much of Manhattan without a telephone system during a workday. The disruption forced two major financial markets to close.[42] Even such negative occurrences indicate, however, how extensive is the impact of this technology and how much organization is required. "Organization is key in business. Just as bad information is useless, even good information is useless if you can't get at it quickly and easily."[43]

In addition to such formal internal channels of communication, informal channels such as the grapevine or the "rumor mill" serve important functions. The grapevine, which channels information informally from person to person, is regarded by some as a harmful influence because it spreads rumors, destroys morale and reputations, leads to irresponsible actions, and challenges authority. Others recognize, however, that the grapevine is a fast, effective way to pass along information quickly. The grapevine can also serve as a safety valve when people need to react strongly—what may not be communicated through formal channels may usefully be communicated through the informal grapevine. Organizations that have had to lay off workers, for instance, have found it useful to communicate the impending need to do so through the informal grapevine so that employees are prepared for the bad news before it is officially conveyed. Although this approach seems questionable, legal restrictions may necessitate it.

Clearly, both informal and formal internal channels of communication are an important part of any organization. One major key to organizational productivity and effectiveness is the extent to which these channels are operational and open for both upward and downward communication. Indeed, many organizations today have in-house communication departments with specialists who focus on the organization's internal communication functions and external communication needs. The Bank of America, IBM, Northwestern Mutual Life (insurance company), and Southern California Edison Co. are just four examples of such corporations.[44]

External Communication

An organization depends not only on internal communication channels but also on external communication with its publics. Because increasing corporate competition has brought about the need to communicate corporate messages effectively, public relations have become more important in recent years. As organizations have come to recognize the value of communicating their mission, services, and products, public relations departments have grown in size and importance. So has the industry of public relations and advertising firms that contract as consultants. The formal efforts of public relations professionals can include television promotions, magazine and newspaper ads, direct-mail campaigns, speakers' bureaus, and radio announcements.

Chief executive officers frequently receive special training in public speaking and television presentational techniques. Many corporations even use executives and employees in their television commercials. In the late 1980s the president of the Chrysler Corporation became closely identified with his corporation through television commercials. The automaker's commercials, which stressed the contention that "I am the president of Chrysler, and I am giving you my assurance that we are producing quality products," were credited with being one of the major factors in the company's economic recovery.

**Employee
Communication
Training**

Organizations place a high value on the external and internal communication skills of their employees because these skills yield increased productivity and, ultimately, increased profits and services. In summarizing the research on organizational communication skills, one researcher discovered that the most important communication skills employees and managers need are listening, written communication, oral reporting, motivating/persuading, interpersonal skills, informational interviewing, and small-group problem solving.[45]

Because "workers often lack communication skills, such as the ability to express themselves accurately,"[46] corporate training has grown to be a $30 billion per year industry.[47] This lack of communication and technical skills has led to the creation of extensive training programs to develop the competencies of employees at all levels in the organization, from entry-level to executive personnel. For example, the U.S. government's training organization, the Office of Personnel Management, offers training for federal workers in such areas as basic communication skills, effective listening, effective briefing techniques, telephone strategies, voice and diction, interpersonal communication, and techniques for negotiating.

The training in and use of communication skills in the context of the organization's internal and external channels of communication have application in many specialized career fields. Just as corporate America has recognized the importance of communication in organizations, so, too, have health care professionals, educators, and a host of other specialists.

*Communication in
the Health Care
Field*

Serious problems in the delivery of health care services have surfaced within recent years. There is evidence that these problems are at least partially due to frequent miscommunication, unrealistic expectations, lack of sensitivity, and widespread dissatisfaction with the level of care offered to patients.

Health care professionals need effective communication skills if they are to work with patients in identifying the causes of disease, creating strategies for treatment, and gaining cooperation from colleagues, patients, and families for continued care. The clarity, timeliness, and sensitivity of communication in health care are often critical to the physical and emotional well-being of patients. Because communication has become so closely identified with good patient care, health care professionals are continually reminded to use effective communication with their patients. "When you see a withdrawn patient open up . . . to a comic situation," advised one nurse, "that's your chance to open a channel of communication. Jump at the opportunity."[48] In identifying the communication skills characteristic of physicians who communicate effectively with patients, one specialist concluded that situational adaptation, role flexibility, language choice, nonverbal behavior, questioning, listening, organizing, presenting, discussing, and managing are all important to the successful physician.[49]

Physicians and other health care professionals are aware that **pseudo-communication** (going through the motions of communicating without truly connecting) is a common problem, particularly during the course of a highly pressured day of treating many different patients. To counter this problem, health care professionals are advised: "If your conversations with patients are routine, superficial, or mechanical, chances are that static is obscuring the messages. And you're running the risk of being tuned out."[50] Dentists are also getting serious about improving their communication with patients. Some dentists now employ communication directors, and one Toronto dental office features a health communication area with comfortable chairs "where people can talk about their expectations without feeling threatened by dental equipment."[51]

"Communicating isn't so difficult," explained one nursing expert, "but it must be more than reciting verbal techniques. When a nurse (or any other health career professional) really cares about her patient, she should try to ensure an honest exchange of feelings. Good communication skills aren't built at the chart rack. They happen at the bedside."[52]

Effective communication between the patient and the medical practitioner is also a two-way street. Just as medical personnel are advised to improve their communication skills at the bedside, patients are also encouraged to speak up, ask questions, and listen more carefully to their physicians and nurses. The role of the patient in effective health care has become so prominent that the *Washington Post* includes a column, "The Patient's Advocate," in its health section each week. The column routinely offers suggestions to patients for gaining all the information they can about their condition before agreeing to any particular treatment prescribed or recommended by the health care professional. Patients need skill in asking for information and reassurance. And patients need to be certain that all their questions are answered.[53]

Communication in the health care field has gained considerable attention in the last few years. Other professional fields also recognize the value of effective communication with their clients and their publics.

Communication in the Service Industries

Corporate America has realized that the "competitive edge" for organizations today is the ability to offer solid service to their customers. Japanese management techniques provide the model for this stress on customer service. Nissan and Toyota automotive corporations, for instance, have established teams of automotive mechanics to service automobiles at dealerships. A customer deals directly with a service manager who is responsible for the team that will always work on that customer's auto. Thus what traditionally has been an impersonal activity becomes a per-

Students and teachers should be prepared to function effectively as communicators in the educational process.

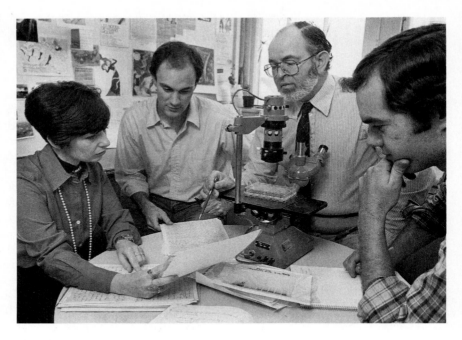

sonal service where the customer communicates with an identifiable person. The Seattle-based upscale department store chain, Nordstrom, stresses customer service as the main responsibility of all employees. The staff gets training that stresses how to communicate in a way that provides personalized service to each customer.

The key to delivering customer service is the utilization of personal communication channels. The service manager or sales associate who makes that extra effort to interact with customers and make them feel that their business is important to the company buys customer loyalty. And that loyalty affects profits, for research has found that it costs five times more to go out and get a new customer than it does to maintain any already existing customer.[54] Now that technology has depersonalized much of the way business is conducted, the human touch through effective interpersonal communication does make a difference to consumers in every industry.

Communication in Education

Another field where communication is recognized as critical to success is education. Educators depend on communication skills to fulfill their purpose—disseminating information, developing attitudes, and reinforcing and/or changing their students' behavior. The effective teacher is an effective communicator. Many schools of education require prospective teachers to take courses in speech communication, and teacher in-service programs frequently focus on such communication needs as parent-teacher interaction, classroom questioning techniques, and effective listening skills. One prominent educator characterized the skillful teacher as one who recognizes that "the heart of the teaching transaction is skilled oral communications. Teachers must consistently practice communication skills and encourage the practice of them by their students. The effective teacher is both a good speaker and a good listener. The latter may, indeed, be more important than the former."[55]

Educators have been challenged to provide speech communication training—much like the course you may currently be taking—in school systems. The 1978 federal Primary and Secondary Education Act added listening and speaking to the skills of reading, writing, and arithmetic as measures of literacy and as necessary basic competencies of all students. The Carnegie Commission reports on secondary and on higher education curricula called for more stress on oral communication skills and required courses in the field to prepare students as speakers and listeners.[56]

Because the effectiveness of the learning process depends to a high degree on teacher-learner interaction, it makes sense that all the participants in the educational process be prepared to function effectively as communicators. Students are expected to participate in class discussions, ask and answer questions, present reports, and listen extensively. Solid communication skills can be the key to academic as well as career success.

Communication in Law and Law Enforcement

Professionals in the legal field also function as communicators. They spend the majority of their time researching cases and preparing and presenting legal briefs in courtrooms throughout the nation. This profession requires considerable skill not only in presenting speeches but also in analyzing audiences for jury selection, interviewing, counseling, and listening to others. Recognizing the critical role of communication in the field, the American Bar Association's Legal Education Committee recommended that students entering the study of law "master, at the undergraduate level, advanced writing skills and effective oral communication."[57]

Despite the obvious importance of effective communication in the legal field, the typical law school curriculum sets aside little time for developing communication skills. As a result, some communication specialists consult extensively with attorneys and paralegal workers to assist them in gaining the background and abilities necessary to function skillfully as communicators. In a revealing study of criminal juror understanding, researchers discovered that the average juror comprehension of a typical set of standard instructions was only 72 percent, which led the investigators to conclude that "if lawyers are unable to communicate and understand the dynamics of complex communication processes, their clients will be ill-served and the public's need unfulfilled."[58]

Law enforcement officers are also constantly confronting situations in which communication skills may be much more than the basis for just completing their job responsibilities. Communication may literally be a matter of life or death. Police officers find themselves involved in family conflicts, suicide intervention, racial confrontations, hostage crises, and chain-of-command relationships that require skillful one-to-one communication. In addition, law enforcement personnel need good interviewing skills to gather and transmit information, process grievance procedures, reprimand subordinates, and appraise the accuracy of information. Testifying in court and speaking in public are also part of most police officers' job description.

Communication in Technical Fields

Yet another field that has come to recognize the important role of effective communication is the high-technology industry. Engineers, scientists, and computer specialists all must communicate their technical research concepts and findings to a variety of different publics. Of this need for effective communication, one technical writer said, "The work of the scientist and technician is not translated from potential (blueprints, equations, etc.) to actuality (superhighways, sun-powered generators, new antidotes for disease, etc.), until, and unless, the scientist can communicate to other scientists and to the general public."[59]

The technical specialist does indeed have a twofold communication challenge. He or she must communicate technical information to others in a clear, organized way that is appropriate to the listeners' backgrounds, knowledge, and expertise. But the specialist must also communicate technical information to a greater public—people who must be able to understand and potentially use the information. The agricultural research scientist, for instance, faces the problem of making his or her findings understandable to those that will actually apply the findings—working farmers. And the consumer may need to know something of research findings to understand how a particular commodity is processed or priced.

At all levels, the technician must communicate clearly, accurately, and effectively. Misinterpretations and incomplete messages can significantly alter the technical information and cause it to be ignored or misused. The technician, caught up in the procedures, processes, and language of his or her particular field, should always be aware of the potential for miscommunication and should strive for clarity and precision.

All professional fields have their own language and their own perspectives on basic concepts. It is only through effective communication that those in any particular field can function successfully with colleagues, supervisors, and the public.

Summary Social and career communication is a major part of human life. In this chapter, we explored the role of communication through several dimensions. The following list summarizes the major ideas presented in this chapter:

☐ We are constantly participating in the act of communicating.

☐ We go through various passages during our life that result in changes in our communication.

☐ The more prepared a person is to deal with the communication necessary to pass through life's stages, the more likely that person is to experience a positive transition.

☐ Couples in an intimate relationship must develop a bond of trust if they are to communicate openly with each other about their thoughts, desires, and feelings.

☐ Maintaining an intimate relationship requires continued adaptation and effective communication.

☐ Much of the success of a marriage, or any intimate relationship, may stem from having open channels of communication in which the partners can honestly express desires and feelings as their needs and wants change.

☐ The creation of a family with children brings about a new and different unit of communication.

☐ Maintenance of effective family communication requires adaptation to the needs and expectations of family members.

☐ Intercultural communication requires an understanding of a particular culture and its communication patterns.

☐ Our notion of social relationships is influenced greatly by the view communicated through the mass media, especially television.

☐ Buying patterns as well as social attitudes are developed through television.

☐ We normally succeed in a career through good work and through the communication of that good work to supervisors, peers, and subordinates.

☐ Communication skills are needed in all occupations.

☐ Management has come to recognize the increasingly vital role of communication in the functioning of any government, business, or industrial organization; thus the need for communication training is great.

☐ People in organizations communicate both internally and externally.

☐ Organizational channels of communication may be formal or informal.

☐ Advanced technology has had a significant impact on the communication channels in organizations.

☐ The grapevine, a common informal channel, often plays an important role in organizations.

☐ Effective communication is crucial in the dealings that health care professionals have with patients.

☐ Communication is critical to competencies in the service industry.

☐ Educators depend on communication skills to disseminate information, develop attitudes, and reinforce and/or change student behavior.

☐ Lawyers and law enforcement officers confront situations in which communication skills may make the difference between life and death.

☐ The technical specialist must use clear, accurate, and effective communication to convey technical information to those with varying levels of understanding.

☐ Communication is critical to effective functioning in all dimensions of human life.

Key Terms

human communication   extended family
intrapersonal communication   intercultural communication
interpersonal communication   top-down process
public communication   bottom-up process
marker event   quality circles
nuclear family   pseudocommunication

Learn by Doing

1. Discuss an experience you are going through or have gone through that illustrates one of the passages of life.

2. How open do you feel a couple's channels of communication should be? Do you feel these channels change with marriage? With cohabitation?

3. Think back to a relationship you have had that has ended. Why did it end? How did you communicate the ending of this relationship?

4. Do you feel the effect of television on the average American as described in this chapter is accurate or overstated? Cite some specific examples in support of your argument.

5. Contact an individual who holds a position similar to the one you would like to have. Set up an interview with this person to find out what communication skills are necessary for success in the position. Try to ascertain what percentage of this person's time is spent speaking and listening.

6. What is your image of such organizations as General Motors, Ex-

xon, Apple, IBM, American Telephone & Telegraph, Sony Corp., the U.S. Department of State, and the New York City government? How did you develop these images? Compare your images with those of other class members. To what extent are these images the result of accurate/inaccurate communication?

7. Do you feel that police officers are effective communicators? What is the basis for your views on this issue? How about physicians?

8. Observe an instructor you feel is an effective teacher. What communication skills make this person effective?

9. Reflect on the impact on communication of such technologies as the computer and the videocassette recorder. How have they changed the life of the average communicator? Have they changed your life?

10. Find literature about your major field (journals, popular magazines) and select an article that addresses communication in that field. Prepare a two-minute presentation that summarizes the article.

Notes

1. Paul Tory Rankin, "Listening Ability: Its Importance, Measurement, and Development," *Chicago School Journal,* 12 (January 1930), 177–179.
2. Lee Iacocca, *Iacocca: An Autobiography* (New York: Bantam Books, 1984), p. 57.
3. Jane Brody, "Effective Communication Involves More Than Talking," *Wichita Eagle-Beacon,* July 21, 1981.
4. Virginia P. Richmond and James C. McCroskey, *Communication: Apprehension, Avoidance, and Effectiveness* (Scottsdale, Ariz.: Grosuch, Scarisbrick, 1985), Chapter 1.
5. Based on David K. Berlo, *The Process of Communication* (New York: Holt, Rinehart and Winston, 1960).
6. Gail Sheehy, *Passages: Predictable Crises of Adult Life* (New York: Bantam Books, 1976), p. 30. The life stages discussed in this section are based on Sheehy's work.
7. Ibid., p. 39.
8. Al Pagel, "Mid-Life Crises: A Time of Great Anguish," *Omaha Sunday World Herald Magazine of the Midlands,* June 24, 1979, pp. 22–26.
9. Ibid., p. 22.
10. Sheehy, pp. 29–30, 395.
11. Pagel, p. 23.
12. U.S. Bureau of the Census, *Current Population Reports,* Series P-25, no. 1017 (Washington, D.C.: GPO, 1988).
13. The U.S. National Center for Health Statistics has noted that the divorce rate has leveled off and that since 1980 has even been declining; in 1986, it was at its lowest point since 1975. See "How to Stay Married," *Newsweek,* August 24, 1987, pp. 52–57.
14. Kathleen M. Galvin and Bernard J. Brommel, *Family Communication,* 2nd ed. (Glenview, Ill.: Scott, Foresman, 1986).

15. John Naisbitt, *Megatrends* (New York: Warner Books, 1982), p. 233.

16. Judy Goldberg, "Family Communications: Insideness and Outsideness," unpublished paper, Arapahoe Community College, Littleton, Colo.

17. Thomas Gordon, *P.E.T.: Parent Effectiveness Training* (New York: New American Library, 1975), p. 11.

18. Adele Faber and Elaine Mazlish, *How to Talk so Kids Will Listen and Listen so Kids Will Talk* (New York: Avon Books, 1980).

19. For an extended discussion about family systems, see Galvin and Brommel, pp. 27–41.

20. John Naisbitt and Patricia Aburdene, *Megatrends 2000* (New York: William Morrow, 1990), pp. 14–15.

21. Edward T. Hall, *The Silent Language* (New York: Doubleday/Anchor Press, 1973), p. 190.

22. L. Robert Kohls, *Survival Kit for Overseas Living* (Chicago: Intercultural Press, 1979), p. 2.

23. Lennie Copeland and Lewis Griggs, *Going International* (New York: Random House, 1985), p. 101.

24. Allan Kennedy, "Back-Yard Conversations: New Tools for Quality Conversations," *Communication World* (November 1984), 26.

25. Jack Mabley, "Blame It All on Television," *Elyria Chronicle-Telegram.* March 29, 1981, p. A-3, as reprinted from the *Chicago Tribune* report on Neil Postman's research.

26. *1990 Nielsen Report on Television* (New York: Nielsen Media Research, 1990), p. 3.

27. Mabley.

28. "Changing Public Attitudes Toward Television and Other Mass Media, 1959–1976" (New York: Roper Organization, 1976), p. 3.

29. The three major commercial networks (NBC, ABC, and CBS) charged $121,860 for an average thirty-second prime-time commercial in October 1987. NBC's "Cosby Show" was the most expensive, with an average of $369,500 for a thirty-second spot. For details, see Verne Gay, "Time Is Money to Nets," *Advertising Age,* January 4, 1988, pp. 3, 44.

30. George Gerbner and Larry Gross, "The Scary World of TV's Heavy Viewer," *Psychology Today,* 10 (April 1976), 45.

31. John Splaine, *The Critical Viewing of Television* (South Hamilton, Mass.: Critical Thinking Press, 1987), p. 61.

32. Thomas Gerdel, "Stress Verbal Arts, Consultant Advises," *Cleveland Plain Dealer,* September 18, 1973, p. C-1.

33. John Costello, "What You Need to Climb the Business Ladder," *Nation's Business,* 64 (June 1976), 6, 8.

34. "Education in Industry: Synopsis of the Joint ECAC-RWI Feedback Committee Report," *Journal of Engineering Education,* 55 (May 1965), 254–256.

35. Rosabeth Moss Kanter, "The New Managerial Work," *Harvard Business Review* (November–December 1989), 92.

36. Bob Fayfich, "The Changing Role of Internal Communications," *Intercom* (Westinghouse Corporation), as reprinted in *Syntax Newsletter,* no. 15 (Winter 1990–1991), 2.

37. Ibid.

38. Tom Peters and Nancy Austin, *A Passion for Excellence* (New York: Warner Books, 1985), Chapter 2.

39. U.S. General Accounting Office, "Difficulties in Evaluating Public Affairs Government-Wide and at the Department of Health, Education and Welfare," L:CD-79-405 (Washington, D.C.: General Accounting Office, January 18, 1979), p. 5.

40. John Baird, *Positive Personnel Practices: Quality Circles Leaders' Manual* (Prospect Heights, Ill.: Waveland Press, 1982).

41. Don Nichols, "Bottom-Up Strategies: Asking the Employees for Advice." *Management Review* (December 1989), 44.

42. John Burgess, "Severed Cable Disables N.Y. Markets, Airports," *Washington Post,* January 5, 1991, p. A3.

43. Dan Gutman, "The Automation Edge," *Success,* 34 (October 1987), 38. For a discussion of the effects of computers on human communication, see James W. Chesebro and Donald G. Bonsall, *Computer-Mediated Communication* (Tuscaloosa: University of Alabama Press, 1989).

44. Roy M. Berko, Andrew D. Wolvin, and Ray Curtis, *This Business of Communicating,* 4th ed. (Dubuque, Iowa: William C. Brown, 1990), pp. 138–142.

45. Vincent S. DiSalvo, "A Summary of Current Research Identifying Communication Skills in Various Organizational Contexts," *Communication Education,* 29 (July 1980), 283–290.

46. Seymour Lusterman, *Education in Industry* (New York: Conference Board, 1977), p. 2.

47. Anthony Patrick Carnevale, "The Learning Enterprise," *Training and Development Journal* (January 1986), 18.

48. Victor Cohn, "Putting Humor to Work," *Washington Post Health,* August 25, 1987, p. 8.

49. Barbara F. Sharf, *The Physician's Guide to Better Communication* (Glenview, Ill.: Scott, Foresman, 1984), p. 10.

50. Luanne Mercer, "Pseudo-Communication with Patients." *Nursing 80 Career Guide,* 10 (February 1980), 105–106.

51. Rona Maynard, "The Cavity Crisis," *Report on Business Magazine* (August 1987), 60.

52. Mercer.

53. Marilyn Elias, "Honesty's the Best Medicine for Doctor, Patient," *USA Today,* October 13, 1983, p. D-6.

54. Study by Technical Assistance Research Programs as reported in Tom Peters, *Thriving on Chaos* (New York: Knopf, 1988), p. 91.

55. Donald N. Dedmon, "Education: Confirming What We Know," speech presented to Radford University Faculty Convocation, September 6, 1983, reprinted in *Vital Speeches,* 50 (October 15, 1983), 14–20.

56. See Don M. Boileau, "Communication Competencies," paper presented at the International Listening Association Summer Conference, St. Paul, Minn., July 1984.

57. *Law Schools and Professional Education* (Chicago: American Bar Association, 1980), p. 104.

58. K. Phillip Taylor, Raymond W. Buchanan, and David U. Strawn, *Communication Strategies for Trial Attorneys* (Glenview, Ill.: Scott, Foresman, 1984), p. xi.

59. Harold Weiss and J. B. McGrath, Jr., *Technically Speaking* (New York: McGraw-Hill, 1963), p. 1.

2 *The Human Communication Process*

Chapter Outline

Learning Outcomes

After reading this chapter, you should be able to:

List and explain the components of human communication

Explain the effects of perceptions on the human communication process

Detail the roles of the perceptual filter, channel capacity, and cognitive style in the human communication process

Identify, define, and give examples of the noise factors that affect the human communication process

Illustrate, define, and give examples of the linear model of communication

Illustrate, define, and give examples of the interactional model of communication

Illustrate, define, and give examples of the transactional model of communication

Distinguish among the reasoning to conclusion processes of Western logic, theological reasoning, and philosophical thought

Expound on the results of the conflict between reasoning systems as they affect the communication process

Explain the role of ethics in the communication process.

To be an effective communicator you need to understand how the communication process operates and how you not only send and process information, but how you reason your way to conclusions and evaluate the ideas others send. In addition, good communicators know what ethical standards they use in making their decisions.

The Components of Human Communication

As human beings, we are capable of selective communication. That is, from the wide repertory available to us we can choose the symbol we feel best represents the idea or concept we wish to express. We can think in abstractions, plan events in the future, and store and recall information. Selective communication allows us to express emotion, describe events and objects, and combine sounds into complicated structures.[1]

We communicate through our **primary signal system,** the senses: seeing, hearing, tasting, smelling, and touching. We express our reac-

We communicate through our primary signal system, the senses.

tions to what we have sensed by both verbal and nonverbal signs. You may say "I heard the bell"; "It smells sweet"; or "It feels soft." These are examples of verbal communications that are responses to what your senses have received. When you touch a hot stove and pull your finger away quickly, your eyes welling with tears, these responses are examples of nonverbal communication. In any communication process, the degree to which the communication is effective depends on the communicators' mutual understanding of the signals being used. A sign hanging on the bulletin board in our office reads. "I know that you believe you understand what you think I said, but I am not sure you realize that what you heard is not what I meant." To which, one day, a student added, "Are you sure?"

Suppose you are about to take an examination and suddenly realize you forgot to bring a pencil to class. You say to one of your friends, "May I please borrow a pencil?" He or she says, "Yes" and gives you a pencil. You have just participated in an effective communication transaction. You (communicator A) encoded a message ("May I please borrow a pencil?") and sent it out over a channel (vocal tones carried on sound waves) to your friend (communicator B). Your friend received the message (by using sensory agents, ears) and decoded it (understood that you wanted a pencil). Your friend's feedback (word "yes" and the handing of the pencil to you) indicated that the message was successfully received and decoded. Thus what may at first seem a simple process is actually quite complex.

Now suppose that the person sitting next to you is from France and speaks no English. The symbol that he or she uses for pencil is *le crayon*. And unless both of you know French, that person will be unable to decode your message. Or suppose that just as you start to ask your question, the public-address system goes on and a loud screech invades the room. In this case, the receiver may not be able to hear the question, and so no successful communication will take place.

Remember that the act of speech itself is not communication. Speech is only a biological act: the utterance of sounds, possibly of vocal symbols of language. Communication, however, is broader: it involves the development of a relationship among people that results in the sending (encoding) and receiving (decoding) of messages in which there is shared meaning among the participants. That is, the intent of the message received is basically the same as the intent of the message sent.

As you can see, communication can be a very complicated process. Technology allows us to send an idea around the world in a fraction of a second, yet it may take years for that idea to penetrate the quarter-inch-thick layer of cortex in a person's brain and influence his or her behavior. "When communication is effective," one expert said, "problems are solved and systems run smoothly. When communication is ineffective, the results are waste, inefficiency, frustration and misunderstanding."[2]

Figure 2.1 illustrates how the components of the communication process work. The circles representing the **communicator/source** (the originator of the message) and the **communicator/receiver** (the recipient of the message) overlap as each person sends **messages** (communication) and **feedback** (response to a message) to the other through a **frame of reference** (a perceptual screen). The overlapping circles in Figure 2.1 suggest that communication is possible only when each communicator understands the other's message. The variables that affect the frame of reference—such as physical state, emotional state, experiences, attitudes, communication skills, memory, and expectations—all make up the perceptual screen through which verbal and nonverbal messages are communicated.

Communicator Perceptions

Your **perceptions**—the way you view the world—affect your interpretation of a communication stimulus. Many factors make up your perceptual filter and represent what you, as a communicator, bring to any communication. These factors, as enumerated in Figure 2.1, include your culture (the background world view you hold), communication skills (as developed from experience and training), physical and emo-

Figure 2.1

The Components of Communication

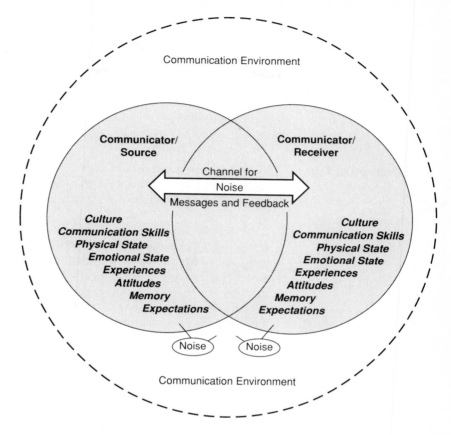

Communication Environment

Communicator/
Source

Communicator/
Receiver

Channel for
Noise
Messages and Feedback

Culture
Communication Skills
Physical State
Emotional State
Experiences
Attitudes
Memory
Expectations

Culture
Communication Skills
Physical State
Emotional State
Experiences
Attitudes
Memory
Expectations

Noise   Noise

Communication Environment

Communicator/Source	**Communicator/Receiver**
1. Senses aroused by idea or need to communicate	1. Senses aroused by stimuli or need to communicate
2. Chooses to communicate the message using language symbols (the code)	2. Receives symbols (the code) in distorted form
3. Uses memory and past experiences to find language symbols to communicate the message (encoding)	3. Uses memory and past experiences to attach meaning to symbols (decoding)
	4. Stores information
	5. Sends feedback

tional state, experiences, attitudes (your negative and positive predispositions to respond to any particular stimulus), memory (your ability to store and recall information), and expectations (what you anticipate will occur). Two people reporting on an incident they have both seen will most likely report some, if not all, of the information differently. These alterations are accounted for by their perceptual differences, which grow out of differing perceptual filters, channel capacities, and cognitive styles.

Perceptual Filter   Through our **perceptual filter** (our attitudinal belief system) we channel the messages we have received and evaluate them based on the concepts we hold. These perceptions reflect all our past experiences and learning and our language.

The perceptual filter, developing as it does from our experience, is affected by several variables, the most important of which are our own needs and wants. In other words in the perceptual process we see and hear what we want to see and hear. We then often express these observations and attitudes with our language. During the U.N.-Iraqi war, for example, much of what we heard and how we understood and interpreted language messages were based on our cultural backgrounds, biases, needs, and wants. Hearing the same message, Iraqis and some other Arabs did not process or believe the news in the same way as many Americans or British did. Even Americans perceived the language they were hearing differently. Those opposed to the conflict heard the same information as those in favor of the clash but assigned different meaning to those duplicate language messages.

Channel Capacity   Our **channel capacity**—that is, the amount of information we can handle at one time—also affects our ability to perceive. Neurological damage, fatigue, or information overload can cause us to miss or misperceive language and other stimuli. As listeners, we can handle and internally process just so much information, and then we must take a mental break. When we consider that most people are now geared to a mental time-out for a short commercial after five to seven minutes of a television show, it is not surprising that speakers have problems with presentations in longer time frames, no matter how clear their language.

Medical professionals are amazing examples of channel capacity. Consider the general practitioner who must continually listen to and diagnose patients' health problems on a schedule of twenty- to thirty-minute appointments. By the end of the day, she or he must be psychologically exhausted, for in this case careful listening can be a matter of life or death.

Cognitive Style

Cognitive style, the way in which we become aware of concepts as well as comprehend, organize, and store information, affects how we learn and how we use language. Some people learn best by hearing information, whereas others grasp it more readily by reading. Because we all have different cognitive learning styles, the way we sort and organize received information may be different from the way it is presented. Some educational researchers are attempting to identify the cognitive learning styles of students so as to match them with the styles of teachers. Thus students who appear to organize information in one style are placed with a teacher who takes a similar approach. This research assumes that a teacher who organizes in a certain cognitive style probably presents material in the same way. Matching teachers and students according to learning style can therefore establish a common base of understanding.

In any case, however, communicators bring to communicative situations speaking and listening skills based on their experiences. In these situations, the environment either helps or interferes with the communication. Noise factors—interference in the sending-receiving system—are always present and always affect the communication. To understand this complex process fully, let us examine in more detail how communication operates.

The Communicator/ Source and the Message

The communication process starts when the communicator/source is consciously or unconsciously stimulated by some event, object, or idea. A need to send a message is then followed by a memory search to find the appropriate language (verbal and/or nonverbal) with which to encode the message. Such factors as perceptions, expectations, attitudes, and physical state affect the sending of messages.

Our perceptions affect our interpretations of the communication stimulus; so do our expectations. For example, how many times have we heard someone say, "I can't do it" even before he or she tries to do anything? Our communication patterns are also influenced by our attitudes, which are the result of our predispositions (positive and negative impressions). How we respond to a person's clothing or to someone's ideas reflects our preconceived attitudes. And just as attitudes have a bearing on the effectiveness of communication, so, too, does the physical state of the communicators. If one person is not feeling well, for instance, she or he may have difficulty concentrating on clearly encoding a message.

The communication process is complex because it uses symbols to represent the objects and ideas that are behind the communication. Unfortunately, symbols can be misunderstood, particularly when a specialist such as an aeronautical engineer must communicate technical information concerning the principles of wind velocity to a layperson. Words that are too abstract or theoretical may confuse the communicator/receiver and lead to misunderstanding.

The Channel During a communication, the encoded message is carried through a **channel** or channels. If the communication occurs face to face, these channels may be some or all of the five senses. Typically, we rely on sight and sound for channels in speaking and listening. Instead of communicating face to face, however, we may choose to use an electronic channel that utilizes sound (the telephone, for instance) or sight (television). In some instances, we may choose to send a message to someone by means of physical contact, such as tapping the person on the shoulder. In this case, we are utilizing the touch channel.

When acting as the communicator/source, we must exercise as much care in using the channel as in choosing the symbols because different channels require different methods of developing ideas. For example, the choice of electronic channels has changed the nature of political communication. Presidential candidates once traveled throughout the country giving speeches from the backs of campaign trains, but today, through the use of television, they can reach a larger number of people without traveling at all. Consequently, campaign advisers must determine the best methods for sending a message via an electronic channel instead of a face-to-face channel. The end result has been short, repeated advertisements rather than one-time speeches. Ads are the tool of television sales and can get a message across by repeating an idea over and over using researched electronic techniques not possible in face-to-face presentations.

The Communicator/ At the end of the channel, the message must be decoded before communi-
Receiver and nication can be accomplished. On receiving verbal and nonverbal sig-
the Message nals, the communicator/receiver processes them through a memory search so that the signals are translated into the receiver's language system. This decoded message is not identical to the one encoded by the communicator/source because each person's symbol system is shaped by a unique set of perceptions.

A home economist, for instance, has one concept of what "season to taste" means in a recipe. In response to the same recipe, a bank executive who enjoys being a weekend barbecue chef seasons lightly and lets the guests add more seasonings. Someone with more cooking experience decodes the message as "season highly."

Human beings are special because they are the only animals that can selectively communicate.

Feedback   Once meaning is assigned to the received message, the communicator/ receiver is in a position to respond. This response, called feedback, can be a verbal or a nonverbal reaction to the message (or both). The feedback indicates whether the communicator/receiver understands (e.g., nodding), misunderstands (e.g., shrugging the shoulders and saying, "I don't understand"), encourages the communicator/source to continue (e.g., leaning forward and saying, "Yes"), or disagrees (e.g., pulling back and saying, "No way!"). The act of responding, by which the communicator/receiver sends feedback to the communicator/source, actually shifts the role of the communicator/receiver to that of communicator/ source.

Feedback is a verbal or non-verbal reaction to the message.

Noise

Messages are influenced not only by the interpretations of each communicator but also by **noise,** which is any internal or external interference in the communication process.[3] Noise can be caused by environmental factors, physiological impairment, semantic problems, syntactic problems, organizational confusion, social noise, or psychological problems.[4]

Environmental Noise

Environmental noise comprises outside interference that prevents the communicator/receiver from receiving the message. This can happen during a lecture when the students around you are talking so loudly that you cannot hear the instructor. Or it can happen when you are in the kitchen running water to wash dishes and the sound muffles your brother's voice when he asks you a question from the next room. In each of these cases, some form of environmental noise is blocking clear reception of the message.

Physiological Impairment

A **physiological impairment** can also block the effective sending or receiving of a message. For example, deaf persons do not have the sensory capabilities to receive a message in the same way as do people with normal hearing. Unless they use some mechanical device, such as a hearing aid, or unless they are able to read lips, deaf people cannot receive oral messages. Similarly, a person with a speech impediment may be difficult to understand.

Semantic Problems   Problems may also arise regarding the meaning of words, or semantics. For example, **semantic problems** may result when people use language that is common only to one specific group, to a particular part of a country, to another country, or to a particular field, profession, or organization.

Travelers frequently encounter semantic problems. The midwesterner who goes into a store in many parts of the East and asks for a soda will probably get a soft drink rather than a mixture of ice cream, fruit flavoring, and soda water. An American in London who asks for the location of the subway will not be directed to the underground railroad or the "tube." Instead, the unknowing American will be led to an underground passageway that allows a pedestrian to walk from one side of the street to the other.

Experts—professors, physicists, mechanics—sometimes forget that those who do not have as much knowledge of their field may not be familiar with its vocabulary. For example, legal clients often complain that lawyers fail to communicate clearly because they use confusing legal jargon.

Similarly, people sometimes use the initials of organizations, equipment, or activities rather than their names. Agencies in Washington are referred to by their initials, such as SEC (Securities and Exchange Commission) and NASA (National Aeronautics and Space Administration), and federal executives become so accustomed to this usage that they forget that most Americans do not recognize this "alphabet soup." To avoid semantic problems, communicators must be aware that although they know the meanings of the words they use, those at the receiving end must assign similar meanings for a communication to be effective.

Ambiguity, the use of obscure or meaningless words, can also cause unclear communication. Consider the following sentences: "That's an interesting idea." "That was quite some theme you wrote." "I need my space." What do "interesting," "quite some," and "space" mean? Or consider these propositions: "Employees should interface with each other." "Relationships can be debugged." "The newspaper is user friendly." What do these assertions mean? Even though all communication contains some ambiguity, it can be minimized when communicators remain aware of the need for clarity and select their words accordingly.

Syntactical Problems   Each language has a syntax—a customary way of putting words together into sentences. If a source uses a syntax unfamiliar to the receiver, the latter may be confused. "Throw Mama from the train a kiss" may not be readily understandable to a native Californian, but the Pennsylvania Dutch know exactly what it means because this is a perfectly correct Germanic word order on which American English semantics has been superimposed.

Various types of **syntactical problems,** flawed grammatical usage, can interfere with communication. For example, receivers may become confused if someone changes tenses in the middle of a story ("She went down the street and says to him . . ."). Or they may be confused by the use of double negatives ("He don't have no business doing that") or by incorrect grammar.

Foreigners who are learning English often put words in the wrong order. The usual sequence of a grammatically correct English sentence is noun-verb-object (I give him the book). But other languages— Spanish, for example—do not follow this pattern. In Spanish the same sentence reads, *Le doy el libro* (To him I give the book). Thus someone who is learning a new language must master not only the vocabulary but an entirely different system of grammar as well. Until this new system becomes natural, the language may be quite difficult both to encode and decode.

Organizational Confusion

When the communicator/source fails to realize that certain ideas are best grasped when presented in a structured order, **organizational confusion** may be the result. One geography instructor presents ideas in a random fashion: first he talks about India, then China, then Greece, and then back to India. After awhile, his students become so confused they have absolutely no idea which country he is presently discussing.

Many methods of organization can provide a clear structure. In giving directions, for example, a person may set a pattern by starting at the departure point and proceeding in geographical order ("Go to the first street, turn right, proceed three blocks, and turn left"). This type of organization follows a spatial arrangement. Some ideas, however, are best explained chronologically ("On Monday go shopping, on Wednesday pick up the laundry, and on Thursday clean the house). If material is presented in a specific pattern, the communicator/receiver can directly process the ideas so as to grasp the meaning. If the material is not organized, the receiver must not only try to figure out what is said but must also sort out the information.

Social Noise

"Nice people don't do things like that." "That's the way it has always been, and that's the way it is always going to be." "Boys are supposed to act like boys." These sentences are all examples of **social noise,** which is made up of preconceived, unyielding attitudes derived from a group or society that are preventing the communicator/receiver from dealing with a message.

A prime example of social noise is the attitude that any action by a representative of one's own group is always right, whereas the same action by a member of another group may well be wrong. Thus a person who has always voted for one political party may well block negative input about the party while accepting negative input about its opponents. Because of this social noise, a listener often does not receive and interpret a message effectively.

Social noise can also result from the topic chosen for communication. Through experience we all learn that some topics are usually not discussed with certain people or in special circumstances. One study indicated that among college students, talking about their current relationship actually headed the list of taboo topics for both Platonic and intimate couples. Other forbidden topics for college couples included "extrarelationship" activities, rules and expected behavior, previous relationships, subjects known from past experience to cause conflict, and self-disclosures that might cast a person in a negative light.[5]

Psychological Problems

We sometimes find ourselves in situations where stress, frustration, or irritation causes us to either send or receive messages ineffectively. Think of what happens when you are so angry that you "can't think straight." Or perhaps you have said something you really did not mean because you "just couldn't control" yourself. You may not listen to the other communicator simply because you do not want to hear what he or she has to say. In all these cases, normal **psychological problems** are getting in the way of effective communication.

Unfortunately, some people have more severe psychological problems that cause them to communicate in unusual ways. Those afflicted with schizophrenia (a disintegration of personality) or catatonia (immobility and speechlessness) may have great difficulty communicating. Such people may talk in riddles and rhymes, make up words, switch personalities, or simply not try to communicate at all.

People involved in nursing, social work, and counseling often find that one of their major responsibilities is to deal with patients or clients who are fearful or under stress. To do so, these professionals use stress-management techniques designed to enable a person to cope with stress and still perform his or her work effectively. These techniques also help people communicate with those who are under stress.

Dealing with Noise

Although noise interferes with communication, we must learn to adapt to it because it is always present. We must also seek ways to compensate for it. For example, a communicator/source should offer opportunities for feedback to make sure that the message has been received and understood. Rather than simply assuming, say, that someone in another room has heard your message, word the statement so that it requires an

A communicator source should offer opportunities for feedback to make sure that the message has been received and understood.

answer: "The phone is for you; are you going to answer it?" Another way to compensate for noise is to define terms that might be misunderstood or that may not be part of the communicator/receiver's vocabulary. Rather than repeating exactly the same words in a message that has obviously been misunderstood, you can change the terms or the sentence structure to aid the receiver in decoding the message. In the same way, a communicator/receiver should ask questions or repeat the message's general ideas to be sure that distractions have not interfered with comprehension.

The way a person does or does not respond may give you some clues as to how to compensate for the noise problem. For instance, consider what happens if you request a sheet of paper and the person does not do anything. Environmental noise may have stopped the message from being received, or the person may not have been paying attention because of psychological or social noise. Or the person may say, "I'm having difficulty hearing. I didn't catch what you said. Could you repeat it and speak up a little?" In this case, you must increase the volume level when you repeat the message. A response of "No comprende" may indicate that the person does not speak English. You may then want to switch to Spanish, if you know the language, or else repeat the message in very simple English while pointing to what you want. Raising the volume level when you repeat the message is not appropriate in this instance because the person obviously heard you but could not understand. In other words, there is no apparent physiological noise, only semantic noise. As a sender of messages, you must keep eyes and ears open to anticipate a problem and, if one exists, to adjust your communication accordingly.

The Environment   Communication does not occur in a vacuum; it always takes place in some context, some **environment.** Where we are and who is with us affect our communication. Such factors as the size of the room, the color of the walls, the decorations, the type and placement of the furniture, the type of lighting, and the number of people in the room can all affect how we feel, the way in which we communicate, and the type of communicating we engage in. For example, placing a large number of people in a small work area, as is often the case with the typing pool in large businesses, may bring about strained communication. We also react to such factors as temperature, smell, and sound.

Models of Human Communication

In the complex process of human communication, it is not enough simply to be able to identify the component parts. We must also understand how these components fit together. A useful way of doing this is to look at the process of communication through a model that can illustrate how the various elements relate to each other.

Any model must necessarily be a simplification; communication does not have the clear-cut beginning and end that a model suggests. Nevertheless, despite these limitations, models can help us to see the components of communication from a perspective that will help us analyze and understand them.

Though there are many ways to describe the act of communication, the following three are used to illustrate the process: the linear, the interactional, and the transactional.[6]

The Linear Model   The early theoretical work concerning verbal communication evolved
of Communication   from ancient Greek and Roman rhetoricians who were concerned with the proper training of an orator. For this reason, early theories of communication stressed the role of the public speaker. They reflected what might be called a one-directional view of communication according to which a person performs specific actions in a specific sequence during a speech and elicits specific desired responses from listeners. This view can be expressed as a **linear model of communication** (see Figure 2.2).

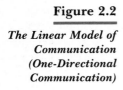

Figure 2.2

*The Linear Model of
Communication
(One-Directional
Communication)*

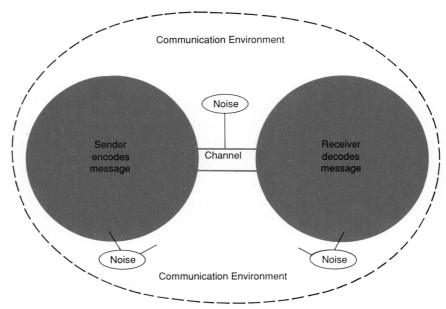

In the linear model of communication, a speaker encodes a message and sends it to a listener through one or more of the sensory channels. The listener then receives and decodes the message. For example, after you buy a computer, you listen to the tape-recorded message produced by the manufacturer of your newly purchased machine. The tape explains how to insert the operating system disk and turn the computer on. When you follow the directions and the computer comes on, the communication has been successful.

Nevertheless, although one-directional communication is often necessary, its effectiveness is limited. To illustrate this, let us consider another example. Brad (the speaker) says, "Please put the book on the table." He then turns and walks from the room. Brooke (the listener) has a stack of books in front of her, but she is not certain which one to place on the table.

In this example, Brad is making a rather common assumption. Many people assume that if they say (or write) something, this sending of a message is all there is to communicating. But this assumption, according to one source, "ignores the important role of the listener in responding to (and consequently affecting) the sender and the message in order to provide feedback. This feedback can enable the sender to check to see if an order is understood, a policy accepted, a message clear, a channel open.[7]

Whenever possible, communicators should attempt to interact with each other so they can find out how effective their communication actually is. For example, Brad's analysis of the number of books available from which to choose might have led him to the conclusion that he had to be more specific. In addition, he might have wanted to ask, "Do you know which book I want?" Or he might have waited until Brooke put down the book to see whether she understood him. If she did not, he could then have corrected his error by being more specific in his directions. When it is impossible to open the interaction for feedback—as it is, say, for the newscaster on radio or television, the newspaper reporter, and the author of books—special consideration must be given to careful prior analysis of the audience so that the communicator/source can use the most appropriate language, clarify examples, and provide a clear structure so as to avoid communication noise.

The Interactional Model of Communication

The linear model of communication does not take into account all the variables in the communication process. Rather, it is a simple speaker-listener model. For this reason, some early behavioral scientists influenced by research in psychology expanded the notion of the process to encompass greater interaction and to demonstrate the dynamic, ongoing nature of communication. This **interactional model of communication** is displayed in Figure 2.3.

In the interactional model of communication, the source encodes a message and sends it to the receiver through one or more of the sensory

Figure 2.3

The Interactional Model of Communication (Two-Directional Communication)

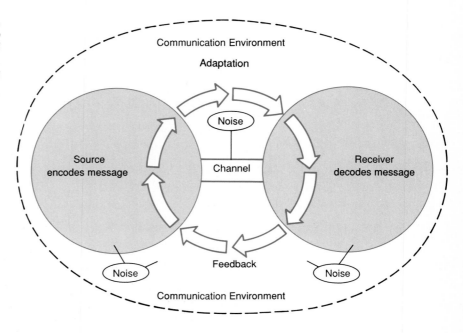

channels. The receiver receives and decodes the message as in linear communication but then encodes feedback (a reaction or reactions) and sends the feedback to the source, thus making the process two-directional. The source then decodes the feedback message. Based on the original message sent and the feedback received, the source then encodes a new message that adapts to the feedback **(adaptation).** For example, Brad says to Brooke, "Please hand me the book." Brooke looks at the pile of books in front of her and says, "Which one?" (feedback). Brad responds, "The red one on the top of the pile" (adaptation).

This view of communication accounts for the influence of the receiver's responses. It thus suggests a process that is somewhat circular: sending and receiving, sending and receiving, and so on.

The Transactional Model of Communication

Some specialists are now suggesting that communication may not be as simple a process of stimulus and response as the linear and interactional models suggest.[8] This view supports the idea that communication is a transaction in which source and receiver play interchangeable roles throughout the act of communication. Thus a clear-cut model of the process is not easy to construct.

Figure 2.4 illustrates the **transactional model of communication.** In this model, which best represents what we now know about human com-

Figure 2.4

The Transactional Model of Communication (Multidirectional Communication)

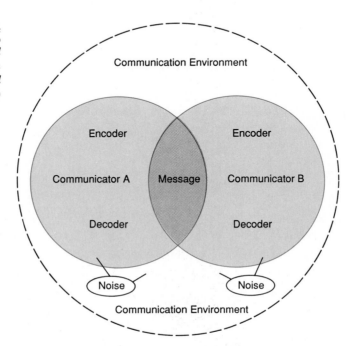

munication, variables are found simultaneously within both communicators. Communicator A encodes a message and sends it. Communicator B then encodes the feedback and sends it to A, who decodes it. But these steps are not mutually exclusive because encoding and decoding may occur simultaneously. Speakers may send a verbal message and at the same time may receive and decode a nonverbal feedback message from listeners. This process of encoding and decoding can occur continuously throughout a communication. Because messages can be sent and received at the same time, this model is multidirectional.

Notice that one person is not labeled as the source and the other as the receiver; instead, both communicators assume the roles of sender and receiver in the transaction. Thus this model most nearly represents simultaneous communication.

Consider the simultaneous communication in this transaction:

Brad (the source) says, "I love you";
  while
Brad (the receiver) sees Brooke walk away as he speaks to her;
  while
Brook (the source) walks away from Brad;
  while
Brook (the receiver) says, "I love you";
  while
Brooke (the source) stops, turns, frowns, and says, "I'm not sure you mean that";
  while
Brook (the receiver) sees Brad nod his head and walk toward her as she speaks;
  while
Brad (the receiver) hears her words;
  while
Brad (the source) nods his head and walks toward Brooke as she speaks.

Throughout the encounter, both Brad and Brooke are simultaneously sending and receiving (encoding and decoding) verbal and nonverbal messages.

From a listening perspective, the transactional process can be understood by recognizing that

> "As I listen, I simultaneously speak to you with my nonverbal responses, and periodically provide you with verbal responses. As you speak, you simultaneously listen to the nonverbal messages, periodically tune in to the verbal messages, and continuously adapt your communicative behaviors according to your assessment of the extent to which you feel you have been understood. I do the same."[9]

*The Models   Comparing the three models in action will give you an understanding
Compared*   of how each one differs from the others. Let us begin with the following
                  scenario.

A director of public relations of a major corporation presents a speech
over closed-circuit television from the headquarters' media studio to the
marketing personnel at the various district offices located throughout
the country. This is an example of the linear model of communication.

Next the director gives the same presentation in the corporation's
board room. She sticks exactly to the manuscript that she had prepared
and makes no effort to seek any feedback. Following the speech, she
asks if there are any questions. One of the board members asks a question, which she answers. This demonstrates the interactional model of
communication.

Then the sales staff enters the room. The public relations director
starts to speak. As she does so, a salesperson asks a question. While the
question is being asked, the speaker nods her head. She then verbally
agrees with the salesperson. While this is happening, the salesperson
also nods his head, indicating that he understood what was just explained, and says, "I get it." This is an example of the transactional
model of communication.

The communication transaction is highly complex. To be effective, a
communicator must understand the complexities of that process and be
able to apply that understanding to the development of the skills necessary to function effectively as a communicator source and receiver.

Communication as a System

Communication takes place within a context. Think of your daily interactions. There is a **system,** a pattern, to the way in which you interact
with others. The pattern centers on who speaks, what the speaker says
or is allowed to say, and the way in which the message is sent. The
participants, the setting, and the purpose form the basis of this communication system. The operation of communication in a consistent pattern
allows communication to be regular and predictable, not random, and
gives everyone who participates a sense of assurance and security. Identify a communication system with which you are familiar (your family
unit or your job environment, for example). You can probably anticipate
what is going to happen and how your actions will affect others before
you actually participate. Your awareness of how well your ideas will be
accepted or of how much encouragement or discouragement you will
receive may well dictate what you do or do not say.

The type of communication system being used affects who speaks. In
a strongly parent-dominated home, for example, the father or mother
may place restrictions on what the children say, the language they use,

Communication takes place within a system.

and the topics they discuss. Any attempt by the children to change the system may be met with strongly negative reactions and may result in physical or verbal punishment.

A communication system can be shaped by the communicators' age, status, gender, attraction for each other, and cultural heritage. For example, in a family system, the rules for the male members may be different from the rules for the female members, the regulations may alter as the children get older, and the "favorite" children may be allowed more freedoms. Certain families may be influenced by a historical ethnic pattern that dictates how much public display of emotions is allowable and whether opinions may be expressed. Typically, in many households, when children reach adolescence their attempts to change the rules and not to be treated as "little kids" are at the core of many family conflicts.

A particular setting may also encourage or discourage communication. In some settings people may feel free to disagree, whereas in others they may feel restricted. Some instructors, for example, encourage differences of opinion in their classroom; others demand adherence to their philosophy and interpretations. Students quickly learn the rules in various classrooms and conform accordingly; if not, they may be faced with lower grades or with verbal insults.

The purpose of the communicative act may also result in limits to the system. Trying to tell someone about what you believe is a different task and experience from attempting to persuade that person to take some action you desire. Parents may be more than willing to hear children talk about what curfews their friends have, but when children try to persuade their parents to extend the curfew, the attempt usually meets with little success. Similarly, discussing with your boss the participatory system used in another business is not the same as asking your boss to put that management process into practice.

Once a system is set up and operating any attempt to change that system and its pattern of rules will often impair the system or cause it to stop functioning. In other words, unless the participants in the communication environment are willing to adjust or alter the rules, the system may stop working. This does not mean that all systems that are working are good. It merely suggests that when a system is functioning, regardless of whether the participants are happy with the pattern, at least there is a basis for understanding how the communication of the people within that system will take place. For example, although children may not like a "be seen-but-not-heard" rule, at least they know what actions are and are not acceptable and what the penalties will be for overstepping the boundaries. In a work environment, if you are aware that your boss is not going to accept anyone else's ideas, you learn to live with the system or know you must get out.

Good can result from a system not working well because the awareness of the problem may halt a negative system. For example, if a family unit has been operating under a reign of physical and verbal abuse, something happening to stop the abuse could result in a much-needed change or could bring the system to an end.

Once rules become nonexistent or fuzzy, chaos may result. The basis of good communication patterns between any two people or among several people is the ability to alter the system with the least amount of chaos. The inability to adjust within a reasonable period of time is often the basis for communicative ineffectiveness, arguments, and conflict. It may also indicate that the relationship is not capable of being repaired or that outside help, such as a marriage counselor, management consultant, or psychologist, may be needed.

Besides understanding the components of the human communication process, the models of how communication takes place, and the fact that communication is system bound, we must develop an awareness of how we reason to conclusions and the role ethics plays in our intrapersonal and interpersonal communications to fully appreciate the human communication process.

Reasoning to Conclusions

Because of our differing backgrounds and experiences, we process information differently; therefore, we solve problems in a wide variety of ways. To understand these variances and comprehend how you personally reach conclusions, familiarity with some common systems of thinking—namely, Western logic, theological reasoning, and philosophical thought—is quite useful. Of course, other approaches exist, including those proposed by persons who seem to believe that no formal system is necessary. Generally, however, knowing the methods presented here will give you a basis for understanding the varying approaches to many of the arguments you hear in daily life and for responding to these arguments.

Western Logic
The word *logic* derives from the Greek verb *legin,* which means "say, speak, or discourse." The Greeks defined a human being as a "rational animal," which literally means "logical animal" or an "animal who has language."[10]

Western logic is based on the belief that "it is only when we have both a formally correct pattern of reasoning and true premises that the truth of our conclusion is assured."[11] Accordingly, those of us who accept this system contend "this type of reasoning promises (without guaranteeing) the best chances of success. Our lives become more and more adjusted, secure, peaceful, harmonious, pleasurable and satisfactory to the extent that the method of intelligence gains effective control."[12] In other words, if we reach conclusions by approaching the end result through a pattern of step-by-step, provable concepts, then the conclusion we reach should be accurate and defensible.

Western logic is based in part on the use of a reasoning process. It is the purpose of reason to discover patterns of causal connection in the world through observation and successful testing. By using the patterns of cause and effect, we can infer the presence of the causes if the facts leading to the effect are available or determine a certain kind of effect if the cause is given.

Of course, there are varying definitions of "fact." Nevertheless, a **fact** is generally defined as something proved by scientific evidence, something about which there is universal agreement, or something observable that has not changed. What is essential in logical reasoning is the presentation of evidence that justifiably supports the conclusion drawn.

Using this reasoning, Western logic reaches its highest form in the statement "A proposition is true if it corresponds to a fact."[13] For example, if you get a rash every time you eat strawberries, you will probably reason that strawberries cause you to get a rash. In other words, if y results every time procedure x is repeated, you can "reason to the conclusion" that "x (your eating strawberries) brings about y (your rash)." The process of putting the concept of critical thinking into action is an important part of the Western logical system.

Critical Thinking for Communicators

An increasing bombardment of information and appeals from sources such as the media and advertising and a disenchantment with the values and actions of our politicians and religious leaders have caused many people to reject or accept without evaluation too much of what is communicatively presented. To be an effective communicator, whether as a sender or a receiver, people must understand and use critical thinking. **Critical thinking** is reasonable, reflective thinking that is focused on deciding what to believe and do.[14] It is essential for competent problem solving, clear understanding, efficient processing of information, and evaluation of received information. If understood and put into effect, critical thinking allows people to recognize that problems can be solved in multiple ways and that many possible conclusions can be reached from the same data or combination of data.

Through critical thinking, evidence can be presented and allegations can be substantiated or disproved. **Evidence** in critical thinking is all the means by which any alleged matter of facts is established or disproved. Evidence includes testimony, records, documents, and objects that assist in building a logical case. Remember that the purpose of this information is not to decorate but to prove. Just because there is a lot of information (quotes, for example) does not in and of itself prove that the information is valid or leads to a particular conclusion. The relevant issue is whether the information helps develop the specific contention, is valid, and is presented in a reliable way.

To apply critical thinking, use the following principles of the Western logical system to establish a basis on which to send and receive messages:[15]

1. Seek a clear statement of the thesis or questions.
2. Seek reasons.
3. Try to be well informed on the topic/issue.
4. Use and mention credible sources.
5. Take into account the total situation.
6. Try to keep to the main point.
7. Bear in mind the original or basic concern/issue/topic.
8. Look for alternatives.
9. Be open-minded.
10. Take a position (and change a position) when the evidence and reasons are sufficient to do so.
11. Seek as much precision as the subject permits.
12. Deal in an orderly manner with the parts of a complex whole.
13. Use critical thinking abilities.
14. Be sensitive to the feelings, level of knowledge, and degree of sophistication of others.

15. Be aware of the strategies of manipulation speakers are likely to employ: the use of doublespeak, false facts, partial information, and biased stands; the telling of only one side of an issue; and the substitution of emotion dressed up as logic for logical ideas.

By applying a critical thinking format, the receiver of information can diagnose (identify the reasonableness of the information based on personal experience, expert opinion, and the factuality of the data), evaluate (determine how close to the desired goal or concept the information is), and implement a plan or idea. This implementation comes from the positive sense of understanding how and why the plan or idea was derived.

Theological Reasoning

Theological reasoning is based on the concept that a prime mover causes things to happen in a prescribed manner. According to this view, the prime mover may be God, natural forces, or even the devil. This concept acknowledges that "the belief in the existence of a supreme personal being is the necessary foundation of this entire scheme of thought."[16]

Theological reasoning is concerned with determining whether an action is right or wrong according to a rule, a law, or an outcome of a moral debate, all of which are defended on theological grounds.[17] Most of the world's established religions have a tradition of revelation that is usually incorporated into sacred scriptures such as the Old and New Testaments, the Torah, and the Koran. Believers in these scriptures turn to them for the theological defense of a particular argument. For example, a theologically reasoned stand against the use of birth-control devices could center on the God-given procreative nature of the sexual act. Thus according to this reasoning, any form of contraception that alters the outcome of the sexual act would be wrong.

People who base their decision making on theological reasoning often advance the idea that "since belief is measured by action, he who forbids us to believe religion to be true, necessarily forbids us to act as we should if we did believe it to be true." Furthermore, "the religious hypothesis gives to the world an expression which specifically determines our reactions, and makes them unlike what they might be on a purely naturalistic scheme of belief."[18]

Philosophical Thought

There are those who have reservations about the use of reason as the principal guide to life, whether that reason be logical or theological in nature. This group of thinkers represents those who use **philosophical thought.** "They point to the positive value of certain levels of human existence that lie beyond the province of conceptual analysis and the practical uses of intelligence altogether, and yet that should also be given their due weight in an adequate philosophy of life."[19]

Some philosophers present alternate ways of thinking about life that are similar to those espoused by religions, most notably Hinduism and Buddhism, found in countries such as India, China, and Japan. These traditions have always stressed certain kinds of "insights" or "modes of awareness" not normally found in the dominant religious traditions of the West; these modes include, for example, transcendentalism, metaphysical speculation, intuition, and the transmigration of souls. The enlightenment sought by Eastern sages such as the Buddha or Lao-tse was, in their view, not to be found through severely intellectual and logical training but through other kinds of training of the mind and the awareness. In recent decades, this perspective has begun to command a considerable amount of attention in the West.

Conflicts Between Reasoning Systems

Not all people come to conclusions based on the same reasoning system. In fact, each person's reasoning process is neither neatly categorized nor entirely understood. When we do not take these differences into account, conflicts often result. Perhaps you have been involved in a disagreement with someone but could not reach agreement. Did you stop to think that the difficulty might result from differences in the reasoning process used to form conclusions? Efforts to change the opinion of a devout religious believer by use of scientific proof may be futile, for example, as may be the reverse. One side counters with quotations from religious scholars and the Bible, while the other answers with findings of prominent scientists.

In confronting a similar problem, different persons may select different solutions because they use different reasoning processes. For example, consider an actual situation in which a husband and wife were expecting their first child. Knowing that he had Rh-positive blood and that she had Rh-negative blood, they were aware of the possibility that their child might die. They were told by their doctor that the baby might have to fight off the blood incompatibility or undergo transfusions. On the advice of their physician, the couple arranged for the birth to take place in a hospital noted for its excellent pediatric care, even though it was a considerable distance from their home.

At the same time, friends of theirs, with the same incompatible blood types, were also expecting a child. They were Christian Scientists. Because their religion taught them to consider a person a God-created spiritual entity and not a material being, the parents believed that their baby would not be made of material elements such as blood, brain, and bones but rather of spiritual qualities such as intelligence, love, kindness, and health. Their solution to the problem was to contact their teacher of

Christian Science, who helped them do prayerful work for their unborn child.[20]

Each couple used a different reasoning process to arrive at a solution. Each was satisfied with the solution that was chosen, though neither would have chosen the other's solution.

A major breakthrough in understanding the communication process both intrapersonally and interpersonally takes place when we accept the concept that it is possible to respect others' beliefs without actually believing as they do. This does not mean, however, that we should blindly accept others' contentions; they must earn our respect through consistency of idea development and clarity of ideas.

As we communicate with others in our daily and professional lives, the underlying core of what we say and the way we act is not only our reasoning system but also our ethical system.

Ethics

Your **ethics** are the values that have been instilled in you, that you have knowingly or unknowingly accepted, and that determine how you act. Your ethical value system is the basis for your decision making and for

Your ethical value system determines whether you will or will not take a particular stand or action.

your personal clarification of why you will or will not take a particular stand or action.

Ethics and Society   Ethics are action oriented. A logical personal ethics system that leads to consistent decision making based on the ability to explain and defend your words and deeds calls for logical agreement among your beliefs, words, and actions. Your ethical system shows itself in how you resolve the conflicts that arise in your life. Your communication ethics are evidenced in the words you select, the ideas you present, and the manner in which you defend and develop your ideas. To understand your own ethical system, you must comprehend that ethical values arise from issues of self-understanding and self-determination.

Recent current events have demonstrated a strong preoccupation with ethics in communication, professional responsibilities, and decision making. The reasons for this concern are complex: perhaps it has occurred because "large sections of the nation's ethical roofing have been sagging badly, from the White House to churches, schools, industries, medical centers, law firms and stock brokerages. . . . [There is a] pressing down on the institutions and enterprises that make up the body and blood of America."[21]

Recent years offer many examples of questionable ethical conduct among those in public life. Presidential candidates have withdrawn because of questionable moral actions (Gary Hart) and because of plagiarism (Joseph Biden). A national newscaster has been chastised by his own affiliates for unfair treatment of interviewees (Dan Rather for his interview with Vice President George Bush during the 1988 presidential campaign). A president and a vice president have resigned from office because of questionable ethical actions (Richard Nixon and Spiro Agnew). Religious leaders have been removed from their positions because of financial and sexual misadventures (the Reverend Jim Bakker, founder of the PTL).

Reports of corporate bribery and white-collar crime have contributed to a sense of uneasiness within the country about the state of professional and private virtue in American life. Medical malpractice and the use of unnecessary operations have led many Americans to wonder about the ethical standards of the professions generally.[22] As one philosopher stated, "Most professions claim some moral purpose and link themselves with some moral goal—law with justice, medicine with preserving life, journalism with truth. But at present few pay explicit attention to what these claims mean."[23] This sense of uneasiness is further fueled by recent technological changes—reproduction and organ replacement techniques, computer use, machinery for prolonging life, space technology—additional moral dilemmas arise. Law and order issues, journalistic rights, and the sexual revolution have also added to the dilemma.

What we and others do and believe is expressed in our communication. Our ethical values form the basis for our communication about our actions and deeds.

Ethics and You

Because ethical questions are so basic to effective communication in today's complex world, understanding your own ethical system can yield several benefits. First, it helps you in making sense of your life. Consistent and coherent beliefs and actions derive from an understanding that your ethics are the basis for what you do and refrain from doing, what you communicate about and refrain from communicating about. Have you ever asked yourself why you believe or do not believe in the death penalty? How would you react if a friend of yours told you he had AIDS? Why would you take that action?

Second, an understanding of your ethics aids you in fulfilling personal, professional, and social responsibilities. Life is a pattern of setting goals and carrying them out. To do so, you must understand how these goals affect your daily life, your work environment, and your interaction with others. Why have you chosen your college major? Why do you want to do that type of work? If you have chosen a career that involves helping other people, such as psychology or counseling, do you really want the responsibility for assisting others to make life decisions? How would you react if your intervention did not prevent a person from committing suicide or fatally attacking someone? It is, of course, difficult to say precisely what constitutes the "moral life," but consistent principles that govern words and deeds and are applied uniformly in all areas of human responsibilities are a significant part of such a life.

Third, knowing your ethical system assists you in making informed political judgments. As a member of a democratic society, you have an obligation to realize your role as a voter and a citizen. How do you select the candidate you decide to vote for in an election? How much of that decision is based on an understanding of your ethical system, and how much is influenced by well-contrived advertisements emphasizing such extraneous factors as the candidate's physical appearance? Or do you select a candidate on a single issue that is not the primary purpose of the office, such as voting for candidate X because she or he has the same religion as you? Understanding why you make the political decisions you do helps preserve your integrity and autonomy as a member of a democratic society.

Fourth, being aware of your ethics helps you in guarding against social or political excesses that promote bigotry and repression. Other people's ethics will not always be similar to yours. To guard against your unknowing participation in acts of hatred and control of others, you must be aware of your value system. What are your prejudices? Would you be willing to put your career or even your life on the line by taking part in civil disobedience for civil rights, women's rights, or animal rights?

A Code of Ethics   Because there is no universal code of morals and ethics, we sometimes become confused about what is right and what is wrong. We are forced to think about what price we are willing to pay for decency, compassion, and sensitivity to others as well as to our personal needs. We must ask ourselves whether words such as "honesty" and "integrity" form the basis for the way we want to live.

There seem to be five driving forces behind the way we apply ethics.[24] The first force is the stimulation of the moral imagination. Each moral choice we make has repercussions for ourselves as well as for others. This is true regardless of our occupation or role in society. Questions such as the following lead to moral decisions: How would I decide whether extraordinary means should be used to keep someone alive? What effect does the grading system used by my instructor have on my entrance into graduate school? What is wrong with "cheating" the government by adjusting my income tax for my benefit because I need the money more than the government does? If I believe and carry out the adage "Spare the rod and spoil the child," what effect will this have on my children's lives? As a businessperson who must make money to stay in business, do I believe that pollution control should take a back seat to profits?

The second force is recognition of ethical issues. Ethical issues are by their very nature overriding—once we recognize an issue as an ethical matter, we attach more significance to it than we did previously. Thus we need to recognize when a moral decision is being made. When we do so, we may attempt to identify hidden assumptions and determine whether a reasonable ground exists for making a judgment or for reaching a conclusion. We may ask ourselves if we have enough evidence to reach a decision, if the person giving advice or counsel is a credible source, and if the decision is the correct one.

The third force is the development of analytical skills. Words such as "justice," "dignity," "privacy," and "virtue" are not always used with clarity and consistency, even though at some time or another we all have to examine and make distinctions among concepts that center on ethical principles and moral rules. Therefore we must be willing to challenge concepts so that we apply them consistently. We need to understand the logical and practical consequences of these applications and the extent to which such consequences are worth considering.

The fourth force is the eliciting of a sense of moral responsibility. Part of the process of adopting an ethical system involves reflecting ethical values in personal conduct. When we attempt to act consistently with our values, some basic questions about reaching conclusions arise. Do we have the freedom to make moral choices? If so, how should we go about making decisions? What is the connection between thinking about ethics and acting? How would we decide, or advise a lover, about whether to get an abortion? Why would we make that decision? Do we have the right to make that decision? If we were in the position to do so, how would we make a decision regarding participation in the denial of life maintenance? Should our tax dollars be used for birth control? Such questions about moral responsibility cannot be set aside. They concern matters that affect us daily.

The fifth force is the toleration of—and resistance to—disagreement and ambiguity. Even if ethical certainty is impossible, ethical reasoning about choice can be precise. In other words, even though there may not always be "right" answers, we can reason clearly about the issues. If we know how we reached a conclusion, we can explain how the decision was made, thus bringing some consistency and coherence to our decision-making process.

Differing Ethical Views

To understand your own ethical system and those of others, you should ask yourself some basic questions regarding the choices you make and those that others make that affect you: Do I understand that it is possible to tolerate differences of choice and to refrain from labeling opposite choices as immoral? What are the exact points of difference between my beliefs and those of the other person?

As you process ideas and then communicate with others, you will encounter dilemmas of principles—situations in which you are torn between conflicting moral obligations that cannot be fulfilled at the same time. You will probably be faced with situations in which what you want to do may not be what you believe you should do or in which you must choose between lying and telling the truth. Is the "little white lie" that protects you from punishment at home or at work really a harmless action? Is your appraisal of whether you will get caught the factor that determines if you tell the truth?

In your decision-making process, you will probably come face to face with utilitarianism, a moral theory that bases the "rightness" of an action on its results. If you come into contact with utilitarianism you may be asked to confront your moral beliefs. For example, if you were a worker in a chemical processing plant who became aware that the materials being produced were causing birth defects and cancer and had additional long-term fatal effects, you might have to answer such questions as, Should I continue to work for an organization that is producing a product that can and has resulted in human destruction? Does my need for financial security force me to aid in the destruction of others?

This is not to suggest that utilitarianism is consistently, or inherently, selfish. Depending on the level of the group whose utility is to be served (society rather than the individual, for example), the time frame (long term as opposed to immediate), and other relevant factors, utilitarianism can produce very humane policies.

Although utilitarians believe that ethics have to do with achieving some desired goal or result, followers of the eighteenth-century philosopher Immanuel Kant believe that morality is the fulfillment of duties and obligations. In other words, according to Kant, our obligations to ourselves should never be given moral priority over our obligations to others merely for the sake of achieving personal goals. For Kant, being moral means having a concern for others simply because they are persons, not because they contribute to some goal or because they are part of a particular group—as utilitarianism would allow. If as a worker in the chemical processing plant you were a follower of Kant, your decision would be clear—the destruction of others is indefensible no matter what the personal gain. You would therefore have to quit your job or take some action to stop the dangerous product from being produced. This stand puts others ahead of personal gain.

The idea of "being moral" as meaning "having a tendency to be concerned about happiness in general" has a long history in Western cultures. This viewpoint is summarized in the Golden Rule. In contrast, Eastern philosophies such as Buddhism and Confucianism see "morality" more in terms of not harming people rather than helping them; thus these philosophies hold the essence of morality to be what is sometimes referred to as the Silver Rule—"What you do not want done to yourself, do not do unto others." According to these views, the essence of morality is the achievement of peace, contentment, and tranquility—not a concern for others.[25]

Because of the dramatic breakdown in traditional value systems in this country during the past twenty years, a stable framework of moral consensus no longer exists to help us decide what is the "right" action to take, the "right" way to live. Therefore each of us must become increasingly aware of the nature of morality and must engage in self-examination. Only through such self-examination can we bring consistency and coherence to our ethical decisions and actions.

The Ethics of Communicating

According to a generally accepted principle, the spoken word can have a significant effect on us as listeners. We are aware that the use of language develops, enlarges, and enhances human personalities. Furthermore, we all acknowledge that a speaker who uses language that degrades or injures human personality by exaggeration, pseudotruths, twisting of words, and name calling is clearly acting unethically.[26]

Over the decades, speech communication instructors have stressed that competent speakers should, by necessity, be ethical speakers; that a speaker should give the audience assistance in making wise decisions; that the speaker's decisions about what to say should be based on moral principles. Speech instructions have also stressed that, although Adolf Hitler and other propagandists were certainly persuasive and compelling speakers, their ultimate downfall was their lack of ethical values.

Ethical communicators are generally defined as those who conform to the moral standards the society establishes for its communicators. Though this definition seems plausible, it contains a major flaw: the words ring hollow because it is impossible to list and gain acceptance for universal moral standards. Nevertheless, research in the field of speech has isolated the specific traits of an "ethical speaker." According to this research, an ethical speaker:

Speaks with sincerity

Does not knowingly expose an audience to falsehoods or half-truths that cause significant harm

Does not premeditatedly alter the truth

Presents the truth as he or she understands it

Raises the listeners' level of expertise by supplying the necessary facts, definitions, descriptions, and substantiating information

Employs a message that is free from mental as well as physical coercion

Does not invent or fabricate statistics or other information intended to serve as a basis for proof of a contention or belief

Gives credit to the source of information and does not pretend that the information is original when it is not.

The basic premise of ethical speaking can be stated as, "You must understand that you are a moral agent, and when you communicate with others and make decisions that affect yourself and others, you have a moral responsibility because your actions have human consequences.[27]

Test how you would put this premise into action as a communicator. What would you do in each of these situations?

1. You are taking a public-speaking course. The instructor requires three quoted references in the speech that you are to present in about five minutes, but you did not have time to do the necessary research. Would you make up three references, not give the speech and get a failing grade, give the speech without the references and hope for the best, or take some other action? If you would take another action, what would it be?

2. You have just finished eating in a restaurant. You check the bill and realize that the waiter has made a $10 error in your favor. The waiter sees your reaction and asks if anything is wrong. How do you respond?

3. You look up during a test and see that your best friend, who needs a passing grade in this class to get off academic probation, is using cheat notes. You think the instructor also saw the action. As you hand in your paper, the instructor says, "Remember, this class operates on the honor system. Is there anything you want to say to me?" How do you respond?

Major problems confront communicators who attempt to exercise ethical standards. Because ethics are not black and white and cannot be easily proven correct or incorrect, people are often faced with making decisions about how ethical is ethical. As a communicator, you will be faced with such dilemmas. What decisions would you make in the following situations?

1. The business you own is illegally storing chemical waste. If the practice was discovered, the fine to the business would bankrupt it. If asked, would you tell the truth?

2. As a lawyer, would you go into court and plead the case for a client who has admitted to you that he had raped a six-year-old?

3. As a politician, would you tell the whole truth and face assured defeat for exposing fund-raising manipulation for much-needed funds, staff indiscretions, or questionable personal moral actions?

4. As a nurse, you know a patient has a terminal illness. The hospital policy is for such information to be conveyed only by the attending doctor. The patient says, "I trust you. Tell me the truth. Am I terminally ill?" How do you respond?

As communicators, we are constantly making judgments concerning what to communicate and to whom. Rhetoric is neither moral nor immoral. Communication itself is neither good nor bad. It is what we do with our communication skills that is good or bad.

Summary

In this chapter, we investigated the process of human communication. The major ideas presented can be summarized as:

☐ People are capable of selective communication.

☐ People communicate through the primary signal system, the senses: seeing, hearing, tasting, smelling, and touching.

☐ The degree to which communication is effective depends on the communicators' mutual understanding of the signals being used.

☐ The communicator/source is the originator of a message.

☐ The communicator/receiver is the recipient of the message.

☐ A person's perceptions affect his or her interpretation of the communication stimulus.

☐ Perceptions are accounted for by the perceptual filter, channel capacity, and cognitive style.

☐ The communication process is complex because it is symbolic.

☐ Messages are carried through a channel or channels.

☐ Feedback is a verbal and/or nonverbal reaction to a message.

☐ Noise is any internal or external interference in the communication process.

☐ Noise can be caused by environmental factors, physiological impairment, semantic problems, syntactical problems, organizational confusion, social factors, or psychological problems.

☐ Communication takes place in a context, in an environment.

☐ The linear model of communication explains the communication process as being one-directional.

☐ The interactional model of communication explains the communication process in terms of encoding, sending, receiving, decoding, providing feedback, and adapting to feedback—that is, this model presents communication as a circular process.

☐ The transactional model of communication represents communication as continuous and indicates that the roles communicators play in the process are simultaneous.

☐ Communication takes places within a system.

☐ The participants, the place, and the purpose help form the basis of the communication system.

☐ People process information and solve problems in a wide variety of ways.

☐ Common systems of thinking are Western logic, theological reasoning, and philosophical thought.

☐ Western logic is based on the concept that it is only when a person employs a formally correct pattern of reasoning and true premises can the truth of her or his conclusion be assured.

☐ Critical thinking is reasonable, reflective thinking that is focused on deciding what to believe and do.

☐ Evidence is all the means by which any alleged matter of facts is established or disproved.

☐ Theological reasoning is based on the concept that there is a prime mover that causes things to happen in a prescribed manner.

☐ Philosophical thought centers on the "positive value of certain levels of human existence that lie beyond the province of conceptual analysis and the practical uses of intelligence altogether"; it examines alternative ways of thinking about life.

☐ It is possible to respect others' beliefs without actually believing as they do.

☐ Ethics are the values that have been instilled in people, that they have knowingly or unknowingly accepted, and that shape their actions.

☐ Ethics are action oriented.

☐ Communicators must understand their own ethical systems so as to make sense of their lives; fulfill their personal, professional, and social responsibilities; make informed political judgments; and safeguard against social or political excesses.

☐ There is no universal code of ethics.

☐ A dilemma of principle occurs when a person is torn between conflicting moral obligations that cannot be fulfilled at the same time.

☐ An unethical speaker uses language that degrades or injures human personality by exaggeration, pseudotruths, twisting of words, and name calling.

☐ Ethical communicators are those who conform to the moral standards the society establishes for its communicators.

☐ A communicator is constantly making judgments about what to communicate and to whom.

☐ Communication itself is neither good nor bad. It is what a person does with communicative skills that is good or bad.

Key Terms

selective communication
primary signal system
communicator/source
communicator/receiver
messages
feedback
frame of reference
perceptions
perceptual filter
channel capacity
cognitive style
channel
noise
environmental noise
physiological impairment
semantic problems
syntactical problems

organizational confusion
social noise
psychological problems
environment
linear model of communication
interactional model of communication
adaptation
transactional model of communication system
Western logic
fact
critical thinking
evidence
theological reasoning
philosophical thought
ethics

Learn by Doing

1. a. Your instructor places a three-by-five-inch card on your desk, blank side up. On the reverse side of the card is a symbol (letter, word, or drawing). There are at least two other people in the room with the same symbol on their cards. When you are told to do so, stand up and find all those who have the same symbol. When you get everyone with the same symbol together, form a group and produce something that represents you as a group. While doing this activity, you may not speak. After you have completed your task, raise your hands so that the instructor knows you are finished.

    b. After all the groups are finished, return to your desks and make a list of what you learned about the process of communication: how groups work, what difficulties you encountered, what it feels like to have your verbal language taken away, and so forth.

2. Design a model of communication that differs from any of the three presented in this chapter, and explain it to the other members of the class.

3. Your class is divided into groups of four to six students. In your groups, share your answers to the list of situations on pages 67–68. After the discussion, write a short paper or share orally what you have learned about your personal ethics as a result of the assignment.

4. Identify an experience in which your attempt to communicate was a failure. Use the classification of sources of noise given in the text to label the type of interference you encountered. Why did this happen? What, if anything, could you have done to correct the interference problem?

5. Describe an environment in which you find it difficult to communicate. Describe an environment in which you find it easy to communicate. Why did you select each one? What implications for communication are involved in your choice?

6. Write down one phrase or expression that is unique to your family or group of friends. It should be an expression that has meaning only for a select group and is not commonly used in the society as a whole. It may be an ethnic expression, an in-group reference, or some other special phrase. The other students then read the expression and try to figure out what it means. Draw inferences about semantic noise from this activity.

7. Your class is divided into groups of four to six students. Use the communication dilemmas on page 68 to select one issue for discussion. After the discussion, write a short paper or share orally what you have learned about your personal ethics as a result of the assignment.

8. Identify an experience you had in which you were involved in a conversation with a person who used a reasoning system different from yours. What happened? If you resolved your differences, indicate how this was done.

9. Do you think it is possible to have political and social harmony in a world in which different reasoning systems are used?

10. Describe the system of communication by which your family operates or operated by investigating the patterns of communication and the rules of operation. What were the advantages and disadvantages of that system?

11. Read each of the following statements and indicate if the statement is *T (true)*—is proven accurate by information provided in the story; *F (false)*—is proven inaccurate by the information provided in the story; or *I (inconclusive)*—cannot be proven accurate or inaccurate because the story does not indicate whether the information is true or false.

    Dale went to a travel agency to arrange some plane reservations. When Dale arrived in St. Louis, it was only two days before the wedding. After the wedding the bride and groom took a trip to Hawaii.

    _____ 1. Dale arrived in St. Louis two days before the wedding.

    _____ 2. Dale got married in St. Louis.

    _____ 3. She went to a travel agency.

    _____ 4. The plane reservation to get to the wedding in St. Louis was made by a travel agent.

    _____ 5. Dale went to Hawaii on her honeymoon.

12. Each class member is to bring a letter to the editor from a local paper. The class is divided into groups. Group members read the letters and decide whether they illustrate positive critical thinking. Be prepared to explain why or why not to the other members of the class.

Notes

1. Robert Hopper and Rita C. Noremore, *Children's Speech* (New York: Harper & Row, 1973), pp. 9–10.
2. Gregory Makst, "Can Your Technicians Communicate?" *American Technical Education Association Journal,* 6 (January-February 1979), 7–9.
3. Factors that cause communication difficulties are sometimes called interference. In this text, these factors are referred to as noise.
4. These categories were identified, in part, by Gerald Phillips in class lectures at Pennsylvania State University in 1970.
5. Carol Austin Bridgewater, "Tabu Topics," *Psychology Today* (October 1985), 16.

6. The models presented here are based on the views of communication agreed on by the participants of the Eastern States Beginning Course Conference, University of Maryland, November 1974. They were presented to the Speech Communication Association to serve as the standard view of speech communication.

7. Roy Berko, Andrew Wolvin, and Ray Curtis, *This Business of Communicating*, 4th ed. (Dubuque, Iowa: William C. Brown, 1990), p. 9.

8. For an extended discussion of the transactional communication perspective, see John Stewart, *Bridges, Not Walls* (Reading, Mass.: Addison-Wesley, 1986).

9. Steven C. Rhodes, "A Study of Effective and Ineffective Listening Dyads Using the Systems Theory Principle of Entropy," *Journal of the International Listening Association,* 1 (Spring 1987), 32.

10. William Barrett, *Irrational Man: A Study of Existential Philosophy* (Garden City, N.Y.: Doubleday, 1962), p. 78.

11. Rem B. Edwards, *Reason and Religion* (New York: Harcourt Brace Jovanovich, 1972), p. 66.

12. Milton K. Munitz, *The Ways of Philosophy* (New York: Macmillan, 1979), p. 322.

13. Reuben Abel, *Man Is the Measure* (New York: Free Press, 1976), p. 78.

14. Lorenz Boehm quoting Robert Ennis, *Critical Thinking/Critical Literacy: Teaching—As If It Matters* (Des Plaines, Ill.: Critical Literacy Project, Oakton Community College, 1990), p. 2.

15. These principles are based in part on Robert Ennis, "A Taxonomy of Critical Thinking Dispositions and Abilities," in J. Baron and R. Sternberg, eds., *Teaching for Thinking* (New York: Freeman, 1987).

16. William P. Alston, *Religious Belief and Philosophical Thought* (New York: Harcourt Brace Jovanovich, 1963), p. 15.

17. For more information on theological reasoning, see R. W. Mulligan, "St. Thomas Aquinas," *Encyclopedia International* (New York: Grolier, 1966), pp. 500–501.

18. Alston, pp. 454, 455.

19. Munitz, p. 323.

20. This is a true story, with the Christian Science explanation given by Mary Mona Fisher, the mother.

21. Ezra Bowen, "Ethics—Looking to Its Roots," *Time,* May 25, 1987, p. 26.

22. "Applied Ethics: A Strategy for Fostering Professional Responsibility," *Carnegie Quarterly,* 28 (Spring-Summer 1980), 2.

23. Ibid.

24. Ibid., pp. 3–4.

25. These distinctions are based on the concepts and writings of Professor Charles Buckalew, Department of Philosophy, Lorain County Community College, Elyria, Ohio.

26. Synthesized from an unpublished paper entitled "Ethics and Effectiveness," which refers generally to J. W. Gibson, C. R. Grunner, M. S. Janna, M. Smythe, and M. T. Hayes, "The Basic Course in Speech at U.S. Colleges and Universities," *Communication Education,* 29 (1980), 1–9.

27. Thomas Nilsen, *Ethics in Speech Communication* (Indianapolis: Bobbs-Merrill, 1966), p. 139.

3 *Self-Communication*

Chapter Outline

*Learning
Outcomes*

After reading this chapter, you should be able to:

Define and explain the concept of intrapersonal communication

Explain self-concept and its role as a guiding factor in a person's actions

Reveal your concept of self, patterns of disclosure, and acceptance of feedback

Define self-talk and demonstrate its impact on a person's emotional well-being

Explain the concepts of "I" and "me"

List some options and sources for improving self-concept

State and detail the theory of basic drive forces as they affect inner communication

Define and explain the causes, results, and help for communication apprehension.

Communication scholars and researchers have come to realize that the sensible way to begin improving our communication skills is by understanding our own self-communication. This processing of internal messages—called **intrapersonal communication**—involves the internal communication patterns we use to "talk to ourselves" either consciously or unconsciously on both verbal and nonverbal levels.

As you lie in bed at night, before you fall asleep, you may review the events of the day. As you take a test, you may read the questions and carry on a conversation with yourself to arrive at the answers. In both cases, you are communicating intrapersonally.

The basis for communication with others is the ability to communicate with oneself. Those people who tend to know who they are, what they believe in, and what their attitudes are and who have a clear understanding of their beliefs, values, and expectations are much more likely to be able to communicate these ideas to others.

Self-Concept

Your understanding of yourself is known as your **self-concept.** It represents your psychological self—all the experiences, beliefs, attitudes, and values that make up the self. It includes how you perceive the world and how you think the world perceives you. "Self-concept is the guiding factor in a person's actions," noted one source. "How a human being

*The more positively you per-
ceive yourself, the more likely
it is that you will have
self-confidence.*

views oneself will determine most of his or her actions and choices in life. Essentially a person is going to choose what he or she feels he or she is worth."[1] Thus the more positively you perceive yourself, the more likely it is that you will have self-confidence—that is, a sense of competence and effectiveness.

We know that the development of self-esteem is the primary prerequisite of learning. When we feel good about ourselves, we can become involved in the world of other people and things. We can risk learning something new, meeting new friends, engaging in a new venture; we realize that even if we fail, we can handle that possibility.[2]

Much of our self-concept stems from what we learn and how we process it. Because each of us has wants and needs that must be met, our early experiences, including whether our needs were met, influence how we view ourselves and others.

This recognition of the importance of self-esteem is not a new development. In fact, American psychologists and educators have been interested in the study of the self for many years. One classic theory indicates that the self has a number of different aspects, most notably the spiritual (thinking and feeling), the material (clothing and possessions), the social (interactions with others), and the bodily.[3]

Another theory of self-concept stresses that the self evolves from the

Our concept of self involves adapting to different roles.

interactions a person has with other people. This evolution takes place in stages. For example, the young child works for a sense of self as a separate person while developing a gender identity, the adolescent tries to establish a stable sense of identity, the middle-aged person emphasizes independence while adjusting to changes in body competence, and the elderly person seeks to come to terms with being old.[4] As we go through these various changes, our self-communication reflects the alterations that are taking place, and for this reason we experience a multiple, rather than a single, concept of who we are. Thus at any one time in our lives we may perceive ourselves to be a different person than at another time in our lives. You are not the same person today that you were five years ago, and you are not the same person today that you will perceive yourself to be five years from now.

Likewise, who you are with one person—that is, the self-concept you express—may not be the same as who you are with someone else. In one relationship you may take on the role of student and in another the role of friend. Each role requires different adapters and influences your self-concept accordingly. Thus you may have a highly positive self-concept as a spouse, for instance, but lack an equally high sense of self-esteem in your career.

Our self-esteem is constantly on display as we interact with others. In many ways, we are essentially putting on a show, managing the impressions we present to others about ourselves. This projection of an image results from cues that others give to us as to which role is appropriate at any given time. A new secretary coming into an organization, for instance, must quickly make decisions about the image the company is attempting to project to the public and determine the proper dress code, suitable telephone decorum, and acceptable interactions with the managers and executives. By using this sort of feedback, we learn the roles we must play to satisfy these individuals, usually so that we can ultimately satisfy ourselves. The result is a positive self-concept on our part.

The study of the self has recently spawned a whole new industry, image management, in which specialists help people to improve the image they project so they will receive positive feedback from others, thereby improving self-esteem. Image consultants work on all aspects of communication skills—developing public-speaking abilities, monitoring body language, improving listening, and even wearing particular styles and colors of clothing.

To be an effective intrapersonal communicator, a person should have a clear concept of self. But he or she must also recognize that self-concept changes and may well be different in the very near future.

Understanding Yourself

Most people have only a general idea of what or who they are, what they believe in, and how others perceive them. In many instances, their perceptions of themselves remain unsubstantiated, for few people really probe into themselves. Often they are unnerved when challenged to explain an action because they find that they do not really know or understand their motives or real commitments. In *The Education of a WASP,* the author recounted just such a dilemma in coming to grips with the conflict she felt trying to live a life of actualities rather than intentions.[5] She found herself challenged to demonstrate her professed love for humanity and her belief that fellowship should exist between black people and white people. Suddenly she could no longer give lip service to her ideas; she had to prove them with actions and deeds. But like so many others, she found it easy to philosophize and difficult actually to live the role.

Are you the type of person who wants to find out more about yourself? If so, investigate your motives and beliefs. Think for a moment. Who are you? What is your self-concept? Most people never bother to ask themselves these questions. Or if they do, they do not answer them in an orderly manner. But here is an experiment that might get you started.

To begin with, complete the following statements on a sheet of paper:

I am

I would like to be

I like to

I am a
I believe that
I have been
I don't like to
I wouldn't want to
The quality I am most proud of is
My biggest flaw is
Something that I would prefer others not know is

After you have finished, go back over your list of answers and write a one- or two-sentence description of yourself based on the statements you just completed. It has been said that you are what you are—based on your verb *to be*.[6] What you have done in the activity you just completed is to describe yourself based on your present verb *to be*. Your understanding of these two words includes a concept of yourself based on your past experiences (I have been/done), present attitudes and actions (I am), and future expectations (I would like to). You have just disclosed this concept—if you were honest and revealed what you really felt.

The questionnaire that follows can help you develop a clearer understanding of your disclosure and acceptance of feedback.

Before each item in the Part I place a number from 1 to 6 to indicate how much you are willing to reveal. A 1 indicates that you are willing to self-disclose nothing or almost nothing, and a 6 indicates that you are willing to reveal everything or almost everything. Use the values 2, 3, 4, and 5 to represent the points between these extremes.

Before each item in the second part, place a number from 1 to 6 to indicate how willing you are to receive feedback about what you self-disclose. A 1 indicates that you refuse or resist feedback, and a 6 indicates that you consistently encourage feedback. Use the values 2, 3, 4, and 5 to represent the points between these extremes.

PART 1: Extent to which I am willing to self-disclose my

_____ 1. goals

_____ 2. strengths

_____ 3. weaknesses

_____ 4. positive feelings

_____ 5. negative feelings

_____ 6. values

_____ 7. ideas

_____ 8. beliefs

_____ 9. fears and insecurities

_____ 10. mistakes

_____   Total

PART 2: Extent to which I am willing to receive feedback about my

_____ 1. goals

_____ 2. strengths

_____ 3. weaknesses

_____ 4. positive feelings

_____ 5. negative feelings

_____ 6. values

_____ 7. ideas

_____ 8. beliefs

_____ 9. fears and insecurities

_____ 10. mistakes

_____   Total

In general, scores of forty and above are considered high, while those below forty are considered low. If you score high on the first part and low on the second, you are probably more willing to disclose than you are to listen to feedback. If you scored low on the first part and high on the second, you are probably more willing to listen to what others have to say than you are to disclose things about yourself. And if you scored high on both, you are probably willing to disclose and receive feedback—a perfect candidate for a high-information-sharing relationship.[7]

Another way of looking at yourself is through the model known as the **Johari window**[8] (Figure 3.1). Your willingness to or not to disclose as well as listen to feedback from others has a great deal to do with your understanding of yourself as well as other's understanding of you.

The Johari window is a framework for defining self-concept. Area I, the **free area,** includes everything you know and understand about yourself and all other people know and understand about you—your values, personality characteristics, perceptions. For example, you may enjoy wearing nice clothes, and so you spend time selecting a wardrobe. This is communicated to others through the clothes you wear. Others, in turn, are aware of your enjoyment of wearing nice clothing because they observe what you wear and the care you take in selecting it.

	Known to Self	Not Known to Self
Known to Others	I. Free Area	II. Blind Area
Not Known to Others	III. Hidden Area	IV. Unknown Area

The **blind area,** area II, represents all those things about you that others recognize but that you do not see in yourself. You may, for example, make a poor first impression on certain people because you are boisterous or aggressive. Unless this behavior is pointed out, it will remain in the blind area and detract from the effectiveness of your communication. Information in the blind area is revealed only when you have the opportunity to investigate other people's perceptions of you. Unfortunately, problems can arise in your relationships with others if you do not know about these aspects of yourself.

In the **hidden area,** area III, you recognize something about yourself but choose not to share it with others. If you are a man, for example, you may have learned not to show certain types of emotions, such as crying; yet you sometimes face situations in which crying would express your true feelings. It seems necessary to you to control yourself so as to avoid an "ummanly" display of tears.

The **unknown area,** area IV, represents all those things that neither you nor others know about you. If you do not sit down and analyze who you are, why you act the way you do, or what internal drives trigger or control your actions, many aspects of yourself may remain unknown. Often they are so well concealed that they never even surface. These aspects remain unknown not only to you but to everyone else. They can inspire you to take certain actions and participate in certain activities; yet you are unaware of the part they play in your life. For example, in therapy you may suddenly remember that you were sexually abused as a child. This may explain a strong aversion to being touched.

Almost no one finds that all the panels in his or her window are of equal size. For example, people who are very open and easily share themselves with others normally have a large free area and smaller blind, hidden, and unknown areas. Because these kinds of people share, they are known to themselves and to others. People who are apprehensive about communicating with others probably have a small free area and large hidden and unknown areas.

You may want to use the Johari window to analyze yourself. Consider the four areas and determine which may be most dominant in your communication patterns, especially in your self-communication. In the self-disclosure experiment based on your verb *to be,* did you reveal a great deal about yourself? If so, area I may be the largest in your Johari window. If not, which of the other three areas may be the most dominant? If your window reflects a very open, free individual (that is, an extremely large area I), your communication patterns are quite different from those of a person with a very large area III. That person probably speaks less, attempts to conceal his or her real feelings, and avoids opportunities to "tell it like it is." Much of this self-concept and these self-understandings are communicated through self-talk.

Self-Talk   There is an old saying that it is okay to talk to yourself but that when you start answering back, it is time to worry. That contention is basically incorrect. Emerging research shows that there are indelible links between what we say to ourselves and what we accomplish. In addition, our **self-talk,** the inner conversations we have with ourselves, has a powerful impact on our emotional well-being.

Regardless of whether we know it, we are all engaged in a nearly constant subconscious monologue with ourselves. Sometimes we vocalize the monologue aloud, but often it is silent thinking or an internal whisper we are scarcely aware of. Even though it may be quiet, its impact can be enormous. "Your behavior, your feelings, your sense of self-esteem, and even your level of stress are influenced by your inner speech."[9] Everything that you do begins as self-talk. "Self-talk shapes our inner attitudes, our attitudes shape our behavior, and of course our behavior—what we do—shapes the results we get."[10]

Think of the inner struggles you often have concerning whether you believe something, will take a particular action, or will make a certain decision. Awake and asleep you are constantly in touch with yourself. You mumble, daydream, dream, fantasize, and feel tension. These are all forms of inner speech. "The subconscious will work for or against you. It's up to you. Tell yourself you're clumsy, can't use a computer, or aren't good with people, and that is what you probably will be."[11]

This belief has infiltrated the arts, sports, and even public speaking. People such as ballet dancer Rudolf Nureyev and superstar hockey player Wayne Gretzky, along with numerous baseball, football and basketball team members, have worked to get in touch with their inner voices and change negative messages to positive ones. People who get nervous before and during speeches have been taught to get in touch with their inner voices and alter self-defeating messages.

A process that allows you to get in touch with your inner voice is to get relaxed, breathe deeply for fifteen minutes while tuning out the hubbub around you, and let your mind wander. You will get a good appreciation for what you are feeding your mind.[12] "We have a choice each time we think, to think positively or negatively. Many of us don't believe it, but that absolutely is our choice. Once we understand that our private thoughts are ours alone to determine, we can select to program our brains with empowering, confidence-building thoughts."[13] According to one method on how to overcome negative self-talk, (1) be aware of your negative messages; (2) collect your recycled negatives, write them down, and regularly read them to yourself; (3) replace the negative thoughts with a positive one by flooding your brain with such statements as "I'm graceful," "I'm a people person," or "I can pass statistics." Once you start focusing on the positives, the negative side has to go away. It can't survive if you don't feed it.[14]

This method has been used extensively with sports personalities to overcome negatives. In one study, basket foul-shot shooters were divided into three groups. The first group used imagery and negative message elimination but did not practice shooting, the second group practiced shooting, and the third group did both corrective imaging and practicing. Though all three groups improved, the first and third groups improved at the same rate, while the second group improved proportionately less. "Positive self-talk really can turn your life around and make any life more successful."[15]

The Self and Others

Your image of yourself[16] may be referred to as your "I."[17] The **I** is the image you project, the way you perceive yourself. It is sent out through the words, ideas, actions, clothing, and lifestyle you choose. All these communicate your I to others.

Those with whom you come in contact build their own image of you for themselves, and they sometimes communicate this image to you. For example, friends comment about what they like and dislike about you, teachers criticize, parents praise and damn, spouses and bosses evaluate. These collective judgments by significant others develop into a "Me." The **Me** is the person others perceive you to be.

One of the best ways to understand how the I-Me dichotomy affects your communication is to examine the entire process as a mathematical formula. Under ideal conditions, we come as close to I = Me (I equals Me) as we can. Just as in algebra, when the equation balances, there is no basic error. If your perception of self (I) and the perception of you

held by significant others (Me) are basically the same—if these perceptions balance out—then you maintain your equilibrium and continue to
function as before. As a result, you continue to communicate in the same
manner as before.

If your friend tells you what a cooperative, bright person you are, and
then you go to work and your supervisor reaffirms this through positive
praise, you are likely to feel at peace with yourself. But you may feel
psychologically uncomfortable if you hear one thing from one source
and something else from another. In other words, when I does not equal
Me, confusion sets in.

Basically, when the I and the Me are not in balance, you have the
following four options of how to react:

1. *You can alter your communication actions.* In doing so, you are attempting to make the specific changes the significant other has indicated. If, for example, your best friend says that you are acting in an
   unacceptable manner and that you should alter your behavior to be
   a better person, a decision has to be made. Do you change? In Thorn-
   ton Wilder's play *Our Town,* George, one of the play's young lovers,
   must decide whether to alter his behavior as a result of a conversation
   with his girlfriend, Emily. She tells George that he is spending all his
   time playing baseball, that he does not speak to people anymore,
   and that he has become stuck-up and conceited. As the conversation
   continues, George offers to buy Emily an ice cream soda to celebrate
   not only their recent election as class officers but also his good fortune
   in having a friend who tells him what he should be told. The scene
   ends as George promises to take Emily's advice and change his ways.

   Often we need help in making these alterations, and we turn to
   psychiatrists, counselors, trusted friends, teachers, or relatives. You
   have probably known someone whose personality changed suddenly,
   or even over a period of time, because of an alteration of attitudes
   and ideas as expressed through verbal and nonverbal communication.

2. *You can accept an evaluation by acknowledging that it exists, but for some
   reason you feel the recommended change is not desirable.* Consequently,
   you accept the evaluation but do not change. For example, a group
   member may take the leadership role after the group flounders for
   several weeks and makes no progress toward accomplishing its goal.
   Another member of the group may accuse the newly emerged leader
   of exerting too much power. Because the group made no previous
   progress and is now well on its way to fulfilling its goal, the newly
   emerged leader may decide to accept the evaluation but not make
   any changes in his or her behavior pattern.

3. *You completely reject the input.* You consider the information, decide it
   is not true or of value, and do nothing about making any changes.

Students should feel comfortable asking teachers and counselors for advice.

This happens, for example, when a young man doesn't change his portrayal of a character in a play in spite of the director's criticism; or when the student in a speech class, rather than accepting comments about her presentation, refuses to consider any criticisms; or when you counter a friend's evaluation with, "If that's the way you feel about it, tough. I don't need friends like you."

4. *You can ignore any evaluation.* You don't seek out criticism and, if someone attempts to give it, you refuse to even listen to what is said. Ignorers use statements such as "Don't even bother to tell me what you think. I'm not interested." Sometimes you block out all criticism because you find it so self-defeating. Think, for example, of people who adopt this attitude: "I am what I am, and I'll be that way no matter what you say!" In the same way, employees sometimes refuse

to listen to suggestions for improving their work habits. "I've done it this way for years," they seem to say, "so there's no reason even to talk about it."

Developing the Self   Emphasis on the self (and self-improvement) became a characteristic of American society in the late 1970s and continues on into the 1990s. A wide range of books have been published stressing such topics as asserting oneself, thinking positively, handling interpersonal and intrapersonal conflict, overcoming shyness, becoming a liberated man or woman, and controlling self-doubt. These have been accompanied by numerous workshops and programs in which experts have attempted to help individuals become the people they want to be. Self-help groups and such programs as Adventures in Attitudes, Marriage Encounter, and Gestalt workshops have all become available to people seeking self-improvement. In addition, academic institutions have added to their curricula courses in interpersonal, intrapersonal, and family communication. Many private counselors, social workers, and psychologists are concentrating on assisting their clients in developing self-worth so as to be more self-fulfilled. Thus persons with negative self-concepts have numerous opportunities and sources for working to improve matters. But the first step, of course, is to have the desire to seek out the available assistance.

Besides your self-concept, which you learned through feedback from important people in your life, plus media influences, you are affected by interpersonal drives. These **drive forces** manifest inner communication and are expressed in outer communication. We think of ideas, consciously or unconsciously, and then act on them through verbal and nonverbal means. When our drives are fulfilled, we feel good—in other words, we communicate positively to ourselves and to others.

Intrapersonal Drives

We are each born with certain biological tools that allow us to communicate—a brain, sound-producing organs (mouth, tongue, voice box), and a receiving apparatus (ears, eyes). We also have basic drives within us that must be satisfied. These drives cause us to respond intrapersonally and to react in various ways, and we express these drives through our communication. Some communication theorists feel that these intrapersonal drives *are* the bases for our communication—what we express, what inspires us to act the way we do, and how we react to the way others express and use their drives.

From a social science viewpoint, the basic forces that determine human behavior are survival of the species, pleasure seeking, security, and territoriality.[18] These intrapersonal drives directly affect human communication. Theorists also assert that these drives are not manifested equally in each person. Some people may have a pleasure need that is stronger than any of the other forces, whereas another person may have strong need for both security and territoriality. This view offers a contrast to theories that posit a hierarchy of needs, each of which must be satisfied before a person can move on to another.

Survival of the Species

A person who is threatened screams out for help; a mother who cannot swim jumps into the water in an attempt to save her child, who has just fallen off a pier; a boy ducks behind a barrel on hearing an explosion he presumes to be a rifle shot; a father places his child behind him for protection against an attacker. All these are examples of attempts to ensure **survival of the species.**

Our ability to communicate selectively gives us a distinct survival advantage. We can call for help, plead, explain our need for food, or try to convince attackers that their action is unwise. In addition, we are aware of our own evolution, an awareness that is probably not possessed by other animals. Because of this, we can communicate about how we reproduce, what causes us to die, and how we can attempt to alter conditions so as to prolong our lives and those of our descendants. We have been able to communicate these ideas from person to person and thus to build on the experience of the past in developing intrapersonal understanding.

The sexual act intended for reproduction is a survival endeavor. Our concern with sex, however, goes beyond the need to ensure survival of the species. Indeed, we may be the only animals that use sex as a communication tool. Because we alone among all animals participate in the sex act outside of biological mating cycles, it is obvious that we use sex for more than reproduction. We use the act to show affection, punish (as in the cases of rape or the withholding of sex so as to penalize), reward, and bond together. The contrast with having sex and making love illustrates this. Having sex is a biological act. Making love entails concern for another and communicating before, during, and after the sexual act so that both people reach emotional or physical satisfaction. In addition, a great deal of male-to-male, female-to-female, and male-to-female interpersonal communication centers on descriptions of activities that are related directly or indirectly to sexual concerns.

Pleasure Seeking

We are basically **pleasure-seeking** and need-satisfying beings. A good part of our lives is devoted to communicating our pleasure or lack of pleasure as we exploit our conquests, stress our influences, and reinforce our accomplishments. We create awards, citations, and grades to communicate to others that we have succeeded, thus satisfying our intrapersonal messages.

But even if we accept the view that all of us do what we do because we seek pleasure, we may not be able to predict exactly how others will behave, for what will or will not give pleasure is not always obvious. Various people find different events pleasurable, and each of us may find both pleasure and pain in a single event. Moreover, we may find pleasure in satisfying not only our own needs but also the needs of others or in fulfilling long-term goals as well as immediate desires. What pleases one person may well torture another. One person happily gives a speech before a large audience; another is petrified by any speaking situation.

Think over your activities of the past several days. How much of what you did was performed in the hope that you would get some kind of pleasurable response from others, and how much was for your own satisfaction? Imagine that you are sitting in class and the teacher asks, "What is the numerical value of pi?" You raise your hand and are called on, give the correct answer of 3.14, and the teacher says, "Good." The experience has been pleasurable—you got a positive reaction. Now the teacher asks, "What is the square root of 23.557?" You do not raise your hand. In other words, you fail to give a signal that you want to participate. Thus the teacher does not call on you, and you avoid a possibly negative reaction.

Each time we participate in such an experience, we put into action the **pleasure principle,** deciding whether to open ourselves to an evaluation. We usually do so if we assume we will be right rather than wrong. The least we hope for is that we will come out no worse than neutral, neither winning nor losing.

We can compare this to a meter with a plus on the right side, a minus on the left, and an N (standing for neutral) in the center. We start out each selectively controlled communication situation in the neutral position. Each time we volunteer to participate, we hope for no worse than a neutral reaction ("OK, but . . ."), although our desire is for a positive one ("Right" or "Good"). If we pile up enough of these positive reactions, we open ourselves up to more opportunities, thereby building confidence and feeling freer to gamble, to take part in the communication. If we receive numerous negative reactions, however, we may decide that we do not want to participate anymore, and we may shy away from communication situations. For example, the speaker who has received positive reactions from an audience is much more likely to try the experience again than the speaker who received negative reactions.

Unfortunately, not all communication situations allow us to control what goes on. In many classes, for instance, the teacher decides who will

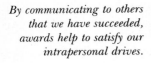

By communicating to others that we have succeeded, awards help to satisfy our intrapersonal drives.

answer and when. Thus if you are assured of negative reactions and you find them extremely painful, you may decide not to participate by skipping class, faking an illness, or disrupting the lesson.

You can see, then, that through our experiences, we gradually build up an attitude about ourselves that we communicate intrapersonally. This attitude controls our self-confidence and often our willingness to take part in communication transactions.

Security   You enter a classroom for the first meeting of a class. You see a place that is unfamiliar, people you do not know, a professor who is an unknown quantity. You feel insecure. Your desire to participate and your comfort in this situation can be affected directly by the messages you send yourself.

Security is a basic human need. Because of it, we seek equilibrium, a keeping of balance. When security is absent, when we feel a lack of control, most of us are uneasy, overly cautious, uncertain.

Our concept of ourselves in situations of security or insecurity motivates our verbal and nonverbal communication. Fear causes the vocal pitch to rise, the body to shake, and the stomach to churn. We find ourselves afraid to speak or speaking incessantly or stammering. But as we feel more comfortable in a situation, as we learn the rules of the game, we find ourselves acting quite differently as we send ourselves positive messages. The first day of class, for instance, you may not say a word. But later, as you acclimate yourself to the situation, you may feel relaxed or knowledgeable enough to participate.

Many people cling to the security of traditions and past accomplishments because they fear what change may bring. Indeed, much of what is referred to as the generation gap may well be the result of past experiences that led to the sending of interpersonal messages of security on the part of adults, establishing for those adults what was right and wrong. In contrast, the young lack this measuring stick and are therefore sometimes willing to gamble on what the outcome of their behavior may be.

Hearing intrapersonal messages of the fear of the unknown explains why some people will not wander down the unmapped paths of life. In a similar fashion, the fear of not being accepted because of differences in dress style, speech pattern, or moral attitudes causes uncertainty in many people. Rules about what is right and wrong that are set up by "society" are often used by such individuals to make their own decisions.

Territory   We intrapersonally define a particular **territory,** whether physical or perceptual, and then feel secure within that territory; we defend it from invasion and use it for protection. We mark off land by defining it precisely with deeds that indicate exactly how long a plot is, how wide it is, and where it is located. We also mark the plot off with fences and shrubbery, with signs and numbers that specifically say, "This belongs to me." We feel secure when we are in our own territory, and we often identify ourselves by our hometown, our school, our academic degrees, and our social groups—all of which are territorial markers.

We act differently in different territories. When friends come to visit you, conditions are not the same as when you go to visit them. The friend you invite over for dinner does not act the same at your house as when you go to his or her house for dinner. In the same way, there is a definite difference in playing an athletic game at home and playing it on the road. The home team is estimated to have an advantage of about one touchdown in football and ten points in basketball. In discussing the success of a professional basketball team, which had just won two playoff games on their home court after having lost two earlier games in their opponents' facility, superstar Michael Jordan said, "Now we've got them at home, which is what we wanted. I hope the crowd will do (for us) what it did for them. The crowd helped them."[19] Being familiar with the surroundings and having cheering friends, rather than

Human beings define a particular territory, whether physical or perceptual, and then feel secure within that territory.

booing enemies, in the stands produce a definite psychological effect on the team members' feelings of security. In addition to physical territory, we also have ideas and areas of expertise we identify as ours. Inventors obtain patents to protect their inventions; writers copyright their books. Both are attempts to establish a territory and to communicate this establishment to others.

Have you ever raised your hand in class and asked your instructor a question he or she could not answer? You might have been surprised when the instructor became irritated. Have you ever asked your boss for an explanation of a particular company policy only to have him or her verbally attack you? Think about it. The reaction could have occurred because you invaded the person's area of expertise, thereby causing a defensive response.

Parents may react in a similar way at home when children force them to relinquish their beliefs or show them to be wrong. There are strong reasons for the feelings underlying such statements as "When you're living in my home, you'll do as I tell you. When you're in your own house, you can do what you want; but as long as I'm supporting you, you'll do what I say." It is obvious here that the possessor of the territory feels she or he has the power to set the rules, enforce them, and maintain established territorial rights.

The more insecure a person is within a territory, the greater is that person's intrapersonal fear of losing that territory. Once people have defined something as theirs, they will tend to defend it. Thus an invasion of someone else's territory is likely to invite a counterattack.

Anxiety: Communication Apprehension

Anxiety—excessive worry or concern—is another important variable that may affect our perceptions and performance. Communication anxiety (or communication apprehension) can affect our processing of information. Though many think of communication anxiety only in regard to public speaking, it is much broader. Worries, concerns, and fears interfere with efficient listening, communicating in groups, talking in class and on the telephone, and verbalizing during interviews. Anxiety can make us so preoccupied we do not get the message that is being communicated or we become incapable of sending the message.

Anxiety about communicating often reflects negative feelings about one's self. Some people have difficulty sharing themselves with others and feel uncomfortable about communicating in selected situations. Other people have difficulty communicating at all. This sort of apprehension has become such a general problem that it has been called the "new social disease" of the American populace.[20]

As terms, "shyness" and "communication apprehension" have been used by various authors to explain what may or may not be the same phenomenon. **Shyness** has been defined as "quietness" or has been used to refer to "someone who doesn't talk much,"[21] whereas **communication apprehension** describes "fear or anxiety about or in communication."[22] This discussion uses the latter term and defines it as "the fear or anxiety associated with either real or anticipated communication with another person or persons."[23] People with this trait are referred to as **communication apprehensives, or CAs.**

No matter what label is used to describe the problem, the evidence is conclusive: most people seem to possess this sort of apprehension at least to some extent. One study estimated that 80 percent of the people in this country confess to being shy and that only about 7 percent of all Americans have never felt shy.[24] Other researchers indicated that virtually 100 percent of us experience communication apprehension from time to time and almost 95 percent of the population reports having apprehension about communicating with some person or group in their lives.[25]

People vary in the degree to which they are apprehensive about oral communication with others. Many feel comfortable in a one-on-one situation and yet are fearful of public speaking.

Identifying and Describing Communication Apprehensives

Most communication apprehensives are aware that they have this characteristic. If they are unsure, there are standardized tests, which can be taken to identify all apprehensive persons.[26]

Who are communication apprehensives? How do they participate in communication? How are they perceived by others? Five theoretical proposals can help us answer these questions.[27]

1. People vary in the degree to which they are apprehensive about oral communication with others.
2. People with high oral communication apprehension seek to avoid oral communication.
3. People with high oral communication apprehension engage in less oral communication than do less orally apprehensive people.
4. When people with high oral communication apprehension do communicate, their behavior differs from that of people who are less apprehensive.
5. As a result of their oral communication behavior, high oral communication apprehensives are perceived less positively than are less apprehensive people.

CAs do appear to share some general characteristics. "Moderate communication apprehensives," said one source, "recognize that some situations bother them but not other situations, and assume that most people are bothered by fewer situations than they are."[28] "High communication apprehensive individuals," noted another source, "evidenced a lack of self-esteem and self-acceptance. While this is not universally true, it is a very common pattern."[29]

Research shows that certain people have a predisposition to fear participation in most communication situations; these people are called "Trait A CAs." Others are fearful only of a specific situation, such as public speaking; they are called "Trait B CAs." One study asked adults to pick items from a list of representative situations in which they had some degree of fear.[30] The results indicated that 40.6 percent identified their major fear to be speaking before groups. This figure, surprisingly, was the highest total of the survey, far exceeding fear of heights (32 percent), death (18.7 percent), and loneliness (13.6 percent).

Still others are apprehensive about a specific person (a boss, a teacher, a parent) or a special group (a class, fellow employees). They are called "State A CAs." Most people fear some specific situation—for example, communicating in a setting where they do not know anyone or being forced to perform when they do not feel prepared. "State B CAs" become apprehensive only when they find themselves in that specific situation.[31]

CAs seem to possess some general characteristics. They tend (1) to be afraid of giving wrong answers and of receiving any type of evaluation, (2) to focus on the correctness of the material, (3) to feel that they do not have the ability to control themselves and the environment in which they are to speak, (4) to be anxious about reading aloud, (5) to feel emotionally unprepared to talk, (6) to be unable to organize their thoughts and ideas, (7) and to be unable to figure out rhetorical strategies for dealing with their audience.[32]

Causes of Communication Apprehension

Why does a person become a communication apprehensive? There appear to be four general causes: heredity, modeling, reinforcement, and expectancy learning. Specific causes also apply.

Heredity

According to one source:

> Researchers in the area of social biology have established that significant social traits can be measured in infants shortly after birth, and that infants differ sharply from each other on these traits. One of these traits is referred to as **sociability,** which is believed to be a predisposition directly related to adult sociability—the degree to which we reach out to other people and respond positively to contact with other people.[33]

According to a recent theory, about "10% to 15% of babies are born to be shy."[34] Those who believe this theory accept the idea that "a person might be born with a sensitive nervous system resulting in heightened awareness of themselves and other people's responses to them."[35] The biological explanation for this birth-centered shyness is that when emotional centers in the brain are activated, chemical messengers are released into the bloodstream that trigger a state of heightened bodily arousal to cope with the challenging situation.[36] Most of the researchers who have posed this inherent inhibition theory have reported that the apprehension can usually be overcome either through panic disorder medication or through some type of training.

Modeling   Children observe the communication behavior of others in their environment and attempt to emulate it. Thus if they are surrounded by people who fear communication, they are likely to follow that pattern. This imitation is called **modeling.**

Reinforcement   The most popular explanation for communication apprehension is **reinforcement.** The basic premise behind this theory is that behavior that is reinforced will increase but behavior that is not reinforced will decline. Therefore because few children are encouraged to present their point of view and many children are actively discouraged from communicating, they learn to *not* present their views and remain quiet on into adulthood.

Expectancy Learning   People are always trying to discover what consequences are likely to result from their behavior—to learn what to expect. They then adapt their behavior so as to increase positive outcomes and avoid negative outcomes (**expectancy learning**). For example, if a person receives negative feedback from her or his communication efforts, that person learns not to speak out. In this way, the person avoids unnecessary pain and sets a pattern designed to protect her or him from future negative experiences.

Other Causes   Communication apprehension may result from more specific causes. For example, a person who is deficient in communication skills, such as vocabulary or the ability to organize ideas, may withdraw from communicating. Or not speaking English as a native language or feeling socially alienated from other people may also cause difficulties. Because their nationality or religious backgrounds differ from the patterns of the general society, some people may find that they simply cannot communicate in the presence of those who are not members of their group. For example, a member of a fundamentalist religious sect may have been negatively perceived because of the ideas he or she presented; as a result, that person may be very apprehensive in future situations that require oral participation when these ideas may again come forth.

Authoritarian homes, authoritarian schools, and authoritarian religions all tend to produce communication apprehensives because people in such environments have not been given the opportunity to ask questions, make decisions, or express their feelings and because they are constantly being told what to do. They have not been allowed to test their communication abilities and are very unsure of how to put their ideas into action.

Social pressures to be the best, to be good, and to conform blindly to rules and regulations all help produce people who find it difficult to express their ideas. The more a person fears rejection and criticism and the more he or she is dependent on others for praise and reassurance, the more likely that person will be to have little self-confidence and prove reticent to communicate for fear of not receiving praise and reassurance.

Results of Communication Apprehension

"Communication apprehension," reported one source, "has been shown to have negative impact on an individual's communication behavior as well as on other essential aspects of their lives."[37] Many people dislike being communication apprehensives. They describe it as a personal problem of serious proportions, one that can lead to other difficulties. For example, an apprehensive person usually cannot make eye contact with another person because it is a form of visual touching.[38] Because of this, the apprehensive person may be perceived as unfriendly, dishonest, and aloof.

The apprehensive person may also become frustrated because he or she often finds it necessary to avoid oral communication. Communication apprehensive people have been known to drop out of classes that require speaking, avoid social situations that might require talking to someone, or not apply for a job for which they may otherwise be qualified if they suspect it may require interpersonal communication.

Communication apprehensives sometimes find that the most simple task—reading out loud, eating in a public restaurant where they have to order their meal, using a pay telephone, returning unwanted goods to a store, or talking to an answering machine—may create trauma. CAs are noted for switching jobs if the work requires social or communicative interactions, relying on spouses or relatives to do their communicating, and becoming introverted to avoid risking social blunders.

Shy people sometimes become phobic about meeting strangers and encountering new environments. There even appears to be a difference in their ability to get physically close to others. One research study indicated that "shyer people preferred a distance 8 inches farther apart, on the average, than did the less shy."[39]

As one communication apprehensive expressed it, "I find it difficult to meet new people, never speak up for my rights or express my opinions or values, find it difficult to communicate effectively, feel depressed, hold a low opinion of myself. I feel the necessity to rehearse everything I say, and feel that everyone is noticing me."[40] Apprehensives often lack the ability to share their true selves with someone else and are less effective in shaping their own world because they hide from themselves and from others.

Help for Communication Apprehension

For the person who is uncomfortable being a communication apprehensive and wants to do something about it, skill training, systematic desensitization, cognitive modification, and self-help are possible forms of aid.

Skill Training

One obvious way to overcome shyness is to learn the skills needed to be an effective communicator—how to organize ideas, how to analyze an audience, how to gain the rhetorical strategies for dealing with people as individuals. If you are a communication apprehensive, many of the theories and skills stressed in this book and taught in the class you are now taking can help you overcome your difficulties. For example, knowing the techniques of developing and presenting a speech goes a long way toward aiding those who have speech apprehension to overcome their anxiety.

Systematic Desensitization

Through systematic desensitization people are taught to recognize tension in their bodies and then to relax. In this technique, the person being treated is "asked to imagine a series of communication situations, progressing from those that previously have aroused little tension to those that normally would cause great tension. The person learns to completely relax while imagining one situation before moving on to a more difficult one."[41] As many as 80 or 90 percent of the people treated professionally by this system report the complete elimination of their apprehension.[42] Nevertheless, such a program will work only if the person wants to change and has the skills to allow modification of his or her behavior. If the person does not have the necessary skills, then training must precede systematic desensitization.

Cognitive Modification

The basic concept behind cognitive modification is that people have learned to think negatively and must be retaught to think positively. The first step in this process is for people to learn how to recognize when they are thinking negatively and identify their own negative statements about their communication. Then they learn to replace negative statements with positive ones. Rather than saying, for example, "I really say stupid things," they may substitute, "I can present clear ideas; it isn't that hard." The last stage of the training is to practice substituting positive statements for negative ones. According to researchers, the success of this technique is quite high.[43]

Self-Help Communication apprehensives may be able to help themselves through the following strategies:

1. *Identify if they really are communicative apprehensive and, if so, what type of communication makes them apprehensive (groups, conversations, meetings, public speaking).* This identification aids CAs in developing a plan to learn the specific skills or understandings to be more effective or to deal with negative internal messages.

2. *Make an effort to learn about the communication process, and gain skills in public speaking, conversation, and group membership.* One of the major techniques that most CAs need to acquire is assertiveness because its lack is a major cause of the uneasiness and the inadequacy that many people experience. Assertiveness is the product of a set of learned attitudes and communication skills used to identify situations in which change is both an important and a realistic goal. In addition, improving self-esteem and learning specific skills for relating to others, such as keeping a conversation active, can aid a communication apprehensive. Signing up for classes or taking workshops that include instruction in these areas is an excellent first step toward overcoming apprehension.

3. *Learn to recognize bodily tension and learn to relax.* People can often feel the tension. Learning to give self-relaxing messages and to engage in self-hypnosis or other relaxation techniques often helps communication apprehensives to cope with and/or overcome their fear.

4. *Learn to identify negative statements and eliminate them.* "I can't do it" is a self-defeating statement that can be replaced by "I'll try to do it the best I can." "I'll fail" can be replaced by "I don't have to be perfect." Self-defeating statements help produce the negative mindsets that almost always ensure defeat.

5. *Practice communication techniques.* The more speeches a person gives, the less likely is the speaking situation to be endangering. The more social interactions a person participates in, the less fear becomes associated with those interactions. People are often afraid of the unknown and of those situations in which they are inexperienced. The more a

person learns about a subject and practices carrying out what has been learned, the less likely that person is to fear participation in similar events.

Shy people are often helped when they accept the adage that a person should not worry about being liked by everyone or being the most popular. Although all people can work to improve themselves, becoming emotionally immobilized because of the fear of not being the best is self-defeating. Learning to give and take compliments often helps CAs to avoid cringing under a word of praise. Rather than putting their heads down and twisting their toes into the carpet, CAs can look their praisers in the eye and say, "Thank you"; this technique can open the doors of friendship and allow communication apprehensives to realize that they are really okay. In addition, mental rehearsal for a conversation, a telephone call, or a meeting can make the situation easier to handle. The rehearsal may take the edge off the unknown.

The most important piece of information for communication apprehensives to keep in mind is that in almost all cases their apprehension is not an illness but is learned behavior that can be unlearned. Although the unlearning takes determination and work, it can be done and indeed has been done by many.

Using Intrapersonal Communication

Developing your own repertoire of communication skills involves, as a first step, understanding your self-concept, intrapersonal drives, and perceptual variables and determining whether you are communicatively apprehensive. If you are aware of your own processing as a sender and as a receiver and can monitor your own communication, you can build your communication strengths and work for improvement of those areas that should be developed.

Much of this intrapersonal awareness is based on a willingness to communicate—to take risks in the process, analyze it, and deal with the results. If you think about some of the effective communicators you know, you can probably characterize them as willing to communicate, aware of the process, and strong in their self-knowledge and communication abilities. In contrast, consider someone who seems to lack these communication characteristics and consequently seems uncomfortable and ineffective as a communicator.

Coming to terms with yourself as a communicator, then, forms the basis for communicating in career and in social settings. The manager who knows herself as a communicator can make decisions that capitalize on her strengths in dealing with others in the office. The father who is in touch with his communication attitudes will know how to take advantage of dinner table conversations with his children and further their growth as people. The foundation must be built, however, from within.

Summary

In this chapter, self-communication, as displayed in self-concept, intrapersonal drives, perceptions, and anxiety, was investigated. The major ideas presented were:

- Intrapersonal communication involves the internal communication patterns we use to talk to ourselves either consciously or unconsciously on both verbal and nonverbal levels.
- Your understanding of yourself is known as your self-concept.
- Each person is a different person to different people.
- To be an effective intrapersonal communicator, a person must have a clear concept of self.
- You are what you are based on your verb *to be*—your past experiences and learning, present attitudes and practices, and future desires.
- Our communication and our actions are based on our self-talk.
- The Johari window is an effective device for looking at yourself.
- The "I" is your image of yourself; the "Me" is the person others perceive you to be.
- If the "I" and the "Me" are not in balance, we respond to that imbalance by altering, accepting and not changing, rejecting, or ignoring.
- Drive forces manifest themselves in inner communication and are expressed in outer communication.
- The drive forces are survival of the species, pleasure seeking, security, and territoriality.
- Communication anxiety is the fear or anxiety associated with either real or anticipated communication with another person or persons.
- Communication anxiety has been shown to have negative impact on people's communication behavior as well as on other essential aspects of their lives.
- Help for communication apprehension can be found in skill training, systematic desensitization, cognitive modification, and self-help.
- An understanding of yourself as a communicator can be the useful first step in developing a repertoire of communication skills.

Key Terms

intrapersonal communication
self-concept
Johari window
free area
blind area
hidden area
unknown area
self-talk
I
Me
drive forces
survival of the species
pleasure seeking

pleasure principle
security
territory
anxiety
shyness
communication apprehension
communication apprehensives
CAs
sociability
modeling
reinforcement
expectancy learning

Learn by Doing

1. Prepare a list of ten questions an interviewer should ask so as to get an accurate picture of who you really are. These questions should allow the interviewer to understand your personal history, beliefs, and future plans. Phrase the questions so they require more than a one- or two-word reply. Your instructor then matches you with another member of the class, and you interview each other, using the questions each of you has prepared. Then you introduce each other in a two- to three-minute presentation to the class. After the class presentation, answer the following questions:

    a. What did it feel like to reveal yourself to a stranger?
    b. Did you conceal things about yourself during the interview? If so, why?
    c. How did you feel while your partner was introducing you to the class? How were you responding nonverbally? (Were you looking at the floor? Did you blush?) Why did you react the way you did?

2. Bring to class a painting, poem, or piece of music you like. Share it with the class and indicate why you have positive feelings about it. What does your choice indicate about you? What did you learn about your classmates from their selections?

3. Your friend asks you to define intrapersonal communication and explain how understanding the theories about it is valuable. What is your response?

4. Do you agree or disagree with the following statements: "A person is changeable and can alter behavior patterns if she or he really wants to do so." "No one can change anyone; only the individual can change himself or herself." Explain the reason for your answers.

5. Select one of the four options—altering, accepting and not changing, rejecting, or ignoring—that are available when the I and the Me are not in balance. Cite a personal example of a situation in which you found the I and Me out of balance and chose this option; describe what you did.

6. Use the illustration and explanation of the Johari window in this chapter to fill in as much of it as you can. If possible, get one of your best friends to fill in the "known to others" part of the window. What did you learn about yourself from this activity?

7. Design a coat of arms for yourself. Place at least four pictures, symbols, or words on the coat of arms. Produce the coat on paper large enough for the class to see all the parts clearly. Explain the coat of arms and why you have selected these things to represent you.

Notes

1. Sveri Wahlross, *Family Communication* (New York: Macmillan, 1974), p. xi.
2. Caroline Donnelly, "Writing an Advertisement for Yourself," *Money,* 4 (January 1974), 308.
3. William James, *The Principles of Psychology* (New York: Holt, Rinehart and Winston, 1890).
4. Ruth C. Wyle, *The Self Concept* (Lincoln: University of Nebraska Press, 1979), p. 9.
5. Lois Stalvey, *The Education of a WASP* (New York: Bantam Books, 1971).
6. The verb *to be* provides us with our basic label of our selves. Native Americans and those from some other cultures, such as West Africans, may have difficulty understanding and applying this concept because of linguistic and other cultural differences. Most North Americans, however, should find it easy to grasp.
7. Lawrence B. Rosenfeld and Roy M. Berko, *Communicating with Competency* (Glenview, Ill.: Scott, Foresman and Co., Little Brown High Education, 1990), pp. 184–185.
8. Joseph A. Luft, *Group Process: An Introduction to Group Dynamics* (Palo Alto, Calif.: National Press, 1963), Chapter 3.
9. Pamela Butler, as noted in Robert McGarvey, "Talk Yourself Up," *USAIR Magazine* (March 1990), 90.
10. Ibid.
11. David Thornburg, as noted in McGarvey, p. 90.
12. Myrna Hartley, as noted in McGarvey, p. 92.

13. Gail Dusa, as noted in McGarvey, p. 90.

14. Dave Grant, as noted in McGarvey, p. 93.

15. Bernie Zilbergeld, as noted in McGarvey, p. 94.

16. For a further discussion of the self and others, see George Herbert Mead, *Selected Writings* (Indianapolis: Bobbs-Merrill, 1964), pp. 244–247, 312–313.

17. For a further discussion of the "I," see Calvin S. Hall and Gardner Lindzey, *Theories of Personality* (New York: Wiley, 1957), p. 483.

18. These categories were identified by Gerald Phillips in a class lecture at Pennsylvania State University in 1969.

19. Roger Nevin, "Jordan: Crowd Inspired Cavs," *Elyria Chronicle-Telegram* (Ohio), May 6, 1988, p. B-2.

20. Phillip Zimbardo, *Shyness: What It Is; What to Do About It* (Reading, Mass.: Addison-Wesley, 1977), p. 92.

21. Comments made by James McCroskey during a panel discussion concerning communication apprehension, Eastern Communication Association, Ocean City, Maryland, April 1980.

22. Ibid.

23. James McCroskey, "Validity of the PRCA as an Index of Oral Communication Apprehension," *Communication Monographs,* 45 (August 1978), 192.

24. Zimbardo, p. 92.

25. James McCroskey and Virginia Richmond, *The Quiet Ones: Communication Apprehension and Shyness* (Dubuque, Iowa: CommComp, Gorsuch Scaresbuck, 1980), p. 21.

26. For copies and discussions of communication apprehensive scales, see Virginia Richmond and James McCroskey, *Communication: Apprehension, Avoidance, and Effectiveness* (Scottsdale, Ariz.: Gorsuch Scaresbuck, 1985).

27. McCroskey, "Validity," pp. 193–198.

28. McCroskey and Richmond, p. 17.

29. McCroskey, "Validity," p. 99.

30. *The Bruskin Report* (New Brunswick, N.J.: R. H. Bruskin Associates, 1973).

31. Comments made by McCroskey.

32. Roy M. Berko, *Interaction = Speaker + Listener,* 2nd ed. (Dubuque, Iowa: Kendall-Hunt, 1975), p. 9.

33. McCroskey and Richmond, p. 6.

34. "Extreme Shyness Linked to Biology, Researchers Say," *Cleveland Plain Dealer,* June 28, 1987, p. A-15, reporting the work of psychologists Jerome Kagan, Robert Plomin, David Rowe, and Stephen Suomi.

35. Frederic Koeppel, *Elyria Chronicle-Telegram* (Ohio), February 5, 1987, p. B-4, reporting the work of Mary Streete.

36. Jules Asher, "Born to Be Shy?" *Psychology Today,* 21 (April 1987), 59.

37. Judy Pearson, "The Relationship Between Communication Apprehension and Assertiveness," presentation delivered at the Eastern Communication Association Convention, Ocean City, Maryland, April 1980.

38. "Shyness: New National Malady?" *Elyria Chronicle-Telegram* (Ohio), April 29, 1975, p. 5.

39. Based on the work of Bernardo Carducci and Arthur Webber.

40. Cleta M. Diamond, "Shyness—A Closer Look," paper, Lorain County Community College, Elyria, Ohio, November 29, 1977.
41. McCroskey and Richmond, p. 36. For a further discussion of systematic desensitization, see Susan R. Glaser, "Oral Communication Apprehension and Avoidance: The Current Status of Treatment Research," *Communication Education,* 30 (1981), 323–329.
42. McCroskey and Richmond, p. 36.
43. McCroskey and Richmond, p. 37.

4 *Listening*

Chapter Outline

Learning Outcomes

After reading this chapter, you should be able to:

Explain the importance of listening in daily communication

Contrast hearing and listening

Define and state the role of reception, perception, attention, the assignment of meaning, and response as they relate to the listening process

List and explain some of the listening influencers

Define the discrimination, comprehension, therapeutic, critical, and appreciative levels of listening

Identify and explain some of the techniques available for improving personal listening.

One of the earliest studies in the field of communication discovered that listening may take up as much as 45 percent of our communication time.[1] It has also been revealed that those of us in organizations spend as much as 80 percent of our time listening and speaking to each other.[2] Furthermore, in the United States we spend as much as twenty-two thousand hours listening to and watching television before we reach the age of nineteen.[3] Indeed, a Nielsen report estimated that the daily television viewing total of American households may be as high as seven hours and two minutes per day.[4] And we certainly spend a great deal of time as listeners in social conversations, family discussions, and interactions with fellow workers.

The Importance of Listening

Because we devote so much time to this activity, many schools and corporations have come to recognize the need for preparing us to listen more effectively. Elementary school reading teachers are increasingly training children in the skill of listening so as to prepare them to be better communicators and readers. (You may not have thought about it, but reading is much like listening with the eyes rather than the ears, although in reading, you can reexamine the information if you do not understand it.) And listening is certainly an important means for learning at the college level. It is estimated that college women spend 42 percent of their daily communication time listening; when questioned, 82 percent of the women in one study considered listening to be equal to or more important than reading as a means for learning at the college level.[5] This finding was reinforced by a study revealing that both male and female college students spent 52.5 percent of their total communication time listening, whereas they spent 17.3 percent reading, 16.3 percent speaking, and 13.9 percent writing.[6] Indeed, research has revealed that skill in listening is more critical to academic success than reading or academic aptitude.[7]

In the business world, attention is being paid to evaluating and enhancing listening efficiency. Several researchers have investigated the amount of time business personnel spend listening. The research indicated that most employees of major American corporations spend about 60 percent of their day listening; executives spend as much as 63 percent of their workday as listeners.[8] Several years ago, the Sperry Corporation (which has since become part of Unisys) launched a major newspaper, magazine, and television advertising campaign to point out how important it is to listen effectively and to persuade Americans to be more concerned with this communication skill. One of these advertisements is shown in Figure 4.1. Like many other American corporations, Unisys has instituted training programs to prepare its executives, managers, and employees to be better listeners. Control Data, 3M, Ford, and AT&T are just a few other major companies that provide training in listening. In responding to the recognized need for improved listening skills, Fortune 500 training directors indicated that poor listening was "one of the most important problems facing them and that ineffective listening leads to ineffective performance or low productivity."[9]

> As educated people, we have an obligation to strive to become responsible listeners. Responsible means responsiveness; instead of being passive we treat listening as part of ongoing communication with the other person. We make decisions about how to listen based on the nature of our relationship with the other person. In making those decisions however, we need to take special care to listen to and appreciate points of view other than our own.[10]

The Listening Process

Many people assume that hearing and listening are the same, but they are not. **Hearing** is a biological activity that involves reception of a message through sensory channels; as such, it may be affected by all of the senses. But hearing—the active processing of all auditory stimuli—is only one part of listening. **Listening** also involves reception, perception, attention, the assignment of meaning, and response by the listener to the message presented.

Reception   The initial step in the listening process is the **reception** of the stimulus or message, which includes both the auditory message and the visual,

KNOWING HOW TO LISTEN COULD DOUBLE THE EFFICIENCY OF AMERICAN BUSINESS. DID YOU HEAR THAT?

Business today is held together by its communication system. And listening is undoubtedly its weakest link.

Most of us spend about half our business hours listening. Listening poorly. Research studies show that on the average we listen at a 25% level of efficiency.

A statistic that is not only surprisingly low, but terribly costly.

With more than 100 million workers in America, a simple ten dollar listening mistake by each of them would cost a billion dollars.

Letters have to be retyped; appointments rescheduled; shipments reshipped.

And when people in large corporations fail to listen to one another, the results are even costlier.

Ideas get distorted by as much as 80% as they travel through the unwieldy chain of command.

Employees feel more and more distant, and ultimately alienated from top management.

Well, as one of the world's largest corporations—with 87,000 employees and five divisions—we at Sperry simply can't afford to pay the price of poor listening.

So we've set up extensive listening programs that Sperry personnel throughout the world can take part in. From sales representatives to computer engineers to the Chairman of the Board.

These programs are making us a lot better at listening to each other. And when you do business with Sperry Univac, or any of our other divisions, you'll discover that they're making us a lot better at listening to you.

We understand how important it is to listen.
Sperry is Sperry Univac computers, Sperry New Holland farm equipment, Sperry Vickers fluid power systems, and guidance and control equipment from Sperry division and Sperry Flight Systems.

Figure 4.1

The Importance of Listening

(Reprinted with permission, Unisys Corporation)

nonverbal message. The hearing process is a very complex one, for the human ear has the capacity to distinguish approximately 340,000 different tones. Obviously, proper care of the ear is important because auditory acuity enhances the ability to listen efficiently. The National Institutes of Health estimated that approximately 13 million Americans (almost 1 out of every 20 people) have some type of hearing impairment.[11] To keep these statistics from rising, people who work near loud machinery are now required to wear ear protectors. But the workplace is not the only source of potential danger. For example, individuals who expose themselves to loud rock music or listen to such music through earphones should also be aware that they can damage their hearing mechanism. Indeed, the use of earphones to listen to music is considered to be the source of much of the ear damage suffered by Americans.[12]

In addition to using the hearing mechanism, people listen through the visual system. Barring physical defects, the eyes have the phenomenal capacity of 5 million discriminations per second. People listen through

*Listening involves much
more than just hearing.*

the eyes a great deal because a person's facial expression, posture, movement, and appearance all provide important cues that may not be obvious merely by listening to the verbal part of the message. It has been
estimated that 93 percent of the total meaning of a message can emerge
from nonverbal and visual cues.[13] Thus sensitivity to these visual cues
becomes a very important part of effective listening behavior. Studying
nonverbal communication makes it possible to learn how to distinguish
and interpret others' nonverbal behaviors.

Perception   After the stimulus or message is received, the listener's perceptions come
into play. **Perception** is a screening process through which the message
is filtered by the listener's background, experience, role, mental and

Reading is listening with the eyes rather than with ears.

physical state, beliefs, attitudes, and values—in short, by everything that makes up that person's orientation to the world. Listeners are constantly influenced by this perceptual filter. Studies on listening perception suggest that "the louder, the more relevant, the more novel the stimuli, the more likely they are to be perceived by the listener."[14] The good listener should recognize the influences on his or her perceptions of speakers' messages and deal with these influences accordingly. The listener who understands that, to Americans, someone who speaks with a British accent sounds more authoritative than those who speak American-English, for example, may want to work more carefully to understand the content of the person's message before drawing any conclusions about it.

Attention

Once the stimulus—the word and/or the visual symbol—is received and sent through the perceptual filter, it reaches the attention stage of the human processing system. **Attention** represents the focus on a specific stimulus selected from all the stimuli received at any given moment. In this phase, all other stimuli recede in consciousness so that we can concentrate on a specific word or visual symbol. Consider, for example, what happens if you are attending a theater production. Perhaps the person next to you is wearing too much perfume, and perhaps you had an argument with a friend just before you arrived and it is still bothering you. In addition to this, the sound system is humming, and you are worried because you left your car in a no-parking zone. Obviously, your attention is being pulled in several directions. But if the play is performed effectively, you will focus on what is happening on the stage, and all the other factors will be relegated to the back of your consciousness.

Attention to a stimulus occurs in a person's short-term memory system. It has been suggested that the capacity of the short-term memory—our attention span—is about twenty seconds.[15] Therefore the ability of the listener to focus attention is indeed limited. In fact, professional speakers and teachers have observed that the listeners with whom they work cannot handle much beyond a fifteen-minute time frame. The reasons for this have not yet been traced, although one pair of experts stated that "it's entirely possible that our capacity for sustained attention and deliberate thought is being altered by television viewing."[16] Most of us who have been raised on television have come to expect a seven- to ten-minute viewing format followed by a commercial break.

Undoubtedly, one of the most difficult tasks we have to perform as listeners is concentration. Clearly, motivation plays a great part in the acquisition of this skill. For example, efforts to anticipate the next point or sequence in a message can sometimes assist in the reception of that message (although if you anticipate a message and the speaker takes a different approach, you can be thrown off the track). In the same way, constructing internal summaries throughout the communication and concentrating on isolating the main points should also help.

Paraphrasing—making a summary of the ideas you have just received—will provide you with a concise restatement of what has been presented. It will also allow you to determine whether you understand the material. After all, if you cannot repeat or write down a summary of what was said, then you probably did not get the whole message or did not understand it. Keep this in mind when you are in class listening to the instructor and taking notes. Try to mentally paraphrase the material instead of writing down direct quotes. If you cannot do so, that ought to be a clue that you should ask for clarification or make a note to look up that particular material later on.

Try paraphrasing the next time you are involved in a demanding conversation. In doing so, you will find that you have to concentrate on the message and that as a result you will not be so likely to interrupt the person because you will be concentrating so hard. In addition, following the interaction you will probably remember more of what was said. This is one of the benefits of paraphrasing, for it eliminates the common complaint, "You weren't listening." Giving people back the ideas they just presented makes it impossible for them to support the claim that you were not paying attention.

Two other factors that affect listening concentration are the interest level and the difficulty of the message. Some messages may be just plain boring, but if you need to get the information, careful concentration is imperative. You may not find the chemistry professor's ideas fascinating, but if you do not listen effectively, you will probably fail the next test. You may also find the information so difficult that you turn it off, thereby avoiding it altogether. Again, if it is imperative for you to understand the ideas, then you have to force yourself to figure out what you do not understand and find a way of grasping the meaning through additional reading, tutoring, or asking for clarification.

We can think three to four times faster than the normal conversation rate of 125 to 150 words per minute.[17] And because we can receive messages much more quickly than the other person can talk, we tend to tune in and out throughout a message. The mind can absorb only so much material. Indeed, the brain operates much like a computer; it turns off, recycles itself, and turns back on to avoid information overload.[18] It is no wonder, then, that our attention fluctuates even when we are actively involved as listeners. Think back to the last class lecture you attended. Do you recall a slight gap in your listening at times? Were you conscious of the moment when your mind tuned out? This is a natural part of the listening process, but you must remember to make a conscious effort to tune back in so that you can concentrate on the message. When you turn off, the major danger is that you will daydream rather than quickly turn back to the message. But by taking notes and forcing yourself to paraphrase, you will avoid this difficulty.

Some interesting research with compressed speech illustrates the human capacity for more efficient listening. In this technique, taped material is speeded up mechanically to more than three hundred words per minute. Incredibly, there is no loss of comprehension at these faster rates. Some tests even reveal increased comprehension, much as the tests given to people who have been taught to speed-read show an increase in their retention of information. Because of the rapid speeds, the test subjects anticipated retention problems and thus forced themselves to listen more attentively and concentrate more fully than they would otherwise have done.[19] The compressed-speech technique has become popular with advertisers who want to put as much of an oral message into a fifteen-, thirty-, or sixty-second commercial as they can without distorting the quality of the sound. That research also indicates a high level of recall of the message makes this method of advertising even more appealing.

Clearly, concentration on any particular message is an important key to effective listening. Developing the skills of concentration requires physical and mental effort. The listener must be thoroughly engaged in the communication and must be able to focus his or her energies on the message presented. Indeed, good listening can be exhausting, but the reward of achieving successful communication is well worth the effort.

The Assignment of Meaning

Once we have paid attention to the material that has been presented, the next stage in the listening process is to categorize the message so as to assign meanings to its verbal and nonverbal stimuli. Only recently have researchers begun to understand something about this assignment naming. Some researchers suggest that once we receive a stimulus, we process it mentally and put the stimulus into some predetermined category.[20] This process, the **assignment of meaning,** develops as we acquire our language system, which provides us with the mental categories for interpreting the messages we receive. For instance, our categorizing system for the word *cheese* may include such factors as food, dairy products, taste, and nourishment—all of which help us to relate the word *cheese* to the context in which it is used.

The categorical assignment of meaning that provides listeners with the interpretation of the message is affected by the human cognitive process. This categorical context creates what cognitive psychologists have identified as a **schema**—a script for processing information. The cognitive process draws on all of a person's schemas for the purpose of interpretation, and these schemas provide the mental links for understanding and creating meaning from the stimuli we receive.[21]

Today's research suggests that the two hemispheres of our brain handle information differently and have different functions. The left hemisphere deals with verbal and numerical information in a linear form, providing the analytical process, whereas the right hemisphere specializes in processing shapes and images and in treating nonverbal, intuitive matters.[22] As researchers come to understand the implications of this division in more detail, we communicators will better understand why we assign the meanings we do to the messages we receive. This understanding could also allow us to become better listeners because we may be able to learn how to better utilize whatever part of the brain deals with particular materials.

One of the greatest barriers we face in the listening process is our tendency to evaluate all the stimuli that we receive, regardless of whether they are relevant to the message. Psychotherapist Carl Rogers has stressed that this tendency is the most persistent barrier to communication that we have to overcome.[23] Although assigning meaning to stimuli often requires a quick evaluation, a listener should attempt to avoid instant judgments based primarily on factors such as a speaker's ability to communicate a logical and effective message. This, of course, is much easier for the theorist to recommend than for the average person to carry out.

A strategy useful to listeners in assigning meaning to messages is to differentiate factual statements (those based on observable phenomena or common acceptance) from opinions (inferences or judgments made by the speaker).[24] The speaker who has a strong, assertive style is likely to sound very authoritative and factual, but the message may be based more on opinion than fact. The listener should be alert to such phrases as "In my opinion," "It seems to me," "I think," and "It would appear"; these are indicators that the content of the message is based primarily on the speaker's opinions.

Likewise, it is helpful for the listener to filter through the verbal obscurity of messages and work for clarification of meanings. Unclear terms and phrases, euphemisms, and evasive language make interpretation difficult. The effective listener, however, asks questions and seeks clarification from speakers and from context cues in their messages.

Listeners also benefit from recognizing what their emotional biases are and how they affect interpretations of messages. One way to discover such biases is to draw up a list of terms and phrases that serve as "red flags" for particular emotional responses. Recognition of such emotional barriers is a good first step toward compensating for the knee-jerk reactions that effectively tune out the speaker. Some people have strong reactions, for example, to such words and concepts as *communist, redneck, AIDS,* and perhaps even *homework!*

Thus the assignment of meaning is a complex process involving linguistic and cognitive categories and responses. The effective listener is able to recognize how and why he or she is interpreting a message and use that self-monitoring to understand the influence of messages on his or her listening behavior. Even though the message as interpreted is going to be different from the speaker's original message, the listener is responsible for arriving at an interpretation that comes as close as possible to the original intent of the speaker.

Response   Once we have assigned meaning to the message, we continue the information processing with an internal or external **response** (intellectual or emotional reaction) to the message. In general, the nature of this response may be seen as information storage. Indeed, some psychologists hypothesize that every stimulus we receive is stored somewhere in our brain.

Memory development courses and special learning techniques are popular today as we work to increase our capacity to recall the vast amount of information we must handle and store away for future use. The authors of a popular study skills program for students recommended using the following techniques: (1) choosing to remember, (2) visualizing what is to be remembered, (3) associating that information with something familiar to assist in its recall, and (4) practicing with the material so that its recall becomes easy.[25] For example, when you are introduced to someone, you must first decide that you want to remember this person's name and then get ready to remember it. You can picture the person in a particular setting, perhaps right where you are meeting him or her. Then tie the person's name to something familiar or to a word with which the name rhymes. Finally, repeat the name several times as you speak to the person. If you carry through this process, the odds of your remembering the name increase greatly.

One area of response that can assist the listener in storing information in long-term memory and at the same time provide meaningful feedback to the speaker is the asking of questions. This enables the listener to ensure that the message he or she has received and interpreted is consistent with the original intent of the speaker. Questions provide clarification and demonstrate to the speaker that the listener is involved in the communication transaction.

To be effective, however, questions must be relevant to the message presented by the speaker. The listener who asks questions that are off the topic or beyond the scope of the speaker's message can disrupt the communication flow. Questions intended to increase the listener's understanding must be direct and to the point. Too frequently, listeners use a question and answer opportunity to take stands on issues and present their own messages rather than clarify the speaker's intentions. This, of course, does little to aid in listener understanding of the

Attention to feedback skills is a critical part of effective communication.

speaker's points. Likewise, questions meant to increase listener comprehension should be appropriate in tone. A hostile vocal tone, for instance, will probably put the speaker on the defensive, interrupt the communication transaction, and fail to elicit clarification.

Of course, a listener's response may very well go beyond storing information. He or she may want some sort of internal response, such as a change in attitude or behavior (especially in the case of a persuasive message). And the listener may want to complete the communication process by sending appropriate feedback to the source of the message. Good listeners are conscious of the feedback cues they are sending and work to keep them consistent with the original message and with the originator of that message.

Attention to feedback skills is a critical part of effective communication. Good feedback should be appropriate to the speaker, the message, and the situation, and it should be clearly presented to the speaker. The effective listener is sensitive to the nonverbal cues that he or she is sending and adjusts them accordingly so as not to distract the speaker or distort the listener's original intent for sending the feedback. Listeners are wise to do an inventory of what feedback signals they send, intentionally and unintentionally, and assess how useful and effective these signals are in communication. Persons who tend to not stifle yawns, for example, communicate boredom (or worse!) while engaged in conversations or even while listening to briefings or lectures.

Listening Influencers

The process of listening, through which the listener receives, perceives, concentrates on, assigns meaning to, and responds to messages, is clearly a complex process. To be effective, the listener must be actively involved throughout this complex process and work to overcome any barriers that may arise during the listening experience. Research in listening has demonstrated that certain key influencers can facilitate or deter the process at almost any point in the listening sequence.[26]

The speaker is, of course, one major influencer. How much the listener knows about the speaker and how much regard the listener has for the speaker can enhance or detract from listening. The speaker's credibility (which is the listener's perception of the speaker's trustworthiness, competence, and dynamism) can lead the listener to accept or reject a message. Unfortunately, some listeners are so in awe of a particular speaker (because of his or her outstanding credentials, perhaps) that they lose all objectivity in analyzing the message the person presents. The speaker's physical presentation (animation, appearance, dress) can have an instantaneous effect on listener attention.

Another major influencer is the message itself. If the message presentation is not clearly organized—if the arguments are not well ordered—

the listener will have that much difficulty concentrating and staying tuned to the message. Likewise, the tone and the treatment of the message can affect a person's listening abilities. If a listener does not agree with the speaker's point of view, or if the speaker is too strident (or too ambivalent) in presenting arguments, listening comprehension is affected.

The communication channel also influences listening ability. Some people are more auditory and some are more visual in orientation, so channel preference can be a factor. The speaker who couples the message with some clear visual aids may assist listeners in comprehending the material. And electronic channels have an effect. Some people are very uncomfortable with telephone answering machines, for instance, and prefer not to deal with them.

Noise (any sort of interference) in the communication channel certainly diminishes the effectiveness of the listener. Static on the telephone or distortions on the television screen can interrupt good listening. Noise from the environment also affects listeners. If the lighting is poor or the room temperature is too cold or too hot, the listener has greater difficulty attending to the speaker and the message.

Listeners are influenced not only by a vast array of external factors but also by internal variables. Receivers are affected by their physical state (general health, gender, age), experiences (background, life history, training, culture), attitudes (predispositions), memory, and expectations. These internal factors are always present and can enhance or detract from good listening. The listener who does not feel well, for example, has difficulty focusing on the message, and some research illustrates that men and women listen differently, as do people at different age levels.[27] Life experiences, which make up the listener's culture, can be influential. People from different cultures have different ways of attending to each other (as indicated by amount of eye contact, distance between each other, and amount of patience, for example), and those who have had some direct training in listening are affected in their listening behaviors.

The positive or negative attitude the listener carries into a listening situation (in conjunction with the listener's expectations of the experience) is important. A listener who goes to a training session, for example, convinced beforehand that it will be a waste of time will probably carry that negative attitude into the session and refuse to suspend judgment and listen comprehensively. And the listener's positive or negative attitude extends to himself or herself as a listener. Just as speakers have self-concepts, so, too, do listeners, and these affect listening behavior. Most people have had very little praise or external reward for good listening but have probably heard lots of negative messages: "Sit down and listen." "Keep quiet and listen." "Why don't you ever listen to me?" These negative messages, which are received from a very early age onward, can create a negative attitude in listeners about their own listening abilities; most listeners programmed in this way probably have poor images of themselves as listeners.

Throughout the entire process, memory plays an important role. The listener must be willing and able to hold the message received in short-term memory long enough to perceive, attend to, and assign meaning to it. This activity requires sufficient auditory and visual memory to maintain the focus long enough to process the message.

Coupled with the influence of memory throughout this process is the influence of time. The listener has to have the time, and take the time, to listen with discrimination and comprehension to respond appropriately to the message. Time for listening is becoming a fleeting factor. People lead busy lives and frequently have little time to engage in active listening with another person. Parents are busy outside the home, managers are busy with burgeoning paperwork in the office, educators must cope with a wide range of distractions every day, and students at all age levels have lots of homework to complete. Finding the time to truly listen is no easy task.

Clearly, however, the effective listener receives, perceives, attends to, assigns meaning to, and responds to messages while being influenced by numerous factors that can enhance or detract from the process at any given point in the system. The listener who wishes to be effective must recognize the personal influence these factors can have on the listening process and then work to compensate for them. Only then can that listener engage in meaningful communication.

Levels of Listening

To be an efficient listener, you must have strong motivation and a clear purpose throughout the entire process of receiving, perceiving, concentrating, assigning meaning, and responding. Reading specialists suggest that if we establish a clear goal before beginning to read, we will read more effectively.[28] The same principle applies to listeners.

We listen on a number of levels. Researchers have come to understand that as listeners we probably function differently depending on our particular level of listening or on our objectives. These objectives represent a taxonomy, or hierarchy, on which listening skills are built.[29]

Discrimination Level

At the basic level, the **discrimination level,** we listen to distinguish auditory and visual stimuli. This distinction of the message stimuli is at the base of all the listening we do. Because we are concerned with identifying auditory and visual cues at this level, experience and practice are our best strategies for improving our listening discrimination. We tend not to discern subtle shades of meaning and vocal nuances until we become accustomed to the communication style of a particular person, so it takes some time to develop these skills.

Discrimination of both auditory and visual cues can help us to be more sensitive as communicators. Through discrimination we can come to understand differences in verbal sounds (dialects, pronunciation) and nonverbal behavior (gestures, facial reactions). By understanding such differences, we gain sensitivity to the sights and sounds of our world. We can then determine, for example, if a person is being sarcastic, negative, or uncooperative, realizing that the same set of words can be taken in a variety of ways. If we do not listen discriminatively to how something is said, we may miss the entire meaning of the message.

Discriminative listening is also important to us as we come in contact with the nonhuman features of our everyday lives. We listen, for instance, to household appliances to determine whether they are functioning properly. And we often listen to our cars to figure out if they need mechanical repairs. In a similar way, we listen to the sounds made by our pets, who tell us what they need through their vocalizations.

Comprehension Level

A second level of listening is the **comprehension level,** at which the objective is to recognize and retain the information in a message. To comprehend a message, the listener must first discriminate the message to recognize its auditory and visual components. But listening with comprehension goes beyond the objective of discriminating the message. At this point in the process, heightened concentration is needed. Comprehensive listening is what students do most in college classes. Because of this, educators have come to recognize its importance and have provided students with further training in this type of listening. Indeed, a very significant study on this issue revealed that listening comprehension was a critical factor in the success or failure of college students. "Among the students who fail," the study stated, "deficient listening skills were a stronger factor than reading skills or academic aptitude."[30]

Some techniques have been found to enhance listening comprehension. One such helpful strategy is to concentrate on getting the main points of a message rather than all the supporting details. A student listening to an instructor discuss an idea in class should focus on the main point being made rather than on the elaboration and the details being presented. Even when taking notes, it is wise to sort the main points and the supporting details into two columns; this can be done, for example, by drawing a vertical line down the middle of the paper, putting the main points in the left-hand column, and noting the supporting ideas in the right-hand column. Abbreviation of commonly used

At the comprehension level of listening, the objective is to recognize and retain the information in a message.

words saves time in writing, which allows for more listening time. For example, if this chapter had been given as a lecture, the notes for it thus far might look like those shown in Figure 4.2.

The note-taker in Figure 4.2 clearly felt there were sufficient cues for understanding the material so that examples were not essential. Nevertheless, many note-takers like to provide examples to help clarify material. Each note-taker has to determine for herself or himself how much detail and how much reinforcement are necessary.

Some communication experts recommend a technique called clarifying and confirming to enhance concentration. This strategy calls for the listener to ask for additional information or explanation. This system works well when added to a technique known as acknowledging or bridging—relating one part of the message to another part. Talk show TV personalities use this system when interviewing guests.[31]

Remembering the main points at a later time may also require the development of a number of memory techniques. Some research indicates that a person can lose as much as 50 percent of any given information after the first day unless she or he takes notes and reviews them.[32] Because it is so easy to lose information in memory storage, the good listener will work at concentrating to gain the greatest comprehension

Figure 4.2

Note-taking Format

<u>Lstng</u>

Lstng Process

Hearing – biological process
Lstng – active processing of
    info heard
Reception – get message
Perception – screen info
Attention
    focus on ideas
    anticipate next point
    paraphrase – restate in
      own words
    get ready to lstn rapidly
Assignment of meaning –
    categorize symbols
Response – info storage
    choose to remember
    visualize what is to
      be remembered
    associate info
    practice material

Levels of Lstng

Discrimination
Comprehension
Lstng Influencers
    speaker
    message
    channel
    noise
    internal variables
    attitude
    memory
    time

and retention of the information being presented. Some student listeners have also found that they retain information best if they review the information immediately after it is presented and then go over it daily, rather than waiting to do a cram review session on the night before an examination.

Listeners function, then, to discriminate the sound and visual messages and to comprehend these messages for further understanding and recall. In addition to these two basic listening objectives, people listen for special purposes: to provide a therapeutic sounding board for a person to talk through a problem, critically evaluate a persuasive message, or appreciate aspects of a particular message.

Therapeutic Level   A special third level of listening is the **therapeutic level,** which is important for those in such fields as psychology, social work, speech therapy, and counseling. Therapeutic listening requires a listener to act as a sounding board so that a speaker can talk through a problem and, ideally, reach a solution. This type of listening uses many of the techniques of a counseling interview.

But therapeutic listening is not restricted to professional counselors. In daily life people often need a listener when dealing with a problem; the listener can help the speaker talk through the situation. To be effective in this role, the therapeutic listener must have empathy with the other person, an ability to understand that person's problem. This is achieved, as one source put it, by cultivating the ability to "understand accurately how another person thinks or feels from his [or her] point of view, to put yourself momentarily into his [or her] shoes, to see the world as he [or she] is seeing it."[33]

People who are training to be professional therapeutic listeners must learn special techniques that allow them to actively participate in counseling. For example, they must learn when to ask questions, when to stimulate further discussion, and when to give advice. Although the effective therapeutic listener can profit from the professional training given hotline volunteers, for example, every listener can profit from adapting some of these techniques so as to listen with empathy. The skillful therapeutic listener ought to maintain eye contact with the speaker, truly engage in active listening, and resist the temptation to jump in with statements such as "Yes, when I was in your shoes, I . . ." or "If I were you, I would . . . " Although one friend may ask another for advice and say, "What do you think I should do?" offering advice may not be very helpful—because then the solution does not belong to the friend with the problem. The listening friend can give a list of possible alternatives from which the person may choose, for then he or she will have some commitment to carrying it out.

Therapeutic listening requires faith that the person can solve his or her own problem (and most people can handle their troubles if they just have the chance to articulate the problem), time to truly listen with empathy, and a willingness to suspend judgment so that the other person can communicate the problem. Nothing will stop a communication faster than saying, "Oh, that's ridiculous!" or "Why on earth does that bother you?" The therapeutic listener must adapt these strategies, or the communication will not be very rewarding for either party.

Critical Level   A fourth level of listening is the **critical level,** the level at which the listener comprehends and evaluates the message that has been received. A critical listener assesses the arguments and the appeals in a message and then decides whether to accept or reject them. This analysis should occur, however, only after the listener has recognized, understood, and reflected on the entire message.

An understanding of both the tools of persuasion and the process of logic and reasoning enables critical listeners to make judgments about the merits of the messages they receive. But judgments should be made only after careful analysis of such factors as:

1. *The personal appeal of the speaker.* The speaker's personal appeal, her or his credibility, stems from the level of expertise, trustworthiness, and dynamism she or he is projecting. The critical listener needs to recognize how much this credibility is influencing how the message is being understood and analyzed.

2. *The speaker's arguments and evidence.* Does the speaker present a logical argument that is supported by substantive and relevant data? Faulty arguments can interrupt the listening process and create blocks to the acceptance of messages.

3. *The speaker's motivational appeals.* How is the speaker attempting to get the listener involved in the message? What appeals to the listener's needs are utilized to get the listener to respond to the persuasive message?

4. *Assumptions on the part of the speaker.* Does the speaker assume that something is a fact before it has been established as such? When someone says, "It is readily apparent that . . . " it may not be apparent at all.

5. *What is not said.* In some cases, the speaker implies, rather than states, his or her ideas, so the listener is forced to read between the lines to supply the message. "You know what our objectives are" or "You know what I mean" are two remarks the listener may have to think about very carefully.

6. *Passives.* Sentences stated in the passive voice eliminate the subject and can thus be too vague. "It has been proved" and "It was previously demonstrated" are all too common examples of this kind of reference.

The critical listener analyzes these factors to assess the merits or demerits of a particular message and then acts accordingly. Sales pitches, advertising messages, campaign speeches, radio and television news reporting and commentary, and persuasive briefings all require appropriate critical analysis of the content of the presentation—judgments that follow the careful grasping of the arguments and appeals in the message itself.

Appreciation Level

A fifth level of listening is the **appreciation level,** at which a person engages in listening for the enjoyment of or the sensory stimulation from a message. Appreciation is a highly individual matter, for there are no rules on how to go about it. Some people believe that the more knowledge they have about a particular subject, the more they can appreciate it. Others feel, however, that the more they know about something, the more critical they become, thus losing their ability to appreciate all but the best. Clearly, however, if a person has more positive experiences in a particular field, she or he will probably enjoy it. A parishioner can listen to a minister's style during a sermon, for instance, and appreciate his or her use of memorable passages or rhythmical phrasing.

One of the newest forms of appreciative listening has resulted from the development and popularity of small tape players with headsets. Many lecturers, psychologists, and writers now tape-record their materials as well as have them printed. Libraries and bookstores have tapes that are available on such subjects as shyness, family relationships, assertiveness, and stress management. A critic of written and oral print observed, "The notion of recorded books, which the blind have been enjoying, compliments of the Library of Congress, for a half-century, is becoming more popular among other members of the population, who can rent or buy tapes from several companies around the country."[34]

The popularity of this listening form has led the *Washington Post* to feature a recorded books column in its Sunday book review section. The editor described one application for the appreciative listener as follows:

> Ear phones on, you're lost in the sonic bliss of your beach cassette. Beach cassette? Well, why not? If there are beach books, why not beach tapes—recorded books you tuck into your bag for vacation listening. Beach tapes also have a slight advantage over books: You don't have to wait until you actually get to your vacation spot to begin your escape into literature. The adventure begins in your car's cassette player as you roll the long miles to your destination.[35]

Improving Listening

Effective listening is clearly a complex, involved, and involving process requiring a great deal of commitment on the part of the listener. Despite the complexities of the listening process, you can do a great deal to improve your skill as a listener. Improving listening skills stems from first understanding what is involved in the process so that you can monitor your own listening behavior and recognize what you are and are not doing at any given time in the listening process. Improvement of listening skills then requires breaking old habits, putting new strategies in their place, and practicing these new skills until they feel comfortable. Developing these new skills can result from guided practice that your instructor can provide as you study listening as a communicator. But it will take time, energy, and commitment on your part to work with these skills until they are a natural part of your listening repertoire.

Techniques   The following are some suggestions to help listeners develop greater skill in the process.

1. *Recognize that both the sender and the receiver share the responsibility for effective communication.* If you are sending a message, work to define your terms, structure your message clearly, and give your receiver the necessary background to respond effectively. Remember that communication noise must be eliminated if the transaction between the two of you is to be successful. As a receiver, you should ask questions and provide feedback if you cannot understand the speaker's point. If possible, repeat the major ideas so that the speaker can check to be sure you have grasped his or her meaning.

2. *Suspend judgments.* One of the greatest barriers to human communication is our tendency to form instant judgments about almost everything we encounter. As listeners, we are prone to make premature assessments of speakers before we have even comprehended their entire message. Statements such as "I don't like his voice," "This is a boring lecture," or "I disagree with her point" all set up barriers to effective listening. Instead, good listening involves setting aside these judgments and listening for the message.

3. *Be a patient listener.* Avoid interrupting or tuning out until the entire message has been communicated. We often find ourselves beginning to act before we have totally understood what is being said. Think about how difficult it is to assemble a new product until you have thoroughly comprehended the instructions. Or remember the times when you filled out a form only to realize later on that you had written your name when the directions said to print and that you had put your first name down when your last name should have come first. Patience in listening will help you avoid having to go back over messages you missed the first time around or did not understand because you did not let the whole message come through.

4. *Avoid egospeak.* **Egospeak** is the "art of boosting our own ego by speaking only about what we want to talk about, and not giving a hoot in hell about what the person is speaking about."[36] When you jump into a conversation and speak your piece without noticing what the other person is trying to communicate, or listening only to the beginning of another's sentence before saying, "That's interesting, but what happened to me was . . ." or "Yes, but . . . ," you are egospeaking. As a result, you do not receive the whole message because you are so busy thinking of what you want to say. Although egospeak is a very natural human temptation, it can very easily become a real barrier to communication.

5. *Be careful with emotional responses to words.* Words can bring about instant reactions from you or others. **Inciting words** are those that trigger strong feelings within us, either positive or negative. How do you react to the words *child-beater, rapist,* and *income tax?* Words like these often send us off on tangents. In an everyday situation, you may tighten up and block out the rest of the message when your roommate mentions the name of a person with whom you have just had an argument. Or you could start daydreaming about the beach when your instructor uses the word *sunshine.* Speakers should be aware that listeners can be sent off on tangents by the use of certain words, resulting in interference with our effort to communicate. As receivers we should be aware that we can be led astray and lose our concentration through our emotional responses.

There is no quick way to prevent yourself from reacting to inciting words. By monitoring your body, however, you might catch yourself physically pulling in, feel yourself flushing as you become upset, or catch yourself daydreaming. These responses are typical of the emotional triggers that set us off in a listening situation.

6. *Be aware that your posture affects your listening.* When you listen to an exciting lecture, how do you sit? Usually you lean slightly forward with your feet on the floor and look directly at the presenter. On the other hand, if you slump down and stare out the window, it's unlikely that you're actively participating in the communication act that's taking place. What happens to you when you curl up in a comfortable chair, turn on soft music, and try to read? Most likely, instead of reading you fall asleep or begin to daydream.

Have you ever left a classroom and felt totally exhausted? You may have been concentrating so hard that you became physically tired. After all, good listening is hard work. An effective listener learns when it is necessary to listen in a totally active way and when it is possible to relax. We can explain the concept by using a simple analogy. When you're driving a car with an automatic transmission,

Your posture affects your listening.

the car shifts gears when it needs more or less power. Unfortunately, people don't have automatic transmissions: we have to shift gears for ourselves. When you need to concentrate, you shift into your active listening position (feet on the floor, posture erect, looking directly at the speaker to pick up any necessary nonverbal clues). Once you feel that you understand the point that's being made (a test for this would be the ability to paraphrase what has been said), you may want to shift your posture to a more comfortable position. When a new subject arises, or when you hear transitional words or phrases such as "therefore," "in summary," then you shift back into your active listening position.

7. *Make a conscious effort to listen.* If it is important for you to listen carefully to a message, then you must tune in to that message. As was discussed earlier, hearing and listening are not synonymous. Listening requires a concerted effort on your part to receive, perceive, concentrate, assign meaning, and respond to the message. Listening does not happen automatically.

8. *Control distractions.* All of us are surrounded by noise. Such factors as the sound of machinery, people talking, and music playing can interfere with efficient listening. If the message is important to you, you should try to adjust the interference or control it. If possible,

turn off the machinery or move away from it. Tell someone who is speaking to you while you are answering the telephone that you cannot listen to both people at the same time. Turn off the radio or raise your voice so that others can hear you over the sound. Remember that there is little point in continuing the communication if you cannot hear the other person or that person cannot hear you.

9. *Tune in to the speaker's cues.* An effective speaker provides the listener with all sorts of verbal and nonverbal cues. You should recognize **transitions** (words indicating a change of idea or topic: "therefore," "another idea is," "finally"), **forecasts of ideas** (statements that show a series of ideas will follow: "there are three ideas that," "the next point is"), and **internal summaries** (restatements of ideas that have just been explained: "and so we have seen that"). These are all vehicles for furthering your grasp of the major points that the speaker is presenting.

   The vocal dynamics, or paralanguage (rate, volume, pitch, and pauses), used by the speaker can also help you to understand the points being developed. By stressing words, pausing before an idea, or increasing the volume of a phrase, the speaker is telling you that something is important, unusual, or significant.

   The speaker's physical movements can also carry a meaning that may reinforce or even contradict the verbal message. For example, a speaker who uses a forceful gesture or enumerates points with the fingers can assist listeners in following the main points in a message. We often have to listen with our eyes as well as our ears to pick up all the cues that will help us understand the real message. Look beyond the words themselves for the full intent of the message.

10. *Paraphrase.* When you are responding to a message, paraphrase the speaker's ideas. Indeed, paraphrasing can be one of the most effective ways to sharpen concentration because to do so requires careful focus and storage in short-term memory. By repeating these ideas in your answer, you let the person know what you have received. Then if the paraphrase is not correct, the speaker can clarify and make you understand what was really intended. This use of active feedback allows both of you to be sure that the message sent was the message received.

11. *Listen actively.* A good listener will be aware of what is going on within the entire communication process, including what type of internal and external responses he or she may be having to the message. Know how you are responding, and allow yourself to become actively involved in the entire process by concentrating on understanding the message and then providing meaningful feedback designed to assist the speaker and facilitate the entire communication.

A Willingness to Listen

Once the listener develops a clear understanding of the complexities of the listening process, recognizes how she or he is functioning within that process, and builds some new skills to perform more effectively in listening, that person must still make a commitment to listen. The good listener is one who is willing to listen, who understands that it is important to engage in communication with the other person, and who makes the effort to participate as a listening communicator.

Unfortunately, listening has been the most underrated of the communication modes. Americans have come to associate listening with a passive act in which the speaker can and should bear almost total responsibility for the outcome of the communication. The active, engaged listener is too rare in today's communication society. But the awareness gained through communication training in schools and in corporations offers hope that Americans will come to a more dynamic model of listening.

Finally, the key to effective listening is caring. "If you care about yourself as a listener and if you care about the other person as a human being, you both will feel enriched for the experience. And that intangible reward may be the greatest payoff we have in human relationships at home, at work, and in the world at large."[37]

Summary

Listening is an important part of the communication process. In this chapter, these points about listening effectiveness were developed:

- ☐ A great deal of our communication time is devoted to listening.
- ☐ Hearing is a biological process that involves the reception of a message through sensory channels; it may be affected by all of our senses.
- ☐ Listening is the active processing of the information we receive.
- ☐ Listening involves reception, perception, attention, the assignment of meaning, and response by the listener to the message that has been presented.
- ☐ Auditory acuity enhances a person's ability to listen efficiently.
- ☐ Listeners use the visual system as well as the hearing mechanism.
- ☐ Attention is the focus on a specific stimulus selected from all the stimuli received at any given moment.
- ☐ The capacity of short-term memory constitutes the attention span, whose duration is approximately twenty seconds.
- ☐ Making a summary of what has just been presented—paraphrasing—can be a helpful technique for sharpening concentration.

☐ Both the interest level and the difficulty of the message affect listening concentration.

☐ Studies of compressed speech indicate that people can comprehend at a much faster rate than they normally speak.

☐ Putting a stimulus into some predetermined category enables a listener to assign meaning to a message.

☐ Schemas are scripts for processing information.

☐ Research suggests that the two hemispheres of the human brain process information differently.

☐ Once we have assigned meaning to a message, we continue the listening process with an internal or an external response (feedback) to that message.

☐ A person can increase memory capacity by choosing to remember, visualizing what is to be remembered, associating the information with something familiar, and practicing with the material.

☐ The process of listening is complex.

☐ Listening influences include the speaker, the message, the channel, noise, internal variables, attitude, memory, and time.

☐ The effective listener receives, perceives, attends to, assigns meaning to, and responds to messages while being influenced by a wide range of factors that enhance or detract from the process at any given time.

☐ The levels at which listening occurs are the discrimination level, the comprehension level, the therapeutic level, the critical level, and the appreciation level.

☐ Effective note-taking can assist in listening comprehension.

☐ Egospeak (interrupting rather than listening to the other person) interferes with effective communication.

☐ Inciting words can interrupt good listening.

☐ Effective listening is an active process that requires time, effort, energy, and commitment.

☐ A good listener cares about participating in communication.

Key Terms

hearing	discrimination level
listening	comprehension level
reception	therapeutic level
perception	critical level
attention	appreciation level
paraphrasing	egospeak
assignment of meaning	inciting words
schema	transitions
response	forecasts of ideas
noise	internal summaries

Learn by Doing

1. Contrast hearing and listening. Draw an analogy between listening and reading.

2. Analyze your own listening. Name one listening behavior that you have that does not match the characteristics of a good listener as described in this chapter. Consider how you can change this listening behavior to be more effective.

3. Now that you are aware of some of the principles of effective listening, put them into practice. At the next briefing or lecture you attend, sit up, concentrate on what the speaker is saying, and focus all your attention energy on comprehending the material. Make internal summaries and paraphrases to assist you in concentrating and comprehending. After the session is over, analyze your listening behavior and determine what you can still do to improve your listening comprehension.

4. Attend an appreciative listening experience—a play, a concert, a film, or an oral reading. After the event, reflect on what you particularly enjoyed or did not enjoy and why. Do you appreciate those art forms about which you have some background training, or do you find those events for which you have little technical information more meaningful to you as an appreciative listener?

5. Attend a lecture on a technical topic not within your field of expertise. Work carefully to concentrate on the material so that you can recall the message later. Is it difficult to comprehend new material? What strategies do you use to heighten your concentration?

6. Practice therapeutic listening techniques with a friend. Each of you should discuss a listening problem that you have encountered. Work at listening with empathy and at sending the appropriate feedback to let the other person talk through his or her problem to a solution.

7. Critically analyze some television editorial commentaries. Listen for the arguments and appeals, and determine how those persuasive elements were arranged to get a positive response from you, the listener.

8. Make a list of your "red flags" (terms that stimulate an emotional response). Go back and review these terms. Why do you think they are inciting for you? If class time is available, your instructor will divide the class into groups of four to six students. Discuss your red flags and what implications they have for your communication.

9. a. Indicate whether you thoroughly agree (TA), agree (A), disagree (D), or thoroughly disagree (TD) with each of these statements: "Prayer should be allowed in the public schools." "Children who contract AIDS should not be allowed to attend public schools." "College students should not have to take required courses outside of their major area of concentration."

b. Your class is divided into groups of four to six students. Your task is to reach agreement by geting everyone in the group to accept one of the attitudes (TA, A, D, TD) for each of the statements. You must paraphrase during the entire discussion. You may not give your opinion until you have summarized the statement of the person who preceded you. One member of the group acts as referee and says, "Foul" if anyone speaks without summarizing.

c. When you have completed the exercise, make a list of the positive aspects of paraphrasing as a listening technique and the frustrations caused by paraphrasing. (If time does not allow for a discussion of all three questions, your instructor will randomly select one for discussion.)

Notes

1. Paul Tory Rankin, "Listening Ability: Its Importance, Measurement, and Development," *Chicago School Journal,* 12 (Chicago School Journal, 12 (January 1930), 177–179. Other studies support Rankin's findings; see Donald E. Bird, "Teaching Listening Comprehension," *Journal of Communication,* 3 (November 1953), 127–130; Lila R. Breiter, "Research in Listening and Its Importance to Literature," M.A. thesis, Brooklyn College, 1957; and Elyse K. Werner, "A Study of Communication Time," M.A. thesis, University of Maryland, 1975.

2. E. T. Klemmer and F. W. Snyder, "Measurement of Time Spent Communicating," *Journal of Communication,* 22 (June 1972), 142–158.

3. Sara W. Lundsteen, *Listening: Its Impact on Reading and the Other Language Arts* (Urbana, Ill.: ERIC Clearinghouse on Reading and Communication Skills, 1979).

4. *1990 Nielsen Report on Television* (New York: Neilsen Media Research, 1990).

5. Donald E. Bird, "Teaching Listening Comprehension," *Journal of Communication,* 3 (November 1963), 127–130.

6. Larry Barker et al., "An Investigation of Proportional Time Spent in Various Communication Activities by College Students," *Journal of Applied Communications Research,* 8 (November 1980), 101–109.

7. Margaret Conaway, "Listening: Learning Tool and Retention Agent," in A. S. Algier and K. W. Algier, eds., *Improving Reading and Study Skills* (San Francisco: Jossey-Bass, 1982), pp. 51–63. For a comprehensive review of information on listening, see the 1990 issue of the *Journal of the International Listening Association.*

8. Leland Brown, *Communicating Facts and Ideas in Business* (Englewood Cliffs, N.J.: Prentice-Hall, 1982), p. 380; and William F. Keefe, *Listen, Management!* (New York: McGraw-Hill, 1971), p. 10.

9. Gary T. Hunt and Louis P. Cusella, "A Field Study of Listening Needs in Organizations," *Communication Education,* 32 (1983), 399.

10. William F. Eadie, "Hearing What We Ought to Hear," *Journal of the International Listening Association,* 4 (1990), 4.

11. "Hearing Loss: Ways to Avoid, New Ways to Treat," *U.S. News & World Report,* October 18, 1982, pp. 85–86.

12. Ibid.
13. Albert Mehrabian, *Silent Messages* (Belmont, Calif.: Wadsworth, 1971), p. 41.
14. Larry L. Barker, *Listening Behavior* (Englewood Cliffs, N.J.: Prentice-Hall, 1971), p. 31.
15. D. A. Norman, "Memory While Shadowing," *Quarterly Journal of Experimental Psychology,* 21 (February 1969), 85–93.
16. Dorothy Singer and Jerome Singer, "Is Human Imagination Going Down the Tube?" *Chronicle of Higher Education,* April 29, 1979, p. 56.
17. Ralph G. Nichols and Leonard A. Stevens, *Are You Listening?* (New York: McGraw-Hill, 1957), p. 107.
18. Norbert Wiener, *Cybernetics* (Cambridge, Mass.: MIT Press, 1961); and Norbert Wiener, *The Human Use of Human Beings* (Garden City, N.Y.: Doubleday, 1964).
19. The September 1968 issue of the *Journal of Communication* is devoted to research on time-compressed speech.
20. See Carl H. Weaver, *Human Listening* (Indianapolis: Bobbs-Merrill, 1972), pp. 42–59.
21. Jack C. Richard, "Listening Comprehension: Approach, Design, Procedure," *Tesol Quarterly,* 17 (June 1983), 219–240.
22. See Sally P. Springer and George Deutsch, *Left Brain, Right Brain* (San Francisco: W. H. Freeman, 1981).
23. Carl R. Rogers and F. J. Roethlisberger, "Barriers and Gateways to Communication," *Harvard Business Review,* 30 (July-August 1952), 46–52.
24. William V. Haney, *Communication Patterns and Incidents* (Homewood, Ill.: Richard D. Irwin, 1960).
25. *Harvard Milton College Study Skills Program Level HI* (Reston, Va.: National Association of Secondary School Principals, 1983).
26. Andrew D. Wolvin and Carolyn Gwynn Coakley, *Listening,* 3rd ed. (Dubuque, Iowa: William C. Brown, 1988), Chapter 3, includes an analysis of the major variables that affect the listening process.
27. Ibid.
28. Ivan Quandt, *Self-Concept and Reading* (Newark, Del.: International Reading Association, n.d.), p. 31.
29. See Wolvin and Coakley, Part 2, for a detailed description of this listening taxonomy.
30. Conaway, p. 57.
31. "Your Attention, Please," *Changing Times* (October 1986), 129.
32. H. F. Spitzer, "Studies in Retention," *Journal of Experimental Psychology,* 30 (1939), 641–656.
33. Thomas Gordon, *P.E.T.: Parent Effectiveness Training* (New York: New American Library, 1975), p. 60.
34. Alice Digilio, "The Best Books You've Ever Heard," *Washington Post Book World,* February 20, 1983, p. 4.
35. Vic Sussman, "On the Beach: Tapes to Tan By," *Washington Post Book World,* August 23, 1987, p. 6.
36. Edward Addeo and Robert Burger, *Egospeak* (New York: Bantam Books, 1974), p. xiv.
37. Wolvin and Coakley, p. 367.

5 *The Foundations of Verbal Language*

Chapter Outline

Learning
Outcomes

After reading this chapter, you should be able to:

Name and detail several theories of the origins of human language

Explain and illustrate how people select, process, and learn symbols and indicate the role of the cybernetic process, the language-explosion theory, and the significant-other theory in this learning

Detail the feature common to all languages

Define and illustrate the emotive, phatic, cognitive, rhetorical, and meta-lingual functions of language

Explain the roles of ambiguity, vagueness, inferences, and message adjustment in relation to language distortion

Define dialects, contrast standard versus nonstandard dialects, and relate the effects of speaking a nonstandard dialect

Analyze slang, verbal obscenity, and articulates as they relate to standard dialects

Explain why communication between men and women is cross-cultural communication.

Why are we each unique in how we communicate? Why can we communicate easily with some people but not with others? The answers can be found in the very nature of language, which creates problems. We can never be sure that the messages sent are the messages received. We each have our own perceptions, based on our past experiences, of what words mean, and we often assume that others interpret these words the same way. Sometimes this is the case, but other times it is not.

As they appear on the printed page, words are one-dimensional. But they pick up additional dimensions when they are spoken and even more dimensions when the receiver can see the speaker and note facial expressions, gesture patterns, and body positions. All these are part of the communication process.

The Origins of Human Language

Though there is no one accepted theory of the origins of human language, most theorists generally agree that people first relied on gestures to communicate and then developed a code by which to communicate orally.[1] To account for the shift to vocal language, most explanations center on the probable linking of sounds with gestures because the lips, tongue, and mouth "imitate" hand movements (for example, sticking one's tongue out when threading a needle).[2] Then, because gestural language can develop only limited messages whereas sounds can be altered to form many additional ideas, vocal language must have been used more extensively. Much later, out of the need for an additional way to convey messages, the written code was developed.

Selecting Symbols   One of the major queries about communication is how we are able to select the symbols we want to use. The process can be clarified with an example: if I hold up a cylindrical piece of graphite that is about one-eighth-inch in diameter, is covered with wood, is painted a yellowish gold, and has an eraser on one end and a sharpened point on the other and I ask you what the object is, you will probably answer, "A pencil." Look at the surroundings you are in, focus on an object, and identify it. Did you respond quickly with a word for the object? Now think back to the experience. Did you—as we did with the word *pencil*—think of all the parts that describe the object you just named? Probably not. Instead, you looked at the object, recognized it, assigned a symbol to it if you could, and then spoke or thought the relevant word.

Let us try another experiment. Picture the following objects: a pen, an apple, and a glass of milk. You probably had little trouble "seeing" these objects. This means that you have been exposed to the objects and their symbols so often that you can identify them by name almost automatically. Let us try that experiment again: chalk, book, jerboa. The first two words in the series were probably familiar, but what about the third? Jerboa? A jerboa is a mouselike rodent, found in North Africa and Asia, that has long hind legs for jumping. It looks a little like a miniature kangaroo with the head of a mouse. You had no trouble with the words *chalk* and *book* because you have already come in contact with these objects and have been told what to call them. But few Americans—with the exception of those who have traveled in Asia or Africa or who have stumbled on a book or a television show that included information about this type of rodent—would have had any exposure to the word *jerboa*.

Processing Symbols   A second question now emerges: how do we remember what we have been exposed to in our environment? In the human brain, the area that allows us to communicate selectively is the **cortex,** a layer of gray matter that covers the surface of the cerebral hemisphere and the cerebellum. It is the center for memory and other activities necessary for communicating. The primary language areas of most human brains are thought

*Human language evolved
from gestural language combined with sounds to express
messages.*

to be located in the left hemisphere of the cortex because only rarely does damage to the right hemisphere cause language disorders.[3] Some biologists believe that changes in ribonucleic acid (RNA), a protein molecule, is of great importance in the transmission of hereditary information, and provides the chemical basis for learning.[4]

To illustrate how the brain uses symbols, we can take as an example one of the business machines found in many of today's offices, the word processor. Imagine the difficulty encountered by a new secretary who has not been trained on this kind of equipment. For example, a supervisor who asks the secretary to "bring up the menu" may get a copy of the bill of fare from the snack shop downstairs rather than a list on the video screen of what is stored on the disk. And even after the term has been explained or demonstrated, the new word-processing operator may not be able to recognize the concept it represents. Only when he or she uses the term with understanding and responds correctly when it is used by others has cortical input-output occurred. In other words, the secretary heard the term, identified it with an image stored in the cortex, and put the two together.

Our senses continuously bombard us with signals that are begging to be interpreted and stored in our information banks. In response, the cortex stores, computes, and eventually processes some of these incom-

Figure 5.1

The Cybernetic Process

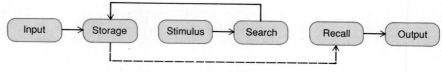

ing signals and puts forth the necessary information. This operation, called the **cybernetic process,** is similar to the input, storage, stimulus, search, recall, and output functions of computers. It is schematized in Figure 5.1.

By investigating the process you used to identify the pencil in the foregoing example, you can gain an understanding of the operation of the cybernetic process. You have been taught the word *pencil* (input), and it has been placed (stored) in your cortex. Thus when you see an object made of graphite, wood, and an eraser, the mere sight of the object is the stimulus. Your storage system sorts the visual signals (search), finds the symbol that represents the image (recall), and you say, "Pencil" (output). You have just experienced the cybernetic process in action.

Norbert Wiener, a mathematician and logician who played an important role in the development of high-speed electronic computers, coined the term *cybernetics.*[5] It comes from the Greek word for "steersman." Wiener noted that the means for internal control and communication in an animal—its nervous system—are similar to those of self-regulating machines, such as furnaces with thermostats. In each one, a measuring device feeds back information about performance. In human beings, the input comes in the form of a sense image (taste, smell, sight, sound, touch) that is tested against stored material (symbols, images); the output (feedback) represents the symbol or image. The major difference between human and machine communication is that "communication is imperfect. You can program a computer to send and receive the messages exactly the way you intended, but this is not the case with human beings."[6]

On the surface, the cybernetic process seems fairly simple. But sometimes there are problems. Sometimes the stored information is incorrect. Sometimes not enough information has been stored. Sometimes an overload occurs. An overload results from the attempt to store too much material in too short a period of time. In other words, sometimes we simply demand too much of our "equipment." Just as machines blow fuses because the demand placed on their circuitry is too great, so, too, can we blow psychological fuses from too much pressure. It is possible to get so nervous and upset that you block messages from coming forth. But when the emotional pressure is removed, the normal flow returns.

That is why experts advise people who are taking a test or are under stress to "turn off" every so often and then return to their work. If you are in that sort of situation, you should look out the window, put your head down on the desk, get up and walk around, shake your hands, or take several deep breaths to break the tension.

Experts seem to agree that cybernetic processing starts to develop in humans at about the third month after birth. It does not become fully operative, however, until a child is capable of processing the image-symbol relationship and select symbols. Another factor is added as a child grows older, for in addition to images and symbols, she or he also acquires values that determine the worth, desirability, or importance of things. An American and a Russian may both be able to define "communism," but how they perceive the value of the communist system may be different.

Learning Symbols

Two views of how we acquire our language, as well as our beliefs, values, and attitudes are known as the language-explosion theory and the significant-other theory.

The Language-Explosion Theory

The **language-explosion theory** proposes that we build future communication skills from the core of language that we develop early in life. If you were asked to name the one person who had the most influence on your ability to communicate, what would your answer be? In most cases, you would name a member of your immediate family, probably your mother. In some homes, however, the mother-infant dyad (pair) is replaced by a father-infant, sibling-infant, or grandparent-infant dyad. And in still other situations, the day care center or a baby sitter may replace the family member.

Whatever the child's primary influence, his or her circles of influence quickly expand to include the communication patterns of many other people (see Figure 5.2). The child's neighborhood, the area of the country in which he or she lives, and the schools he or she attends all influence the total ability to communicate, as does exposure to the media. Indeed, in recent years the influence of television and films has been credited for setting not only communication patterns but also values, beliefs, and attitudes.

The Significant-Other Theory

At a certain stage in our lives, we start selecting the specific people or groups whose ideals and beliefs we allow to influence us. These people become the significant others in our lives, and their effect on us is great. Indeed, social psychologists generally contend that we have no identity whatsoever except in relationship to others. This view is called the significant-other theory.[7]

Figure 5.2

The Language-Explosion Theory—Vocabulary Building Through Circles of Influence

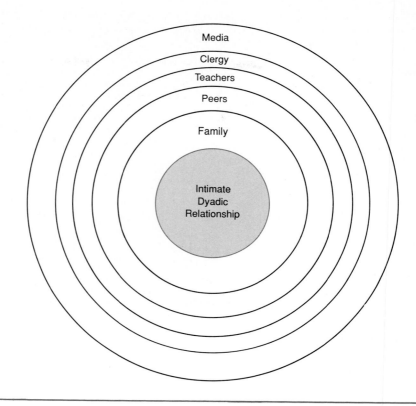

The **significant-other theory** centers on the principle that our understanding of self is built by those who react to and comment on our actions, ideas, beliefs, and mannerisms. Thus if we respect a particular individual, we are likely to adjust our behavior and our messages continually so that we can derive the most encouraging evaluation from that person. Even if we do not like or even personally know such people, we may be influenced by their messages because of the position they hold (as is the case with politicians, sports heroes, or movie stars) or the control they have over us (as is true of a boss, teacher, parent, or spouse).

We are constantly coming into contact with people who have the potential to be significant others in our lives. If you think about who you are today and compare your present language, beliefs, values, and attitudes with those you held five years ago, you will probably find some noticeable differences. These very likely were brought about by your acceptance of someone else's influence. No one can change you except you, but the significant others in your life can alert you to new concepts

The significant-other theory proposes that our understanding of self is built by those who react to and comment on our actions, ideas, beliefs, and talents.

and help lay the foundation for the changes that come when you accept them.

The Concept of Meaning

Understanding what language is gives us an important base for understanding how meaning results. The study of the structure of human language is called **linguistics.** It tells us that there are certain features common to all languages. Among these are the following:

All languages are based on a set of symbols, both verbal and nonverbal. We use the letters s-c-i-s-s-o-r-s, for example, to represent the instrument that is used for cutting paper. Or we form a circle with our thumb and index finger and extend the other three fingers to signify that everything is fine.

All languages recognize a difference between vowels and consonants. In English the vowel sounds are generally represented by the letters *a, e, i, o,* and *u,* singly or in combination. The consonants are such letters as *b, c, r,* and *m.*

All languages have ordered, structural categories, such as verbs, noun phrases and objects. Our language is symbolic in that we use words to represent objects and ideas. The sentence "The car is beautiful" designates the object (car) and expresses the idea about the car ("is beautiful").

Words in and of themselves are not inherently meaningful. The meaning we derive from our language stems from how we as communicators interpret the symbols used in that language. Because words carry no meaning as such, we derive our meaning for the verbal symbols through our own backgrounds, experiences, and perceptions, which shape our interpretations of the language as it is used within any particular communication message and communication context.

The communication message and context help us to achieve some degree of accuracy in interpreting the symbols used. Nevertheless, meaning is not an infallible result of communication. Because we interpret the symbols through our backgrounds, experiences, and perceptions, we can assign meaning according to our frame of reference, which may be far from the intent of the communicator/sender. Thus all communicators in a transaction must work to be as accurate as possible in the interpretation and assignment of meaning from the verbal symbols. These symbols carry both denotative and connotative meanings.

We give words **denotative meanings**—that is, direct, explicit meanings—when we want to categorize them. For instance, the word *dog* may carry the denotative meaning of a four-legged, furry animal. This denotation enables you to classify the animal and to understand the literal characteristics of the term. In contrast, connotative words have an implied or suggested meaning. Words such as "love," "good," "pretty," and "nice" have connotative meanings.

Our language is filled with connotative meanings as well as with connotative words. **Connotative meanings** are those that we associate with certain words or to which we attach particular implications. Thus the word *dog* may carry pleasant connotations—such as lovable, friendly, and warm—if we have had pleasant associations with these animals. Postal carriers, however, may find that the word has negative connotations; to them "dog" may carry the connotative meaning of a mean, snarling, biting animal.

Words, then, may have both denotative (explicit) and connotative (implicit) meanings that influence communication. Connotative meanings in particular may vary greatly from person to person. For this reason, an encoded message and a decoded message can never be identical.

Connotative meanings form the foundation of our communication transactions. Therefore communicators have to exercise care in encoding and decoding messages. People who study **semantics,** the relationship of language and meaning, encourage us to avoid a rigid orientation that sees everything as falling into one of two categories of value: good or bad, right or wrong, black or white. Instead of approaching the world with this either/or, two-valued orientation, we can remember that life is multidimensional and that meanings vary as the backgrounds and experiences of the communicators differ.

Instructors who say someone is a "good student" or a "poor student" reflect a two-valued orientation because such statements do not allow for other dimensions of a student's performance. Perhaps, for example, the student is strong in some subjects but weak in others. Or perhaps he or she has not been motivated to work in school but does have considerable academic ability.

A communicator/source should attempt to use language as precisely as possible so as to reduce misunderstanding and thus avoid semantic noise. Choosing symbols that describe references as precisely as possible is an important part of this process. The use of definitions, examples, synonyms, and explanations can serve to clarify terminology.

As in any type of communication, a successful transaction occurs only if the sender takes into consideration the background, knowledge, and other factors that determine how the particular person or audience receives the message. In other words, consideration must be given to making sure that the message is clearly presented in terms, grammatical structure, and emotional appeals that relate to the receiver.

Consider the following example: a dentist says to an assistant, "Hand me the instrument." The assistant looks at a tray of fifteen different instruments and responds, "Which one?" Obviously, the word *instrument* was so imprecise in this situation that the assistant was unable to determine the intended meaning.

Semanticists encourage us to qualify our statements. What if a friend says to you, "Take the sociology course from Professor Strata. She's great!" What does "great" mean in this context? Does she give all A's? Assign no homework? Cover the material thoroughly? Give an exam every week so you can demonstrate what you know? Miss class regularly? If your friend had said, "Take the sociology course from Professor Strata. She's great because she'll tutor you individually if you don't understand the material," the message would have been clearer.

Remember that the communicator/receiver has a responsibility in the transaction. If you are in this position, you should work to understand the meaning intended by the communicator/source. Giving feedback such as asking questions, noting uncertainties, and repeating the message can aid in clarifying the meaning in a communication transaction. Feedback can also eliminate organizational noise (if you ask the person to structure his or her ideas in a different way) or semantic noise (if you state that the words of the message need defining).

The Functions of Language

The way in which one person uses language to deal with others is affected not only by the available vocabulary but also by the functions of language.[8] These functions are generally classified into five categories—emotive, phatic, cognitive, rhetorical, and metalingual.

Emotive language is used to express the feelings, attitudes, and emotions of the speaker. Emotive language employs a great number of connotative words to get the listener involved through the speaker's own emotional involvement. In discussing a movie, a person who says that it is riveting, stunning, heart-rending, and gripping is using emotive language.

Phatic language is used to reinforce the relationship between the participants in a communicative exchange. Such language functions as

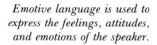

Emotive language is used to express the feelings, attitudes, and emotions of the speaker.

greetings, farewells, and small talk exchanges are phatic aspects of language. The emphasis is on the exchange of pleasantries for the development of good will. The traditional "Hello, how are you?" and "Have a nice day" are examples of phatic language.

The function of **cognitive language** is information. Cognitive language tends to be denotative and allows the listener to learn something he or she does not know. News broadcasts, excluding editorials, center on the cognitive function. This section on the functions of language is an example of cognitive language.

The function of **rhetorical language** is to influence thoughts and behaviors. It is persuasive. The intent is to motivate the listener's attitudes, values, or beliefs. The speaker uses connotative terms to create emotionally vivid pictures and draw implications while developing logical appeals. A media editorial encouraging recycling and a speech supporting donations to a charitable cause are examples of the rhetorical function of language.

Metalingual language discusses language itself. It describes what language is, how it functions, and how people use it. A critique of a speech is an example of the metalingual function of language. Following a speech by the president, for example, experts in the field of communication and current events often dissect how the president presented his materials and analyze the intent of what he said.

Language Distortion

Words stand for different meanings, people intentionally or unintentionally distort information as they process it, and people intentionally or unintentionally use language that is not clear. All these factors lead to language distortion. **Language distortion** is commonly caused by ambiguity, vagueness, inferences, and/or message adjustment.[9]

Ambiguity can be present when a word has more than one interpretation. For example, does the word *hog* mean a fat pig, someone who eats too much, a large car, a motorcycle, or a segment of the Washington Redskins' football team? All these definitions are appropriate, depending on the context. Fortunately, ambiguity can often be overcome if the listener refers to the word's context to determine whether the word means a recent sporting event or the purchase of a Cadillac.

Vagueness takes place when words or sentences lack clarity. Use of words such as "they," "he," and "things like that" are vague unless we specifically know the they, the he, or the things being referred to by the speaker. Many connotative words, because they have no specific definition, are vague. How clear were the statements made early in the Iraqi-U.N. conflict that called bombing raids "successful" and "encompassing"?

A special form of vagueness in which individuals intentionally misuse language, manipulating it to obscure the truth by saying what they do not mean, is **doublespeak.**[10] It is extremely common among politicians and members of the advertising and news media. It is so frequent and negative that the National Council for Teachers of English has set up a committee to monitor political and government verbiage, for which they give a yearly Public Doublespeak Award. The Pentagon was a nominee when it referred to bombing as "routine, limited duration, reinforced, protection-reaction air strikes."[11]

There are no potholes in the streets of Tucson, Arizona, just "pavement deficiencies." There are no longer any street people, just "non–goal-oriented members of society." Americans are not paying any new taxes; they are just being subjected to "revenue enhancements" and "user fees." There are no more poor people, just "fiscal underachievers." Patients do not die from malpractice; "a diagnostic misadventure of a high magnitude" occurs. The U.S. Army does not kill anymore; it just "services the target." Morticians are now sometimes called "grief therapists," a schoolroom desk has become a "learning station," and a secretary is "an administrative assistant in charge of transcribing functions." There are no longer used cars, instead they are "preowned." And some colleges are no longer administering tests. Instead they ask students to participate in "educational opportunities."

> Double-speak is not a slip of the tongue, or a language used out of ignorance, but is instead a very conscious use of language as a weapon or tool by those in power to achieve their ends at our expense. While some double-speak is funny, much of it is frightening. We laugh and dismiss double-speak as empty or meaningless words at our own peril . . . but it is a great weapon of power, exploitation, manipulation, and oppression.[12]

Inferences result when we interpret beyond the available information. Because listening is a creative process, inferences are a natural and inevitable part of processing information. If we do not have enough material, we just complete the idea with what seems logical to us, what we have experienced in the past, or what we hope or fear is the potential outcome. Read the following sentence quickly:

THE COW JUMP OVER

OVER THEE NOON.

Did you see "jump," or did you read it as "jumped"? What about "over" "over" and "thee" and "noon"? Many people simply see the first couple of words and based on their past experience instinctively know what is written and infer the nursery rhyme statement.

Inference also has special forms: leveling, sharpening, and assimilation. In **leveling** the message is shortened. You have probably heard a long, long story and when passing the information on simply left out the "unimportant details." This is sometimes the result of wanting to save time or of simply forgetting some particulars. In **sharpening** certain parts of the information are highlighted at the expense of other parts. You decide what is really important, from your perspective, rather than conveying all the information. News reporters are constantly placed in the position of having to make decisions about what to report regarding a widespread story. In **assimilation** the speaker reorganizes the information to fit her or his personality and needs.[13] The workings of leveling, sharpening, and assimilation can be clearly observed in the spread of a rumor. The concluding story may have little or no relationship to the actual happening or information presented at the start of the rumor trail.

The Languages We Use

Speech, like chemistry, has a structure. There is a limited set of elements—vowels and consonants—and these are combined to produce words which, in turn, compound into sentences.[14] It is the responsibility of a **linguist,** a social scientist who studies the structures of various languages, to provide the concepts that describe these languages. Thus linguists make certain observations and then report on the development of linguistic forms: the words, phrases, and sentences of a language. "Systematic and rule-governed differences exist between languages," reported one linguist. "Each language is a collection of similar dialects. **Dialects,** like languages, differ from each other in terms of pronunciation, vocabulary, grammar and prosody (accent or tone.)"[15] A dialect may be used, for example, by people from the same geographical region, from a certain occupational group, or from a specific social or educational class. The dialects of the English language, for example, have more similarities than differences. For this reason, speakers of different English dialects can communicate with relative ease. But when the systematic rules of pronunciation, vocabulary, and grammar differ enough for communication between individuals to be impossible, then, by definition, two different languages exist.

Each speaker of a language speaks some dialect of it or a combination of dialects. A common mistake is to view one dialect as best. No single dialect of a language is *the* language. But in every language there is a continuation in terms of prestige from the lowest to the highest. High-prestige dialects are called **standard dialects,** and low-prestige dialects are called **nonstandard dialects.** A dialect derives its prestige from those who speak it. The dialects of those who are in power, have influence, and are educated become the standard dialects of a language, and the literature, science, and records are written using the vocabulary and grammar that approximate the standard dialects.[16]

Standard American
English

Such variance in word selection and pronunciation exists from one part of the United States to another that some communication theorists include a discussion of this country's language patterns under the topic of intercultural communication, a category usually reserved for information about different countries' patterns. These linguists feel that **intercultural communication** occurs whenever "a message producer is a member of one culture and a message receiver is a member of another."[17]

Because culture manifests itself in patterns of both language and thought and in forms of activity and behavior, persons from a given society within a given geographical area, such as a country or a part of a country, are culturebound.[18] Thus each of the various American English dialects creates a subculture, and cultural binding makes people in one area of the country think and act differently from people in other parts of the country. A northerner who travels to the South quickly notes the difference in the pace of spoken language and the actions of the people. Basic midwestern values such as "show me" or "prove it to me" are expressed differently from the West Coast's "do what feels good" attitude.

The question, then, is what is "Standard American English"?[19] **Standard American English** is the language generally recognized by linguists as being representative of the general society of the United States. It is considered the oral form usually spoken by national news personalities and generally characterized by the oral sounds of the residents of the Middle West (Midwest) and the West.

The pronunciation generally used in the Middle West and the West is identified by distinctions of pronunciation such as that of pronouncing the final *r* (as in "father" versus "fa'da") and the *r* before consonants in words (as in "park" versus "pok"). In these and other respects, Standard American English differs from the dialects spoken in the other principal regional pronunciation areas—the Midland, New England, and the South (see Figure 5.3). In New England and the Midland, the *a* in such words as "fast" and "path" is generally pronounced like the *a* in "father," and the *r* is not pronounced when it is a final consonant or when it precedes a final consonant. In the South, the *r* is not pronounced after vowels ("for" becomes "fo"), and simple stressed vowels are dipthongized ("him" becomes "he-im").

Although there may not be a one "best" way of pronunciation, there do appear to be some generally accepted standards of American pronunciation. The words *pitcher* and *picture* do not have the same meaning and are not pronounced the same way. Such words as "hunderd" (hundred), "liberry" (library), "secatary" (secretary), and "alls" (all) do not exist. Words ending with *ing,* such as "going," "coming," and "doing," are not generally pronounced "goin," "comin," and "doin." Saying "jeet yit?" is not a substitute for "Did you eat yet?" "Many" should not be pronounced "minnie," and "didn't" is not "dint."

Figure 5.3

Principal Regional Pronunciation Areas

(Wilbur Zelinsky, *The Cultural Geography of the United States,* © 1973, p. 113. Adapted by permission of Prentice Hall, Englewood Cliffs, New Jersey.)

The general American word selection and grammatical form are those of educated citizenry and nationally published magazines (such as *Time* and *Newsweek*) and newspapers (*USA Today,* the *New York Times,* and the *Washington Post*). These words tend to represent the vocabulary of the West, the Midwest, the Midland, and the southern section of New England.

There are some linguists, however, who contend that as long as no single pattern of language has been legalized, there is no such thing as a standard by which American English can be judged. That notwithstanding, a considerable segment of American society may consider people who pronounce words, use grammar, and select words outside of the generally accepted pattern to be uneducated and less-than-desirable employees or social participants.

Slang   The English language comprises somewhere between 600,000 and 1 million words, as shown in Figure 5.4. But the average American's vocabulary consists of only about 20,000 words, 2,000 of which may be slang.[20] **Slang** comprises words that are related to a specific activity or incident and are immediately understood by members of a particular group. In logger lingo, for example, "drag'er" means "quite," a "faller" is a logger who cuts down trees, and "Give 'er snoose" means "Hurry up."[21] Slang can also be recreationally oriented; in rock music "gonzo"

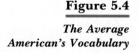

Figure 5.4

The Average American's Vocabulary

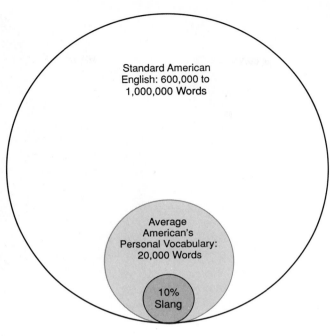

connotes the ultimate in craziness, "heavy metal" means distorted chords, and "R&B" means "rhythm and blues."[22] Or slang can be age oriented, as in the collegiate study that found that "schween," "feeb," "slug," and "nudley" are all terms for an unintelligent or dull person, whereas a "dizzweeny" is the ultimate blockhead. Order a "za" and a pizza will appear. A "ferny" is a person whose diet consists of nothing but vegetables and organic foods; a "quiche eater" is a dizzweeny who eats only expensive food.[23]

In some instances, slang takes on the form of **psychobabble,** which can be described as "telling it like it is."[24] This basically means that the person uses whatever terms he or she feels will carry the meaning, no matter the language form. As a result, psychobabble often consists of obscure phrases ("Find your own space" or "Get back to square one") and complicated terminology ("eventuated," "feasibility," "viable").

Technobabble is a specific type of psychobabble in which computerese (computer language) takes on daily meaning. Technobabblers "interface" with each other, "debug" their relationships, and want their newspapers to be "user friendly." A short glossary of computerese includes "access"—in computerese, to gain access to a computer, in technobabble, to get into anything. "Database"—in computerese, a basic store of com-

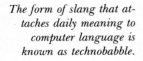

The form of slang that attaches daily meaning to computer language is known as technobabble.

puter information; in technobabble, intelligence or common sense. "Interface"—in computerese, a system for making computer parts compatible; in technobabble, to talk or communicate.[25] Because of the prevalence of computers in our society, technobabble is fast becoming a permanent part of our vocabulary.

The U.N.-Iraqi war brought military slang to the civilian population. Through newscasts civilians became familiar with such terms as "juke"—moving quickly to evade enemy fire; "smart bombs"—bombs guided to their targets by video and laser systems; and "wing weenie"—an air force officer with no combat duties.

There is also regional slang. In New England a "flatlander" is anybody who does not live in Vermont, New Hampshire, or Massachusetts. The people who reside in those areas are often called "pine needles." People in the Midwest refer to a brown paperbag as a "sack," whereas in some parts of the South the same item is referred to as a "poke."

Verbal Obscenity

Another way that people find a meaningful set of symbols is by using the language of the general society but altering it with rhetorical devices. One of the most profound of these is **verbal obscenity,** or swearing that uses offensive words and phrases. Despite centuries of criticism, verbal obscenity has become a frequently used device to attract attention, discredit an enemy, provoke violence, and foster identification.

Historically, verbal obscenity has had its effect. Just as physical acts of violence, such as throwing bricks and bottles, may provoke violent retaliation, verbal obscenity has also been an effective rhetorical method for inciting a violent response. The book *Kent State,* which reconstructs the historic confrontation between the National Guard and students at Kent State University in 1969, notes the value of this device:

> It should be added that, although we fully understand and agree with the principle of law that words alone are never sufficient to justify the use of lethal force, the verbal abuse directed at the Guardsmen by the students during the period in question represented a level of obscenity and vulgarity which we have never before witnessed. The epithets directed at the Guardsmen and members of their families by male and female rioters alike would have been unbelievable had they not been confirmed by the testimony from every quarter and by audio tapes made available to the grand jury.[26]

Though obscenity is often construed as merely an attention-getting device, its use can also provide a catharsis, a release of pent-up frustrations. Vulgar speech can give people a "psychologically suitable vehicle for the ventilation of fury and despair, the elimination of anger and aggression, the expression of rebellion and the suppression of fear."[27] Tennis professional John McEnroe, for example, is noted for his emotional outbursts during a match, which allow him to vent his feelings and calm himself down.

Profanity can also enable those with a limited vocabulary to express their feelings. Consider the frustration of being unable to describe one's emotions, present action-oriented concepts, or explain ideas. The natural response is to become infuriated. Just as kicking a rock one has tripped over allows a person to attack an outside source and blame it for a problem, so the use of obscenity can provide a similar outlet. Verbal obscenity may also be used for humor, as can be observed by the number of comedians who rely on this device.

Five different kinds of talk have traditionally been considered to be obscene:

1. Words, mostly of four letters, dealing with human sexual processes.
2. Words, mostly of four letters, dealing with human elimination processes.
3. Words that suggest that others are appropriate for eternal damnation and "curse" words ("damn" and "hell").
4. The inappropriate use of divine names (so-called profane words, that is, unnecessary or irrelevant use of divine names).
5. Uncharitable language or words that attack other people's character, personality, reputation, or integrity.[28]

Though often construed as merely an attention-getting device, the use of obscenity can also provide a release of pent-up frustrations.

Over the last twenty-five years, beginning with the Vietnam War, many conventions and traditions concerning language and what is and is not verbal obscenity have broken down. It may well be that with the decline of patriotism and family values has come a decline in traditional standards of language. Language that was unacceptable in the "good old days" is no longer even questioned. Newspapers and other media, once the pillars of protection of language, have broadened their language use extensively. Newspaper style books devote pages to the subtle distinctions among obscenities, profanities, vulgarities, and merely indecent language. Even as editors thumb through their style books, they often find that the rules are already out of date.[29]

The use of language in the popular culture—specifically in music and comedy—as well as the broadening use of what was called obscenity in past generations by the news media has branded the 1990s as the Filth Decade.[30] This use of nontraditional language has become so much an issue that a major magazine bannered a front cover story with the theme: "It's a four-letter world out there: in rock and rap, in movies and on TV, in comedy clubs and real life. Many love it, especially kids. Many others hate it or don't get it."[31]

Inarticulates

Inarticulates are sounds, words, or phrases uttered during speech that have no meaning or that do not help the listener gain a clear understanding of the message. Inarticulates are fillers that cover up the speaker's inability to think of what to say, fill in thinking time, or are bad vocal habits.

Vocalized filler sounds include "um," "and-uh," "ur," and "well-uh." Common inarticulate phrases are "you know" and "stuff like that." None of these sounds or phrases aids the listener's understanding. If the receiver already knew, the speaker would not have to say "you know." And what is "stuff like that"? A speaker who uses inarticulates is often construed either to be lacking in language skills or to be deliberately evasive.

Nonstandard English/Dialects

Many people in this country speak languages and/or dialects that differ from Standard American English. Some of these speakers use a recognizable alternate language form such as Spanish, French, Chinese, or one of the Native American tongues. In some cases, speakers present their ideas in identifiable dialects of Standard American English, such as Spanglish. Still another group speaks a separate but definite rule-based language called Black English, which fulfills the definition of language because it has a distinct grammatical and symbolic system; but because it has so many similarities to Standard American English, Black English is considered by some to be a dialect.

Many Americans assume that only one form of English—the form spoken by the educated white majority—is "right." Accordingly, schoolchildren whose speech patterns differ from the standard forms—whether they are blacks, Hispanics, Native Americans, Europeans, Caribbeans, or Orientals—are encouraged to discard their familiar patterns and adopt those of Standard American English as a means of gaining social acceptance within the larger community. One of the arguments for elimination of other language systems is that this country is a melting pot and that all citizens should learn Standard American English just as earlier immigrants did. In addition, because Standard English is the language of business, the language that must be used to succeed in most segments of the world of work, all members of society must be able to speak Standard American English. Another contention is that because a society is what its language is, there is a need for all residents of a country to speak the same language. This view is controversial; some linguists have argued that such attitudes are unsound and racist.[32]

One of the major problems confronting today's schools is how to handle non-Standard American English speakers. In 1979, a Michigan federal court ruled that a group of black children in predominantly white Ann Arbor, Michigan, had been denied equal educational opportunity because teachers failed to recognize or accommodate their black dialect.[33] As a result of that ruling, programs developed in many parts of the country to investigate the most appropriate ways to teach and to test students who speak various dialects and non-English languages. Most schools adopted the attitude that "we accept the language the students bring from home, but we teach them that standard English is a tool they must have. They may not use it all the time, but when you need it, you need it."[34]

Any discussion of dialects must recognize that "there are many dialects and some get a lot of respect and some don't get any. In some cases, the respect given to the dialect is in the same amount that is given to the people who speak it."[35] The contention well may be, "If you accept my language, you accept me." A brief examination of Black English, Spanglish, and Asian-American English may lead to some understanding of their nature, their history, the speakers who use them, and the perceived effects of speaking an alternative language or a dialect.

Black English   "After years of controversy, linguists and educators have come to agree that a separate black vernacular exists."[36] Besides the professional recognition, a 1979 ruling by a federal judge legally acknowledged the existence of **Black English.**[37] Linguistic researchers refer to the semantic and syntactic pattern as Black English, Vernacular Black English,[38] or Ebonics (ebony phonics).[39] "Black English is rooted in a historical past that spans Africa, the Caribbean, the Creole heritage, the South and now the northern U.S. cities. Many of the grammatical elements of Black English can be traced directly to these earlier speech and language influences."[40]

Linguists cite fifty characteristics of Black English that differentiate it from Standard English, many of which have parallels in the linguistic structure of West African languages.[41] Among the most common speech markers is the use of what linguists call the "invariant be" to denote an ongoing action ("He be going to work"). This usage is not present in Standard English grammar but is parallel to the indefinite or habitual tense of languages such as French and Spanish. In addition, there is the zero copula ("You crazy"); the nonredundant plural, or dropping of the *s* at the end of some words (twenty cent); the consonant cluster, or dropping or adding of letters to words ("firs" instead of "first" or "des" instead of "desk"); and the absence of the *th* sound at the ending of a word ("wif" for "with").[42]

"Vernacular Black English is the most common dialect used by African Americans. . . . This is not street talk; it is not broken English and it is not slang."[43] It is "a private vocabulary of Black people which serves the users as a powerful medium."[44] "Moreover, Black English is not a regional dialect. It reflects the common national culture of the American black community. The grammar used by many black adults in Los Angeles in their home setting is virtually the same as that used by adolescent groups in New York. As an important black writer stated, 'Black English is a vivid and crucial key to Black identity.' "[45]

Spanglish takes a variety of forms.

Spanglish

A significant group of Americans speaks a dialect referred to as **Spanglish.**[46] It is a common linguistic currency wherever concentrations of Hispanic Americans are found. Spanglish takes a variety of forms, from the humorous "hasta la bye-bye" to the serious invitation to "lonche" (a quick lunch rather than a leisurely luncheon), the description of a group of "los teenagers," and the almost universally used "no problema." Spanglish sentences are mostly Spanish, with a quick detour for a few English words and some fractured syntax.

A professor of linguistics who speaks Spanglish with relatives and neighbors said, "Among Latinos, Spanglish conversations often flow easily from Spanish into several sentences of English and back again. It's unconscious. I couldn't even tell you minutes later if I said something in Spanish or in English."[47]

Major advertisers, like Miller Lite Beer, eager to tap the estimated $134 billion in spending power wielded by Spanish-speaking Americans, have ventured into Spanglish to promote their products. Although the exact number of Hispanic speakers in this country is not known, it is estimated that about 10 percent of the U.S. population speaks some form of Spanish-based dialect. This makes Hispanics the nation's second-largest speaking group, surpassed only by Standard American English speakers.

To speak Standard English, the Hispanic speaker, in addition to learning English vocabulary, is confronted with acquiring a language quite different in form.[48] For example, English is not as phonetic as Spanish—it is not necessarily pronounced the way it is written. A Spanish speaker, according to his or her language background, will normally pronounce an English word with all the letters as they are ordered. For example, in English the letters *i-n-t-e-r-e-s-t-i-n-g* are usually pronounced "in' trasting," whereas the same letters in Spanish would be pronounced "in ter est' ing." An additional problem is that in Spanish there are five vowel sounds (*a* as in *paso, e* as in *peso, i* as in *piso, o* as in *pozo, u* as in *puso*); English contains the same five vowels, but they have fifteen different vowel sounds. This creates confusion; for instance, in English the letters *r-e-a-d* could mean "to read" or "having read" (same spelling, different vowel sound).

In English pronunciation, vowel sounds are often prolonged, whereas in Spanish they are rapid and clipped. In English, the word *no* sounds like n-o-o-o; in Spanish it is a clipped no! In addition, Spanish speakers use many more upward inflections while speaking. Furthermore, most Spanish words end in vowels, not consonants, thus leading to difficulty in adding *ed* and *ing* sounds at the ends of words; thus "going" becomes "goen" and "based" becomes "baysa." The *th* sound is almost nonexistent in Spanish at the beginning of words, so "I think so" becomes "I sink so." Thus the errors in English pronunciation made by native Spanish speakers seem logical in the context of their original language.[49]

Asian-American   The last several decades have seen a large immigration of Asian speakers into the United States. People have come from such countries as Vietnam, China, Korea, Taiwan, Japan, and Cambodia. They bring with them languages that differ from English and often differ from each other. There are four general classifications of Asian language: Tai (Southeast Asia), Ainu (western China), Altaic (Korea and Japan), and Sino-Tibetan (China and Russia).[50]

As with Hispanic speakers, as Asian speakers develop an **Asian-American** dialect by combining their language with English, vocabulary *and* pronunciation are major stumbling blocks. Most significant are the letters *r* and *1*. There is generally no Asian sound like either of these; thus *"run"* becomes *"wun"* and *"lady"* becomes *"aedi."* Also, many Asian words are monosyllabic and end in vowels, which creates problems with multisyllabic words and terms ending with consonants. Thus *ed, s,* and *ing* word endings are dropped from English words. The *sh* sound does not exist, so *ch* may be substituted, and "shopping" becomes "choppin."

Japanese and Korean speakers, who have a consonant-vowel language in which a consonant sound is always followed by a vowel, have a tendency to add an extra vowel sound after words ending in consonants. Thus "walk" becomes "walka" and "and" sounds like "anda."[51]

The Effects of Speaking a Dialect

Recent studies have reinforced the concept that speaking a dialect, rather than Standard American English, can be detrimental to a person's educational and economic health. Children entering schools with weak Standard English skills are at a definite disadvantage.[52] In economic terms, nonstandard speakers are given shorter interviews and fewer job offers than Standard-English speakers. When job offers are presented, nonstandard speakers are offered positions paying as much as 35 percent less than Standard-English speakers.[53] In social terms, speakers of nonstandard dialects are often mistakenly confronted with negative assumptions concerning their intelligence, dependability, and creativity. Standard English even contains prejudicial terms to describe those who speak non-Standard English; these terms refer to the speaker's place of origin or physical characteristics.

People speaking dialects should be aware that in some instances education, speech therapy, and other types of training can make alterations in their vocabulary and speaking patterns—if they are desirous of change. That desire is usually based on a person's awareness that her or his career and social needs include particular language requirements.

People and their abilities to communicate are not only affected by dialects, they are also affected by gender.

Male-Female Communication

Two issues arise as we examine male-female communication. One is whether there is a bias toward "male" language in American English and, if so, how it has affected the roles men and women adopt in society; the other is whether men and women speak differently.

Psychologists believe that "roles are patterns of expectation by the self and others about appropriate behavior of an individual in given social settings."[54] These roles are learned by means of our symbolic interactions, through which we also acquire the norms of culture and society. Roles are defined in the language of the society, and once we acquire them, we believe in them.[55] Though these usages may seem unimportant to some, they affect children as they are growing up and learning roles according to the language that surrounds them. Eventually children learn to play out the roles indicated by the labels attached to men and women.[56]

English is one of the few languages that does not have three words to refer to humans. Other languages have one term for humanity in general, with no regard to sex; a term for males; and a term for females. Traditionally, in English, all people have been considered in a general way and have been referred to with such words as "man," "he," "him," or "his." This has resulted in women feeling dismissed, defined, and determined.

The language, as it has been traditionally used, dismissed women through the general use of male terms such as "spokesman," "chairman," "working man." For many, this has become a past-tense issue as the society generally becomes more accepting of the need for more neutral terms, such as "spokesperson," "chair," and "worker."

The language also defined women in terms of their relationships to others, especially to men ("the doctor's wife and mother of three" or "Mrs. John Smith"), whereas men were known by their occupations ("the Florida banker"). Again, as the educational system and the media, the major sources of language dissemination, have become aware of the implications of this language usage, the concern with this issue has diminished.

The language also had a determining effect. Certain jobs and roles were long identified with certain sexes—mechanics, doctors, carpenters, and truck drivers were male domains; secretaries, nurses, social workers, and teachers were female occupations. Boys used language and were encouraged to play male roles and girls to play female parts, thus determining their expectations of what parts to play in life. These usages have changed in response to the attack on sexism in the English language.

As for the second issue, whether men or women do speak differently, "some people become agitated as soon as they hear a reference to gender. A few become angry at the mere suggestion that women and men are different";[57] nevertheless, "a decade's worth of research has shown that men and women in our culture use distinctive styles of speech and also tend to play different roles when talking with one another."[58] And though it is accepted that every person is unlike anyone else, and that the desire to affirm that women are equal has made some scholars reluctant to show there is a difference, there are gender differences in ways of speaking that need to be identified and understood.

Communication between men and women is cross-cultural communication; it is as confusion-ridden as talk between people from two different countries. Because men and women approach one another from distinct worlds, the simplest phrase can carry separate, sometimes conflicting meanings to members of the opposite sex.[59] Men and women use language to contrary purposes and effect. Women tend to use language to create intimacy and connection, and men use language to preserve their independence and negotiate their status. "The question overriding women's interactions is, 'Do you love me?' or, if it's not a close relationship, 'Do you like me?' And the question in men's minds is, 'Are you trying to dominate me?' "[60]

How do these differences develop? Girls and boys grow up in different worlds of words. Boys and girls have very different ways of talking to their friends. Boys tend to play in large groups that are hierarchically structured: there is a leader and/or there is a competition for leadership; there are winners and losers in the games they play as well as complex rules. The emphasis is on skill and who is best. Girls play in small groups or pairs and usually have a best friend; intimacy is the key; everyone gets a turn, there are usually no winners and losers, and girls are not expected to boast about successes. Girls don't give orders; they express their preferences as suggestions. Boys say, "Gimme that!" and "Get out of here!" Girls say, "Can we do this?" and "How about doing that?" Gender differences in language can be observed in children as young as age three.[61]

Both male and female styles are valid in their own ways. Misunderstandings arise because the styles are different. An examination of how problems are handled illustrates the vast difference in language usage. Women wish to talk about their problems, share information with others, and seek advice. Men want to get the problem out and be done with it, either by finding a solution or by laughing the matter off.

There are general patterns of communication that are identifiably male and female. For example, which of the following are true?

"Women use more words to make their point."

"Men are more competitive in their speaking."

"Men tend to be more task oriented."

"Women are more supportive conversationalists."

"Men are more direct."

"Women disclose more personal information to others than men do."

"Women have larger vocabularies for describing emotions and aesthetics."

Yes, women do use more words to make their point. Much of this centers on their desire to fill in details and to explain more fully. They tend to be more sensitive to the needs of the listener. Men tend to say what they have to say, assume that the message is clear, and proceed from that point. Therefore men may believe that women are wasting time, talking too much, or not getting to the point because of the additional effort women spend in clarifying and enlarging.[62]

Partners in successful relationships are able to overcome the inherent differences in the way that women and men communicate.

Yes, men are more competitive in their speaking. They have been socialized to "take charge" and get things done. "Typically men engage in competitive turn-taking, or grabbing the floor by interrupting another speaker. Women have been conditioned from childhood to believe that to interrupt is impolite."[63] Indeed, research on male-female communication patterns found that 96 percent of the interruptions and 100 percent of the overlaps in mixed pairs in daily conversations were induced by men.[64]

Yes, men do tend to be more task oriented, whereas women tend to be more maintenance oriented. Men tend to want results at any cost. Women are usually more concerned about the process used, about keeping things going smoothly, and about doing business in the least disruptive manner. Women characteristically use tentative phrases such as "I guess" and turn direct statements into indirect statements. For example, a woman may say, "Don't you think it would be better to send that report first?" A man will typically say, "Send the report."[65] Men will say, "Who's next on the agenda?" and "What's the bottom line?" Women tend to ask, "You haven't spoken; what do you think?" or "How does everyone feel about this?"

Yes, women are more supportive conversationalists. They are much more likely to check the connectedness of conversations. Women tend to ask more questions and work harder than men do to keep the conversational ball rolling. In fact, women ask questions three times as often as men.[66] Women often feel that it is their role to make sure that the conversation goes well, and they assume that if it is not proceeding well, they have to do something to remedy the situation.[67]

Yes, men are more direct. When men want something, they ask for it directly; women tend to be more indirect.[68] A man may ask a woman, "Will you please go to the store?" He wants something; he feels that he has the status to ask for it and get it. But a woman asking a man may say, "Gee, I really need a few things from the store, but I'm so tired." Often she speaks this way because she feels in a low-status position that does not include the right to make a request.[69] A man may well describe the manner in which a woman makes a request as "beating around the bush," and he may ask, "Why, if you want something, don't you just ask for it?"

Yes, findings indicate that women disclose more personal information than men do. In their vocabulary selections, females tend to be people oriented and concerned with internal psychological and emotional states, whereas men are self oriented and concerned with action.

Yes, women have larger vocabularies for describing emotions and aesthetics. Women have been taught to express their feelings, men to hide or disregard theirs. Therefore women have a larger repertoire of words to describe what they are feeling. Women also have broader vocabularies that can finitely separate aesthetics, such as colors. Men tend to describe the color as red; women describe specific shadings, such as ruby, magenta, and rose.

What are the implications of these differences in male and female speech? One implication is that the divide between the speeches needs to be crossed. The women's movement has looked to androgyny as one solution. **Androgyny** is the internalization of both masculine and feminine language and characteristics so that both men's and women's speech falls further from sex-type counterparts but instead falls in between the stereotypical roles of each. Although those interested in gender communication want to believe there have been drastic changes, and although a softening of some of the stereotypical language usages and roles has taken place, there is little conclusive research to prove that a true elimination of sex-role communication differences has occurred.

Accepting the theory that men and women live in different worlds, even under the same roof, means that for men and women to understand and accept each other, both must try to take each other on their own terms rather than applying the standards of one group to the language usage of the other.

Habitual ways of talking are hard to change. Learning to respect others' ways of talking may be a bit easier. Men should accept that many women regard exchanging details about personal lives as a basic ingredient of intimacy, and women should accept that many men do not share this view. Mutual acceptance will at least prevent the pain of being told you are doing something wrong when you are only doing things your way.[70]

Summary

In this chapter the foundations of verbal language and the language we use were discussed. The important concepts included:

☐ There is no one accepted theory of the origins of human language.

☐ Gestural language seems to have preceded verbal language.

☐ The processing of language can be explained by the cybernetic process, in which there are input, storage, stimulus, search, recall, and output functions.

☐ We can describe how we acquired our language, beliefs, values, and attitudes by investigating the language-explosion theory.

☐ The significant others in our lives are those people or groups whose ideas and beliefs we allow to influence us.

☐ The study of the structure of language is called linguistics.

☐ All languages are based on a set of symbols, both verbal and nonverbal.

☐ The meaning we derive from our language stems from our perceptions, experiences, and backgrounds.

☐ Denotative meanings are direct and explicit.

☐ Connotative meanings are those that we associate with certain words.

☐ A successful communication transaction takes place only when the sender adapts the message to the background, knowledge, and other necessary factors of the particular person or audience being addressed.

☐ Language has emotive, phatic, cognitive, rhetorical, and metalingual functions.

☐ Ambiguity, vagueness, inferences and/or message adjustment can distort language.

☐ Systematic and rule-governed differences exist between languages.

☐ A dialect is used by people from the same geographical region, a certain occupational group, or a specific social or educational class.

☐ No single dialect of a language is *the* language.

☐ Intercultural communication occurs whenever a message producer is a member of one culture and a message receiver is a member of another.

☐ Standard American English is the language generally recognized by linguists as being representative of the general society of the United States.

☐ Slang is words that are related to a specific activity or incident and are immediately understood by other members of the affected group.

☐ Psychobabble is "telling it like it is" by using whatever terms the sender feels will carry the meaning.

☐ Verbal obscenity is swearing that uses offensive words and phrases.

☐ Verbal obscenity may be used to get attention, express feelings when the language is not available for other expression, and communicate humor.

☐ Inarticulates are sounds, words, or phrases uttered during speech that have no meaning or do not help the listener gain a clear understanding of meaning.

☐ Ebonics, or ebony phonics, is a term used to refer to Black English, black language, or black dialect.

☐ Linguists have identified characteristics of Black English that differentiate that language from Standard English.

☐ Spanglish is a blending of Spanish and English.

☐ There are four general classifications of Asian languages: Tai, Ainu, Altaic, and Sino-Tibetan.

☐ Recent studies reinforce the concept that speaking a dialect, rather than Standard American English, can be detrimental to a person's economic and social health.

☐ The sexist nature of Standard American English has affected the roles and expectations of men and women.

☐ The sexist nature of English results in the dismissing, defining, and determining of women.

☐ The attack on sexist language has brought significant changes in the way Americans write and speak.

☐ There is a difference between the way men communicate and the way women do.

☐ Communication between men and women is a cross-cultural activity.

Key Terms

cortex	denotative meanings
cybernetic process	leveling
language-explosion theory	sharpening
dyad	assimilation
significant-other theory	linguist
linguistics	dialects

standard dialects
connotative meanings
semantics
emotive language
phatic language
cognitive language
rhetorical language
metalingual language
ambiguity
language distortion
vagueness
doublespeak
inferences

nonstandard dialects
intercultural communication
Standard American English
slang
psychobabble
verbal obscenity
inarticulates
Black English
Spanglish
Asian-American
androgyny

Learn by Doing

1. Do you feel that the growth of the women's liberation movement has had an effect on the way people use language? If so, what specific effect(s) have you noticed?

2. Carry on a class discussion based on the concepts presented in this chapter regarding the problems confronted by those whose basic language is other than Standard American English.

3. Find an example of doublespeak in a political speech, a letter to the editor, or a newspaper or magazine article, and bring it to class. Discuss what you feel the speaker was trying to hide by using doublespeak.

4. Write down one phrase or expression that is unique to your family or group of friends. It should be an expression that has meaning only for a select group and is not commonly used in the society as a whole. It may be an ethnic expression, an in-group reference, or some other special phrase. The other students then read the expression and try to figure out what it means.

5. Make a list of five people who have had a significant effect on your present values and attitudes. Identify which of these people was the most influential. What effect have that person's values and attitudes had on your life?

6. List five words that have different meanings depending on the people who use them or the place in which they are used. See how many different definitions you can develop for each word.

Notes

1. For a further discussion of this subject, see Charles F. Hockett, "The Origins of Speech," *Scientific American*, 203 (September 1960), 89–96.

2. Gordon Heives, "How Language Began," *Current Anthropology*, 14, no. 1 (1973), 1–2.

3. Norman Geschwind, "Language and the Brain," *Scientific American,* 226 (April 1972), 76–83.
4. Ibid.
5. Norbert Wiener, *The Human Use of Human Beings* (New York: Anchor Books, 1950).
6. T. R. Tortioriello, *Communication in the Organization* (New York: McGraw-Hill, 1978), p. 13.
7. George Herbert Mead, *Mind, Self and Society* (Chicago: University of Chicago Press, 1934).
8. Barbara Warnick and Edward S. Inch, *Critical Thinking and Communication* (New York: Macmillan, 1989), pp. 257–259.
9. Blaine Goss and Dan O'Hair, *Communication in Interpersonal Relationships* (New York: Macmillan, 1988), pp. 67–69.
10. For a complete discussion of doublespeak, see William Lutz, *Double-Speak* (New York: Harper Penennial, 1990).
11. "The Humbug Patrol," *Newsweek,* March 25, 1974, p. 108.
12. Lutz, pp. xii, xiii.
13. G. Allport and L. Postman, *The Psychology of Rumors* (New York: Holt, Rinehart and Winston, 1948).
14. Roger Brown, *Words and Things* (New York: Free Press, 1959), p. 22.
15. Howard A. Mims, "On Black English, A Language with Rules," *Cleveland Plain Dealer,* August 31, 1979, p. A-21.
16. Ibid.
17. R. E. Porter and L. A. Samovar, "Basic Principles of Intercultural Communication," in L. A. Samovar and R. E. Porter, eds., *Intercultural Communication* (Belmont, Calif.: Wadsworth, 1991), p. 10.
18. Ibid., p. 10.
19. Material in this section is based on the work of W. Zelinsky, as discussed in Peter A. Andersen, Myron W. Lustig, and Janis F. Andersen, "Regional Patterns of Communication in the United States: A Theoretical Perspective," *Communication Monographs,* 54 (June 1987), 128–144.
20. "People, Etc.," *Elyria Chronicle-Telegram Scene* (Ohio), April 10, 1977, p. 2.
21. Judy Frutig, "It's Called Logger Talk," *Elyria Chronicle-Telegram* (Ohio), April 10, 1977, p. 3.
22. Jane Scott, "Don't Throw Stones—Learn Rock Talk," *Cleveland Plain Dealer,* February 26, 1978, p. C-2.
23. Steve Novak, "Dizzweeny Defined," *Elyria Chronicle-Telegram* (Ohio), October 19, 1983, p. A-9.
24. Sheila Wellerp, "How to Make Your Point—Not Bury It: An Interview with Edwin Newman and John Molloy," *Self* (April 1981), 88–91.
25. Muriel Dobbin, "Computer Words Permeate English," *Cleveland Plain Dealer,* December 23, 1984, p. P-26.
26. James A. Michener, *Kent State* (New York: Random House, 1971), p. 242.
27. "Now It Can Be Said," *Cleveland Plain Dealer,* November 27, 1977, sec. 7, p. 1.
28. Andrew Greeley, "Is Dirty Talk Dirty?" *Lorain Journal* (Ohio), March 15, 1982, p. 25.

29. Mitchell Stephens and Eliot Frankel, "All the Obscenity That's Fit to Print," *Washington Journalism Review* (April 1981), 16.

30. "X-Rated," *Time*, May 7, 1990, pp. 92–100.

31. Ibid.

32. Olivia Mellan, "Black English," in Raymond D. Liedlich, ed., *Coming to Terms with Language* (New York: Wiley, 1973).

33. Sandy Banks, "Ebonics Is a Language with Its Own Set of Rules—An Interview with Orlando Taylor, Acting Dean of Communication Department, Howard University," *Cleveland Plain Dealer,* January 14, 1986, p. B-2. For a discussion of the Ann Arbor case, see David Yellin, "The Black English Controversy: Implications from the Ann Arbor Case," *Journal of Reading* (November 1980), 150–154.

34. Banks.

35. Robin Henry, " 'Black English' Causes Confusion in the Classroom—An Interview with Dr. Howard Mims, Associate Professor of Speech and Hearing, Cleveland State University," *Elyria Chronicle-Telegram* (Ohio), July 26, 1987, p. G-2.

36. Banks.

37. "Black English Must Be Recognized, Judge Rules," *Elyria Chronicle-Telegram* (Ohio), July 13, 1979, p. A-3.

38. "Teaching Standard English: A Sociolinguistic Approach," unpublished handout based on the syllabus for the Basic Communication Strategies course at LaGuardia Community College, New York, Speech Communication Association Convention, Chicago, November 1987.

39. Banks.

40. William Labov, "Allow Black English in Schools? Yes—The Most Important Thing Is to Encourage Children to Talk Freely," *U.S. News & World Report,* March 31, 1980, pp. 63–64.

41. Banks. For an in-depth discussion of the syntactic and phonological features of Black English, see Robert Hopper and Rita J. Naremore, *Children's Speech: A Practical Introduction to Communication Development,* 2nd ed. (New York: Harper & Row, 1978), pp. 161–164, 168–171.

42. Banks.

43. "Teaching Standard English."

44. Ibid., with reference to Clarence Major, *Dictionary of Afro-American Slang* (New York: International Publishers, 1971).

45. Rachel L. Jones quoting Black writer James Baldwin, "What's Wrong with Black English," *Newsweek,* December 27, 1982, p. 7.

46. Janice Castro, "Spanglish Spoken Here," *Time,* July 11, 1988, p. 53.

47. Ibid., as stated by Carmen Silva-Corvalan, professor, University of Southern California.

48. Examples in this discussion provided by Helen Sheppard, associate professor of Spanish, Lorain County Community College, Elyria, Ohio.

49. Richard Hoehn, *The Art and Practice of Public Speaking* (forthcoming).

50. Ibid.

51. Ibid.

52. Hopper and Naremore, pp. 159–174; Naremore and Hopper, pp. 156–158; Labov, pp. 63–64; and the work of Howard A. Mims, associate profes-

sor of speech and hearing, Cleveland State University, as described in a series of lectures presented at Cleveland State University, 1979, and on Cleveland radio.

53. "Black English Hazardous to Job Prospects," *Elyria Chronicle-Telegram* (Ohio), November 18, 1982, p. A-2, based on research by Sandra Terrell and Francis Terrell.

54. Sandra Pu, "Sex Roles in Communication: Teaching and Researching," *Western Speech Communication,* 40 (Spring 1976), 111–120.

55. Nancy Henley, *Body Politics* (Englewood Cliffs, N.J.: Prentice-Hall, 1977), p. 156.

56. Ibid.

57. Deborah Tannen, *You Just Don't Understand* (New York: Morrow, 1990), p. 14.

58. Stephanie Gilbert, "Girl Talk, BOY TALK," *City Paper,* November 9, 1990, p. 20.

59. Alfie Kohn, "Girl Talk, Guy Talk," *Psychology Today* (February 1988), p. 65.

60. Gilbert, p. 20.

61. Tannen, pp. 43–44.

62. Carol Krucoff, "Sexes: Who's Talking," *New York Times Style,* November 9, 1981, p. D-5, based on a series of interviews with and research by psychiatrist H. G. Whittington; psychologist James P. Smith; Leonad Kriegel, author of *On Men and Manhood;* pathologist Lillian Glass; and Hilary Lips, co-author of *The Psychology of Sex Differences.*

63. Georgia Dullea, "Garble Gap: Men, Women Just Don't Talk the Same Language," *Cleveland Plain Dealer,* March 31, 1984, p. B-1.

64. These statistics are based on research conducted by Barrie Thorne and reported in Barrie Thorne, *Womanspeak and Manspeak: Sex Differences and Sex Roles* (St. Paul: West, 1976); in Barrie Thorne and N. Henley, eds., *Language and Sex: Difference and Dominance* (Rowley, Mass.: New Burg House, 1975); and in N. Henley and Barrie Thorne, *She Said/He Said: An Annotated Bibliography of Language, Speech and Nonverbal Communication* (Pittsburg: KNOW, 1975).

65. Thorne.

66. Krucoff.

67. Glen Collins, "Men's and Women's Speech: How They Differ," *New York Times Style,* November 17, 1980, p. C-19, based on interviews with sociolinguist Cheris Kramarae, sociologist Candace West, and sociologist Pamela Fishman.

68. Krucoff.

69. Ibid., p. 65.

70. Tannen, p. 122.

6 *Nonverbal Communication*

Chapter Outline

Sources of Nonverbal Signs

Neurological Programs

Cultural/Intercultural Behavior

Emotional Influences on Nonverbal Communication

Verbal and Nonverbal Relationships

The Substitution Relationship

The Complementing Relationship

The Conflict Relationship

The Accenting Relationship

Channels of Nonverbal Communication

Kinesics
  Emblems
  Illustrators
  Affect Displays
  Regulators

Adaptors
Walk and Stance
The Face and Eyes
Open and Closed Channels

Paralanguage

Proxemics
  Space Distances
  Small-Group Ecology

Chronemics

Olfactics
  Smell Blindness
  Smell Adaptation
  Smell Memory
  Smell Overload
  Smell Discrimination

Aesthetics

Physical Characteristics
  Attractiveness
  Height

Artifacts

Learning   After reading this chapter, you should be able to:
Outcomes   Define nonverbal signs

Explain the role of clusters and congruency in the reading of nonverbal communication

Identify the sources of nonverbal signals

State and explain verbal and nonverbal relationships

List and illustrate the channels of nonverbal communication

Analyze the role of intercultural differences in nonverbal communication

Illustrate the emotional influences on nonverbal communication.

We have long been aware that it is possible to communicate a great deal without using verbal language. The **nonverbal signs** we use to do so have been defined as "all external stimuli other than spoken or written words and including body motion, characteristics of appearance, characteristics of voice, and use of space and distance."[1] We all have interpreted body talk, perhaps without knowing we were doing so, but only in recent years have attempts been made to analyze and explain nonverbal communication in a scientific manner.

Research has established that nonverbal language is an important means of expression. In documenting this, experts in the field have identified patterns of body-language usage through the study of films and videotape recordings and through personal observations.[2]

Because the study of nonverbal communication is newer than the study of verbal communication, we do not as yet have a dictionary of its terms or a thorough understanding of the process involved in it. But attempts are already being made to apply the information that has been collected. One such attempt, known as **neurolinguistic programming,** has been developed to codify and synthesize research on nonverbal communication with that of other fields of communication, including cybernetics (the study of how the human brain processes information) and language study. Researchers in this area hope to set up a system for training individuals in the concepts and techniques of nonverbal communication to improve the performance of those employed in such fields as business relations and psychotherapy.[3]

Experts tend to agree that nonverbal communication carries the impact of a message. In fact, it has been established that in a communica-

Nonverbal language is an important means of communication.

tion situation 35 percent of a message is carried verbally, whereas 65 percent is conveyed nonverbally.[4] A message's impact is 7 percent verbal, 38 percent vocal, and 55 percent nonverbal.[5]

In attempting to read nonverbal communication, we must remember that no one signal carries much meaning. Instead, such factors as gestures, posture, eye contact, clothing styles, and movement must all be regarded together. This grouping of factors is called a **cluster**.

We must also remember that, just as in verbal communication, nonverbal signs can have many different meanings. For example, crossing the arms over the chest may suggest that a person is cold. But crossed arms accompanied by erect posture, tightened body muscles, setting of the jaw, and narrowing of the eyes probably indicate anger.

A person's background and past pattern of behavior must also be considered when we analyze nonverbal communication. The relationship between present and past patterns of behavior as well as the harmony between verbal and nonverbal communication is termed **congruency**. When you say to a friend, "You don't look well today," you are basing your statement on an evaluation of present appearance compared with past appearance. In other words, something has changed, and you have become aware of a difference. If you did not have past experience to draw on, you would not have noticed the change.

Sources of Nonverbal Signs

We learn to read words through a step-by-step process in which we are taught to use our written form of communication. But how do we acquire nonverbal signs? For these, there are two basic sources: innate neurological programs and behavior that is common to a culture, social class, or family.

Neurological Programs

Innate neurological programs are those automatic nonverbal reactions to stimuli with which we are born. For example, we blink our eyes automatically when we hear a loud noise or when hands are clapped in our face or when a pebble hits the windshield of the car we are driving. Our stomach muscles tighten and our hands sweat when we feel insecure. These are all examples of innate neurological reactions.

"Moving while you talk is a biological requirement," said one expert. "You have to move to think. You have to know you exist, to stay on the beam, to exclude interference."[6] That we are born with some of our nonverbal tendencies is clearly illustrated by the tendency of "people born blind [to] move their hands when they talk, although they've never seen anyone do it."[7] Paralyzed individuals also seem to respond neurologically even if they are unable to do so physically. To a certain extent, then, we are born with the tendency to react physically in particular ways, and control of these innate actions seems almost impossible.

Cultural/ Intercultural Behavior

Some nonverbal behavior is learned in the same way as spoken language is. By observing and imitating people around us as we grow up, we learn not only to speak but to behave as they do. Every culture has its own body language, and the young learn its patterns along with those of the spoken language. As a research anthropologist indicated, "The important thing to remember is that culture is very persistent. In this country, we've noted the existence of culture patterns that determine [physical] distance between people in the third and fourth generations of some families, despite their prolonged contact with people of very different cultural heritages."[8] These cultural patterns are readily identifiable. Italians, for example, are noted for using their hands when they speak. In contrast, the British are noted for controlling their gestures and emotions.

A person who uses more than one language gestures according to the language he or she is speaking. Fiorello LaGuardia, New York City's mayor in the 1930s and early 1940s, carried on his political campaigns by speaking English, Italian, and Yiddish—the languages of the major voting blocs in the city. He used one set of gestures for speaking English, another for Italian, and still another for Yiddish.

Nonverbal gestures and behaviors convey different messages throughout the world. A Neopolitan communicates "No!" by jerking the head upward and sticking out the lower lip. An Arab man commonly strokes his chin to show appreciation for a woman, whereas a Portuguese man does it by pulling his ear. But in Italy a similar kind of ear tugging is a deliberate insult. In Tibet, when members of hill tribes meet, they exchange greetings by protruding their tongues, much as Westerners shake hands.

In communicating nonverbally, people also operate on different **action chains**. "An action chain," according to Hall, "is a behavioral sequence with two or more participating organisms, in which there are standard steps for reaching a goal. If an individual leaves out a step, the chain gets broken, and you have to start all over again."[9] For example, in this country a formal greeting has a certain set procedure, and if one person does not follow the expected steps, the other person may become confused or upset. If a person does not say, "Hello" when introduced or if businesspeople do not shake hands when they meet, the participant who has not received the normal greeting can become disoriented.

Of course, different cultures operate under different action chains. For example, to an American, to be "on time" normally means making contact within five minutes or so of a designated hour. To a Mexican, however, "on time" often means within a reasonable time. An American businessperson, having been kept waiting for twenty minutes in a Mexico City client's office, may decide to leave the office, feeling that she or he is being ignored and that the client's lateness is a sign of lack of interest in the business dealing. But the Mexican client may not consider himself or herself at all tardy and may be totally confused by the American's quick exit. Such cross-cultural differences in action chains may cause conflicts. For this reason, diplomats, businesspeople, and even tourists are wise to learn the action chains of the persons they will be dealing with in different parts of the world.

Whenever there is a great cultural distance between people, problems will arise from differences in behavior and expectations—and from misinterpretation of behavior and expectations. For instance, the thumb-and-forefinger-in-a-circle gesture is a friendly sign in the United States. In France or Belgium, however, it means "You're worth zero." The same gesture in Greece and Turkey is a sexual invitation. Likewise, an index finger to the temple with the other fingers curled usually means "He is smart" in the United States, whereas it communicates "He's stupid" in most of Europe. And an American who assumes that a vertical movement of the head is a universal gesture for "yes" may be surprised in parts of Greece and Turkey, where the motion is intended to communicate "no"![10]

The use of space varies widely around the world. Arabs, South Americans, and Eastern Europeans favor close conversational encounters that may make Americans feel somewhat uncomfortable. Asians and Northern Europeans, like Americans, tend to keep their distance while talking with each other.

Americans engaged in business dealings with Arabs, for instance, are smart to understand their customs of hospitality and adhere to them so as to be successful in conducting business. The initial meeting with an Arab businessperson is typically devoted to fact-finding. No commitments are implied or made. But the initial session is usually lengthy and thorough. Americans often feel, based on their pattern of working quickly so as not to waste time, that the process is tedious. The next meeting is taken up with additional rituals. It is not unusual, then, for a business deal to take as long as thirty days to be completed. And even after agreement is reached, a contract is seldom signed as a verbal agreement is considered to be a person's pledge of honor.

Clearly, the pace of the business process is slower in Arab culture. And the lines of authority are important, for control of business is tightly held at the top. As a result, a company that sends a lower-management person to a business meeting with Arabs could be making a mistake. Dealing with those from other cultures, particularly in business settings, requires the effective communicator to take into account, before initiating contact, all the nonverbal variables. Possible questions to answer about variables that will influence the nonverbal communication include:

- What are the roles and relationships of the participants?
- What are the time patterns of the others? Is time an important factor in the culture?
- How are successful encounters concluded? What is the proper time to end the conversation?
- What is the pattern of listening and talking in conversations? Do people interrupt? Do people listen patiently?[11]

As you can see, conversational distance, eye contact, head nodding, and even odors can make the difference between a friendly interaction and a hostile reaction.

We tend to read nonverbal signs on the basis of our own personal background and experiences, having been taught how to interpret specific movements, and we assume that others share the same interpretations. But this assumption can be misleading, even dangerous. We must remember that in all forms of communication, an understanding of the receiver or the audience is necessary before we can engage in effective transactions. And as if matters were not complicated enough, we must also be aware that although cultural patterns are reported to be persistent, not all the people within a given culture share identical patterns.

As communicators become more familiar with people from many different cultures through student exchange programs, travel, television, and other means, they should become more proficient at adapting nonverbal channels so as to communicate successfully in the global village.

Emotional Influences on Nonverbal Communication

Emotions have a direct effect on the size of people's territory and their resulting nonverbal responses. When people are tense and afraid, they tend to avoid closeness. People who are emotionally upset may even become violent if someone invades their territory.

When people are upset, their bodies become rigid. For example, many people who are nervous about public speaking report that their throats tighten and their stomach muscles contract when they must present a speech. Under high tension, the pitch of the voice also rises because the vocal cords tighten.

Those who attempt to mask their emotional upsets may become physically ill. Doctors explain this by emphasizing that the body must release its pent-up feelings. Suppressed emotions must get out somehow, and the result may be a migraine headache, an upset stomach, ulcers, or a heart attack.

People under stress also find that other people loom larger and closer than they actually are. To a frightened child, an adult can seem like a giant. Because of this, child psychologists recommend that in dealing with crying or hysterical children, adults should kneel to talk with them. By the same token, police interrogators and trial lawyers know that moving in close to an inverviewee may cause him or her to get upset and say something that would be controlled under normal conditions. This emotional pressure may result in the breaking down of defenses and an admission of guilt.

Sometimes nonverbal patterns change because of outside influences. For instance, a vast difference exists between normal nonverbal communication and deviant communication such as that caused by drugs, alcohol, or shock. Patterns change as people lose conscious and unconscious controls that affect their ability to make decisions and value judgments. A person under the influence of alcohol or drugs does not walk, talk, or have the same bodily controls as when sober.

Verbal and Nonverbal Relationships

Obviously a link exists between verbal and nonverbal communication. Because they are so tightly interwoven, it is necessary to identify, analyze, and understand their various relationships. The main relationships of nonverbal to verbal communication can be described as substitution, complementing, conflict, and accenting.[12]

The Substitution Relationship

Suppose someone asks you a question. Instead of answering verbally, you nod your head up and down. In doing so, you have substituted the action meaning yes for the word *yes*. Or suppose your best friend walks into the room. You look at the expression on her or his face and say, "What's the matter?" Though your friend has not said a word, the message "Something's wrong" has been transmitted. In both these examples, there has been a **substitution relationship** in which nonverbal signs are substituted for verbal signs.

The Complementing Relationship

Body language can complement a verbal message. For example, shaking your head from side to side while saying "no" reinforces the negative verbalization. In a similar way, an angler's brag that "the fish was three feet long" may be accompanied by hands held three feet apart. Such a nonverbal **complementing relationship,** in which the nonverbal message accompanies the verbal message, adds further dimensions to communication.

The Conflict Relationship

A person's physical movements can sometimes conflict with his or her verbal message. For example, suppose a professor is confronted by a student after a class session. The student asks, "May I speak with you?" The professor says, "Sure, I have lots of time." While making this reply, however, the professor is packing books and glancing at the clock. Clearly, a conflict exists between the verbal and nonverbal messages.

When actions conflict with verbal messages, thus forming a **conflict relationship** between the verbal and nonverbal, as a receiver you should rely more on the nonverbal aspect of communication because nonverbal clues are often more difficult to fake than verbal ones. When you were young, you might have been surprised to find that your parents knew when you were not telling the truth. Think about it. There you stood—looking at the floor, twisting your hands, with a flushed face—as you insisted, "I didn't do it." Sigmund Freud once said, "He that has eyes to see and ears to hear may convince himself that no mortal can keep a secret. If his lips are silent he chatters with his fingertips; betrayal oozes out of him at every pore."[13] If you tend to blush when you are embarrassed, no matter how often you say to yourself, "I will not blush," your face still burns when something embarrassing happens.

Lie detectors read the body's nonverbal reactions by measuring changes in blood pressure, respiration, and skin response—in other words, by attempting to detect a conflicting relationship between the verbal and the nonverbal.[14] This is accomplished by hooking up a meter to the fingers, by measuring the perspiration, or by attaching the person to an electrocardiograph machine and checking the heart rate. Both government and private industry now regularly use these devices for job screening and for detecting suspected leaks of classified information, even though their accuracy is still in doubt. "The polygraph is not infallible," claimed one source, "but it could be as high as 90 percent accurate in the hands of a good examiner."[15] Other estimates range from 50 to 70 percent.

The Accenting Relationship

Nonverbal behavior may accent parts of a verbal message, much as underlining emphasizes written ideas. In the **accenting relationship,** the nonverbal message stresses the verbal one. Jabbing someone's shoulder with a finger as you turn the person to look at you while commanding, "When I speak to you, look at me!" obviously accents the verbal message with nonverbal signs.

Channels of Nonverbal Communication

Nonverbal messages, like other forms of communication, are conveyed through channels (see Figure 6.1). Though these nonverbal channels can be defined in many ways, let us look at them in terms of kinesics (body language), paralanguage (vocal sounds), proxemics (space), chronemics (time), olfactics (smell), aesthetics (music and color), physical characteristics (body shape and size, skin color), and artifacts (clothes, make-up, eyeglasses, jewelry).[16]

Kinesics

Kinesics is the study of communication through body movement. We communicate through the gestures we use, the way we walk and stand, the expression on our faces and in our eyes, and the manner in which we combine these variables to open or close channels.

As people attempt to communicate, they make gestures. These gestures carry meaning and may be interpreted by an alert communicator. Researchers have been able to classify them into five nonverbal categories: emblems, illustrators, affect displays, regulators, and adaptors.[17] An

Figure 6.1

Channels of Nonverbal Communication

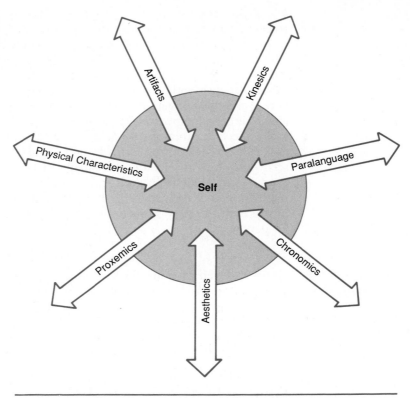

understanding of these classifications can aid us in deciphering the code of nonverbal meaning.

Emblems

Emblems are nonverbal acts that have a direct verbal translation or dictionary definition. For example, using the thumb and index finger to form a circle, with the other three fingers outstretched, is a signal meaning "Everything is all right." Emblems like this are nonverbal signs that a specific society or identifiable group holds in common. The sign language of the deaf, nonverbal gestures used by behind-the-scenes television personnel, and signals between two underwater swimmers are all examples of the use of emblems.

Illustrators

Illustrators are gestures that are tied directly to speech or that accompany it. They are used to sketch a path, to point to an object, or to show spatial relationships. Pointing to a specific place on the map while describing the geography of an area is an example of using an illustrator.

An emblem is a nonverbal act that has a direct verbal translation.

Affect Displays   **Affect displays** are facial configurations that show emotions and feelings such as sadness or happiness. Pouting, winking, and raising or lowering the eyelids and eyebrows are examples of affect displays.

Regulators   **Regulators** are nonverbal acts that maintain and control the back-and-forth nature of speaking and listening between two or more people. Nods of the head, eye movements, and body shifts are all regulators that are used to encourage or discourage conversation. Imagine, for example, a conversation between a department manager and an employee who has come to ask for a raise. The appeal has been made, and the employee continues to restate his case. The manager glances at her watch, her fingers fidget with the telephone, she slides out her desk drawer and glances through some materials in it. The manager has indicated that the conversation is over as far as she is concerned. In other words, her regulator signs indicate that the transaction is completed. Unfortunately, the employee, not being alert to nonverbal regulators, has not picked up the message. Most people have had similar conversations in which the intended receiver of the "it's all over" signals simply ignored them. These receivers may not acknowledge such signals intentionally, or they may be unable to read them easily.

Adaptors   **Adaptors,** such as restless movements of the hands and feet, tongue movements, kicking movements of the legs, and finger tapping, are used to manage emotions. They are movements that accompany boredom, show internal feelings, or regulate a situation. For example, those who are bored often tap their fingers on a table or bounce a crossed leg. Consider the typical situation in which a person is waiting on a street corner for someone who is late: he or she often stands with arms crossed—fingers tapping on upper arms, foot tapping the pavement— checking the time every few seconds.

Walk and Stance

Does the way a person walks say something about that person? Nonverbal research indicates that it most decidedly does. A person's walk can give us clues about his or her status, mood, ethnic and cultural affiliation, and self-perception.

Detectives and airline security personnel are trained to pick out suspicious people by the way they walk, and blind people can identify others by the sound of their footsteps. Interestingly, walking even follows certain cultural patterns, for Europeans, Americans, and Orientals may all have different walks. Europeans coming to the United States often ask why Americans are in such a hurry so much of the time—an image that comes from the quick pace at which they walk.

In general, the way you walk tells more about you than you probably realize. Think about it: when someone enters a room, you instantly form conclusions about that person. Some people walk with confidence—head high, shoulders back, jaw set, assurance in every movement.Others walk with sloping shoulders, eyes down, withdrawing within their bodies. This posture may indicate lack of confidence or lack of self-assurance.

The Face and Eyes

A number of nonverbal studies have concentrated solely on the face and the eyes. Indeed, we have more data about these features than about any other physical nonverbal communication tool.[18]

The eye, unlike other organs of the body, is an extension of the brain.[19] Because of this, it is almost impossible for an individual to disguise eye meaning from someone who is a member of the same culture. Sayings such as "Look at the sparkle in her eye," "He looked me straight in the eye," and "He must be sick because his eyes don't look good" have meaning for each of us. Of all our features, our eyes are the most revealing. Often they communicate without our even knowing it. For example, when the pupils of our eyes are dilated, we may appear friendlier, warmer, and more attractive. In one experiment, a hundred men were shown a picture of a pretty woman. In this picture, the pupils of the woman's eyes had been touched up to appear very large. When asked to give their first impression of her, 80 percent of the men described her as warm and nurturing. When the same picture but with the pupils touched up to appear very small was shown to another hundred men, 80 percent of this second group said the woman was cold and

The way a person walks or stands says a great deal about that person.

selfish. Obviously, the difference in the pupils of the woman's eyes seemed to make clear statements to the observers.[20]

A theory known as **pupilometrics** indicates that the pupils dilate when the eyes are focused on a pleasurable object and contract when focused on an unpleasurable object.[21] Numerous tests support the contention that enlarged pupils signify interest and contracted pupils reflect boredom. Thus knowledgeable teachers often watch the pupils of their students' eyes to ascertain their interest in a particular lesson. This idea of wide-eyed wonder and interest is not new. In Napoleon's time, women placed a drug called belladonna in their eyes to keep their pupils wide and make them look both interested and interesting.

Members of different social classes, generations, ethnic groups, and cultures use their eyes to express different messages. Americans often complain when they feel foreigners stare at them too intensely or hold a glance too long. This is because a gaze of longer than ten seconds is likely to induce discomfort in an American.[22]

Lengthy eye contact is comfortable as long as the communicating people have sufficient distance between them. As you walk down a corridor, notice that you can look at someone for a long period of time until you suddenly feel uncomfortable and glance away. This usually happens at a distance of about ten feet.

When some individuals in Western cultures are intent on hiding an aspect of their inner feelings, they may try to avoid eye contact. Thus the child who has eaten forbidden candy will not look at a questioning parent during the interrogation. Remember when you were told, "Look me in the eye and say that"? Law enforcement officers use an eye-to-eye test as a guide in ascertaining whether a suspect is telling the truth or trying to be deceptive.

People in many cultures are very aware of the part played by eyes in communicating. This awareness has led some people to try masking their eyes. "Since people can't control the responses of their eyes," reported one source, "many Arabs, like [the Palestine Liberation Organization's Yasir] Arafat, wear dark glasses, even indoors."[23]

In addition to watching a person's actions, an astute observer can ascertain what that person is doing by watching his or her eyes. Generally, when ninety percent of people look up and to the left, they are recalling a memory. Eyes up and to the right register a future thought.[24]

The fine art of observing eyes has even invaded the political field. During the presidential election of 1976, researchers studied whether Gerald Ford or his opponent, Jimmy Carter, was revealing anything unconsciously during televised debates. The findings indicated that if Carter was in trouble he would look down at the lectern, shift his gaze randomly, and smile inappropriately. Ford would look away from the camera in similar situations.[25]

Open and Closed Channels

Few of us realize how much we depend on nonverbal communication to encourage and discourage conversations and transactions. For instance, we consciously wave at waiters, raise our hands to get a teacher's attention, and otherwise signal someone when we want to talk to her or him. Much of our opening and closing of channels, however, occur without our consciously realizing it.

If you observe people conversing, you notice that they indicate they are listening by moving their heads. If they agree with what is said, they nod affirmatively. They may also smile to show pleasure or agreement. If, however, they glance several times at their watches, start to bob their feet, divert their gaze from the speaker, cross and uncross their legs, and stand up, they are signaling that they have closed the channel and wish an end to the transaction.

Paralanguage

All the vocal effects we make to accompany words (such as the tone of the voice), except for the words themselves, are called **paralanguage.** Vocal quality communicates nonverbally to the listening ear. The rate (speed), volume (power), pitch (such as soprano or bass), pause (stopping), and stress (intensity) of sounds all have particular meanings. These paralinguistic tools are often referred to as **vocal cues.**

Often we can use vocal cues to tell the sex, age, and status of a speaker. We can also make some pretty accurate judgments about the emotions and feelings of the people with whom we communicate by their paralinguistic presentation. When you get excited, what happens to the pitch of your voice? Usually, it goes up. If you are very angry, the pitch of your voice also often goes up. And when you are very, very angry, you sometimes say words slowly and distinctly, pausing between each word to gain a special effect.

By observing a person's paralanguage, we can often gain insights into his or her personality. Former California governor Jerry Brown's manner of speaking is slow and deliberate, deep, loud, and lacking in melody. In studying Brown and others, one expert noted that the **metamessage** (paralinguistic implications) of his speech suggests an authoritative person, one who is dull and lacking emotion. To the same expert, former president Carter's speaking style is characterized by an extremely uneven tempo and an excessively flat tone, an absence of melody and strong Southern regionalism, and pauses that are not logical. The metamessage Carter's speech conveys is uncertainty, depression and a strong sense that he is unsure of himself.[26]

Research findings indicate that the voice may also be important in some aspects of persuasion.[27] A higher rate of speech, more intonation, more volume, and a less halting manner seem to be related to successful attempts at persuasion. If a person sounds assured, the receiver credits the speaker with a higher degree of credibility.

Vocal cues can provide much information about a speaker, and our total reaction to another person is at least somewhat colored by our reactions to these cues. Our perceptions of vocal cues combined with other verbal and nonverbal stimuli mold the conceptions we use as a basis for communicating.[28]

Proxemics   A basic difference among people can be seen in how they operate within the space around them—in how they use their territory. The study of how people use and perceive their social and personal space is called **proxemics.** Much of what is known about this field is based on the studies of Edward Hall.[29]

According to Hall, every person is surrounded by a psychological bubble of space. This bubble contracts and expands depending on the person's cultural background and emotional state as well as the activity in which he or she is participating. Northern Europeans—the English, Scandinavians, and Germans—tend to have a larger zone of personal space and often avoid touching and contact. They require more room around them and structure their lifestyles to meet the need for this room. Thus the English are stereotyped as being distant and impersonal, not showing great emotion through hugging, kissing, and touching. This stereotype derives from the respect they exhibit for each other's territory. In contrast, Italians, Russians, Spaniards, Israelis, Latin Americans, Middle Easterners, and the French all tend to like close personal contact.

Some marriage counselors have indicated that a major cause of marital conflicts in the United States is the lack of spatial and emotional compatibility between spouses. Consider, for example, what happens when a woman from a family with an English heritage marries a man with an Italian background. If they follow stereotypical patterns, she is physically and emotionally controlled, whereas he wants to touch and invade her territory. He expects her to kiss and hug, soothe him after a hard day, sit close to him, and show outward emotion. She does not understand the "loud" voices and "exaggerated" gestures of his family. And he cannot understand why members of her family never touch each other. Thus a conflict results from differences in these two partners' proxemic patterns and expectations.

Informal space or personal space is important to us because we feel that if someone touches our bodies, he or she is attacking us—for we are our bodies.[30] Many of us do not like to be touched but do not really know why. This dislike may well stem not from something unique to us but from cultural training. When someone who does not like to be fondled is confronted by a "toucher," the situation can be quite uncomfortable. If the toucher places a hand on the arm of the nontoucher and the second person jerks away, the first person may well get the idea that a rejection has taken place when in fact it is the touch, not the person, that has been scorned.

Space Distances   Most middle-class Americans maintain four principal areas of distance in their business and social relationships. These distances are classified as intimate, personal, social, and public.[31]

Intimate distance covers a space that varies from direct physical contact with another person to a distance of six to eighteen inches. It is used for our most private activities—caressing, making love, and sharing intimate ideas and emotions. We can often get clues about a relationship by noticing whether another person allows us to use his or her intimate space. For example, if you have been on a hand-holding or physically touching basis with someone and suddenly that person will not let you near, or pulls away when you get very close, a change in the relationship may have occurred. If, however, the other person suddenly encourages close body proximity, this may also indicate a change in attitude.

Personal distance, eighteen inches to four feet, is sometimes called the "comfort bubble." We normally feel most comfortable keeping at

Personal distance is the "comfort bubble" that surrounds Americans.

this distance when talking with others, and invasion of this personal territory will cause us to back away. If we are backed into a corner, are sitting in a chair, or are somehow trapped, we will lean away, pull in, and tense up. To avoid invasion of our territory, we might place a leg on the rung of a chair or on a stair. Some of us even arrange our furniture so that our territory cannot be invaded. For example, businesspeople place their desks so that employees must sit on one side and the boss on the other. In contrast, interviewers have reported a completely different atmosphere when talking to job applicants if the chairs are placed side by side instead of on opposite sides of the desk.

Similarly, we can learn a great deal about courtship behavior in observing how people place themselves physically. For example, on a date the choice of where the passenger sits in the car has much communicative significance. Obviously, if the passenger holds on to the door handle opposite the driver's side of the car, the message is different from that sent if the passenger sits so close to the driver's side that the driver has trouble steering. Not a word may have been said, but a great deal of communication has taken place.

Social distance covers a four- to twelve-foot zone that is used during business transactions or social exchanges. Also part of social distance is the standing-seated interaction, in which the person in charge stands and the other person sits. Standing-seated positions occur, among others, in teacher-pupil, boss-secretary, and police officer–arrestee transactions.

In general, however, social distance encompasses enough space so that persons do not invade each other's territory.

Public distance may dictate a separation of as little as twelve feet, but it is usually more than twenty-five. It is used by teachers in lecture rooms and by speakers at public gatherings as well as by public figures who wish to place a barrier between themselves and their audience. When people from different cultural backgrounds come into contact, they often assume they have the same concept of space. This, of course, is not true. For example, Asians and Americans are at opposite ends of the spatial-distance scale. Most Asians are accustomed to close contact and face-to-face interaction, whereas most Americans want more space around them.

Even within our own culture, the space bubble varies according to our emotional state and the activity being performed. Though Americans usually keep well beyond the three-foot personal circle of space, this can change very quickly. If you are on a crowded bus and someone presses against you, you may tolerate it. If, however, you are standing at the bus stop and someone presses against you, you will probably object to the action. Thus the situation affects your idea of public distance.

Your emotional state can also change your idea of space. For instance, when some males are angry, they may grab someone by the front of the shirt, step in close, get "nose to nose," and shout.

Small-Group Ecology

The physical placement of members of small groups in relation to one another has an effect on their behavior. This **small-group ecology**—the placement of chairs, the placement of the person conducting a meeting, and the setting for a small-group encounter—clearly influences the method of the group's operation.

If, for example, people are seated in a tight circle, they will probably feel more comfortable and interact more than they would if they were sitting in straight rows. They will be able to see each other's nonverbal reactions, and because there is no inhibiting physical distance, they will lose their self-consciousness as they become members of the group.

Business organizations make considerable use of such nonverbal strategies in small-scale conferences. One technique is to seat key members of the group in prominent positions to stimulate discussion or even direct it.

Chronemics

The way that people handle and structure their time is known as **chronemics.** As a nonverbal sign, this whole subject area is sometimes greatly misunderstood. Only within certain societies, for example, is precise time of great significance. In most Western societies, punctuality is a part of good manners. Thus tardiness can be a sign that a person wants to avoid something or that the activity or person to be met is not important enough to warrant the effort to be on time.

Time has become a critical factor in the American workplace. Throughout a person's career, punctuality is used as a measure of effectiveness. A person who arrives late for a job interview will probably have difficulty overcoming such a negative first impression, and employees who arrive late for work may be reprimanded and even dismissed. The American employer expects promptness in attendance and in the finishing of work.

Americans traveling abroad are often amazed and irritated by the seeming lack of concern for time commitments among residents of some countries. Tours are late; buses arrive sporadically; guides fail to indicate the correct arrival and departure times. Yet in other places, such as Switzerland, a traveler can set her or his watch by the promptness of the trains.

Within cultures that value promptness, one of the questions often raised about time centers on the person who is constantly late. What does habitual tardiness reveal about the person? "Chronic lateness," said one expert, "is deeply rooted in a person's psyche. Compulsive tardiness is rewarding on some level. A key emotional conflict for the chronically late person involves his or her need to feel special."[32] Presumably, such a person does not gain enough recognition in other ways. People must be special in some way, so the person is special by being late. Other reasons include needs for punishment, for power, for expression of hostility, or for attention.

Olfactics   **Olfactics** is the study of smell. Our sense of smell is extraordinarily precise. Indeed, our sense of smell may be the most direct of all our senses. Growing evidence also suggests that we remember what we smell longer than what we see and hear.[33]

Smells fall into seven basic categories. As you read each of the examples in this list be aware of your ability to smell each. The categories are minty (peppermint), floral (roses), ethereal (pears), musky (musk), resinous (camphor), foul (rotten eggs), and acrid (vinegar).[34]

Our sense of smell is very selective and helps us reach conclusions. We are attracted by the scents of certain colognes and repulsed by others. We find certain body odors offensive. Thus we often make decisions about people without realizing that these decisions are based on odors. Several phenomena provide insight into how smell serves as a nonverbal communication tool: smell blindness, smell adaptation, smell memory, smell overload, and smell discrimination.[35]

Smell Blindness   Each person is uniquely different in his or her ability to identify and distinguish smells. **Smell blindness** occurs when a person is unable to detect smells. It parallels color blindness because it is a physiological blockage. It accounts for the fact that some people do not smell their own or others' body odors or detect the differences in the odors of various foods. Because smell and taste are so closely aligned, this can explain why people who are smell blind may also have taste-identification difficulties.

Smell Adaptation   **Smell adaptation** occurs when we gradually lose the distinctiveness of a particular smell through repeated association with it. As a customer, when you walk into a bakery, you may be aware of the wonderful odors. The clerk, however, may have become so used to the odors that he or she is not aware of them. The speed at which the odor message is adapted depends on the strength of the odor and the length of time we are in contact with it.

Smell Memory   As a child your grandmother may have baked you a favorite dessert. Walking into someone's home years later and smelling that same odor may cause you to flash back to memories of your grandmother. This ability to recall previous situations when encountering a particular smell associated with them is **smell memory.** Smelling a crayon may trigger experiences of kindergarten, the odors of a dentist's office may cause your teeth to ache, or passing a perfume counter with samples of a cologne a former lover wore may trigger intrapersonal smell memories.

Smell Overload   Have you ever entered an elevator and been bombarded by the heavy dose of perfume another passenger is wearing? Onions in a salad are fine, but slicing several at the sink may cause you to cry. These are both examples of smell overload. **Smell overload** takes place when an exceptionally large number of odors or one extremely powerful odor overpowers you. Walking down a detergent aisle in a supermarket or standing in a small room with several people who are smoking can also trigger smell overload—too much smell for you to comfortably manage.

Smell Discrimination   The ability to identify people, places, and things on the basis of their smell is **smell discrimination.** Tests have shown that young children can identify their mothers by smelling clothing they have worn. You may have been able to distinguish someone who comes up behind you unde-tected by the smell of her or his hair. We can detect more than ten thousand different odors.[36] The identification takes place through smell discrimination, which allows us to tell the difference between cinnamon and garlic, bananas and oranges, and one person and another.

Aesthetics   The communication of a message or mood through color or music is called **aesthetics.** As you stroll through the supermarket, you may not

Our sense of smell may be the most direct of all our senses.

even be aware that this principle is in force. But just listen to the music on the supermarket's sound system. The owner wants you to move slowly through the store and see everything on the shelves. Therefore the music is slow, comfortable. But near closing time it may speed up to stimulate you to move more quickly.

The music may also affect buying patterns. During a nine-week test, the music in one supermarket was randomly played at a slow 60 beats a minute on some days and at 108 beats a minute on others. Not surprisingly, on slow-tempo days the store's gross receipts were 38.2 percent higher.[37]

Effects like this can be observed in many situations. For example, when you are driving a car, the type of music on the radio affects your driving, alertness, and concentration. And the music in an elevator is almost never loud and pulsating because such strong sounds would be too emotionally stressful for a contained area. A study on the impact of rock music tested more than twenty thousand records for their effect on muscle strength. (This sort of activity is part of a science entitled **behavioral kinesiology,**[38] which holds that particular kinds of food, clothes, thoughts, and music strengthen or weaken the muscles of the body.) According to a behavioral kinesiological study, "listening to rock music frequently causes all the muscles in the body to go weak."[39] This relationship may well account for the drugged and dreamlike feelings of some people who attend rock concerts. It is theorized that some rock music has a stopped quality that is not present in other types of music. That is, the beat is stopped at the end of each bar or measure. Because the music stops and then must start again, the listener subconsciously comes to a halt at the end of each measure.

Other studies indicate that music's effect is also based on tempo, rhythm, and instrumentation. They can heighten a person's attention or induce boredom, thereby creating a nonverbal language that can change or stimulate various activities.[40] These effects, combined with the behavioral kinesiology studies, suggest that music can serve as a type of drug in regulating behavior.

Colors also affect people, and many institutions are putting into practice this awareness, which has been gained through studies on the association between color and mood. For example, hospitals are experimenting with using various colors for rooms in hopes that these colors may motivate sick people to get well. These days fewer hospital rooms are being painted green because green is often associated with sickness and nausea. Hospitals are also painting large pieces of equipment, such as X-ray machines, the same color as the background walls so they do not appear as frightening to patients. In addition, food trays are being arranged more attractively, with bright accents such as red water pitchers. Sheets and blankets are now made in softer colors—pinks, blues, and pastels—rather than sterile, cold white. Prisons are also using pale pink shades because it is the most calming of colors. Similarly, bright colors are being added to classrooms to make students feel alert but not in such amounts that these colors become overpowering.

One of the newest trends is followed by color analysts, people whose knowledge of color concepts and images is used to advise others on the right hues to wear. Organizations such as Neiman Marcus and J. C. Penney Company have trained their staffs in color concepts so they can assist customers in purchasing clothing. Amway and Mary Kay Cosmetics are promoting the idea of color and its effect in their home sales campaigns. Consultants are teaching courses in color choice. The recognition that the right color selection can play a role in business success has brought about new rules in occupational dress. Because colors can make a person look sick or powerful depending on that person's skin tone and hair color, careful analysis can assist him or her in selecting the most advantageous shades.

Physical Characteristics

General attractiveness, body and breath odors, and height are all nonverbal communication signs.

Attractiveness   We are often drawn to or repulsed by people according to how they appear physically. For example, an informal survey at a recent speech contest indicated that, all other factors being equal, the more attractive the contestant, the greater were his or her chances of being judged the winner.

The prejudice against unattractive people is deeply ingrained in our society. In one study with preschoolers who were shown pictures of children their own age and asked to pick potential friends and enemies, children as young as three discriminated between attractive and unattractive peers in the same way that adults do.[41]

Clarence Darrow, a famous trial attorney, once noted that jury members seldom convicted a person they liked or acquitted one they disliked.[42] And a study at a major university determined that a jury's decision could be affected by the plaintiff's and the defendant's physical appearances. In this study, students served as jurors in a mock automobile negligence trial during which they heard tape-recorded testimony. The first set of jurors was shown photographs of an attractive male plaintiff and an unattractive male defendant; the second set of jurors saw the reverse. A third panel saw no pictures but heard the testimony. The results: the attractive plaintiff received a 49 percent positive vote from the first jury, the unattractive plaintiff got only a 17 percent positive vote from the second jury, and 41 percent of the third group, which did not see any pictures, ruled for the plaintiff.[43]

Height   A television star once told a talk-show audience that because of his large size and weight, he was often confronted by men trying to "prove something" by being able to "whup" him. Law enforcement departments, however, often set minimum height requirements because some offenders lack respect for small police officers.

It should not be surprising, then, that a recent study indicated that "to be of less than average height in American society is to fall short of the mark in almost all aspects of everyday life."[44] One sociologist concluded that "being short isn't always funny. A short man is subjected to more sidewalk psychiatric evaluations than most tall psychotics. Every personality quirk is blamed on his height."[45] This researcher set five feet, four inches as his standard for shortness but also noted that "the height at which a man begins to suffer discrimination can range from 5'9" down."[46]

Discrimination against short men also extends to career settings. Who is most likely to be more successful in business? Studies indicate that men who are taller than six feet, two inches receive a starting salary of 12.4 percent higher than graduates of the same school who are shorter than six feet and that shorter men have a harder time finding a job in the first place.[47] Although American society seems to show a preference for taller men, "tall women are often labeled 'ungainly'; short busi-nesswomen, in fact, may have an advantage in not acquiring whatever threatening overtones may attend to increasing height."[48]

Artifacts   The clothing that a person wears—as well as that person's make-up, eyeglasses, jewelry, and so forth—carries distinct messages. These items, classified as **artifacts,** express their meanings through **object language.**

Clothing is probably the most obvious of the artifact communicators. It is almost like a substitute body, telling an observer something about who you are. Because you have made a choice about what to wear, it follows that this is the image you want to portray, this is the attitude you want to present about the type of person you are, and this is the way you want others to perceive you. Clothes also say something about your judgment. For example, if you wear something inappropriate to the office, people may worry that you will do something inappropriate in your job.[49]

Numerous books have been written instructing job applicants and those interested in climbing the corporate ladder on what to wear and how to dress for success. One expert, author John T. Malloy, makes his living by counseling individuals who are worried about the image their clothing conveys.[50] Malloy's pioneering efforts have spawned an industry of wardrobe consultants.

Legal professionals are also aware of the effect of clothing for them-selves and their clients. Consider, for example, the following advice from a lawyer:

> Though a slovenly appearance won't land you a bigger fine in a courtroom, judges are more likely to listen attentively to what you have to say if you look your best. The appearance of a defendant in a criminal case is one of the most important factors in a trial. There are some people who just naturally look like a stereotype of the person who would commit the crime charged—others look the exact opposite. You can get some kooky results in that type of situation.[51]

If you are to appear in a courtroom, attending to your appearance may prove beneficial. If you have a beard or a mustache, think seriously about shaving it off. Dress conservatively but appropriately for your age and social standing. And do not wear sunglasses.

Summary   In this chapter, nonverbal communication was investigated. The major ideas presented were:

☐ Nonverbal communication is communication through "all external stimuli other than spoken or written words and including body motion, characteristics of appearance, characteristics of voice, and use of space and distance."

☐ Experts tend to agree that nonverbal communication carries the impact of a message.

☐ Clusters are groups of signs—such as gestures, posture, eye contact, clothing styles, and movements—that are taken together as factors in nonverbal communication.

☐ Congruency is the relationship between present and past patterns of behavior as well as the harmony between verbal and nonverbal communication.

☐ Nonverbal signs can be caused either by innate neurological programs or by learned behavior that is common to a culture.

☐ Every culture has its own body language.

☐ A behavioral sequence that includes standard steps for reaching a goal is known as an action chain.

☐ Whenever there is a great cultural distance between people, problems will arise from differences in behavior and expectations.

☐ There is a vast difference between normal nonverbal communication and deviant communication such as that caused by drugs, alcohol, or shock.

☐ The main relationships between verbal and nonverbal communication are substitution, complementing, conflict, and accenting.

☐ The channels of nonverbal communication are kinesics, paralanguage, proxemics, chronemics, olfactics, aesthetics, physical characteristics, and artifacts.

☐ Nonverbal gestures can be divided into the following classifications: emblems, illustrators, affect displays, regulators, and adaptors.

☐ Nonverbal research indicates that a person's walk gives clues about his or her status, mood, ethnic and cultural affiliation, and self-perception.

☐ We depend on nonverbal communication to encourage and discourage conversations and transitions.

☐ The factors involved in the sounds we make (our paralanguage) are rate, volume, pitch, pause, and stress.

☐ A basic difference among people can be seen in how they operate within the space around them—in how they use their territory.

☐ Most middle-class Americans maintain four principal distances in their business and social relationships: intimate, personal, social, and public.

☐ Emotions have a direct effect on the size of people's territory and their resulting nonverbal responses.

☐ The way people handle and structure their time is known as chronemics.

☐ Olfactics is the study of smell.

☐ Behavioral kinesiology holds that particular kinds of food, clothes, thoughts, and music strengthen or weaken the muscles of our bodies.

☐ We are often drawn to or repulsed by people according to how they appear physically.

☐ The clothing that a person wears—as well as that person's make-up, eyeglasses, and beauty aids—carries messages.

Key Terms

nonverbal communication
neurolinguistic programming
cluster
congruency
innate neurological programs
action chains
substitution relationship
complementing relationship
conflict relationship
accenting relationship
kinesics
emblems
illustrators
affect displays
regulators
adaptors
pupilometrics
paralanguage
vocal cues

metamessage
proxemics
intimate distance
personal distance
social distance
public distance
small-group ecology
chronemics
olfactics
smell blindness
smell adaptation
smell memory
smell overload
smell discrimination
aesthetics
behavioral kinesiology
artifacts
object language

Learn by Doing

1. Research one of the following and be prepared to give a two-minute speech on what you have learned: neurolinguistic programming, Ray Birdwhistell, Albert Mehrabian, Edward Hall, pupilometrics, biorhythms, Muzak, behavioral kinesiology.

2. Give examples of your own recent use of substitution, complementing, conflict, and accenting.

3. Carefully observe members of your family or think of the nonverbal patterns they display. Can you find any similarities between their patterns and your own? Do you think these patterns are innate, or are they learned from common experience?

4. Identify a cultural nonverbal trait and describe it to the class.

5. Make a list of five emblems used in America. Be prepared to demonstrate them. Compare your explanations of what they mean with those of your classmates.

6. Be prepared to read a sentence to the class at least twice in such a way that the meaning of the sentence changes because you have varied the paralanguage.

7. Carry on a conversation with a person outside your classroom. As you speak, slowly move closer to him or her. Continue to move in on the person gradually. Observe his or her reaction. Did the person back up? Cross his or her arms? Report to the class on the results of this experiment.

Notes

1. K. K. Sereno and E. M. Bodaken, *Trans-Per: Understanding Human Communication* (Boston: Houghton Mifflin, 1975), p. 277.

2. For an in-depth discussion, see Ray L. Birdwhistell, *Kinesics and Context* (New York: Ballantine Books, 1970); and Albert Mehrabian, *Silent Message* (Belmont, Calif.: Wadsworth, 1971).

3. Dan Coleman, "People Who Read People," *Psychology Today,* 13 (July 1979), 66.

4. Ray L. Birdwhistell, as cited in Mark Knapp, *Nonverbal Communication in Human Interaction* (New York: Holt, Rinehart and Winston, 1972), p. 12.

5. Ibid., p. 149.

6. Norbert Freedman, "You Have to Move to Think," circulated by the Clinical Behavioral Research Unit at Downstate Medical Center, Brooklyn, New York, n.d.

7. Ibid.

8. Edward Hall and Mildred Hall, "The Sounds of Silence," *Playboy,* 18 (June 1971), 148.

9. Edward Hall, as interviewed by Kenneth Freedman, "Learning the Arabs' Silent Language," *Psychology Today,* 13 (August 1979), 53.

10. This discussion is based on research reported by Paul Ekman, Wallace Friesen, and John Bear, "The International Language of Gestures," *Psychology Today,* 18 (May 1984), 64–69.

11. An excellent learning aid for gaining awareness of intercultural characteristics is *Intercultural Communicating* (Provo, Utah: Language Research Center, Brigham Young University); another is the Language Research Center's "Culturegram" series, which is intended to offer briefings to aid understanding of, feeling for, and communication with people around the world.

12. Mark Knapp notes researcher Paul Ekman's original designation of such relationships in Mark L. Knapp, *Nonverbal Communication in Human Interaction,* 2nd ed. (New York: Holt, Rinehart and Winston, 1978), pp. 9–12.

13. Cited in Knapp, 1st ed., p. 103.

14. Rice Berkeley, "Beating the Polygraph at Its Own Game," *Psychology Today,* 12 (July 1978), 107.

15. Louise Sweeney, "Now Who's Telling Us the Truth About Lie Detectors," *Elyria Chronicle-Telegram* (Ohio), October 30, 1983, Sunday Scene, p. 10.

16. No specific identifying channels of nonverbal communication have been universally defined. The names used here are a compilation of those that have appeared in various textbooks on communication.

17. Knapp, 2nd ed., pp. 13–17.

18. Hall and Hall, p. 204.

19. Ibid.

20. Jeannette Belleveau, "Gobbledygook Is an Occupational Hazard Here," *Montgomery County Journal* (Maryland), August 19, 1981, p. 1.

21. For a discussion of pupilometrics, see E. H. Hess, A. L. Seltzer, and J. M. Shlien, "Pupil Response of Hetero- and Homosexual Males to Pictures of Men and Women: A Pilot Study," *Journal of Abnormal Psychology,* 70 (1965), 165–168; and E. H. Hess and J. M. Polt, "Pupil Size as Related to Interest Value of Visual Stimuli," *Sciences,* 132 (1960), 349–350.

22. Knapp, 1st ed., p. 135.

23. Hall, pp. 47–48.

24. Based on the theories of Milton Erickson as presented by Ron Klein, as part of the training units of the American Hypnosis Training Academy, Inc., June, 1991.

25. "Body Talk: Uhs and Ers Debate Watchers Clues," *Cleveland Plain Dealer,* October 22, 1976, p. A-2.

26. Dinah Prince, "Did You Know You Speak More Than One Language?" *Elyria Chronicle-Telegram* (Ohio), October 28, 1982, p. D-2.

27. Knapp, 2nd ed., pp. 351–353.

28. For a discussion of vocal cues, see ibid., Chapter 10.

29. Much of the information in this section is based on Edward Hall's research and writing, particularly Edward Hall, *The Silent Language* (Garden City, N.Y.: Doubleday, 1959); Edward Hall, *The Hidden Dimension* (Garden City, N.Y.: Doubleday, 1966); and Hall and Hall, note 6.

30. Some research classifies touch separately as tactile-cutaneous rather than as part of proxemics. This discussion, although recognizing this distinction, includes touch within proxemics.

31. Hall and Hall, p. 148.

32. Constance Rosenblum, "Johnny Come Latelies: Tardiness Hides a Hangup," *Elyria Chronicle-Telegram* (Ohio), January 12, 1979, Encore, p. 15.

33. Diane Ackerman, "Our Most Mysterious Sense," *Parade Magazine,* June 10, 1990, p. 8.

34. Ibid.

35. This section is based on Joseph DeVito, *Nonverbal Communication Workbook* (Prospect Heights, Ill.: Waveland Press, 1989), pp. 187–189.

36. Ackerman, p. 8.

37. Carol Austin Bridgewater, "Slow Music Sells," *Psychology Today,* 17 (January 1983), 56.

38. Patricia McCormick, "Rock Music Can Weaken Muscles," *Elyria Chronicle-Telegram* (Ohio), January 12, 1979, Encore, p. 15.

39. Ibid.

40. Muzak research, unpublished materials.

41. Lawrence Rosenfeld and Jean Civikly, *With Words Unspoken* (New York: Holt, Rinehart and Winston, 1976), p. 25.

42. "The Eyes Have It," *Newsweek,* December 3, 1973, p. 85.

43. Ibid.

44. Carol Kramer, "Bigot's Last Refuge: Putting Down Short Men," *Elyria Chronicle-Telegram* (Ohio), March 31, 1975, p. 3.

45. Ibid.

46. Ibid.

47. Rosenfeld and Civikly, p. 23.

48. Knapp, 2nd ed., pp. 166–167.

49. Amy Gross and Nancy Comer, "Power Dressing," *Mademoiselle* (September 1977), 188.

50. John Molloy, *Dress for Success* (New York: Warner Books, 1978).

51. Mike Benbow, "Dressing for Success in the Courtroom," *Elyria Chronicle-Telegram* (Ohio), February 26, 1978, pp. A-1, A-3.

PART TWO

Personal Communication

7 The Theory of Interpersonal Communication

Chapter Outline

*Learning
Outcomes*

After reading this chapter, you should be able to:

Define interpersonal communication and list and explain some of its basic concepts

Clarify the role of self-concept as the starting point of a person's interpersonal communication

Illustrate how self-disclosure plays a role in both self-understanding and understanding of another

Explain the roles of trust, approval seeking, emotions, and power as they relate to interpersonal communication

Define what relationships are and demonstrate how they develop, continue, and end

List and explain the principles of fighting fair

Define what criticism and rejection are and explain their role in interpersonal communication.

The term *interpersonal communication* has become popular since it was coined in the early 1950s.[1] **Interpersonal communication** is "an interactional process in which meaning is stimulated through the sending and receiving of messages between two people."[2] Two primary themes underly this process: that communication involves relationships and information and that communication necessitates give and take.

The effectiveness of any one-on-one communication depends greatly on the relationship between the people involved. The more two people trust each other, the more likely they are to share their real feelings. Thus as a relationship develops, so does the ability of the participants to share information—confidences, opinions, values, and beliefs.

As there can be no communication unless the communicators give and take information, the basis for interpersonal transactions is the sending and receiving of messages in such a way that they are successfully encoded and decoded. The more experiences the communicators have in common and the more openness they have between them, the more likely it is that their communication will be successful.

Our interpersonal relationships bring together the most important people, roles, contexts, and energies that we experience. Interpersonal communication functions to combat loneliness, shape self-concepts, confirm world experiences, renew personal and intrapersonal growth, and aid us in understanding who we are and how we relate to others.

Basic Concepts of Interpersonal Communication

As you examine interpersonal communication, keep some basic concepts in mind.

1. *We communicate what and who we are.* Every time we communicate, we tell a great deal about ourselves. Our selection of words, the tone of our voice, and the gestures we use combine to give a picture of our values, likes and dislikes, and self-perceptions. We give clues to our environmental background by the types of gestures we use, the pronunciation patterns we produce, and the attitudes we express. And as receivers we also use communication to form conclusions about senders and their ideas, and we react to these conclusions based on our own background, experiences, and beliefs.

2. *Language can be used to conceal as well as to reveal.* We select what we want to say to another person and what we wish to hold inside of us. We each have certain ideas that we prefer to share with no one, with a single other person, with a few people, or with anyone. It is our right to decide with whom to share and what to share. Often if we reveal too much, we pay the penalty by having others react to us in ways we may not like. For example, have you ever told someone something and had him or her pass it on to others or react to you in an unacceptable way? Once information is revealed, it cannot be grabbed back or made to disappear. Therefore we must constantly make decisions about what we wish to conceal and reveal.

3. *Much of our interpersonal communication centers on our wanting others to act or think or feel as we do; in other words, much of it is an attempt at persuasion.* In our interpersonal relations with parents, children, and friends, we constantly attempt to alter or reinforce behavior, give advice, or elicit some type of action.

4. *"Meaning is in people, not in words.* A word is only a word by virtue of the meaning people give to that word."[3] In communicating with others, we must constantly be aware that what a particular symbol means to us is not necessarily what it means to them. A suburban home owner hearing the word *grass* may think of the lawn that must be cut weekly. A drug counselor probably thinks of marijuana. How many times have you found yourself in a situation in which what you said was misunderstood? You just could not figure out why the other person did not know what you meant. After all, it was perfectly clear to you. Or have you ever been on the receiving end of such an experience—in dealing with a doctor or lawyer, in learning a new job responsibility? From these situations, we know that unless some basis for understanding exists, ineffective communication may be the result. Thus we must define terms and give examples, con-

stantly keeping our audience in mind and adjusting our messages accordingly.

5. *We cannot not communicate.* Communication does not necessarily stop simply because people stop talking and listening. Suppose you do not answer a question your instructor has asked. Or suppose you sit quietly at the dinner table instead of joining in the conversation. Even in these cases, you are still sending messages, although your lips are silent. Remember that much of our communicating is done below the verbal level. We may think that if we do not actively participate, we are not sending messages—but we are!

6. *People react to our actions.* We are constantly demonstrating the **action-reaction principle.**[4] When we smile, others smile back; when we shout, others shout back; and when we display anger, others do so as well. Try a little experiment. The next time you are walking down a hallway or a sidewalk, smile as others come toward you. You will probably find that the people you pass smile back, often saying, "Hello." Think back to the last time you had an argument. If you raised your voice, what did the other person do? No doubt that person also raised his or her voice—thus demonstrating the action-reaction principle.

7. *We do what we do because in the end we expect to achieve happiness.* When we choose to enter into communication, we do so hoping to gain from the experience or at least to come out neutral but certainly to be in no worse psychological shape than when we entered. Consequently many people try to avoid any situation in which they feel they may get negative feedback or be unsuccessful in communicating their ideas.

8. *We cannot always have the same understandings and feelings as others.* As we communicate, we must recognize that because of differences in our environment, the only areas we share are those in which we have a common experiential background. To illustrate this, let us assume that all our knowledge and experience are contained within one circle and that all the knowledge and experience of the person with whom we are communicating are contained within another circle. The only **commonality**—the only place where our ideas, concepts, mores, and vocabulary will overlap—is where we have had similar exposure. Figure 7.1 explains this idea further. Only in the area where the circles overlap are there any common feelings and experiences.

   If we add a third person to the conversation, the problem becomes even greater, as seen in Figure 7.2. Here many areas of overlap exist between persons A and B, between persons A and C, and between persons B and C. But notice the small area of overlap among all three. The difficulty of communicating with large groups

Figure 7.1

Commonality of Experience Between Two Persons

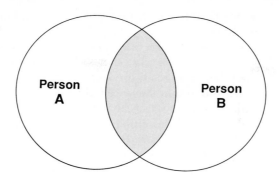

Figure 7.2

Commonality of Experience Among Three Persons

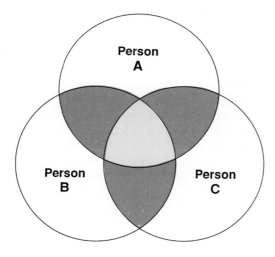

of people can be easily demonstrated when this process of drawing representative circles is continued.

We should also recognize that we have more in common with some people than with others. And it is with these people that we probably have the fewest problems in interacting and understanding. In addition, we must recognize that we often have difficulty sharing ideas or helping others reach conclusions similar to ours because of past encounters that affect their ideas and conceptions. What makes good sense to us is sometimes rejected by others, and in trying to explain why we believe something, we may find it difficult to get others to see our point of view. We must realize that our language is a thought trap and that when certain notions do not fit into our personal framework, they remain unrecognized or unacceptable.

9. *Communication takes place within a system,*[5] *and for that communication to change, the system must change.* In other words, if you change your role, that changes the system. For example, when you were a teenager, you might have felt that your parents were overprotective, and eventually you realized that the only way to make a change in the system was to embark on some action. You might have alerted your parents to your desire to take responsibility for yourself in such matters as curfews and dating and eventually worked out some new arrangement. But if this had not been done, there would have been no way for your parents to know your feelings. If no attempt is made to communicate, there is little chance of any alteration in the status quo. In other words, if you do something now and it is not working, then do something else to change the system.

But also recognize that there may be great resistance to changing the system because this may involve a shift in the power structure. If your parents, boss, husband, wife, or friend like being in control and you are proposing a change, problems may arise. At the other extreme, there may also be situations in which the system requires adjustment so that a person is forced to assume responsibility after having been dependent on someone else. Whatever the case, no changes take place as long as the status quo is maintained. For this reason, people must be alerted to the need for change and the desire for change before the system can be altered.

10. *We each have a "public I" and a "private I."* The **public I** embodies the qualities, beliefs, and personal images we are willing to share with others. The self-concepts, ideas, and experiences we choose to hold to ourselves make up the **private I.** In communicating with others, we are constantly evaluating what we choose to share and what we choose not to share. Some of us are willing to share everything, whereas others are very protective of personal privacy. Neither system is best because only you can decide what you want to share, with whom, and under what conditions. As long as you are satisfied with your pattern of sharing, then that is the best pattern for you. If not, you may want to change your system by learning such skills as assertiveness, self-revelation, or self-control.

Self-Disclosure

The starting point of any interpersonal communication is the **self-concept,** the view we have of ourselves, which determines what we will say and to whom we will say it. We can tag ourselves with this concept or label, or we can be assigned it by others. For example, if we perceive ourselves to be good communicators, then we are likely to feel confident in our communication. But if we label ourselves, or are labeled by others, as shy or apprehensive, then we may find it difficult to assert ourselves. At the heart of this dynamic is the basic truth that if we do not accept ourselves, probably no one else will either, for our lack of confidence is easily caught by those with whom we interact.

Some of us worry about appearing too self-confident and being thought a braggart. Nevertheless, accepting yourself as a worthy person does not necessarily mean you are boasting. Sometimes you have to "blow your own horn" because no one else knows how to play the tune. There is a difference, however, between tooting your own horn and playing a symphony. In this vein, consider the following advice:

> Self-love means accepting yourself as a worthy person because you choose to do so. Self-love has nothing to do with the sort of behavior characterized by telling everyone how wonderful you are. Boastful behavior is motivated by others, by an attempt to gain favor. Self-love means to love yourself; it doesn't demand the love of others.[6]

Self-disclosure is showing what you know about yourself to others. It is, as one expert put it, "any information about [the] self that is intentionally or unintentionally communicated to another person through verbal or nonverbal messages."[7] In other words, it is communicating about yourself to others.

Whether the atmosphere is supportive or defensive is a large factor in determining how much will be revealed and how vulnerable we will allow ourselves to become. The amount and type of disclosure will also be based on the relationship between the people involved. The people to whom you disclose a great deal often wear the label of "friend." The deepest level of self-disclosure occurs when two people open themselves in such a way that each can be hurt by the other's actions. This takes place when both people share part of their private I in such a way that it becomes a public I.

Self-disclosure allows us and others to understand ourselves. This does not mean that people who choose not to self-disclose are deficient. Each of us must determine what and to whom we want to disclose. You must realize that when you disclose to another person, the act makes you vulnerable because that person now knows something about you that you prefer others not know. We are all entitled to private knowledge, secrets, and beliefs.

Seeking Approval

To many of us, the evaluation by others that will result from self-disclosure is a major concern. Much of our **self-defeating behavior**—our erroneous zone—results from our seeking the approval of others through our interpersonal communication. It is hardly surprising that you have found yourself placing too much emphasis on what others think. You have been conditioned to do so throughout your life, and even if your own family is conscious of the need to help you promote self-reliance, cultural factors, such as advertising, that stress dependence on other things or people to satisfy your needs work against your family's efforts. You may be spending far too much of your time trying to win the approval of others or being concerned with some disapproval that you have encountered. "You can never find self-fulfillment if you persist in permitting yourself to be controlled by external forces or persist in thinking that you are controlled by external forces."[8]

If you want to eliminate approval-seeking behavior as a major need in your life, keep the following guidelines in mind:[9]

- If you think someone else is trying to control you by withholding approval, say so.
- When you are faced with disapproval, ask yourself, "If they agreed with me, would I be better off?"
- Accept that many will never understand you and that this situation is perfectly acceptable.
- You can refuse to argue or try convincing anyone of the rightness of your stance and still simply believe it.
- Trust yourself.
- Stop verifying your ideas by having them substantiated.
- Work at eliminating the apologies you make even when you are not really sorry for what you have said or done.

The **self-fulfilled person,** the person who confidently chooses what to reveal and to whom and is not intimidated into a negative self-concept, realizes that there will always be problems, frustrations, and failures in life. But that person knows how to meet and confront such disappointments intelligently and is capable of adjusting to problems. He or she has learned to be happy and is therefore confident of his or her ability in interpersonal communication.

Trust

Because communication takes place in a system dependent on interaction between individuals, trust is among the most important elements in any communication situation. **Trust** is the "generalized expectancy that the word, the promise, the verbal or written statement of another individual or group can be relied upon."[10] In other words, one person ex-

Trust is an integral and important aspect of interpersonal communication.

pects or predicts that another person will act in a positive way; if the latter person does, trust develops.

We all know people we trust and people we distrust. We are willing to confide in some people, whereas we do not feel comfortable in disclosing personal information to other people.

The inclination to trust or distrust is learned over a long period of time, and it results from cumulative experiences. Trust is often cultivated through self-disclosure. Through self-disclosure you put yourself at risk. If your disclosure is met with acceptance and support, trust can be built in the relationship. If, however, your disclosure is ridiculed, rejected, or not held in confidence, trust is destroyed. The result of the distrust is the development of a negative feeling about the person and a lack of confidence in future self-disclosure.

Several factors lend themselves to the development of trust in a relationship:[11]

1. *The consistency or reliability of a person's past behavior.* A person's past behavior affects the degree of confidence you have in predicting that person's present or future behavior. How dependable was this person in the past when you shared confidences?

2. *The belief that another person holds some expertise on a given subject.* You will probably feel more positive about revealing yourself to a person with a proven record of "knowing what he or she is talking about" than to someone with no such knowledge. You probably have more trust in the advice of a doctor, lawyer, or certified mechanic than in a layperson's opinion on medicine, law, or auto repairs.

3. *The degree of power.* Having power over another person, or feeling that someone can influence your behavior, can affect the level of trust. Parents, bosses, instructors, police officers, and judges all hold power positions. In dealing with these people, you may trust them if you want advice, but you may avoid sharing with them if you are dependent on their evaluation of you or on their permission.

4. *The nature and quality of communication.* When lines of communication are open and goals and expectations are easily identified, a trusting situation is likely to develop. When you deal with people you feel comfortable with, who generally want the same things you do, and who have similar likes and dislikes, you are most likely to trust them and share.

Trust becomes especially important in conflict situations. The extent to which you trust the other person involved in the conflict will affect your choice of communication styles and behaviors. If you trust the other person, you may try to mediate, work toward compromise, or share your feelings and needs. But if you feel the other person will take advantage of you, or if you know she or he has not been honest in the past, you are not likely to work cooperatively. Instead you may try to be aggressive, controlling, or divisive in your approach.

One of the advantages of trusting others is that trusting individuals are likely to be regarded as dependable. Research shows that "low trusters are not only perceived as less trustworthy than others but also are actually more likely to lie and cheat."[12] Evidence also suggests that people who are high trusters are both better adjusted psychologically and more likable than people who are less trusting. Although people tend to prefer those who are most like themselves in attitudes, opinions, and personality, in general everyone respects a high truster—even low trusters.

Contrary to the attitude of some that high trusters are "suckers" and are just plain ignorant, research shows that high trusters are no more gullible than anyone else. Also, high trusters tend to be "do-gooders," traditionally involved in community projects, fund-raising, and other activities intended to help others. Low trusters tend to be involved in more self-centered pursuits and in careers dependent on manipulating others, such as advertising or sales.

Trust is an integral and important aspect of interpersonal communication. What we say to others, how we perceive what they say to us, and our ability to care and turn to others are encapsulated in our trusting attitude.

Emotions

Any message we communicate is made up of both logic and emotion. **Emotions** are strong feelings that usually result in internal physical reactions. Emotional states include fear, anger, disgust, grief, joy, surprise, and yearning. We are born with our emotional instincts, and we are taught to be logical in dealing with other people and issues. It has been estimated that 90 percent of our actions are emotional and only 10 percent intellectual. This, then, leads us to the conclusion that we make decisions emotionally, not intellectually.[13]

"You have probably grown up believing that you can't control your emotions, that anger, fear and hate, as well as love, ecstasy and joy are things that happen to you. Feelings are reactions you choose to have."[14] Seen in this way, anger is usually a reaction to hurt. If you were brought up to believe that it is good to control yourself, that nice people do not display their emotions, or that big boys do not cry, then the next statement may startle you: there is nothing wrong in expressing your feelings! **Anger** is emotional excitement induced by intense displeasure, which may take the form of rage, fury, or indignation. "Anger is a

Emotions are strong feelings that usually result in physical reactions.

natural, normal emotion. To react with anger to a given situation or set of events is not bad. . . . Anger serves as an emotional defense mechanism to relieve the stress of an overstressing situation. Suppressed anger leads to ill health, emotional disturbance and a general feeling of unhappiness."[15]

Expressions of anger can be constructive or destructive. Indeed, letting out your anger by saying how you feel while not verbally or physically attacking another person can be a positive outlet. But screaming at another person or physically abusing her or him is not a positive way of showing emotion. If we use someone as a scapegoat, blaming him or her for our own shortcomings, we are not being fair to ourselves or to the other person. Each of us must assume responsibility for our feelings and for our reactions to those feelings.

Dealing with Personal Anger

What can a person do who finds himself or herself unable to control emotional outbursts? In some cases, the problem may be caused by a genetic predisposition to anger, often the result of a biochemical imbalance. More and more, some people, because of their physical make-ups, are more susceptible to quick emotional flares. In some of these cases, medical tests may indicate certain factors that can be controlled with medication or a change in diet. For example, people who anger easily may be advised to avoid sugar, artificial food coloring, red meats, and stimulants such as caffeine. Still other people, because of deep psychological patterning, may need to be put under clinical hypnosis to allow them to focus on their problems and work them through. And yet another approach involves working with a trained therapist who helps the person learn to tolerate unexpected occurrences.[16]

Some of us have to be taught to develop constructive ways to "blow off steam" so we can react constructively rather than destructively. We have to be taught to "do something to interrupt the neurotic behavior."[17] Some of the most common recommendations include playing the radio as loud as you can and singing along at the top of your lungs; running at top speed around the block or until you are exhausted; looking in the mirror and having a serious talk with yourself about what is troubling you; sitting facing an empty chair, imagining someone else sitting there, and telling that person how you really feel; writing a poem or a short story based on your own experience; writing a letter to the person with whom you are having the conflict (you may or may not mail it, depending on the situation); writing a letter to your favorite person explaining what is bothering you; or punching a pillow as you verbalize your feelings.[18]

You can also try to make more positive use of your anger. Consider, for example, the following suggestions:[19]

Anger can be dealt with positively.

1. *Do not react immediately when you are angered.* Although old, the count-to-ten technique is still effective.

2. *Never make important decisions in the heat of an angry moment.* That is not the time to fire anybody or sell your controlling share of the company's stock to the competition.

3. *Recognize your disminished capacity for clear thinking.* You are likely to make mistakes when you are angry; at these times, your memory is not functioning at its best.

4. *Use the extra energy generated by anger constructively.* When you experience anger (or its first cousin, fear), your body activates its fight-or-flight mechanism. This results in an increased flow of adrenalin that makes you temporarily stronger than usual. But instead of throwing the china or beating the office machinery, mow the yard or move a filing cabinet.

5. *Apologize if necessary.* If you really behave badly during a fit of anger, you may decide it is best to apologize to those who have been affected. A simple "I'm sorry; I was angry" will probably do. You will have to decide what is needed and appropriate.

Above all, remember that emotions touch every facet of our lives and that anger and conflict represent a stimulus to action for each of us. "There are no pat answers," said one expert, "no right way or wrong way for working through emotions. Individuals must find their own unique way of coping with the anger and conflict that are part of everyone's life."[20]

Dealing with Another's Anger

To deal with someone's anger, one expert advised, "Don't let them dump on you; it only encourages their craziness."[21] Instead, you must determine what is the best behavior for you and then carry out that behavior. If you give in to another's emotional blackmail (such as threats she or he will leave you or stop being your friend), you have set a pattern by which that person can control you in the future. And the more you give in, the more the person will use the same ploy again.[22]

Remember that in a conflict situation, the other person is often attacking you when you are not really the cause of the problem, cannot solve the problem, or are not directly related to the problem. It may simply be that you are the first person who wandered on the scene after the incident happened. Or it may be that you are the only person who is available. Or by the position you occupy in relation to that person, you become the likely scapegoat. The best approach to follow in any of these situations is to allow the person to vent his or her frustrations, while you remember that the attack is not really against you and try not to react personally.

Power

Because there is growing awareness of the role of power in any type of relationship, the implications of power in interpersonal communication are worth considering.[23] **Power** may be defined as control, or the ability of an individual to change or control the behavior of other members of a social system.[24]

The hierarchy of power may determine the message that is sent and received and the effect of that message. Thus people in positions of power—parents, teachers, judges, police officers, bosses—are often able to obtain a desired response simply because of the position they hold.

The power to reward or punish is always a factor in times of conflict. If you are powerless, you may have very little influence on the outcome of an argument. After all, a parent can physically expel a child from home; a boss can fire an employee; a police officer can issue a ticket. When these symbols and controls are held over the "victim," the weakness of his or her position becomes obvious.

In many disagreements, the power to reward or punish is irrelevant, but in family or labor or legal conflicts, that power becomes significant. When we are involved in interpersonal communication, we must recognize that we can lose a great deal by failing to realize the consequences of what we say and to whom. If a person has the power to control us, we must be willing to pay the price for any show of strength we may make; the price can include being ejected from home, losing a job, failing a class, or getting a traffic ticket. If, however, we are in a position of power, we can, if we so desire, demand obedience based purely on our ability to manipulate, reward, and control.

Ideally, the use of power is controlled to the extent that it becomes a tool of cooperation rather than a weapon of punishment. And here the message of a Hindu proverb should be kept in mind: "There is nothing noble in being superior to another man; true nobility is in being superior to your former self."[25] Realistically, however, we must recognize that many people do not hold this attitude, and we should take this into consideration in our dealings with others.

Relationships and Their Development

Throughout our lives, we find ourselves in relationships with other people—with parents, siblings, and friends. After all, we do not suddenly grow up and no longer need caring and nurturing contact with others. This reality makes it extremely important that we understand how relationships develop, how they continue, what constitutes a positive relationship, why we turn to others, and how to communicate effectively within the structure of a relationship.

The Development of a Relationship

Relationships vary so greatly that it is almost impossible to formulate any rules about them. Nevertheless, some general principles explain how they develop.[26] "Within the first moments of a relationship," wrote one expert, "internal [intrapersonal] decisions are being formulated which can determine the functions and goals of the relationship. Whether the relationship will be primarily task oriented, friendship oriented or intimate oriented will more often than not be formulated with the initial interaction."[27]

When two persons meet for the first time, their levels of uncertainty about each other and themselves are fairly high. This uncertainty is generated because people can behave and believe in a number of ways; thus accurate prediction of behavior and beliefs is difficult. And initial encounters can cause uncertainty in the future as well because predicting behavior is always difficult and because little or no information has been exchanged between the two.

Think back to your first meeting with someone you now consider to be a good friend, with your spouse, or with a coworker. What went on

In the entry phase of a friendship, biographical information and general attitudes are exchanged.

during that first contact? Why did you decide to pursue the relationship? Did your attitudes change as you got to know the person better? How long did it take you to decide to pursue the relationship? We ask all these questions each time we contact others and decide how far to allow the interaction to go.

Because of this, relationships do have some form of sequential pattern: an entry phase (the beginning), a personal phase (the middle), and an exit phase (the end). But "each relationship does not have to move through the stages at the same rate."[28] In the entry phase, biographical information and general attitudes are exchanged. In the personal phase, information about central attitudes and values is exchanged. In the exit stage, questions concerning the future of the relationship are raised and resolved. This stage may include an agreement to continue the affiliation (continuing the personal phase) or terminate it.

Continuing a Relationship

People make judgments about interpersonal contacts by comparing **relational rewards and costs.** Basically, a relationship continues to proceed into greater depths and breadths of communication as long as it is perceived as rewarding. "As long as rewards [are equal to or] exceed costs," said one expert, "the relationship becomes more intimate; however, once costs exceed rewards the relationship begins to stagnate and eventually to dissolve."[29]

In a dating situation, if one person believes that the investment (cost) of money, time, and emotion is met with security and affection (reward), then that person will want to continue the relationship. If, however, he or she is doing all the giving and the partner is only taking, then the relationship will probably end.

With this in mind, examine a friendship you now have. Why have you continued to remain associated with this person? You probably do so because you receive pleasure from knowing and being with him or her. In contrast, if you have recently taken the initiative to end an association with someone, your action was probably caused by your belief that you were giving too much and not receiving enough or that the relationship was one-sided. "When people find reciprocity in relationships rewarding," reported one source, "they will continue to interact in order to maximize their rewards."[30]

Positive Relationships — A good relationship allows freedom of expression and reflects acceptance of the idea that the feelings of both people are important. We should remember, however, that any alliance experiences times of uncertainty and anxiety. "Individuals bound together will inevitably experience periods of tension, anger, or anxiety," wrote one pair of experts. "Indeed, as relational partners cope with the new and stressful situations that present themselves, conflicts can be expected to emerge as needs and desires change or become incompatible."[31] In addition, once a change has taken place, we must recognize that the relationship will never be the same again.

On the basis of your own experience, think back to a time when you had an argument with a friend or a disagreement with a member of your family or broke off a relationship and then reestablished it. After all these events, the feelings and actions between you and the other person were altered. Never again could things be exactly as they were before.

Besides freedom of expression and acceptance, an important consideration in many relationships is love:

> A relationship based on love is one in which each partner allows the other to be what he chooses, with no expectations and no demands. It is a simple association of two people who love each other so much that each would never expect the other to be something that he wouldn't choose for himself. It is a union based on independence, rather than dependence. Unfortunately, that type of relationship is almost mythological.[32]

We must also recognize that we cannot achieve happiness through someone else. If it is to be found, it must be found within. Unfortunately, it is this desire to find happiness in someone else that causes us to try changing people we supposedly love, when in fact our love should allow them to be themselves and do what they feel is best for themselves. "Love is the ability and willingness to allow those that you care for to be what they choose for themselves without any insistence that they satisfy you."[33]

Communication is the key to creating and maintaining positive relationships. "The ability to send clear messages, to be heard and understood, is central to any ongoing relationship—husband and wife, parent and child, employer and employee, friends, siblings, you name it."[34] The more people share their mutual interests, the closer their talk will bring them together as they discuss goals, mutual responsibility, and the joint rewards that will result.

Research shows that couples who are happily married argue no less vigorously for their own positions than do those who are not happily married; but happily married couples come to agreements fairly readily, either through one partner giving in to the other without resentment or through compromise. Unhappily married people tend to get caught in a situation that seems like cross-complaining, and neither partner is willing to come halfway to resolve a dispute. Instead, each must continue to have his or her own way.[35]

Experts in family communication have identified certain qualities that are shared by both healthy families and healthy friendships. At the top of the list is "communication and listening, with affirming and supporting one another running a close second. Also cited were a sense of fair play, shared responsibility, and trust."[36] In a similar vein, consider the following five guidelines for making a relationship flourish:

1. When you are speaking, get into the habit of using "I" messages instead of "you" messages. (Indicate what you are feeling or how you are reacting to the situation rather than accusing the other person.)

2. Always respond to what the other person has said. When you go off on a tangent without first having replied to the original statement, you are catching the other person unaware.

3. Give the other person freedom of speech.

4. Set aside regular and frequent talking time just for the two of you.

5. Do not put labels on either yourself or the other person.[37]

Also watch out for some specific communication patterns that cause conflict in intimate relationships. Included among these are blaming or putting someone down as well as playing psychological games. The latter can involve such activities as trying to make a person measure up to preset expectations, making an individual prove how much he or she loves you, and forcing someone with whom you have a relationship to follow your wishes.[38] Another problem occurs when you attempt to make your partner fuse with you or vice versa. This **fusion** takes place when one partner defines reality for the other. In other words, the controller dictates what is good, right, and acceptable for the partner.

People who are unhappy in their relationships tend to talk at each other, past each other, or through each other but rarely with or to each other.[39] One source described the problem this way: "Though most couples spend a lot of time talking to each other, many lack the skills needed to get their messages across effectively, to express their feelings or resolve conflicts without hurting each other or provoking anger and dissonance."[40]

Communication in Relationships

All relationships have a structure, and each person has a role he or she plays. As long as no one changes the system and each member of the relationship maintains his or her assigned role, everything is fine. But if someone wants alterations, wants to do things that are not normally done, then the system becomes dysfunctional. A system that is operating to the general satisfaction of the participants is a **functional system.** For example, you are dating someone. You and that person look forward to your times together. When conflicts do arise, you are capable of working out the problems without destroying the relationship or building up bad feelings. A **dysfunctional system** is one in which its members are confused about the roles they are to play. For example, if a woman who has been a housewife decides to go to college, there will have to be a distribution within the family of her former chores, and the family's old system of operation will be thrown out of kilter. Some members in the system may not want to change roles: the husband may not want to do the cooking or child care, or the children may resent not having their mother around. Before the system can become normal again, a new balance will have to be established.

This does not mean that dysfunctional systems are not operational. The individuals in the relationship may continue to function quite effectively as they make changes. The usual result of the dysfunction, however, is confusion because each person lacks clarity about what role to play and what rules to follow. For example, questions and protests may arise as to who is responsible for the tasks formerly done by the mother and wife who is now going to college; common complaints may include "Why should I have to make the meals now?" or "I've never cooked before, and it's not fair for that job to be shoved onto me."

Often, as a system is being **recalibrated,** or restructured, growth takes place. People learn to assume new roles, develop new respect for each other, or make a new team effort. Or chaos may result as people fight for new role identities, defend their emotional territories, or feel compelled to make changes not to their liking.

In a positive relationship, the participants attempt to adjust to alterations in the normal patterns so that the dysfunctional period is kept to a minimum. This usually takes place because the partners in the **dyad** (the two people involved) have developed effective communication skills and a positive method for solving problems. "As long as you and your mate are talking with each other," noted one expert, "there is the chance that you will resolve whatever it is that has come between you. But once you stop talking, there's no chance at all. When you're no longer talking with each other, your attitudes become hardened. You become inflexible and immovable. As long as you're talking there is hope."[41]

Fighting Fair   Disagreements can actually end up being constructive if you follow the basic principles of "fighting fair."[42] These include the following strategies:

1. *Get as much information as you can, and attempt to adjust to the problem based on this information.* Fact, rather than hearsay, may show that the supposed cause of the conflict is really not the actual cause.
2. *Keep arguments in the present tense.* You cannot argue about what happened in the past.
3. *Do not try to make the other person change things that cannot be altered.* We cannot, for example, change our parents, extensively alter our physical appearance, easily switch occupations, or become totally different people.
4. *Do not start a fight when it cannot be finished.* Timing is important. It is not appropriate to start a stressful discussion when a person is walking out the door on the way to work, when a person is on a tight schedule, or when one or both parties are extremely tired.
5. *The setting can affect a conflict.* Disagreeing in public, in front of individuals who are not part of the conflict and will not be affected by its result, is not a good strategy unless your purpose is to win at all costs. And if that is your goal, then you are not interested in fighting fair.
6. *A fight can take place only if both parties participate.* If the conflict is getting out of hand or has gone on too long, then one party should simply stop. An estimate of the appropriate length of an argument is twenty minutes or when the participants start repeating the same arguments. Once both of you begin repeating arguments, it is not uncommon for one of you to start attacking the other rather than the issue—and that is unfair fighting.
7. *If time is available, walk through the argument in your head before it starts.* Using this technique, you can often think of strategies or get rid of some of your hostility by thinking out what has happened, what you want to happen, and what you will do if the result is not to your liking.
8. *Listen to your body.* If you feel that you are losing control to the degree that you may say things you do not want to say, or do things you do

not want to do, then get out. Either you can physically leave, or you can limit your role to that of an active listener for a while.

9. *Identify what you need to get out of the transaction and collect the data you will require to explain those needs to the other person.* Often we enter into a fighting situation without having identified our goals, which means we have no clarity of purpose.[43]

Handling Criticism **Criticism,** the act of judging, is often considered a negative act by the receiver. To handle criticism constructively, without feeling the need to justify yourself or to counterattack, you can try several strategies.

1. *When criticized, seek more information.* If someone accuses you of having done something, ask for specifics. If the person cannot supply those specifics, guess about them as a possible way of discovering whether any evidence exists to back up the criticism. For example, if a friend says that you are selfish and do not respect anyone's feelings, ask for some specific examples or for the specific instance that inspired the comment.

2. *Paraphrase the ideas of the person making the criticism to clarify them for both of you.* Repeat the accusation and ask if that is what he or she really meant. That way you will be dealing with exactly what has been said.

3. *Ask what consequences will result from your not altering the behavior being criticized.*

4. *Agree with the speaker.* Listen to the person and accept his or her opinion. To do this, you can use such techniques as agreeing with the truth, agreeing with the odds (if it is a projection into the future, agree with the odds for its occurrence), agreeing in principle (if the criticism comes in the form of an abstract ideal against which you are being unfavorably compared, you can agree with it in principle without agreeing with the comparison), or agreeing with the critic's perception (agreeing with the right of the critic to perceive things the way he or she does). For example, if you are accused of spending too much time studying and not enough socializing, and if you feel this is true, why not simply agree, rather than arguing that you have a right to spend your time as you wish? Or if your parents warn that the odds are against your finding a job if you major in theater at college, you can agree with the odds being on their side. This does not mean you have to give up your plans, only that you are acknowledging the odds.[44]

In dealing with criticism, you are wise to recognize that much of it is well intentioned. Quite often your parents, friends, and boss are telling you how to change "for your own good" or at least as they perceive what is good for you. This does not mean that they are automatically right or wrong or that you have to take their suggestions. Nevertheless, their advice may be well founded, and you may want to follow it. Just remember that no one has a crystal ball that allows him or her to see into the future. Your desires, needs, and goals are ultimately your responsibility.

Handling Rejection

One of the most difficult messages we can receive and attempt to deal with is **rejection,** which takes place when we are made to feel useless or unsatisfactory or when a concept we have presented is refused.[45] It helps to keep some general principles in mind when you are faced with this sort of experience.

1. *Just because someone says no to you does not mean that you are rejected.* If possible, try to find out the specific reason the statement was made.
2. *We often set ourselves up for rejection.* After all, each of us goes through life being refused requests and being told the answer is no. To persevere, you have to give yourself permission to be rejected. Accept that it will happen now and then, and when it does, consider the potential outcomes and how to continue down the path of personal happiness in spite of the rejection.
3. *People sometimes reject you or your ideas based on their needs rather than yours.* The idea you presented may be valid or the act you performed well done. It may, however, not be in the best interest of the other person to accept or admit this is so. The boss, for example, may not

One of the most difficult messages a person can receive and attempt to deal with is rejection.

like the idea one of the subordinates came up with because it was better than the boss's own idea. For these reasons, when being rejected, ask yourself whether the other person really discounted you or whether you were being used as a scapegoat.

Some additional suggestions for handling rejection include:

1. *Give yourself time to recover from the rejection.* Hurt takes time to heal.
2. *Do not react immediately.* Appraise the situation before you decide on a course of action.
3. *If necessary, seek out help.* A friend may provide you with a sympathetic ear; or in more severe cases a therapist may be needed to help you talk through your reactions.
4. *Ask yourself whether your hopes and desires were realistic.* Try to be honest with yourself in answering this question.
5. *If it is not too painful to do so, follow up and see why you were rejected.* Learn from the experience so that you do not repeat the same mistake.
6. *Ask yourself what is the worst thing that can happen from the rejection.* Often there is only a short-term feeling of hurt pride, with no long-term consequences.

Ending Relationships

Whenever we enter any type of relationship, we pay a price for it. A relationship takes time, energy, and commitment. It means giving up freedom, and it means considering another person, adapting to another person, even changing our lives to accommodate another person. When we enter into a relationship, there are not only possibilities for mutual sharing but also for mutual or individual hurt.

Whether we are dealing with dating, friendship, or marriage, we must realize that these relationships will not go on forever. Rather, we must accept that the ending of relationships is part of the life cycle. We grow up, move, change schools, change jobs, have different needs, grow in different directions, and ultimately die. We must realize that just as change is inevitable, so are endings.

The breakup of any relationship can cause hurt. And this hurt usually comes with the realization of the heavy investment, emotionally and sometimes physically, in the tie. At such times, we normally feel loss, question who we are, feel alone, search for the reason for the break, and sometimes experience guilt. These emotional difficulties are compounded when one party wants to terminate the relationship and the other does not.

Of course, endings can take many forms. When a relationship is ailing, it can be renegotiated instead of terminated. But this can occur only if the issue is confronted before either party has decided there is no point in continuing.

It is also possible to leave a relationship, if not on a positive note, at least with a feeling of not being rejected or with some gain from the experience. This sort of ending is most likely to occur in a face-to-face meeting in which the participants take time to discuss their own observations and inferences about the relationship and each other in a productive fashion. Though this is seldom done, it can be an insightful experience. Unfortunately, the endings of most relationships tend to be charged with tension and hostility over feelings of failure and rejection.[46]

Divorce   "Present nationwide statistics show that one out of every two marriages ends in divorce."[47] And these statistics only begin to suggest a reality known intimately by marriage counselors—namely, that "divorce is the death of a marriage: the husband and wife together with their children are the mourners, the lawyers are the undertakers, the court is the cemetery where the coffin is sealed and the dead marriage buried."[48]

Divorce is a painful process, especially when one person wants to leave and the other wants to stay together and nothing can be done to stop the split. "A lot of people don't seem to realize how angry people can get when there is no power to hold the other party. It is easy to flip out, to go over the brink."[49]

As in any termination of a relationship, the divorced person goes through adjustment stages. These include denial ("I really don't believe this is happening to me"), bitterness ("Life isn't fair"), counterattack ("He or she was a rotten human being"), acceptance ("This is the way it is; I'm just going to go on from here"), loneliness ("What do I do now with all my time?"), and healing ("I'm going to make new friends and get on with my life"). A radio-talk-show psychologist, in giving advice to a recently divorced woman who had called her program, indicated that the most important thing to remember is that "we need time to grieve over the death of a relationship."[50]

Death   A fatal illness may be long and drawn out, or death may be very sudden. In a prolonged death, the dying person goes through various stages that eventually lead to the separation. In *On Death and Dying,* Elisabeth Kübler-Ross identified what she considered to be the five stages that a terminally ill patient progresses through and communicates about. These include denial and isolation ("It can't happen to me"), anger ("Why me?"), bargaining ("Please, God, don't let me die"), depression ("I no longer have any hope; all I can do is wait for the end"), and acceptance ("I've had a good life; it's time to die").[51]

In another book, *Questions and Answers on Death and Dying,* Kübler-Ross indicated that family members and friends usually limp behind in the same stages, in both their feelings and their communication about these feelings, so that often the effect does not hit them until after the person has died. The living, however, have an additional burden in that they may be drained, emotionally and physically, and often carry guilt for deeds done or not done for the person who died.[52]

If death is sudden, the dying person does not go through the five stages, but those left behind usually do. The survivors usually acknowledge that it was better for the person who died to go quickly and thus avoid suffering. But the shock may continue to be great for those who are still living.

The ability to talk out the feelings we have, to communicate to ourselves and others, is often the single most important factor in learning to cope with our own impending death or with that of another. As we talk it out, we are sometimes able to put death into a perspective that makes it more manageable. Often, as we communicate about something, we find that we understand it much more fully.

Summary

This chapter dealt with interpersonal communication, with specific emphasis on self-disclosure and relationships. The major points made were:

- ☐ Interpersonal communication is "an interactional process in which meaning is stimulated through the sending and receiving of messages between two people."
- ☐ The primary principles of interpersonal communication involve relationships and information.
- ☐ We communicate what and who we are.
- ☐ Language can be used to conceal as well as to reveal.
- ☐ Much of our interpersonal communication centers on our wanting others to act or think or feel as we do.
- ☐ "Meaning is in people, not in words."
- ☐ We cannot not communicate.
- ☐ People react to our actions.
- ☐ We do what we do because in the end we expect our actions to bring us happiness.
- ☐ We cannot always have the same understandings and feelings as others.
- ☐ Communication takes place within a system. We each have a "public I" and a "private I."
- ☐ The starting point of interpersonal communication is self-concept.
- ☐ "Self-love means accepting yourself as a worthy person because you choose to do so."
- ☐ The self-fulfilling person is the one who realizes that there will be

problems in life but knows how to meet and confront such disappointments.

☐ Trust is the "generalized expectancy that the word, the promise, the verbal or written statement of another individual or group can be relied upon."

☐ Trust is an integral and important aspect of interpersonal communication.

☐ Our communication is made up of both logic and emotion.

☐ There is nothing wrong in expressing your emotions.

☐ Expressions of anger can be constructive or destructive.

☐ The role of power is important in any relationship.

☐ The sequential pattern of a relationship is the entry phase (the beginning), the personal phase (the middle), and the exit phase (the end).

☐ People make judgments about interpersonal relationships based on comparisons of rewards and costs.

☐ "Love is the ability and willingness to allow those that you care for to be what they choose for themselves without any insistence that they satisfy you."

☐ Communication and listening are found in all healthy families.

☐ People involved in unhappy relationships tend to talk at each other or past each other or through each other but rarely with or to each other.

☐ In a functional system, members are clear about the roles they are to play.

☐ In a dysfunctional system, members are confused about the roles they are to play.

☐ Constructive disagreement springs from basic principles of "fighting fair."

☐ To handle criticism constructively, seek more information, clarify, decide on the consequences for not altering behavior, and/or agree with the speaker.

☐ One of the most difficult communication messages to deal with is rejection.

☐ All relationships terminate.

☐ Marriages fail because the partners are unable or unwilling to find methods to relate to each other.

☐ Divorce is a painful process.

☐ A terminally ill patient goes through five stages: denial and isolation, anger, bargaining, depression, and acceptance.

☐ We need time to grieve over the death of a relationship.

Key Terms

interpersonal communication
action-reaction principle
commonality
public I
private I
self-concept
self-disclosure
self-defeating behavior
self-fulfilled person
trust
emotions

anger
power
relational rewards and costs
fusion
functional system
dysfunctional system
recalibrated
dyad
criticism
rejection

Learn by Doing

1. Think of an interpersonal problem you have had. Then on a three-by-five-inch card describe your role and the role taken by the other person. The class will be divided into groups of three. Read your card to the other two people in your group, and find out how each of them would have handled the situation. After the discussion, tell them what you did and what the outcome was.

2. Relate to the class a recent personal experience that illustrates the action-reaction principle.

3. How do your values and attitudes affect your life? Have you ever found yourself in a situation in which you had to defend your values? What happened?

4. Think back to a relationship you have had that has ended. Examine it from the standpoint of the sequential pattern discussed in the chapter.

5. What do you consider the most difficult part of developing a relationship? Give examples to back up your contention.

6. What is your major fear in revealing information about yourself to others?

7. Relate an experience you had in which power was an important element in a relationship. Was the power used to aid or destroy the relationship? If the power structure had been eliminated, would the relationship have been the same? Why? Why not?

8. Relate a personal experience in which your emotions totally dominated your logic and you said or did something for which you were sorry later.

9. Discuss the statement "Sometimes you have to blow your own horn because no one else knows how to play the tune."

Notes

1. Rebecca Cline, "Seminar in Interpersonal Communication," unpublished syllabus, Temple University, n.d.
2. Thomas Tortoriello, S. J. Blatt, and Sue DeWine, *Communication in the Organization* (New York: McGraw-Hill, 1978), p. 90.
3. Ibid., p. 13.
4. Roy Hatten, "How to Handle People," a speech presented at Lorain County Community College, Elyria, Ohio, 1974.
5. An idea expressed and discussed by Susan Forward, media psychologist, Talk Radio, WERE—AM, Cleveland, Ohio.
6. Wayne Dyer, *Your Erroneous Zones* (New York: Avon Books, 1977), p. 52.
7. James McCroskey and Virginia Richmond, "A Predictor of Self-Disclosure," *Communication Quarterly*, 25 (Fall 1977), 40, based on research by P. Ekman and W. V. Friesan.
8. Dyer, pp. 11–16, 58, 71, 151.
9. Ibid., pp. 78–80.
10. Julian B. Rotter, "Trust and Gullibility," *Psychology Today*, 14 (October 1980), 35.
11. This discussion is based on work reported by B. R. Patton and K. Giffin, *Interpersonal Communication: Basic Text and Readings* (New York: Harper & Row, 1974), p. 443.
12. Rotter, p. 36.
13. Murray Banks, speech presented at Lorain County Community College, Elyria, Ohio, 1974.
14. Dyer, p. 20.
15. Marlene Arthur Penkstaff, "Understanding Anger and Conflict," *Self Development Journal*, 2 (November 1979), 8.
16. This is a principle of Gestalt therapy, as explained by Les Wyman of the Gestalt Institute, Cleveland, Ohio.
17. Forward.
18. "How to Blow Off Steam," *Teen*, 24 (July 1980), 76.
19. Penkstaff.
20. Ibid.
21. Forward.
22. Ibid.
23. Mary Anne Fitzpatrick and Jeff Winke, "You Always Hurt the One You Love: Strategies and Tactics in Interpersonal Conflict," *Communication Quarterly*, 27 (Winter 1979), 3.
24. Ibid.
25. Hatten.
26. Jon Nussbaum, "A Goal-Oriented Perspective of Relationship Development," paper delivered at the Eastern Communication Association Convention, Philadelphia, Pennsylvania, May 1979, p. 4.
27. Ibid., p. 9.
28. Ibid., p. 6.
29. Ibid., p. 1.
30. Robert Duran and Marshall Prisbell, "A Theoretical Extension of the Innovation Process in Relational Development," paper delivered at the Eastern

Communication Association Convention, Philadelphia, Pennsylvania, May 1979, p. 3.

31. Fitzpatrick and Winke, p. 3.

32. Dyer, p. 205.

33. Ibid., p. 39.

34. James Brody, "Helping People to Say What They Mean," *New York Times,* July 6, 1981, p. A-10.

35. Anthony Brandt, "Avoiding Couple Karate," *Psychology Today,* 16 (October 1982), 41.

36. Brett Harvey, "The Family That Stays Together," *Psychology Today,* 17 (August 1983), 78.

37. John Diekman, "How to Develop Intimate Conversation," *New Woman,* 12 (November 1982), 70.

38. Judi Marks, "Relationship: Good? Bad? How to Tell," *Teen,* 24 (January 1980), 32.

39. Brandt, p. 42.

40. Brody, p. A-10.

41. Diekman, p. 70.

42. The principles outlined here were included in an interview with Sonya Friedman on the "Morning Exchange" television program, WEWS-TV, Channel 5, Cleveland, Ohio, August 13, 1976.

43. Wyman.

44. Lawrence Rosenfeld, "Conflict's NOT a Four-Letter Word," unpublished workshop manual, 1982, as adapted from Deborah Weider-Hatfield, "A Unit in Conflict Management Communication Skills," *Communication Education,* 30 (1981), 265–273.

45. Paul Neimak, "Rejection, How Well Do You Handle It?" *Success,* 29 (October 1981), 24–27.

46. Jacquelyn Carr, *Communicating and Relating* (Menlo Park, Calif.: Benjamin Cummings, 1979), p. 213.

47. *The World Almanac and Book of Facts—1988* (New York: Rharos Books, 1988), p. 808.

48. Larry Bradford, "The Death of a Dyad," paper presented at the Central States Speech Association, Chicago, Illinois, April 1978, based in part on Esther Fisher, "A Guide to Divorce Counseling," *The Family Counselor,* No. 22.

49. Alan A. A. Seifullah, "Two Desperate Women," *Cleveland Plain Dealer,* November 4, 1979, p. AA-3.

50. Forward.

51. Elisabeth Kübler-Ross, *On Death and Dying* (New York: Macmillan, 1969), Chapters 3–7.

52. Elisabeth Kübler-Ross, *Questions and Answers on Death and Dying* (New York: Macmillan, 1974), pp. 103–104.

8 *Interpersonal Skills*

Chapter Outline

Participating in Conversations

Presentational Skills

Listening Skills

Nonverbal Skills

Giving Directions

Including Details

Organizing Ideas

Using Understandable Terms

Requesting

Requesting Information

Requesting Change

Asking

Asking for Restatement

Asking for Definition

Asking for Clarification

Conflict and Conflict Resolution

Negotiation

Avoidance

Accommodation

Smoothing Over

Compromise

Competition

Integration

Further Considerations

Assertiveness

Assertiveness, Nonassertiveness, and Aggressiveness

Principles of Assertiveness

Assertiveness Skills
  Simple, Empathic, Confronting Assertions
  DESC Scripting

Special Assertiveness Techniques
  The Broken Record
  Fogging
  Negative Assertion
  Self-Disclosure

*E*very day you participate in the act of interpersonal communication. You converse with friends, interact with business associates, negotiate with members of your family, and send messages to and receive messages from your instructors. To participate successfully in all these interactions, you need to master certain skills.

Participating in Conversations

Almost all of us possess basic conversational skills. We use them when we talk to friends, coworkers, and family members. Nevertheless, some people try to avoid conversations. Others have difficulty starting and maintaining social interactions even if they are not shy. Still others need improvement in their conversational skills. If you are one of these people, you can gain the confidence that makes conversation easier through an understanding of the basic principles and skills involved.

*Presentational
Skills*

The key to good conversation is to hit on a common interest shared by you and the other person. One way of doing this is to ask questions. But

The basic principle of good conversation is to hit upon a common interest that is shared by you and the other person.

try to avoid asking a question that can be answered with a simple yes or no. By the same token, try never to answer a question in that manner.

Conversations usually start with small talk and then move to more in-depth sharing. **Small talk** is interaction with someone at a surface-level exchange of information. It is intended to allow the people involved to determine whether they are interested in pursuing a deeper relationship. It is a safe procedure to indicate who each person is and how the other person may get to know him or her. It is usually nonthreatening and tends to avoid disagreement and conflict. It takes place at informal gatherings, cocktail parties, bars, reunions, and meetings. The information exchanged centers on demographics and biographics (name, occupation or college major, marital status, hometown, college attended or attending) or on slightly more personal information (hobbies, interests, likes, dislikes, tastes, future plans, acquaintances, friends). Small talk at parties and the like usually goes on for about fifteen minutes, and then "big talk" starts. The ground level of communication has been passed when people start talking about personal matters, such as attitudes, beliefs, goals, and specific ways of behaving, or express the desire for social or business interaction, such as a date, a business lunch, or a visit to each other's residence.

In the initial engagement with another person, it is safe to begin a conversation by asking about the basics—the person's name, his or her hometown, and other general information. You will find that people usually like to talk about themselves and their experiences. For example, you can ask about where a person lives, what it is like to live there, what his or her job is. You can ask whether a person likes the job and how she or he chose it. Whether the person works at McDonald's or at IBM does not matter; he or she will have an opinion and will probably be eager to share it.

Other approaches can help you to become a good conversationalist. Keep track of current events, which can furnish a rich source of material; remember that having a common opinion on a subject is not necessary; watch nonverbal clues; show interest; if you disagree and want to state your opinion but do not want to offend, try to be tactful—you can say, for instance, "I see your point, but have you considered . . ."[1] Another good approach is to make a comment about an aspect of the situation you are both in or an observation about the person you are talking with. Say something positive about the person's appearance, or compliment the person by asking for advice. Most people are uncomfortable telling another person something good about themselves, but if you mention it and then ask them to discuss it, they usually will because then they do not appear to be bragging.

Questions are powerful devices for building conversations. Asking a question of a person is a form of a compliment. It indicates that this person knows something you do not or that you respect the person enough to want her or his advice.

1. *Questions encourage people to open up by drawing them out.*[2] (For example, "What university do you go to?" "What's your major?" "I've been considering switching my major to communication; do you think that's a good idea?")

2. *Questions aid you in discovering the other's attitudes.* (For example, "Why did you decide to be a communication major?")

3. *Questions keep the conversation to the topic at hand.* Whenever a response is irrelevant, ask a follow-up question that probes for more information about the topic (such as "What do you feel the future job market is for communication majors?").

4. *Questions can be used to direct the conversation.* A question can change the topic, probe for more information, or keep the conversation going.

5. *Questions help you gain information and clarify meanings.* If what the person says is not clear, you can ask for definitions or examples or ask for the source or basis of information.

To use questioning most effectively, start with easy questions, ask short questions, seal your lips after each question and wait for an answer, and let your partner know you are listening by giving nonverbal feedback such as "Uh huh" and "oh," while you are looking at the person.

Throughout the conversation, relax and be yourself. One of the biggest problems for people who are nervous about conversations is staying calm. Periods of silence are all right. If the other person does not want to talk to you, that is his or her loss, not yours. You act as your own worst enemy if you convince yourself that you cannot carry on a conversation and that the other person is superior to you. "Acceptance of your own experience and feelings as valid and worthwhile (equally as much so as everybody else's) is a necessary step in the process of becoming an integrated, fully functioning person."[3]

Remember that some people are difficult to get to know and that there are some people you may not want to get to know any better. The small talk at the start of a conversation often gives you and a new acquaintance an opportunity to determine whether a closer relationship merits exploring.

Listening Skills   Listening is a very important part of conversation. "People who can talk to strangers," noted one expert, "are invariably good listeners."[4] To be a good listener, learn how to paraphrase the speaker's ideas, repeat the person's name as you are introduced, continue to use it during the conversation, maintain eye contact, and listen to important clues for what to say and what topics are of interest. As a person talks, she or he gives you many clues that can serve as the basis for continued interaction. But be sure to allow the speaker to finish her or his point before you respond to it because interruptions can be very annoying. Some specific suggestions about listening in conversations include:[5]

1. *Listen with an inner ear—listen for what is actually meant rather than for what is said.* Observe the other person's actions. Is what is being said parallel to what his or her body is saying to you? Listen to the tone of the voice, the determination or boredom. These are all cues to whether the conversation is really succeeding.

2. *Listen to the concerns of others.* Do not concentrate solely on your own ideas. Conversations are two-sided. Both people should get an opportunity to participate. Often people ask questions only so that they can give their own answers—a practice of little value. You already know what you think. If you are interested in a conversation, and not a personal speech, find out what others think and address their ideas. You may learn something, and others, seeing that you take them seriously, may be moved to take you seriously in return. Nothing is more deadly than an I-I/me-me conversation. Work toward a I-you/we-us interaction if possible.

3. *Assume nothing.* Too often we assume one thing and later find we were completely mistaken. Because physical and oral first impressions

are not always accurate, give the other person a chance to prove he or she is worthy of your conversation or repugnant enough to cast aside.

4. *Before speaking, ask yourself what message is needed.* Many people do not like to participate in small talk because it appears to offer no opportunity for in-depth discussion or because finding out little tidbits about people whom they are not interested in seems a waste of time. These contentions may be true, but you cannot get to know a person to the degree necessary to have in-depth conversations until you get to know that person on a basic level and built rapport. People who start right off by stating strong viewpoints and getting too personal are often rebuffed. The aggressiveness of such acts works against developing conversations. Nevertheless, if you really do want a debate, go ahead . . . fire away, but be ready for the reaction.

Nonverbal Skills   Nonverbal communication plays an important role in conversation. If you do not think so, pay attention to the hands, arms, legs, feet, and shoulders as well as the facial expression and posture of the person you are talking to. For example, quick glances away may indicate that the person is anxious to leave, and the same may be implied when that person glances repeatedly at a watch, looks around the room, or shifts from one foot to the other. If, however, the person leans forward, is intently looking at you, or is directly facing you, then the interaction is probably positive.

Watch for nonverbal feedback. Grunts, smiles, and nods can all serve as signs of encouragement for you to continue. Researchers have also discovered that the last person at whom a speaker looks before ending his or her utterance is the most likely to speak next. Thus eye contact not only synchronizes thoughts and wishes but also passes the focus to a particular member of a group if there is more than one listener.[6]

Giving Directions

We often find ourselves giving other people **directions**.[7] These can include instructions for accomplishing a task, achieving an effect, or getting somewhere. In giving directions, you are wise to include all the necessary details, organize the ideas in a specific order, and use terms that can be clearly understood.

Including Details   How many times have you asked someone for directions and been given only a very general description? Others assume that because they know

When giving directions, try to be as specific as possible.

what they are talking about, you do, too. "Go down the street to the corner and make a right" may be very clear if you know what street and which corner the person means. Unfortunately, such is not always the case.

Have you ever attempted to assemble a child's toy or an electronic device that was accompanied by vague directions? The frustration here can be great because the directions are commonly written by the experts who designed the item. They often assume that you can figure out what to do simply because they can.

In the giving of directions, try to be as specific as possible. Include such information as names, references (north, south; left, right; up, down), descriptions (the size of the item, a sketch of what it looks like), and warnings about where confusion may set in. The procedure should be the same whether you are giving travel directions, assembly information, or a recipe.

Organizing Ideas   Directions are easiest to follow when given in either a chronological or a spatial order. In a chronological order, you indicate the step-by-step procedure by telling what is to be done first, second, third, and so on. This is a good method to use when explaining how something should be assembled or when giving recipes.

Spatial order involves providing descriptions according to geographic directions. A travel plan from the auto club indicating the exact place where you start and the place-by-place order of the cities you will go through is an example of directions that are in spatial order.

It often is a good idea to write down or draw your directions. Some people find it easier to follow written, rather than oral, information.

Using Understandable Terms   If a person cannot understand the directions, then the details are of no value. For this reason, make sure that any scientific and mechanical terms you use are adequately defined. The prospect of operating a computer is often more terrifying than it should be because in many instances the operational procedures are written in computer jargon rather than in Standard English. No wonder so many people have computer phobia! In the same way, an auto repair manual may seem like a foreign language dictionary if you are not familiar with the terms being used. Unfortunately, in the case of many computer and auto repair manuals, the writers appear not to have taken the potential user into consideration, although increased pressure has caused some manufacturers to make manuals more "user friendly" by defining terms and writing from the consumer's standpoint.

Make sure that terms that are familiar to you are clarified in your directions if they may not be clear to someone else. Giving directions that include "turn right at the Smiths' old house" is not going to help if the other person does not know which house that is.

Requesting

"**Requesting** is the process of expressing a desire for something. The request, in some instances, takes on the form of a demand."[8] Requests usually fall into two categories: requesting information and requesting change.

Requesting Information   When you request information, specify the exact nature of the information you want, and make the request in specific language that includes a suggestion as to how the request is to be carried out. If you ask the research librarian, for example, to tell you about Lucerne, Switzerland, she or he can give you volumes of information. But what specifically do you want to know? Maybe you are interested in finding out the most recent population statistics or the general weather conditions in June. Whatever your interest, try to be as specific as possible. And take care to avoid meaningless phrases ("and stuff like that" or "you know") because they add nothing to the specification.

If you are not presenting the request in person, indicate how you wish to receive the reply—by phone, by letter, in person at the end of the day. This rounds off the entire process so that you and the other person both understand exactly what is wanted and how the request is to be processed. If there is a deadline by which the information must be received, be sure to specify this as well.

Requesting Change   When you request change, be as specific as possible. Be sure to indicate what is wrong, what has to be done to correct the situation or bring about a positive outcome, what procedure should be followed to do so, and what consequences are likely to result if the change is not made.

When you explain what is wrong, say so in detail. For example, telling a salesperson that "This thing isn't any good" does not clarify the problem. But saying, "The alarm on the clock I bought always rings ten minutes late" does. Then follow up this statement of the problem with a remark such as "I'd like a new clock with a correctly working alarm." This allows the salesperson to know exactly how you wish the problem solved, and the problem may end here. If not, negotiate a solution through the sort of assertive actions discussed in detail later in this chapter.

One of the errors people who are asking for change often make is to immediately issue a threat. This is a poor tactic because the receiver should be given a chance to fulfill the request before any type of additional action is taken. Remember that a threat is a means of last resort. If you make it too early, you will have no other form of ammunition to use if the request is not granted. By the same token, take care when presenting any type of consequences. Ask yourself if the threat will bring about the desired action, if the threat can realistically be carried out, and if you are really willing to do it. Obviously, threatening to kill someone or suing for an extremely small amount of money is generally not a realistic way to resolve a dispute. Stating that you will never shop in a particular establishment again may have little effect if you are talking about a large department store. Do not make idle threats; be sure any actions you propose are realistic and operational. If, for example, you have purchased a product that is not working well and the store refuses to take it back, indicate that you will withhold payment of your charge until a compromise is reached.

Employees should feel comfortable asking questions.

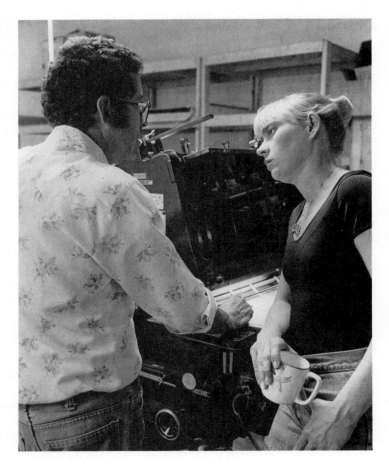

Asking

People often do not ask questions because they are afraid to do so, do not know how to ask them, or do not know what to ask. Gaining the skills involved in **asking,** which entails seeking out information by inquiring, will help you to eliminate misunderstandings, aid you in assuring the receipt of the intent of your message, reassure you that you gained the proper information, and convince the sender that you really do understand.

Asking questions is important in handling a job. If, for example, a person receives directions to institute a new procedure at work, that person may need to ask questions of the supervisor or trainer who is providing the instructions. A worker who is reluctant to ask for clarification for fear of appearing uninformed is probably just creating more problems for himself or herself. Later, when called on to actually perform the new procedure, the worker may be unable to do so. Remember, if it is important for a person to know, it is important for her or him to ask.

When you ask questions, make the sort of request that can be answered and will get at the problem. Determine what it is that you do not seem to understand. If you can identify it, ask a specific question that will clarify your dilemma. If you still cannot identify what you do not understand, recognize that confusion usually centers on the need for restatement, for definition, and for clarification.

Asking for Restatement
Sometimes in explaining things, people state their ideas in such a way that they are unclear. This may be caused by the order in which the ideas are presented. For example, an explanation of an accounting procedure that does not tell the first step, second step, and so on will probably lead to confusion. In this case, ask for the ideas to be presented in a step-by-step sequence.

Asking for Definition
Vocabulary is one major problem in the understanding of information. Asking someone to restate his or her ideas in other words or to define his or her terms often clears up the misunderstanding. This is usually the problem, for example, with physicians who use medical terms to explain a patient's illness. Many professionals forget that the average person does not have much expertise in the subject and therefore does not have access to technical terminology; an explanation appropriate to the layperson's vocabulary is necessary.

Each time you are introduced to a new subject area, you must learn its vocabulary. Chemistry, psychology, and communication, for example, all have a special vocabulary. Students who fail these subjects often do so because they are weak in the subject's vocabulary.

Asking for Clarification
Sometimes the basic information in a communication message is simply not enough. In that case, clarification can be achieved through the use of examples, illustrations, and analogies. For example, in listening to a lecture, you will find that the first few sentences dealing with each new concept tell the idea, and the rest of the statements clarify. Sometimes, however, senders forget to give examples, illustrations, or analogies. If the illustrations used are not clear, ask for new or additional ones.

As you sit in class, as you participate in a sales demonstration, as you are being trained to operate a piece of sophisticated equipment, try to paraphrase what the speaker is saying. If you cannot do so, you probably do not understand the message. If that is the case, ask questions!

Conflict and Conflict Resolution

"**Conflict** is natural, the inevitable result of individual differences, limited resources, and differences in role definitions."[9] The most common sources of conflicts are individual differences in age, sex, attitudes, beliefs, values, experience, and training; limited human, financial, technical, time, and space resources; and differences in the definitions of various relationships.[10]

The process of conflict begins when one person perceives that another person has caused him or her to experience some type of frustration. This frustration, if put into words, would sound like this: "I want (your personal concern, need, want) _____, but (the person perceived as frustrating you) _____ wants (his or her concern, need, want) _____.

From these feelings or statements comes a conflict situation in which incompatible activities occur. These activities prevent, block, or interfere with each other or in some way make the participants irritated. "Any

Conflict is a natural and un-avoidable aspect of interpersonal relationships.

situation in which one person perceives that another person, with whom he or she is interdependent, is interfering with his or her goal achievement may be defined as a **conflict situation**. . . . If it is not expressed in some way, but kept bottled up inside, it is an **intrapersonal conflict**."[11]

Conflict in and of itself is a natural process that can be negative or positive, depending on how it is used. Though some people may try to avoid conflict at any cost, this sort of behavior is generally not desirable. Conflict can be healthy because it allows for the communication of differing points of view, which can lead to important changes, particularly in an organization. After all, if all persons share the same orientation to a policy or procedure, the organization to which they belong may not change and grow.

But just as conflict can serve a useful function, so, too, can it be dysfunctional. Conflict is detrimental when it stops you from doing your work, threatens the integrity of your relationship, is personally destructive, endangers the continuation of your relationship or your ability to function within it, is so upsetting that it causes physical or mental destruction, or leads you simply to give up and become inactive in the relationship or in life in general. Conflicts can be dealt with through negotiation, avoidance, accommodation, smoothing over, compromise, competition, or integration.

Negotiation   **Negotiation** is the act of bargaining to reach an agreement. We all negotiate because we are all involved in situations in which it is necessary to alter a relationship, solve a problem while working with others, or work in a group for the accomplishment of a goal. But to negotiate successfully, we need to be familiar with the methods negotiation involves.

Negotiation is a process used extensively in business and industry. Labor unions negotiate contracts with management, workers negotiate job responsibilities with their supervisors, and customers negotiate purchases with sales representatives. One of the greatest fears involved in this process is the reluctance of some negotiators to engage in conflict to reach a solution. Amateurs in particular are often frightened by negotiations because they feel ill-equipped to handle the process.[12]

When you are negotiating, you must be explicit about what you want and why. And if you are unable to work out an amicable solution, you must accept that invoking the consequences may be necessary. If this is the case, make clear what the consequences will be; also make sure that the consequences are relevant to the other person or organization and can be carried out.

There usually are a number of considerations to bear in mind when you are negotiating. Begin by preplanning. Look closely at the other party's point of view to understand where you differ. Conflict is often cleared up as soon as one party realizes that he or she did not understand the other person's viewpoint or his or her own.

Identify your needs. What do you really want? What does the other person want? Are your needs similar to the other person's or different? Does the subject of the conflict really deal with these needs, or is there a **hidden agenda** (something else that is really motivating the conflict)? In examining the specific topic of the conflict, we sometimes find that it is not really the issue at all. If this turns out to be the case, try to identify the reason you feel the way you do, and deal with that rather than wasting time on a side issue.

Once you have identified your needs, decide on a negotiating style. Remember that the same pattern does not work in all situations. Because of this, one of your basic considerations should be whether you are interested in a win-lose, a lose-lose, or a win-win resolution.

The **win-lose** style of negotiating centers on one person getting what he or she wants, while the other comes up short. In **lose-lose** negotiations, neither person is satisfied with the outcome. In a **win-win** negotiation, the goal is to find a solution that is satisfying to everyone.[13] Although the last seems to be the ideal for which most people strive, some may prefer a different option. There are times when people feel they must win at all costs, and if they cannot win, the other person is not going to win either.

Avoidance

Some people choose to confront conflict by engaging in **avoidance,** or not confronting the conflict at all. They simply put up with the status quo, no matter how unpleasant it may be. While seemingly unproductive, avoidance may actually be a good style if the situation is short term or of minor importance. If, however, the problem is really bothering you or is persistent, then it should be dealt with. "Avoiding the issue often uses up a great deal of energy without resolving the aggravating situation. Very seldom do avoiders feel that they have been in a win-win situation. Avoiders usually lose a chunk of their self-respect since they so clearly downplay their own concerns in favor of the other person's."[14]

Accommodation

A person who attempts to resolve conflict through **accommodation** puts the other person's needs ahead of his or her own, thereby dealing with conflict by giving in. For this reason, the accommodator often feels like the "good guy" for having given the other person his or her own way. This is perfectly acceptable if the other person's needs really are more important. But unfortunately, accommodators tend to follow the pattern no matter what the situation. Thus accommodators are often stepped on by everyone because they simply do not stand up for their rights.

They are often taken advantage of, and they very seldom get what they want. Usually they have the unpleasant feeling of being everyone's doormat, and in a win-lose situation they always come out as losers.

Smoothing Over

"It is the goal of **smoothing over** to preserve the image that everything is OK above all else."[15] By using smoothing over, people sometimes get what they want, but just as often they do not. Usually, they feel they have more to say and have not totally satisfied themselves. Because of this, smoothing over can result in either a win-win or a win-lose situation.

As with avoidance and accommodation, smoothing over can occasionally be useful. If, for example, the relationship between two people is more important than the subject they happen to be arguing about, then smoothing over may be the best approach. Keep in mind, however, that smoothing over does not solve the conflict; it just pushes it aside. It may very well recur in the future.

Compromise

Compromise brings concerns out into the open in an attempt to satisfy the needs of both parties. The definition of the word *compromise*, however, indicates the basic weakness of this approach, for compromise means that both individuals have given in at least to some degree to reach a solution. As a result, neither usually completely achieves what she or he wanted. But this is not to say that compromise is an inherently poor method of conflict resolution. It is not, but it can lead to a lose-lose or a win-lose situation when a win-win situation may have been achievable through another means.

Competition

The main element in **competition** is power—someone has to win, and someone has to lose. This, unfortunately, has become the American way of operation in many situations—in athletic events, business deals, and interpersonal relations. Indeed, many people do not seem to be happy unless they are clear winners. You, of course, realize that if someone wins, someone else must lose. The parent must defeat the child; the professor must be right, while the student is wrong; the overaggressive driver must force the other car off the road. The value of winning at all costs is debatable. For our purposes here, the issue is whether outright winning is the best way to resolve a particular conflict. Must the boss always be right? Must the parent always win?

Sometimes, even though we win, we lose in the long run. The hatred of a child for a parent that was caused by continuous losing and the negative work environment resulting from a supervisor who must always be on top may be much worse than the occasional loss of a battle.

Integration   Communicators who handle their conflicts through **integration** are concerned about their own needs as well as those of the other person, but unlike compromisers, they will not settle for only a partially satisfying solution.[16] Integrators keep in mind that both parties can participate in a win-win conflict resolution. Thus the most important aspect of integration is the realization that the relationship is the most important element of the situation. For this reason, integrative solutions often involve a good deal of time and energy.

People who are competitive by nature, who are communication apprehensive, or who are not assertive find it nearly impossible to use an integrative style of negotiation. They feel that they must win, that they cannot stand up for their rights, or that they have no right to negotiate. In contrast, people who tend to have assertiveness skills and value the nature of relationships usually attempt to work toward integration.

Further
Considerations   No one consistently uses any particular style of negotiation. Instead, most people tend to vary their styles according to the situations in which they find themselves. Because of this, the climate of a situation is always an important factor.

Setting up the climate is a crucial negotiating technique. If the atmosphere is positive, the negotiation will probably go forward. If the atmosphere is negative, however, there may be no way of avoiding a win-lose or a lose-lose situation, both of which are fostered by competition.

For the climate to be positive, conflict resolution may have to be delayed. For example, an accountant who has just received a poor performance evaluation that she feels is unfair may consider taking a "cooldown period" before storming into the supervisor's office. When people are emotionally charged, they often have difficulty handling anything rationally. Instead, a totally emotional conflict may result.

The setting of a negotiation is also an important consideration. For example, trying to negotiate in front of others often places a strain on the participants that can result in a less-than-desirable solution. The timing of the confrontation may also have an effect. If the participants feel rushed, tired, or under pressure to meet a deadline, this can influence both their thinking and their emotional attitude. But if the purpose is to win, no matter what the cost, then high-level emotion on the part of the other person or a pressure-oriented setting and time may be desirable.

Another important negotiating technique is to keep the discussion focused. This can be achieved when there is meaningful communication between the parties involved, when communication is accurate and is kept to the issue being discussed, and when there is an avoidance of game playing.[17]

A final point to remember is that no one has to lose in a negotiation. If both people are satisfied as a result of what has been decided, then their needs are met and a win-win situation results. Ideally, this should be the goal of all conflict resolutions.

Assertiveness

Have you ever found yourself saying, "I didn't want to come here, but she made me," or "I ordered this steak well done and it's rare. Oh well, I guess I'll eat it anyway"? If so, the skill you were probably missing in each of these cases was the ability to be assertive.

"**Assertive behavior** is a direct and honest communication of who you are and what you are," reported one source. "It begins by acknowledging everyone's basic human rights. Once you are aware that you have a right to choose and control your life, you can act assertively."[18] A person who is assertive takes action instead of just thinking about it. Rather than saying, "Why didn't I tell her?" or "If he were here now, I'd say . . . ," the assertive person takes action at the appropriate time.

"A good many communication problems have assertive difficulties at their roots. You may know how you feel but be afraid to state your feelings because you're afraid somebody won't like you or you will make waves."[19] But you must remember that your feelings are you. You must be in contact with your feelings and listen to them. If your stomach is churning, if your body is tightened up, then something is drastically wrong.

> You have to learn to respect your feelings, and in doing so you will not only learn to respect yourself but will also gradually arrive at a clear definition of who, and what, you are. . . . You can't go through life (happily, that is) trying to respond the way you think you should or the way somebody else thinks you should. Eventually your body will rebel and your repressed feelings may express themselves in the form of ulcers, colitis, or tension headaches.[20]

The real point of assertiveness training is to learn to express feelings appropriately and directly.

Assertiveness, Nonassertiveness, and Aggressiveness[21]

As illustrated in Figure 8.1, the goal of assertive behavior is to communicate your needs through honest and direct communication. Nevertheless, assertiveness does not mean taking advantage of others; it means taking charge of yourself and your world. In other words, assertiveness is effective personal caretaking.[22] Thus assertiveness centers on such statements as "It's fine for me to ask for help," "I got myself into this; now I have to get out of it," and "It's my decision to make." In assertive speech, the words *I feel* are crucial.

Figure 8.1

A Comparison of Nonassertive, Assertive, and Aggressive Behavior

	Nonassertive	Assertive	Aggressive
Characteristics of the behavior	Does not express wants, ideas, and feelings, or expresses them in self-deprecating way. Intent: to please.	Expresses wants, ideas, and feelings in direct and appropriate ways. Intent: to communicate.	Expresses wants, ideas and feelings at the expense of others. Intent: to dominate or humiliate
Your feelings when you act this way	Anxious; disappointed with yourself. Often angry and resentful later.	Confident. You feel good about yourself at the time and later.	Self-righteous; superior. Sometimes embarrassed later.
Other people's feelings about themselves when you act this way	Guilty or superior.	Respected, valued.	Humiliated, hurt.
Other people's feelings about you when you act this way	Irritation, pity, disgust.	Usually respect.	Anger, vengefulness.
Outcome	Don't get what you want; anger builds up.	Often get what you want.	Often get what you want at the expense of others. Others feel justified in "getting even."
Payoff	Avoids unpleasant situation, conflict, tension, and confrontation.	Feels good; respected by others. Improved self-confidence. Relationships are improved.	Vents anger; feels superior.

This chart was created by Phillis DeMark and is used with permission.

In contrast, the goal of **nonassertive behavior** is to avoid conflict and tension. Nonassertive statements include "Don't make waves," "Don't be selfish," "Think of others first," "Be modest," "Don't be demanding," "Let's keep the peace," and "Keep it in the family." The consequences of nonassertive behavior are that you do not get what you want. Because of this, anger builds, you suffer, and you are alienated from yourself and others.

The goal of **aggressive behavior** is to dominate, to get your own way. If you are aggressive, you are apt to make such statements as "Get in there and fight," "Win at all costs," "It's a dog-eat-dog world," "Give them what they gave you," and "They only understand being yelled at." Aggressive behavior may well get you what you want, but it will also lead to your alienation, thereby putting emotional distance between yourself and others that can lead to loneliness and frustration.

Principles of Assertiveness   In dealing with assertiveness and learning to be an assertive person, you are wise to keep the following basic principles in mind.

1. *You cannot change other people's behavior; you can only change your reaction to it.* In other words, you can control only one person—you. Until the age of four or five, a child is greatly influenced and controlled by her or his parents. Shortly thereafter, the child starts to be influenced by others and eventually becomes independent. Gradually the parents' role is lessened to the point where the child can be influenced and changed only when she or he wishes to be. One of the valuable lessons of assertiveness is the recognition that you can tell a person what you are feeling and how his or her actions affect you, but you cannot make that person change the way he or she is treating you; only the other person can do that. If you cannot bear to continue a relationship with a person after having asserted your reactions and needs, then it may be best for you to recognize that fact and sever the affiliation, if possible.

2. *People are not mind readers.* You must ask for what you want. You must share your feelings if you are hurt, have been taken advantage of, or need assistance. Others are not capable of reading your mind to find out what is bothering you, what they have done to cause you to feel as you do, or what you do not understand.

3. *Patterned habit is no reason for doing anything.* "That's the way it always has been," "We always do it that way," and "Our family tradition is . . . " are all patterned statements. But the presence of a past pattern does not mean that change cannot occur. Be careful, however, to recognize that once a pattern has been broken, it is difficult, if not impossible, to restore the pattern to what it was before.

4. *You cannot make others happy.* Others make themselves happy, just as you make yourself happy. Much of the guilt we feel has been forced on us by parents and friends who make us believe that if we do not act as they want us to, then we are causing them unhappiness. How many times have you gone somewhere you really did not want to go because your parents or friends felt it was your duty? How many times have you been manipulated by statements such as "Make me

happy and . . ." or "If you don't do that, I'm going to be mad at you"? You have been had if you fell for these lines. Your actions in themselves cannot make anyone glad or sad; only that person can determine her or his reaction to what you do.

5. *Remind yourself that parents, spouses, friends, bosses, children, and others will often disapprove of your behavior and that their disapproval has nothing to do with who or what you are.* In any relationship, you will incur some disapproval.[23] Get ready for it, accept that it will happen, and remember that you can never totally escape disapproval, no matter how much you may want it to go away.

6. *Whenever you find yourself avoiding the unknown, ask yourself, "What's the worst thing that could happen to me?"*[24] It is amazing how often we fail to do or say something because of fear. Before you let fear act on you, determine what the consequences are of the action, of the communication. If you would prefer to avoid these consequences, then by all means avoid the situation. But if you do want the experience, then go ahead!

7. *Do not be victimized.* A **victimizer** is a person or establishment that interferes with another person's right to decide how to live his or her own life, and a **victim** is a person who is denied that right. Victimization may be enacted by others, but it can also take the form of **self-victimization,** in which a person prevents herself or himself from deciding how to live. Self-victimizers often go through life thinking of themselves as failures or losers, with no capability to achieve.

    It is a basic psychological principle that when people are functioning as adults, they use available resources to get out of victimizing situations and victimizing relationships.[25] When they do so, they are deciding for themselves that "this is what I want," "this is what I need," and "this is what I am going to do to get the most out of life."

    One of the basic questions a person who is being victimized must ask is "Why am I playing the victim?" To cure self-victimization, the person must get rid of the self-defeating beliefs and behaviors he or she accepted in the past. Such phrases as "I can't do it right," "I'm a loser," "I tried it before and it didn't work," and "It was too hard for me" must all be eliminated because they almost always ensure that a person will not or cannot succeed.

8. *Worrying about something will not change it.* Worrying will not alter the past, the present, or the future. Instead, you must take some action to relieve yourself of anxiety. It may be necessary to confront someone and share your feelings with him or her. Or it may be necessary to make drastic changes or even dissolve a relationship. But worrying about the problem will not solve it.

Express yourself with confidence.

9. *Adopt the attitude that you will do the best you can, and if someone does not like it, that is her or his problem, not yours.* Remember that no one can satisfy everyone. You are responsible to only one person—you. If others cannot and will not accept that idea, that is their problem, not yours. Dealing with your communication and action from this perspective changes much of your dependence on others for praise and assurance. But this does not mean that you should not seek out information and advice from those whose opinions you respect. Instead, it means that you do not need to seek reassurance for everything you do, think, and feel. For if you become dependent on others for your perceptions of self, then you may lose self-respect. In this vein, consider this advice:

   The important thing is to determine for yourself which rules work, and are necessary to preserve order in our culture, and which can be broken without harm to yourself or others. There is no percentage in rebelling just for the sake of rebelling, but there are great rewards in being your own person and living your life according to your own standards.[26]

10. *Assertion does not mean aggression.* Aggressive people come on too strong and are not sensitive to others' feelings and reactions. They

tend to be poor listeners because they usually spend most of their time talking. Their attitude is "Only I talk; only I need!" And they often want others to play the passive role. What an aggressive person has to do is modify his or her behavior to become sensitive to the feelings and responses of others and become willing to give as well as take.

11. *When you decide to be assertive, be aware of the consequences.*[27] For example, if you are not ready to leave home, telling your parents that the rules they have set up are causing you problems may bring about a reaction you are not ready to handle. And if you threaten to quit your job if you do not get a raise, you should be ready to start looking for another employer. Finally, in deciding to be assertive, you may want to use the sage advice given in the column "Dear Abby": "Is it hurting anyone? Is it harming you? Do you enjoy it?"[28]

Assertiveness Skills

If you are not already assertive, you may have decided that you would like to be. Or if you are basically assertive but have not been extremely successful, it may be because you lack sufficient techniques to handle a variety of situations. In each case, a number of strategies can be of assistance to you.

Simple, Empathic, Confronting Assertions

One assertive technique is known as simple, empathic, confronting assertion. The use of this technique (as illustrated in Figure 8.2) follows several stages. When you feel the need to be assertive, start with a **simple assertion** in which you state the facts that relate to the existence of the problem. This in itself may be enough to solve the problem because people are often not aware that something is bothering you or that they have done something you consider wrong. A simple assertion alerts them to the problem. If they act, the solution is at hand.

Sometimes, however, you need to recognize the other person's position but state your own needs. This is an **empathic assertion.** It may follow a simple assertion or be the first step in the assertive process. By recognizing the other person's problems or rights, you may find that she or he understands that you are not on the attack; that person may then become quite cooperative.

A **confronting assertion** gives a statement of the person's behavior, then states your own position. This assertion is usually a follow-up to a simple or an empathic assertion. The first part of the statement alerts the person to what is wrong; the second usually contains a request for change or states the consequences for not altering the present behavior.

All these assertions are dependent on **descriptive speech,** in which you describe rather than accuse. "Descriptive speech, in contrast to that which is evaluative, tends to arouse a minimum of uneasiness."[29] If

Figure 8.2

Three Types of Responses

1. *Simple assertion:* State the facts.
   If someone shoves ahead of you in the supermarket, you say:
      "I was here first."
   If someone asks to borrow money, you say:
      "I don't want to lend it."
2. *Empathic response:* You recognize the other's position *but* state your own needs.
      "I know you're probably in a hurry, but I was here first."
      "I know you need money, but I prefer not to lend it."
3. *Confronting response:* Repeat a description of the person's behavior, then state your own position.
      "You cut in front of me. I was here first. I'd like you to go to the end of the line."
      "You've asked me three times for money. I won't lend it to you. Please don't ask again."

This material is derived from Judith Spencer, "Assertiveness Training Workshop," a paper delivered at a workshop at Lorain County Community College, Elyria, Ohio, November 14, 1978.

a person does not feel endangered, he or she will likely honor your request.

DESC Scripting

DESC scripting is a way of dealing with interpersonal conflicts that centers on the process of Describing, Expressing, Specifying, and stating Consequences. This process allows you, as one source put it, to "analyze conflicts, determine your needs and rights, propose a resolution to the conflict, and, if necessary, negotiate a contract for change."[30]

This process also allows people to plan ahead, if desirable, to avoid not being able to think of what to say. People who use DESC scripting often find that in addition to using it as a tool for planning, they can actually use it to ad lib as well. Most people, but especially those who are communication apprehensives, tend to feel more secure if they know exactly what they are going to say. This system allows them to rehearse and eliminate bad scripts or self-defeating statements. The four steps of DESC scripting are:

1. *Describe.* Describe as specifically and objectively as possible the behavior that is bothersome to you. For example, you may say, "I was told these repairs would cost $35, and now I'm being charged $100."
2. *Express.* Say what you think and feel about this behavior. For example, you may say, "This makes me angry because I feel I was not told the truth."

3. *Specify.* Ask for a different, specific behavior. For example, you may say, "I want my bill adjusted to the original estimate unless you can clearly justify the extra charges."

4. State *consequences.* Spell out concretely and simply what the reward will be for changing the behavior. For example, you may say, "If you make the change, I'll let the people with whom I work know that I've gotten good, fair service here." Sometimes you may have to specify the negative consequences. For example, you may say, "If the change isn't made, I'll contact the Better Business Bureau, and I'll certainly let people know what bad service you give."

DESC scripting can be used for requesting an adjustment, asking for information or help, clarifying instructions, reconciling with someone, saying no to unreasonable demands, protesting annoying habits, dealing with unjust criticism, combating physical violence, handling emotional outbursts, and even dealing with the silent treatment.[31]

Special Assertiveness Techniques

Sometimes we find ourselves in situations in which we need to take a special assertive approach. The techniques we can use include the broken record, fogging, negative assertion, and self-disclosure.

The Broken Record

When you use the **broken record** technique, you say what you want again and again in a very calm voice. This allows you to avoid getting caught in verbal games because you are continually sending the same message. Be careful, however, that you do not get led off the track. This technique tends to work because the person knows that you are intent on what you are saying, and he or she quickly learns that you are not going to change your mind.

Fogging

In **fogging,** you calmly acknowledge what the other person is saying because there must be some shred of truth in it. Nevertheless, you return to your own position. Examples of fogging are statements such as "I'm sure you feel that way, but I want my refund," or "You may be right, but I want my refund." Fogging can often be used as part of the broken record process.

Negative Assertion

In using a **negative assertion,** you accept your errors and faults but do not give up your position. An example of a negative assertion is "I did it wrong the last time; now if you give me help in planning it, maybe I won't do it wrong this time."

Self-Disclosure

Self-disclosure is an assertive device that centers on inviting others to know you. It makes others deal with you as a person. Two examples of this technique are "I guess I didn't handle that because I really don't know what to do about it," and "Yes, I am a member of a fraternity; I guess that's why I believe in the importance of the college rush policy."

Summary

These points, describing skills in interpersonal communication, were covered in this chapter:

☐ Every day we participate in the act of interpersonal communication.

☐ Nearly everyone possesses basic conversational skills.

☐ Many people shy away from conversation.

☐ The basic principle of good conversation is to hit on a common interest between yourself and the other person.

☐ Conversations usually start with small talk.

☐ Listening and nonverbal communication are important parts of conversation.

☐ Directions include instructions for how to accomplish a task, achieve an effect, or get somewhere.

☐ When you give directions, include all the necessary details, organize the ideas in a specific order, and use terms that can be clearly understood.

☐ Requesting is the process of seeking out information or change.

☐ Gaining skill in asking questions helps to eliminate misunderstandings, aids in assuring the receipt of the intent of the message, reassures you that you did gain the information, and helps the sender to know that you really do understand.

☐ Confusion usually means you need to restate, define, and clarify.

☐ "Conflict is natural, the inevitable result of individual differences, limited resources, and differences in role definitions."

☐ Conflict can be dysfunctional.

☐ Conflict can be resolved through negotiation.

☐ Negotiation is the act of bargaining to reach an agreement.

☐ Styles of negotiating include win-lose, lose-lose, and win-win.

☐ Conflict resolution techniques include negotiation, avoidance, accommodation, smoothing over, compromise, competition, and integration.

☐ "Assertive behavior is a direct and honest communication of who you are and what you are."

☐ People express their feelings through assertive, nonassertive, or aggressive behaviors.

☐ A victim is a person who is denied the right to decide how to live his or her own life.

☐ Knowledge of assertive techniques allows a person to get out of a victimizing situation.

Key Terms

small talk
directions
requesting
asking
conflict
conflict situation
intrapersonal conflict
negotiation
hidden agenda
win-lose
lose-lose
win-win
avoidance
accommodation
smoothing over
compromise
competition

integration
assertive behavior
nonassertive behavior
aggressive behavior
victimizer
victim
self-victimization
simple assertion
empathic assertion
confronting assertion
descriptive speech
DESC scripting
broken record
fogging
negative assertion
self-disclosure

Learn by Doing

1. Select a place on your campus, and write directions from your classroom to that place. Your instructor then divides the class into pairs. One partner is to orally give the directions to the other partner without revealing the chosen destination. See if by following your directions, your partner can figure out the place you have selected. Then reverse roles.

2. Your instructor gives you a drawing of several geometric figures connected together. The class is then divided into pairs, with the partners seated back to back. One person receives the drawing; the other has a pencil and a blank piece of paper the same size as the one the drawing is on. The partner with the drawing describes the geometric configuration, and the other person draws it on the blank paper, attempting to produce an exact duplicate of the original. The first time this experiment is done, the person who is drawing may not ask any questions. After the completion of the drawing,

compare the original sketch to the new one. If they are not exact, discuss what could have been done to improve the directions; then perform the activity again. This time, if the instructor so indicates, the person doing the drawing may ask questions. After the completion of the drawing, discuss whether the questions aided in the process. If so, what implications does this experiment have for the process of giving directions?

3. Select an object. Write a description of the object without revealing its identity. Then read your description to your classmates. At the end of the entire description, they attempt to name the object. When everyone has read his or her description, discuss why the class members could or could not identify certain objects.

4. Make a list of five questions that someone who does not know you could ask so they could become better acquainted with you. Walk around the classroom, exchange questions, and go through the interview process based on the questions. If time is available, introduce someone in class based on the answers you received.

5. Before your next class session, ask three people questions based on a need for information or clarification. Write a short paper indicating the situation that gave rise to each question, what the question was, who was asked, and what response she or he gave. Conclude your paper by indicating what you learned from this exercise about the process of questioning.

6. Task 1. Do something you have wanted to do for yourself but for some reason have not. This is an assertive, selfish act. (Example: call a friend you have wanted to talk to for a while.) Record what you did and how you felt.

    Task 2. Do something you have wanted to do for someone else but for some reason have not. This is an assertive, selfless act. (Example: visit an ill relative.) Record what you did and how you felt.

    Task 3. Think of something that someone is doing that bothers you. Tell that person how you feel, remembering to be assertive, not aggressive. This is an assertive act. (Example: tell your roommate that you would appreciate his or her not borrowing your clothes without asking.) Record what you did and how you felt.

    Do this activity over a period of several days with the tasks done in the order given. When you are finished, share your experiences with the class. A discussion follows on what you learned about the process of assertiveness.

7. After you have read the section in the text on assertiveness, list a specific situation in which you should have been assertive but were not. Why did you not assert yourself? How could you have asserted

yourself? What do you think might have happened if you had asserted yourself? Use your answers as the basis for a discussion on assertiveness.

Notes

1. Kirmet Moore, "Creating Conversation," *American Way* (October 1983), 76–78.
2. Milt Grassell, "The Power of Questions," *Nation's Business* (November 1986), 56.
3. Barbara Powell, *Overcoming Shyness* (New York: McGraw-Hill, 1979), p. 92.
4. Moore, p. 75.
5. Malcolm Boyd, "How to REALLY Talk to Another Person," *Parade Magazine,* February 19, 1989, p. 14.
6. John Gibson, quoting from an Oxford University study, in "Will a Nod Get You Ahead in Conversations?" *Family Weekly,* June 19, 1983, p. 15.
7. For a further discussion of this topic, see Roy Berko, Fran Bostwick, and Maria Miller. *BASIC-ly Communicating: An Activity Approach,* 2nd ed. (Dubuque, Iowa: William C. Brown, 1983), pp. 169–176.
8. Ibid., p. 100.
9. Lawrence Rosenfeld, "Conflict's NOT a Four-Letter Word," unpublished workshop manual, 1982, p. 5, as adapted from Deborah Weider-Hatfield, "A Unit in Conflict Management Communication Skills," *Communication Education,* 30 (1981), 265–273.
10. Ibid., p. 4.
11. Ibid., p. 3.
12. Bill Zehme, "Negotiating," *Success,* 29 (October 1982), 48; based on an interview with Gerard Nieranberg.
13. Rosenfeld, p. 51.
14. R. Adler, L. Rosenfeld, and N. Towne, *Interplay,* 2nd ed. (New York: Holt, Rinehart and Winston, 1983), p. 283.
15. Ibid., p. 284.
16. Ibid.
17. John Diekman, "How to Develop Intimate Conversations," *New Woman,* 12 (November 1982), 71–72.
18. Judith Spencer, "Assertiveness Training Workshop," presentation delivered at a workshop, Lorain County Community College, Elyria, Ohio, November 14, 1978.
19. Powell, p. 94.
20. Ibid.
21. This discussion is based on shyness workshop materials prepared by Phyllis DeMark, Lorain County Community College, Elyria, Ohio, 1980.
22. As discussed by Susan Forward, media psychologist, Talk Radio, WERE—AM, Cleveland, Ohio.
23. Wayne Dyer, *Your Erroneous Zones* (New York: Avon Books, 1977), p. 215 (Funk and Wagnalls). Copyright © 1976 by Wayne W. Dyer. This passage and others reprinted by permission of Harper & Row, Publishers, Inc.

24. Ibid., p. 143.

25. Forward.

26. Dyer, p. 160.

27. DeMark.

28. Abigail Van Buren, "Pregnancies Bear Lively Record," *Elyria Chronicle-Telegram* (Ohio), December 27, 1982, p. A-7.

29. Jack Gibb, "Defensive Communication," *Journal of Communication*, 11 (September 1961), 143.

30. Sharon Bower and Gordon Bower, *Asserting Yourself* (Reading, Mass.: Addison-Wesley, 1976), p. 87.

31. Ibid., p. 106.

9 *The Interview*

Chapter Outline

Learning Outcomes

After reading this chapter, you should be able to:

Define what an interview is

Describe the significance of interviewing in personal and professional interactions

Explain the process of preparing for an interview

Demonstrate the organization for an interview

List and explain the different purposes for interviews and how those purposes affect what happens in the interview

State principles for functioning as an interviewee

State principles for functioning as an interviewer

Identify the types of interviews

List and explain the various parts of the format for an interview

Identify and illustrate the types of questions used in an interview

Explain how to prepare for an interview as the interviewee

Explain how to prepare for an interview as the interviewer.

The general techniques of interpersonal communication find specific application in the formal process of interviewing. An **interview** is a purposeful conversation between two or more persons that follows a basic question-and-answer format. Thus interviewing is more formal than most conversations because the participants share a preset and clear purpose and have a focused structure.

An interview is usually dyadic—that is, it is always centered on two persons—even if more than two persons are involved. This happens because the structure of an interview establishes an interviewer and an interviewee, although more than one person may assume either of these roles during the course of the conversation. For example, a person attempting to sell a computer program to a corporation may conduct an interview with the corporation's entire staff of technical specialists, who may all question the salesperson throughout the proceedings.

Although there are many types of interviews, the employment interview is one of the most prevalent. In fact, some people mistakenly believe that this is all there is to interviewing. There are, however, many other varieties. These include information-gathering interviews (for example, polling, reporting for a newspaper), persuasive interviews (selling door to door), problem-solving interviews (finding a solution to a corporate problem), counseling interviews (participating in psychotherapy sessions), appraisal interviews (evaluating the job performance of an employee), and interrogatory interviews (examining someone suspected of a crime).

Interviewing Roles

An interview involves two or more communicators who assume two fundamental communication roles: the interviewer and the interviewee. In some transactions, of course, the two people involved can reverse roles as the interview proceeds. In many types of interviews, however, the roles remain a bit more fixed: one person maintains the position of interviewer, and the other keeps the role of interviewee.

The Role of the Interviewer

The **interviewer** is responsible for the interview's arrangements. He or she usually establishes the time, the location, and even the purpose of the meeting. Quite often the interviewer also assumes responsibility for the **interview format,** determining some of the procedures that will be used to achieve its purpose. Some interviewers draw up a short checklist or outline of the points they want to cover. This practice can be useful as a memory aid, but it should not be slavishly adhered to. After all, a checklist should be a guide, not an inflexible format. Otherwise the interview will lose its spontaneity and flexibility.

One of the most common mistakes that interviewers have been found to make is that they tend to talk too much.[1] One of the most important functions of the interviewer is to listen. "The general rule is that the interviewee should do about 80% of the talking."[2]

Good interviewing is usually informal and allows the participants to adjust to each other. A good interviewer works at establishing a rapport with the interviewee by providing a climate of trust and support. Putting the interviewee at ease by listening thoughtfully and actively and by responding appropriately is a very important strategy. For this reason, the successful interviewer must be a sensitive communicator, one who is aware of the nonverbal cues of the interviewee and who can adapt to these responses. Careful preparation is also a key to success as an interviewer.

The Role of the Interviewee

The **interviewee** must also prepare carefully, primarily by analyzing the interviewer. What is his or her purpose? What organization does the interviewer represent? What will he or she expect? To provide answers to these and other questions, any potentially helpful background materials and supporting data should be gathered beforehand. Publications by or about the organization or the inteviewer are useful sources of information and can often be obtained from the organization, its employees, or the public library.

As an interviewee, one of the best ways for you to pull together the thoughts and materials you hope to present is to anticipate what you will be asked and think about how you can best respond with detailed answers. A good way to do this is to draw up an outline of possible questions. To illustrate this procedure, let us suppose you are preparing for an employment interview for a position as a computer programmer. In anticipating what you may be asked, you can construct the following outline:

I. Educational Background
   A. *What classes do you think have done the most for you as a programmer?*
      Definitely the assembly language course. I think it taught me the most and made me better as an all-around programmer. It is also the class in which I excelled, and because it is the most involved programming language, it gives me an advantage over other programmers. In addition, my systems project class provided me with an above-average understanding of the place and importance of each program within a given system.
   B. *What has the Computer Learning Center done for you as a programmer?*
      It has given me a more practical, businesslike approach than other entry-level programmers usually have because of its business-oriented atmosphere. And because it was a six-month accelerated learning course, it gave me a thorough introduction to the importance of meeting deadlines and working under pressure.
   C. *Why did you decide to return to college after attending the Computer Learning Center?*
      The center's preparation was focused on gaining entrance into the programming field, whereas I wanted to become the best possible programmer I could be. I went back to college to get a more in-depth and well-rounded approach to programming. That way I could get a job with a greater degree of upward mobility.
   D. *What other classes have you taken that you feel are relevant to programming, and why are they relevant?*
      I have taken many courses in accounting, economics, and psychology. These three disciplines have helped give me a more logical flow of thought and a better understanding of complex, diverse systems.
II. Past Experience
   A. *Give me an example of a past programming experience that has made you a better candidate for this job.*

> While I was in school, I often helped other students trouble-shoot their assembly programs by dump-reading. This made me a quicker, more efficient troubleshooter of my own programs and also helped me perform maintenance more easily on other programs.

The outline can, of course, go on at length, giving examples of non–computer-related experience that has made you a better candidate for the job. The interview will probably also contain questions about personality traits necessary for the job and the reasons for your enthusiasm about the programming field.

Prepare a document like this outline only to get ready for the interview. You want to have your potential responses well in mind, but you do not want to take the outline itself with you. Remember that you must be ready to adapt your responses to the interviewer's actual questions.

Above all, when you are in the interview, concentrate on being a good listener because this will enable you to adapt and respond appropriately. In fact, you must be as sensitive as the interviewer is to nonverbal as well as verbal clues. Listen with empathy by putting yourself in the role of the interviewer. Try to understand his or her position and why his or her questions are being raised as they are. If you can adapt in this way, the interview will be conducted effectively enough to accomplish its objectives.

Because all interviewing is communication, the parties engaged in the interview must remember that at all times they are communicators. As participants in a communication transaction, then, the distinct roles of the interviewer and interviewee can blend and even change as an interview continues. Just as a candidate for a position in an employment interview, for instance, must be the interviewee and respond to the questions asked by the interviewer, so, too, can the candidate shift roles and ask questions about such things as the position, the company, and the benefits, essentially becoming the interviewer at points in the process.

The Interview Format

Once the objectives of the interview are established, the interviewer should do some planning to organize the proceedings. The basic format of any interview, regardless of its purpose, should include an opening, a body, and a closing.

The Opening
of the Interview   The opening of the interview ought to focus on the establishment of a rapport between the two communicators. The interviewer should try to make the interviewee feel at ease and comfortable. One of the best ways

to do this is for the interviewer to do most of the talking at the outset. This technique serves two functions: it establishes the goal of the interview for both communicators, and it puts the interviewee at ease, giving her or him time to become comfortable with the situation and with the interviewer. In addition to putting the interviewee at ease, the opening discussion can establish the interviewer as a responsive, interested person, thus encouraging the interviewee to open up.

A journalist conducting an information-gathering interview, for example, began her fact-finding communication with a conversation about the Oscar-winning film *Dances with Wolves* that both parties had seen and enjoyed. The discussion of how Kevin Costner, star of the movie, had portrayed his character offered the interviewee the opportunity to feel comfortable communicating with the journalist before going into the substance of the interview itself.

The Body of the Interview

The body of the interview is the heart of the process because here the purpose of the interview is developed and explored. At this stage, the interviewer should attempt to get the interviewee to develop the topic under consideration. The basic purpose of the interview will determine the types of questions that will be asked and their sequence.

Types of Questions

A good interviewer uses a variety of questions: direct questions, open questions, closed questions, and bipolar questions. **Direct questions** are explicit and require specific replies. For example, the interviewer may ask, "Where did you last work?" or "How long have you worked in this field?" **Open questions** are less direct and specify only the topic: "What is your educational background?" or "How do you feel about this company?" **Closed questions** provide alternatives, narrowing the possibilities for response and probes for opinions that are on opposite ends of a continuum: "Do you think that knowledge of a product or communication skill is the most important asset of a salesperson?" An extreme form of a closed question is the **bipolar question,** which requires a yes or no response: "Would you like to work for this company?" or "Do you drink alcoholic beverages?"

If an interviewer hopes to foster openness and trust between the participants during the interview, he or she is unlikely to use leading, loaded, or yes-response questions. **Leading questions** strongly imply or encourage a specific answer: "You wouldn't say you favor gun-control legislation, would you?" This is a leading question because it implies that the interviewee should agree with the views of the interviewer. **Loaded questions,** a type of leading question, are designed to elicit a very emotional response. Some interviewers, in an attempt to observe how potential employees will work under pressure, purposely ask emotionally charged questions that bait the interviewee. Asking a job applicant who has been president of the union at a previous job to defend this company's policy of nonunion affiliation would, for example, be a stress-inducing loaded question. Another form of leading question is the **yes-response question,** which is stated in such a way that the respondent is encouraged to agree with the interviewer: "You would agree with me, wouldn't you, that this company's policies are fair?"

By using leading, loaded, and yes-response questions, an interviewer forces an interviewee into responding to queries that may in fact be traps. Ideally, these types of questions should not be used; some interviewers feel, however, that the only way to get responses that show the true personality and beliefs of the interviewee is to put him or her on the spot. For this reason, interviewees should be aware that questions can carry implications that go far beyond what is actually being asked and should consider this fact before they provide an answer. By the same token, interviewers should be aware that these kinds of questions are manipulative.

Two other types of questions—the mirror, or reflective, question and the probe—are used by interviewers to follow up on responses to initial questions. A **mirror,** or **reflective, question** is intended to get a person to expand on a response. For example, the interviewee may say, "I've worked for this corporation for years, and I'm getting nowhere." In this instance, the mirror question can be, "Do you feel you're not moving ahead in the corporation?" Such a response may encourage the interviewee to disclose more about her or his feelings.

The **probe** is used in interviews to gain a deeper, more detailed response. Some examples of probes are "I don't understand. Can you explain that further?" "Can you explain that in more detail?" "I'd like to know more about your thinking on that topic," and "Why do you feel that way?" These questions encourage the interviewee to discuss the point being made with more direction and depth. But for this technique to be effective, the interviewer must know when and how to use such probing questions. She or he must listen carefully and pay close attention to the feedback from the interviewee to know when a probe will result in a deeper response.

Sequence of Questions   Because the use of questions forms the core of the body of the interview, a good technique is to set up a checklist of questions in the categories you want to cover. A checklist for an employment interview may, for example, take the following form.

Employment Interview Format

Interviewer: Personnel director seeking to hire a civilian computer programmer to work on a military base.

Interviewee: Computer programmer applying for a programming position.

I. Open interview
    A. Specify details of position
        1. Duties
        2. Supervisor
        3. Workdays and hours
        4. Pay schedule
        (Transition to next topic)

II. Education
    A. Why did you choose computer science as your educational major?
    B. Which courses do you feel best prepared you for this position? Why?
    C. Did you ever dislike any particular course? Why?
    (Transition to next topic)

III. Experience
    A. Describe one problem of any type for which you devised a solution on your last job.
    B. If you were rushing to meet a deadline, how would you go about completing the assignment with quality work? Can you give a specific example of how you have dealt with such a situation in the past?
    C. What do you perceive to be the advantages and disadvantages of working for the military?
    D. Why do you want to be a junior systems analyst for the government?
    (Transition to next topic)

IV. Job-related outside activities
    A. Do you own a computer? If not, why? If so, tell me about the software you have written that you use most often.
    B. In which computer language or languages are you fluent? Which language do you like the most? Why?
    C. We are very concerned about the security of our computer facilities and programs. What specific computer security measures do you feel should be carried out to protect military information?

V. Communication skills
    A. On our main computer we have sixty gigabytes of random-access memory. How would this affect your job if you are hired?
    B. Our system has been "down" for twenty minutes and already users are asking you for an estimated "up" time, although you

do not yet know what the problem is, much less when it will be fixed. What do you tell the operations manager when she calls?

   C.   We cannot read the VTOC on any of a string of disk drives. The CE is stumped and strongly suggests that it may be a software problem. You are 100 percent sure that it is not a software, but rather a hardware, problem. If I am that CE, convince me that I am wrong and you are right.

   D.   If I were to offer you the following two jobs, which would you choose and why?

   1. One with a $50,000 salary and a job description and responsibility level with which you are not very happy.

   2. One with a $35,000 salary and a job description that fits the type of position you really want.

VI.   Conclude interview

   A.   Summarize briefly.

   B.   Ask for any questions.

   C.   Tell interviewee when he or she can expect to hear from you regarding the final hiring decision.

In drawing up the checklist of questions, the interviewer must first determine the categories that are needed. For example, in the job interview just presented, the interviewer selected four categories: educational background, experience, job-related outside activities, and communication skills. These categories and the questions within them should be set up to move from the more general (those that are easier to answer) to the more specific (those that are more difficult to answer). The interviewer should also set up the questions so that they move from finding facts to seeking attitudes. Notice how the preceding set of questions aims for general information in each area before probing for specifics. Note also that the questions probe for attitudes as well as facts. The interviewer should provide the interviewee with transitions between each category of questions so that he or she knows in what direction the interview is proceeding, can think along with the interviewer, and consequently can provide specific responses. For example, the interviewer can provide a transition by saying, "Now that we've covered your educational background, let's turn to your on-the-job experience."

Answers   Skillful questioning to accomplish the interview's purposes requires careful listening and adaptation by the interviewer; but a successful interview also requires the same characteristics in the interviewee. While the interviewer carries the burden of determining the sequence of questions, the interviewee has the responsibility for responding with accuracy, clarity, and specificity. Just as good public speakers support their points with meaningful data, so do good interviewees back up their statements with supporting material for clarification and evidence.

A trial attorney, for example, when interviewed about the role of listening in his work, detailed its importance in selecting the jury, drawing up the arguments for the brief, and adapting to the responses of witnesses. In addition, he offered statistics, examples, and quotations to illustrate the significance of listening to trial work.

The Closing of the Interview

The closing of an interview should be agreed on and understood by both communicators. It is frustrating to the interviewee, for example, if the interviewer ends the conversation before the interviewee can complete his or her thoughts. Instead, when the interview is nearing its end, the interviewer should give the other person an opportunity to make statements or ask questions. A good concluding question is "Are there any topics we haven't covered, or is there any additional information you'd like me to know before we end this interview?"

A good interview conclusion ought to summarize—to the satisfaction of both parties—what has been accomplished. Time should be spent forming a concise summary and, if appropriate, discussing the next step to be taken after the interview has ended. A real estate broker, for example, ended an interview with a potential buyer with the statement "I'm pleased that you're interested in buying this house. I'll write up the contract at the price you'd like to offer and with the special provision we've discussed. Do you have any further questions before I leave?"

Types of Interviews

The specific principles just discussed can be applied to many different types of interviews, not just the employment interview. Although not all these varieties may be relevant to you at this point in your academic and/or employment career, you may well be called on to participate in them later in your life. Sometimes we participate without even perceiving we are involved in an interview. For example, that persistent telemarketing person who interrupts dinner with a phone call is engaging you in a persuasive interview. Therefore an extensive discussion follows on a multitude of types of interviews.

The Employment Interview

The most crucial interview for many people early in their careers is the employment interview. It is both their way of entering the job market and their means for changing positions. The success of this interview will probably have as much, if not more, effect on whether a potential

Employment interviewing skills are important throughout one's career.

employee is hired than such factors as work experience, grade-point average, and personal recommendations.[3]

Effective communication skills are critical to projecting a positive image for initial employment in an organization and to advancing one's career later on in life. Often to gain promotions to upper-level positions in an organization, an employee has to participate in selection interviews. And, of course, a person must be able to function effectively in interviews to move to a position in a different organization at any point in the span of a career. Thus employment interviewing should be viewed not just as an entry-level skill for young workers but as a valuable tool for people at midlevel and senior-level positions as well. Because more and more people are likely to change jobs and entire careers during their work life, the use of these techniques has become important at all stages of a career. Indeed, promotions and salary increases may result from the use of effective on-the-job interviewing skills.

In an employment interview, the interviewer's purpose is to find out about the job applicant. At the same time, the interviewer attempts to sell the organization or the position. The interviewee must provide clear, complete information about her or his background and experience and at the same time convince the recruiter that she or he is the best applicant for the position.

To accomplish all these goals, both the interviewer and the interviewee have to prepare carefully.[4] The interviewee should provide a complete resume and letter of interest so that the recruiter has the necessary background information, and the recruiter should then thoroughly study the resume before the interview begins.

A resume and cover letter ought to be tailored to the specific company and the particular position for which you are applying. The resume is a vital part of your communication image and can often make the difference in whether you are even called in for an interview for the position. Although the resume requires written communication skills, it is a significant part of your preparation for the employment interview. Therefore some information on preparing the resume and a sample resume are presented in Appendix 1.

Preparing to Be Interviewed   Prepare for an employment interview by doing background research on the company so you can adapt to that company's particular needs. This background research can then provide the basis for answering questions in the interview. In this connection, one expert identified the questions that are most frequently asked in employment interviews, based on a survey of ninety-two companies.[5] These or similar questions can provide a helpful checklist as you are preparing for an employment interview.

According to the survey, the eight most commonly asked questions were

1. What are your future career plans?
2. In what school activities have you participated?
3. How do you spend your spare time?
4. In what type of position are you most interested?
5. Why do you think you may like to work for our company?
6. What jobs have you held?
7. What courses did you like best? What courses did you like least?
8. Why did you choose your particular field of work?

Prospective employees should also be aware of the importance of selecting appropriate clothing for an interview. Males most frequently wear a suit or jacket and tie, and females usually wear a dress or a suit, though the type of position for which one is applying dictates what is appropriate.

Remember, too, that employers are interested in your ability to communicate, your basic social skills, and your general personality as well as your talents and training. Be prepared to answer such questions as whether you would be willing to relocate, what salary you expect, and what specific type of job you are interested in. In general, it is also wise to keep in mind the following advice:[6]

■ Be pleasant and friendly but remain businesslike.

Prospective employees should be aware of the importance of selecting appropriate clothing for the interview.

- Be willing to tell the employer your job preferences as specifically as possible. Avoid comments like "I'll do anything" because they show a lack of clarity about your desires and skills.
- Stress your qualifications without exaggeration.
- When you discuss your previous jobs, avoid criticizing former employers and fellow workers.
- Be prepared to state what salary you want, but do not do so until the employer has introduced the subject.
- Be yourself. Few people can fake a role well. Even if you can, employers will hire you for what they see, and if you are not the kind of person you have pretended to be or cannot perform at that level, your employment will soon be terminated.
- Tell it straight. If you lie and get the job, you will have to do what you say you can do. If you cannot, you will lose the job.
- Ask questions when appropriate. For example, ask about what your initial duties and responsibilities will be, what kind of training you will receive, what the next step will be if you do well, and what the interviewer likes most about working for the company.
- Be enthusiastic; listen for ideas; maintain eye contact; be as natural as you can.

- If the employer does not definitely offer you a job or indicate when you will hear about it, ask when you may call to learn the decision.
- Thank the interviewer for granting you the interview.

Preparing to Interview

The interviewer also has particular responsibilities. For example, an interviewer should generally let the applicant do the talking. He or she should generally avoid questions that can be answered with a yes or a no, questions that are answered on the application form or resume, questions that are leading, questions that contain evaluative responses, questions that trick the applicant, or questions that may violate local, state, or national laws regarding fair employment practices.[7] A modification of this employment selection format is part of many admission processes for colleges and universities, for internships or assistantships, and for graduate programs.

Legal Restrictions on Interviewing

The employment interview is the first opportunity a person has to gain an impression of a particular organization. As a result, it is important that the interview be conducted smoothly and professionally. In addition to interviewing techniques, the legal implications of the entire selection process must be considered. In planning and carrying out an interview, the interviewer must know the legal guidelines to be followed. If this is not the case, or if the person being interviewed feels that he or she has not been dealt with fairly, then the company may be subject to legal action. A Midwestern utility company, for example, was recently judged by the courts to have placed too great a reliance on the subjective judgment of its interviewers. As a result, the firm was required to establish a structured means of conducting interviews and a clear rating system for evaluating job applications to make sure that all people were treated fairly.[8]

Because the legal issue has become so important, guidelines as to what questions can and cannot be asked in employment interviews have been established. Questions that can be asked include:

- How many years' experience do you have?
- (To a homemaker) Why do you want to return to work?
- What are your career goals?
- Who were your prior employers? Why did you leave your previous jobs?
- Are you a veteran? Did the military provide you with job-related experience?
- If you have no phone, where can we reach you?
- What languages do you speak?
- Do you have any objection if we check with your former employer for a reference?

Interviewers may not ask:

- What is your age?
- What is your date of birth?
- What is your race?
- What church do you attend?
- Are you married, divorced, separated, widowed, or single?
- Have you ever been arrested?
- What organizations or clubs do you belong to?
- What does your spouse do?
- Have your wages ever been attached or garnished?
- What was your maiden name?

Unfortunately, in spite of these guidelines, potential job applicants still sometimes report that they have been subjected to a barrage of inappropriate questions. If you have experienced this situation and feel you may have lost a position because of it, you have a right to make a formal complaint against the interviewer and the company. Be certain, however, that you can document the questions that were asked or the procedure that was followed.

Answering the Questions   If we assume that the interviewer is aware of the legal guidelines, the question becomes, "How should I answer the questions?" In reply, a specialist who trains interviewees offered the following recommendations:

Listen to the questions asked.
Avoid making assumptions if you do not understand the question.
Answer ambiguous questions to your best advantage.
Make use of pauses and silences to formulate your thoughts.
Establish a rapport with the interviewer.
Treat every question as an important one.[9]

The Information-Gathering Interview   In an **information-gathering interview,** the interviewer sets out to obtain information from a respondent. This type of interview is important to journalists, for instance, because they must interview other people for stories. An information-gathering interview is also used by a police officer investigating a break-in, a dental assistant getting information from a new patient, and a social worker seeking background information from a new client. Whatever the field, a general rule in conducting this sort of interview is to establish a rapport so the respondent will provide thorough, accurate information. For this reason, open questions are preferred.

In an information-gathering interview, the interviewer sets out to obtain information from a respondent.

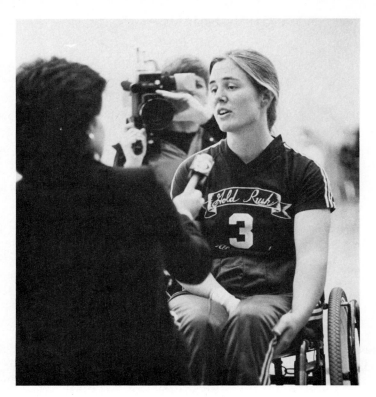

Of course, you may also find yourself in the role of the interviewee, giving information. This position can be a very important one, as, for instance, in the field of law enforcement. If you are a witness, say, to a traffic accident, you must be as thorough and as accurate as possible in providing officials with information. Thus your responses should reconstruct your perceptions of the accident as clearly and completely as possible. Be aware that you should give a factual account of what happened. If you are unable to give facts, make sure the interviewer is aware that you are transmitting an opinion. Remember that there is a vast difference between saying, "The driver turned left on the red light," and "I couldn't see the light clearly, but I think it was red when the driver turned left." Much courtroom testimony becomes of little or questionable value when what was purported to be fact becomes, under cross-examination, merely the interviewee's opinion.

Special Information-Gathering Interviews

The job-hunting guide *What Color Is Your Parachute?* recommends that persons who are seeking career changes begin their job search by interviewing potential employers to find out more about the work and career prospects in their chosen field. And the book recommends doing this before one begins any actual employment interviews. This strategy has been adopted by job seekers, many of whom have benefited from the opportunity to get to know more about the issues and organizations that are involved in particular careers.

If you are planning on conducting such an information-gathering interview, here are four basic questions that should get you started:

1. How did you get into this line of work?
2. What do you like best about it?
3. What do you like least about it?
4. Where else could I find people who share your enthusiasm or interest?[10]

Journalists are constantly involved in information-gathering interviewing, and their style centers on grouping questions by subject area in progression so that they will lead logically from one point to the next. In this way, the interviewees will not have to jump back and forth from one topic to another while they are responding.

Even if you are not a journalist, if you are ever in an information-gathering interview, you can use the journalist's standard formula of questions: who, what, where, when, why, and how? *Who* has to do with the person or persons involved in an event. Normally you would be interested in their names as well as in other basic information, such as their ages, addresses, physical descriptions, and so on. *What* asks for a description or explanation of the event. *Where* indicates the place the incident hapened. *When* provides such information as the date and time of the occurrence. *Why* is an explanation of the reason the event took place. And *how* centers on the exact details of what occurred.

Reporters and others who use information-gathering interviewing set up their interviews by using what one source described as "the open approach; they should ask appropriate questions in a friendly manner, and leave as quickly as possible unless invited to stay on by the interview subject. Above all, they should remember that they are there at the sufferance of the interviewee, and taking up valuable time."[11]

In dealing with difficult interviewees, another source advised that "certain people can be highly evasive, hard to pin down. . . . You just have to persevere and keep after them. 'I understand what you're saying, but you haven't answered my question.' You've got to try to control the interview without alienating the interviewee so he'll cut off the interview."[12] Sometimes, of course, alienating the interviewee is inevitable. If he or she has something to hide, or if the information could be used in legal action, then it will probably be impossible to find out exactly what you want.

The respondent in an information-gathering interview clearly has a good deal at stake. A research survey or a journalistic interview may be designed to ask for more information than you want to reveal. Or you may want to avoid being misinterpreted or misquoted when the information is incorporated into an article or a study. For these reasons, listen carefully to each question, and consider thoroughly the ramifications of your response. Do not allow yourself to be pressured into an answer you may regret later, and remember that you always have the right not to answer at all. Nevertheless, be aware that information-gathering interviewers usually assume you are willing to talk, or you would not have agreed to the interview in the first place.

Another interesting application of the information-gathering interview is known as the collecting of an oral history. The oral history technique is to interview a source who has some knowledge of a historical nature for the purpose of recording it. Just as it is an important strategy for the professional historian and anthropologist, amateur family historians have found that audio- or video-taping an interview of an aging relative can be a valuable way of preserving family heritage and traditions.[13] It is proving to be a highly popular format in many families who want to preserve some record of their backgrounds and pass them on to future generations.

The Problem-Solving Interview

In a **problem-solving interview,** the interviewer and the interviewee meet to solve a mutual problem. Suppose, for example, that you are a poultry specialist for a large feed-manufacturing company and your role is to help farmers solve problems with their poultry. Because of this, you must structure your interviews so that the people you talk to will detail all the symptoms of their problems; then, much like a physician, you can make a proper diagnosis.

Problem-solving interviews are very common in business and industry. If a company has a slump in new-car sales, for instance, it would be good strategy for the marketing division to conduct interviews with sales personnel to determine why sales of new cars are down, and, further, what can be done to recover the business that has been lost.

It is a good idea in a problem-solving interview to structure the questions in the body of the interview so that the dimensions of the problem—its causes and effects—are discussed before specific solutions are addressed. In the previous example, the interviewers may want to focus on the specific details of the slump in auto sales, but if the full implications of the problems are not covered first, then a meaningful solution may never be derived.

Indeed, the greatest drawback to the effective use of the problem-solving format is people's tendency to deliberate about solutions before they have a very clear understanding of the problem. For this reason, it is crucial for both the interviewer and the interviewee to come to terms with the general aspects of a particular issue and to have a thorough understanding of it before systematically discussing potential solutions.

An effective problem-solving format relies on extensive give-and-take in which the interviewer and the interviewee shift roles and pursue a thorough discussion about the matters under consideration. Probing questions can be used to establish an in-depth analysis of the problem, and the funnel schedule (going from the general ramifications of a problem to more specific discussions and solutions) can also be applied.

Managers in organizations frequently use problem-solving interviews to deal with structural problems and problems with specific employees. In this context, both parties are encouraged to identify their "stake" in the problem so as to develop a plan that will be acceptable to both. "The problem solving style is characterized by questions and descriptive language. . . . Questions are used to seek information, probe feelings and discover other points of view. . . . The language is non-judgmental . . . and the amount of time spent talking and listening is equally balanced between the two people."[14]

The Counseling Interview

Closely related to the problem-solving interview is the **counseling interview,** which is designed to provide guidance and support to the interviewee. It is used by professional psychologists, school counselors, and therapists, among others. In the most therapeutic type of counseling interview, the interviewer serves as a sounding board and listens with empathy, while the interviewee talks through a problem.

Managers in organizations have been urged to develop skills in counseling techniques to improve communication with their employees. In this way, observed one source, "counseling can provide a service to both the organization and to individuals within it who have particular problems. Counseling can provide a release for the frustrations that are an inevitable part of human interaction in an organization."[15]

The format for a counseling interview may be like that used in an information-gathering situation. Suppose, for example, that a friend of yours is having difficulty in school and is in danger of flunking out. In discussing the problem, you serve as a therapeutic listener, letting your friend talk through the problem until he finally decides to reach a solution to his problem, such as to drop out of school, stop missing classes, or quit his job to have time to study.

One approach to the counseling interview centers on the concept that it should not include an evaluation by the interviewer. With this approach you would not say to your friend, "Have you considered that your study habits may be the cause of your problem?" Instead, nonpro-

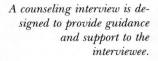

A counseling interview is de-signed to provide guidance and support to the interviewee.

fessional therapeutic interviewers often allow the interviewees to talk until they get to the heart of their difficulties by themselves. Such a strategy can be valuable in reinforcing a positive self-image, helping people see their own problems, and giving them a firm foundation for a commitment to solve them. But such **nondirective techniques,** not taking an active role in recommending a solution, can work only if both communicators accept the problems and deal with them appropriately.

The nondirective approach requires skill on the part of the interviewer. Essentially, only three forms of response are appropriate: nonverbal encouragement to continue, such as a nod of the head; verbalized hmms; and repetition of the interviewee's point as a question ("You feel you don't have the time to study?"). These responses, designed to keep the interviewee talking, must be used very subtly, or the tactic will fail to be of much use.

Professional therapists recognize that "the base of any therapeutic interaction is the interview," that "the therapeutic process requires effective communication."[16] Furthermore, counselors who conduct therapeutic interviews note that these interviews go through a definite series of stages. During these stages, the expectations and objectives of the counseling are spelled out by both the interviewer and the interviewee;

there is an emotional release during which the interviewee elaborates on his or her perceptions of the problem; the problem is explored, and, ideally, all its ramifications are probed; the interviewee is reassured or consoled; there is a confrontation in which the interviewee's contradictions, or "blind spots," are examined; further probing for more information takes place to gain a better perspective about the problem; the interviewee's options are discussed; and finally there comes a time when the interviewee's feeling or behavior may be changed or when the interviewer may wish to refer the person for another type of counseling.[17]

For nondirective techniques to succeed, the interviewee must be willing to self-disclose. In nondirective counseling, emphasis is placed not on what the interviewer would do to solve the problem but on what the client feels she or he should do.[18]

Another approach to the professional counseling session is directive intervention. It has become apparent to some counselors and psychotherapists that allowing unlimited talk by a patient who is not capable of solving his or her own problems in the first place only wastes time and leads to even more problems. Thus **directive intervention** entails the counselor taking a stand that there should be active probing; that homework should be given to the client (specific activities to carry on outside of the counseling session, such as writing a letter to or directly confronting a person who has abused the client); that there should be role playing and activities during counseling (such as the letting out of emotions by envisioning that the person victimizing the client is sitting in a chair, so the client can tell the person exactly how he or she feels); and that therapeutic hypnosis should be used in some cases to deal with certain types of problems.[19]

An effective psychotherapist or counselor fits the nature of the counseling approach to the client and the nature of his or her perceived problem.

The Persuasive Interview	Careful establishment of rapport through empathy can lead to success in a **persuasive interview,** the purpose of which is to change a person's beliefs or behavior. In most persuasive interviews, the interviewee is doing the persuading, which makes the process more difficult for him or her. In this kind of situation, the interviewer still handles most of the questions, but the interviewee must provide persuasive responses. For example, the director of a volunteer organization may conduct individual interviews with volunteers to persuade them to undertake a new fund-raising campaign. Although the volunteer assumes the role of the interviewer and asks questions about the new campaign, the director must attempt to persuade the volunteer to join the campaign, convincing her or him that it is worth the time and energy required.

The selection and organization of persuasive points depend on the initial position of the interviewer. If he or she agrees with the beliefs or purpose of the interviewee, then the interviewee's task is to reinforce the agreement. For instance, if a woman comes to a salesperson already convinced that she needs a new television set, then that salesperson does not have to persuade her that she should buy a new set. Instead, the salesperson can concentrate on showing her the sets that are available.

If, however, the interviewee disagrees with the interviewer's beliefs or purpose, then the interviewer should find some points of agreement and try to build on these to lead the interviewee into the areas of controversy. In this way, the interviewer can build a solid enough argument to secure the interviewee's acceptance of other points. For example, a management consultant may have to begin with praise and recognition for some aspect of a company's management program before attempting to persuade its executives that their organization needs to develop better internal communication.

The uncertain or neutral interviewee may require more background information before persuasive appeals can be introduced. If, for example, a voter does not know anything about your candidate for mayor, you will have to provide that person with some background information on the candidate before giving any reasons to vote for her or him.

A persuasive interview should maintain an informal conversational style so that the interviewee is free to raise questions and respond to the interviewer's message. In addition, the interviewee should apply the principles of critical listening, being alert to biased questions or to leading questions that may condition a certain response.

The Sales Interview

Organizations recognize the tremendous value of the persuasive interview as a sales technique. "In contrast to advertising," wrote one expert, "personal selling establishes a two-way communication between the salesperson and buyer which allows the sales message to be adapted to the special circumstances of the customer."[20]

The format for a good sales interview provides an excellent illustration of the structure of the persuasive interview. It begins by the salesperson establishing rapport, arousing interest, and getting the customer involved; then the salesperson explores the customer's needs through probing, careful listening, and observing so that the product and the presentation can be linked to these needs. The next step is to present the product or service and illustrate how it will meet the customer's needs. This is followed by an acknowledgment of the potential buyer's objections in which the salesperson probes and answers them. Finally, at the closing of the sale, the salesperson reiterates the reasons to decide favorably, asks for a commitment, and paves the way for future business.[21]

An attempt to sell goods or services is an example of a persuasive interview.

Just as the persuasive interviewer must be well organized and able to adapt to the needs of the interviewee, so, too, must the interviewee be carefully prepared to participate. Indeed, it is crucial that the interviewee actively participate in the process, critically analyzing the sales approach and appeals, particularly when a great deal of time and money is at stake.

A prominent type of sales interview that is increasingly used by businesses is the telemarketing sales. A person, or even a computer, employed by the company is given telephone lists and a sales script and is assigned to complete a specified number of calls within a certain time frame. Many of these telemarketing efforts are of the "tell and sell" model, offering little, if any, time for questions. A useful strategy for the receiver of unwanted telephone sales pitches is to firmly but politely interrupt the speaker as soon as the receiver determines that she or he is not interested in the product or service being sold and then hang up. Thus neither the receiver's nor the caller's time is wasted.

An understanding of just what the interviewer is attempting to do to get you to buy a product or an idea can be strong ammunition for dealing with any sales approach. Asking questions, reading any literature that may be available, and going to several different suppliers to compare opposing points of view should prepare you to handle hard-sell techniques.

If the sales pitch is legitimate and the product or proposal is going to meet your needs, then your acceptance of it may well be in order. But remember that many salespersons are trained to close a sale so as to make a commission or reach a quota; thus they have very strong motivations to do whatever they can to disarm you during the negotiation.

The Appraisal Interview

In an **appraisal interview,** the interviewer helps the interviewee to realize the strengths and weaknesses of his or her performance. But to do this, the interviewer must realize her or his own strengths and weaknesses. Furthermore, to be constructive, the interviewer first should build on the interviewee's strengths before moving into areas where improvement is sought.

Appraisal interviews are used often in the education field; in fact, you may have participated in one with your instructor in this course. Supervisors frequently use appraisal interviews. Indeed, federal agencies are required by law to provide every employee with the opportunity to have regular appraisals of his or her performance.

Unfortunately, appraisal interviews may be misunderstood and abused, and sometimes they are used only to create negative criticism instead of to provide positive reinforcement. But when handled well, an appraisal interview can present methods to be used for change while reinforcing positive aspects of a person's performance. In communication classes, for example, the strengths of a student's performance should be emphasized before suggestions are offered for improving it.

The performance appraisal system has become very much a part of the American workplace. Employees in government, education, industry, business, and service jobs throughout the nation are consistently being rated on their performance, and experts have estimated that "over 90 percent of companies and . . . nearly 80 percent of all governmental units have formal systems of personnel assessment."[22]

One management specialist has identified twelve points that characterize effective performance appraisal interviews. These goals should be sought by all good appraisal interviewers.

1. Identify the positive behavior your employees should strive for.
2. Identify the criteria by which you will evaluate their performance.
3. Maintain a balance between positive and negative in the performance assessment.
4. Do not overemphasize differences between ideal and actual job performance.
5. Bring up performance concerns as needed, not just at the scheduled periodic review time.
6. Distinguish between an employee who *will not* work and an employee who *cannot* work.

7. Separate the performance discussion and the salary discussion of the review for counseling purposes.
8. Avoid becoming defensive.
9. Encourage employees to participate in the development of a good performance appraisal system.
10. Keep performance appraisals open, honest, and informal.
11. Develop effective communication channels within the organization so that performance appraisals will be part of an open system of communication.
12. Give employees full, factual, and complete information.[23]

Effective performance appraisals should be thorough two-way communications about the person's work. Neither the supervisor nor the subordinate should dominate the proceedings, but both ought to view the process as a careful analysis and, if necessary, a problem-solving session. This, of course, is very difficult to carry out in practice, simply because of the nature of the boss-employee, supervisor-worker power relationship. Nevertheless, in organizations in which the boss or supervisor has built trust by dealing honestly with his or her employees, there is a better chance for true participatory evaluation. This usually takes place when the person in the position of power indicates what is and what is not negotiable, encourages openness regarding questions of authority and does so without repercussions, and does not feel that she or he is the only one with the ability to think of solutions to problems. Unfortunately, this type of leader is usually quite rare.

Just as it requires skill to present constructive criticism in a performance appraisal, so, too, does it take ability to receive criticism. Unfortunately, criticism can engender a great deal of defensiveness because we all tend to be ego centered. We feel a need to be right, and even when we recognize we are wrong, we tend to defend our actions. It is recommended that in performance appraisals the receiver:

1. Listen carefully to the criticism.
2. Paraphrase the criticism.
3. Ask for specifics.
4. Monitor nonverbal behavior and be aware of the physical signs that indicate upset—hand twisting, teeth grinding, face flushing, wiggling in one's seat or shifting from foot to foot if the person is standing, or feeling sudden tightness in the back of the neck or in the temples.
5. Respond by agreeing to take the steps necessary to change the situation, or if one feels the criticism is not legitimate or beneficial, refuse to take the recommended actions and indicate why.[24]

Remember, however, if you refuse to accept the recommendations or accept the input you may well be punished for that action—be fired, be denied a promotion, be put on a warning for insubordination. Therefore if you chose to take such an action, be sure that you are willing to accept the consequences of your action. This is not to say that you should not act; rather, act with the foregone knowledge of the consequences.

Much of the research on performance appraisal methods deals with the manager in the workplace. It should be clear, however, that the same principles apply to a teacher who is trying to improve a student's performance, a parent who wishes to change or improve a child's behavior, an athletic coach who wishes to motivate a player, or a director trying to get a different characterization from an actor.

The point of performance appraisal in any field is to develop improved performance. But this improvement can result only if a specific plan is established in the interview. For this reason, the performance appraisal interview should conclude with a specific plan in which both parties jointly explore several possible actions; concentrate on one or two specific actions; specify who those actions will happen to, what will happen, and when; provide for follow-up on the work; and set out in writing the plan to be followed.[25]

The Correcting, or Reprimanding, Interview

In a **correcting,** or **reprimanding, interview,** the interviewer helps the interviewee to analyze problems caused by the interviewee so that corrections can be made. Thus the reprimanding interview begins with identification of a problem that must be corrected. Usually the reprimand follows the appraisal interview, so that an employee has had an opportunity to try correcting the situation.

Ideally, the interviewee should suggest a desirable solution to the problem. In fact, some employers like to build counseling techniques into the reprimand, beginning with identification of the problem and then leading to the employee's own disclosure of why the problem persists and how she or he can resolve the difficulty. Suppose, for example, a lab technician continually fails to replace equipment after using it, a practice that causes other technicians to complain to the employer. Through an interview, the employer tries to get the technician to understand the problem, suggests the necessity for correcting the behavior in the future, and encourages the employee to propose an acceptable procedure for behavior alteration.

The National Labor Relations Board and the U.S. Supreme Court have ruled that an employee has the right to have third-party representation in the form of a witness, an attorney, or some other person present at any disciplinary interview.[26] From this provision, it should be clear that the reprimanding interview is one of the most difficult to conduct because the interviewer must carry the burden of establishing the grounds for the disciplinary action. Usually the reprimand is necessary only if performance violations have continued for some time after initial attempts at problem solving or counseling took place. Thus supervisors are encouraged to develop a reprimanding interview format based on the following questions that an employee would want answered:

1. What did I do wrong?
2. Why was it wrong?
3. What is the penalty?
4. Is the penalty fair?
5. What will happen if I do it again?
6. What can I do to improve my performance or behavior?[27]

The reprimanding interview, whether it is used by managers with workers, by parents with children, or by teachers with students, ought to be considered the procedure of last resort. Only when all else has failed should drastic steps be taken. The risk involved in the reprimanding interview is great because the procedures can create considerable defensiveness on the part of the interviewee unless the process is handled skillfully.

To be careful communicators in these situations, interviewers should avoid accusatory statements and use phrases such as "I feel" instead of "you are." Interviewers should ask questions that permit the person to express feelings or explain behavior, should stay away from verbalizing conclusions during the interview, and should conclude the interview on a neutral level.[28] Because the interviewer can be held legally liable for any type of punishment that is given, she or he must use factual evidence in making any final decision. The evidence should also be available for any legal action that may follow.

The Interrogation, or Stress, Interview

An **interrogation,** or **stress, interview** is designed to secure information from the interviewee through extensive use of probing techniques. Lawyers, credit officers, tax specialists, and law enforcement officers all frequently use such interviews. Because of the circumstances, the interviewer is sometimes dealing with an interviewee who is reluctant to respond to questions. Consequently, through the phrasing of questions and the manner in which they are verbally and nonverbally presented, the interviewer uses psychological pressure to elicit responses.

Law Enforcement Interrogation

Law enforcement officers are often trained in interrogation interviewing, a format that is designed to scrutinize the interviewee and, in the case of arrests, to secure a confession to a crime. As a result, the interviewer works to create a climate of stress during the interview so as to pressure the interviewee to admit his or her wrongdoing.

Investigators who must use this interview format are advised to maintain personal control throughout the interrogation. "Remember," wrote one expert, "whatever your personal feelings may be toward the person you are questioning, keep them to yourself. Do not shout and do not scream. Keep yourself even-tempered at all times."[29] There are situations in which strong emotion may be needed to extract the necessary information, but it should be used only as a last resort. Because human beings are emotional animals, what is good as theory may not translate into realistic practice.

Because the interviewee in a police investigation is likely to be quite hostile, the questioning strategy becomes very important. A good interrogator works to break through that hostility and get the information she or he needs to complete the case. The interrogator begins this process by informing the suspect of his or her rights. The U.S. Supreme Court's far-reaching *Miranda* decision requires that police officers inform suspects that they have the right to remain silent, that anything they say may be used as evidence against them, and that they have a right to have an attorney present at the interrogation.

> An interrogator must establish credibility and take control of the situation. By employing different types of questions . . . the officer constructs a picture of the incident depicted by the suspect. Lies are difficult to maintain. By noticing contradictions or improbable statements an interrogator can undermine the suspect's story, which weakens resistance, self-confidence, and makes compliance with the investigator's demands easier.[30]

Obviously, the less practiced a person is in resisting an interrogator's techniques, the less ability will he or she have to lie effectively, and the more likely it is that the interrogator will be successful.

Job Application Interrogation The interrogation interview is sometimes used to screen job applicants. In the most common technique, a potential employee is put into a stressful situation so that those who are conducting the interview can observe how he or she reacts under pressure. This may be an important consideration if the interviewee will have to perform under stressful conditions on the job, but it is a highly controversial strategy for merely "checking out" a potential employee. Many people perceive this to be an unfair test of an applicant, and some applicants are resentful of such an approach.

Legal Interrogation Interrogation in court is a firmly established practice. If you are ever involved in this kind of interrogation, remember that you are responsible for answering only questions for which you have factual answers. Some trial lawyers attempt to trap a witness by asking questions that elicit information outside his or her factual knowledge. For this reason, witnesses should be on guard so they do not place themselves in the position of having answered questions on the basis of opinion rather than proof.

A professor once appeared as a character witness for a former student who was on trial for possession of drugs. The prosecutor asked, "Do you think that the defendant has ever used marijuana?" He also asked, "Would you say that there is a drug problem at the school the defendant attended?" In both questions the prosecutor was asking for information beyond the factual knowledge of the witness. The answers given were, respectively, "I have no way of knowing whether the defendant has used marijuana," and "I don't know what you mean by 'drug problem,' and if I did, I would have no way of knowing whether the school has such a problem." The professor was not trying to be evasive or hostile, but the questions were posed for the purpose of leading the witness to conclusions that the prosecutor could then use to influence the jury. The courtroom interviewee must always be on guard to answer only those questions for which he or she has accurate, factual information.

Interviewing in its many forms is a major communication function in personal and in professional settings. Skill in effective interviewing enables speakers and listeners to readily adapt to the demands of the particular formal and information-interview setting and to respond appropriately to those demands.

Summary

This chapter discussed the interview. Key points made in the chapter were:

- [ ] An interview is a purposeful conversation between two or more people that follows a basic question-and-answer format.
- [ ] An interview is always described as dyadic.
- [ ] An interviewer is responsible for the interview's arrangements and format.
- [ ] The interviewee is the person who has been granted the interview.
- [ ] The interview format includes an opening, a body, and a closing.
- [ ] The types of questions usually asked during interviews are direct questions, open questions, closed questions, and bipolar questions. Other types of questions that may be used are leading questions, loaded questions, yes-response questions, mirror questions, and probing questions.
- [ ] An employment interview is used to enter the job market or change positions.
- [ ] A resume is a document that emphasizes a person's background skills and training.
- [ ] There are legal restrictions that relate to employment interviews.
- [ ] The purpose of an information-gathering interview is to obtain information from a respondent.

☐ Much of the information-gathering process centers on receiving the who, what, where, when, why, and how of a particular occurrence.

☐ The participants in a problem-solving interview attempt to solve a mutual problem.

☐ A counseling interview is designed to provide guidance and support to the interviewee.

☐ The purpose of a persuasive interview is to change beliefs or behavior.

☐ The sales interview is a persuasive interview.

☐ An appraisal interview is intended to help the interviewee to realize the strengths and weaknesses of his or her performance.

☐ The correcting, or reprimanding, interview helps the interviewee to analyze problems she or he has caused so that corrections can be made.

☐ The interrogation, or stress, interview is designed to secure information from the interviewee through the extensive use of probing techniques.

Key Terms

interview
interviewer
interview format
interviewee
direct questions
open questions
closed questions
bipolar question
leading questions
loaded questions
yes-response question
mirror, or reflective, question

probe
information-gathering interview
problem-solving interview
counseling interview
nondirective techniques
directive intervention
persuasive interview
appraisal interview
correcting, or reprimanding,
 interview
interrogation, or stress, interview

Learn by Doing

1. Make an appointment with a person who is or has been engaged in your present career choice. Interview the person to determine what courses she or he took to qualify for the job, what specific skills are required for success in the career, what the specific job responsibilities are, and what helpful hints that person can give you about being successful in the field. Report to the class on not only the results of the interview but also on what you learned about the interviewing process.

2. You are paired with another student according to your academic major. Each student is to independently research job descriptions within the field; employment opportunities; communication skills, special talents, and abilities that are needed; the types of organizations employing people trained in the field; working conditions; and salary. You are given several weeks to complete your research. You and your partner then conduct a seven- to ten-minute information-gathering interview concerning the selected career during one of your class periods. One of you acts as the interviewee and the other as the interviewer. Before you do so, develop an interview agenda and questions.

3. Two students are assigned to read the same book, short story, or magazine article. In class, one of the students interviews the other concerning what she or he has read.

4. Write down the five most important items that you want an interviewer to know about you, and write a sentence about how you plan to convey each of these items. The class is then divided into groups of three, with each group having an interviewee, an interviewer, and an observer. After a ten-minute interview, the observer states what he or she believes the applicant has communicated. The interviewee shares her or his list of five items, and the entire group discusses how the interviewee might have communicated any items that he or she failed to get across. Then change roles and repeat the process until all three members of the group have had a chance to be interviewed.

5. You are paired with another student. You are to select a subject of mutual interest and ask each other a series of questions about the topic. You should first ask each other a direct question, then an open question, then a closed question. Repeat the procedure three times so as to practice the types of questions. Continue the interview by asking a leading question, a loaded question, and a yes-response question. Follow up with a mirror question and a probe.

6. Prepare a resume for yourself, following the format given in Appendix 1.

7. Select an ad from the newspaper for a job that you would be interested in applying for at the present time. It should be one for which you are qualified. Use the advice given in this chapter on how to prepare to be interviewed and write a paper describing with specific examples what you would do to get ready for the interview.

8. Select one of the types of interviews, other than the employment interview, in which you have participated, and be prepared to discuss what happened and whether you felt it was a successful interview. Back up your statements with specific examples.

9. Your instructor assigns sets of two people in your class various segments of Richard Bolles, *What Color Is Your Parachute?* to read. Each pair conducts an information-gathering interview about the segment read. These interviews may be done before the entire class, outside of class, or simultaneously while the class is in session. If either of the latter is done, each team is asked to share observations in a class discussion after the interviews are completed.

Notes

1. Alon Gratch, "The Interview: Who Should be Talking to Whom?" *Wall Street Journal,* February 29, 1988, p. A8.
2. Ibid.
3. Carol Peffley, unpublished survey, Indiana State University, Bloomington, Indiana, 1974.
4. For a review of the communication research on the employment interview, see Donna Bogar Goodall and H. Lloyd Goodall, Jr., "The Employment Interview: A Selective Review of the Literature with Implications for Communications Research," *Communication Quarterly,* 30 (Spring 1982), 116–122.
5. Frank S. Endicott, *Making the Most of Your Job Interview* (New York: New York Life Insurance Company, n.d.).
6. U.S. Department of Labor, Employment and Training Administration, *Merchandising Your Job Talents* (Washington, D.C.: GPO, 1976), pp. 7–8.
7. Charles J. Stewart, *Teaching Interviewing for Career Preparation* (Urbana, Ill.: ERIC Clearinghouse on Reading and Communication Skills, 1976), p. 8.
8. "Keeping Bias Out of Job Interviews," *Association Management,* 29 (August 1977), 89.
9. Anthony Medley, *Sweaty Palms: The Neglected Art of Being Interviewed* (Belmont, Calif.: Lifetime Learning Publications, 1978). Excerpted in "Spring Job Market 81," *Washington Post,* May 3, 1981, pp. 11, 16.
10. Richard N. Bolles, *What Color Is Your Parachute?* (Berkeley, Calif.: Ten Speed Press, 1988), p. 144.
11. Ronald P. Lovell, *The Newspaper* (Belmont, Calif.: Wadsworth, 1980), p. 229.
12. Ibid.
13. See, for instance, William Fletcher, *Recording Your Family History: A Guide to Preserving Oral History with Video Tape and Audio Tape* (New York: Dodd, Mead, 1987).
14. Sandra O'Connell, *The Manager as Communicator* (New York: Harper & Row, 1979), p. 21.
15. Norman C. Hill, *Counseling at the Workplace* (New York: McGraw-Hill, 1981), p. 10.
16. Golda M. Edinburg, Norman E. Zinberg, and Wendy Kelman, *Clinical Interviewing and Counseling: Principles and Techniques* (New York: Appleton-Century-Crofts, 1975), pp. 1, 5.
17. Michael E. Stano and N. L. Reinsch, Jr., *Communication in Interviews* (Englewood Cliffs, N.J.: Prentice-Hall, 1982), pp. 262–267.
18. Lawrence M. Brammer. *The Helping Relationship* (Englewood Cliffs, N.J.: Prentice-Hall, 1973), p. vii.

19. A psychological theory as expressed on several broadcasts by Susan Forward, media psychologist, Talk Radio, WERE—AM, Cleveland, Ohio.

20. Douglas J. Dalyrymple, *Sales Management: Concepts and Cases* (New York: Wiley, 1982), p. 9.

21. These strategies are spelled out in detail in V. R. Buzzotta, R. E. Lefton, and Manuel Sherberg, *Effective Selling Through Psychology* (Cambridge, Mass.: Bellinger, 1982), Chapter 5.

22. Michael E. Stano and N. L. Reinsch, Jr., *Communication in Interviews* (Englewood Cliffs, N.J.: Prentice-Hall, 1982), p. 99.

23. Paul Preston, *Communication for Managers* (Englewood Cliffs, N.J.: Prentice-Hall, 1979), p. 254.

24. This list is based in part on Joan Linder, "Accepting Criticism Gracefully," *The Secretary* (May 1990), 29.

25. Walter R. Mahler, *How Effective Executives Interview* (Homewood, Ill.: Dow Jones—Irwin, 1976), p. 118.

26. Joseph P. Zima, *Effective Interviewing* (Palo Alto, Calif.: SRA, 1983), p. 281.

27. Ibid., p. 284.

28. Charles J. Stewart and William B. Cash, Jr., *Interviewing Principles and Practices* (Dubuque, Iowa: William C. Brown, 1982), pp. 231–232.

29. Harold Mulbar, *Interrogation* (Springfield, Ill.: Charles C Thomas, 1951), p. 23.

30. T. Richard Cheatham and Keith V. Erickson, *The Police Officer's Guide to Better Communication* (Glenview, Ill.: Scott, Foresman, 1984), p. 37.

10 Small-Group Communication

Chapter Outline

Learning Outcomes

After reading this chapter, you should be able to:

Define small-group communication

Explain the purpose of decision making in the group

Compare and contrast closed, informal, and public discussions

Describe the role of the group in family communication

Explain the task and maintenance functions of a group

Reveal the role of listening in group communication

List and explain the responsibilities of group members

Compare and contrast the role of leader and leadership

Be able to describe at least two techniques for group problem solving.

*T*he **small group** is a form of communication that usually involves three or more persons (ideally five people and generally not more than twelve) who are brought together for some common purpose or goal. Much of our communication occurs within small groups.

At work, we may be called on to participate in conferences, to join our colleagues for lunch, and to meet with out-of-town clients. Some research suggests that managers spend as many as seven hundred hours a year in meetings; this phenomenal figure accounts for two or three working days a week devoted to meetings![1]

Because meetings are recognized as such an important part of business, the 3M Corporation has developed a Meeting Management Institute to help units of 3M and other interested organizations conduct meetings more effectively. The institute has identified six "secrets" for effective meetings:[2]

1. *The right reasons*—a meeting should be called only when it is necessary and has a clear objective.
2. *The right participants*—participants should be truly involved in and prepared to discuss the issues on the agenda.
3. *The right room*—a setting that facilitates good communication is important.
4. *The right equipment*—if visual material is going to be used, the equipment that supports the visuals should be included.
5. *The right visuals*—the use of the visual channel can facilitate retention of the information, so such devices as overheads, flip charts, and slides should be used when necessary to clarify and reinforce ideas.

6. *The right skills*—meeting leaders must have the communication strategies that allow them to conduct effective sessions, and the participants require the skills to be active and meaningful participants.

At home, we function within family and social groups while dining, while spending an evening with friends, and even while completing household chores. Communication specialists have come to recognize the importance of viewing the family as a group and working out communication patterns within the group for healthy family dynamics.[3]

The health care profession provides evidence of the importance of effective communication in occupational groups. Hospital personnel, for instance, must make up an effective team, and the key to effective teamwork is good communication. Researchers studied the teamwork in intensive-care units in major hospitals and concluded that "whether patients survive in the intensive care unit depends less on the amount of high-tech equipment available than on effective coordination between doctors and nurses."[4]

An effective transaction with other people on a one-to-one basis within a small group requires systematic analysis and adaptation to other communicators at all times. You can even view your communication within the group as a series of short interviews within a more complex interaction. Thus the adaptation, organization, and development of your remarks should be as thorough as your communication in an interview. And, just like interviewees, small-group participants should be active listeners throughout the process.

Decision Making in the Group

One of the most prominent functions of the small-group communication process is that of decision making. Groups of all types utilize the discussion format as a basis for resolving problems and arriving at decisions about issues and questions confronting them.

The group decision-making process has been shown to occur in four phases. In phase one, the *orientation phase,* introductions are offered and the purpose of this group is established. Phase two is the *conflict stage,* in which different positions are advanced in an attempt to sway the other members of the group from individual positions. The third phase, *emergence,* results when the group shifts from conflicts to considerations as to how best to formulate a recommendation and what the recommendation must incorporate. The fourth phase, *reinforcement,* occurs when the group forms a strong sense of unity and cooperation as the final decision is shaped, reported, and considered for implementation.[5]

The phases of the decision-making process occur over the course of time and vary according to the nature of the group. A new group, of course, takes more time in the orientation phase than does a group that has a prior history as a group. It is helpful for group members to be able to identify where they are in the decision-making process so that they can utilize their collective time more productively. As it plays out through the series of phases, the decision-making process requires step-by-step procedures that allow group members to locate and explore the dimension of the program before selecting a conclusion.

Types of Discussions

Because we spend so much of our time communicating in groups, it is helpful to look at the various types of discussions in which we participate. These include closed discussions, informal meetings, and public discussions.

Closed Discussions

A **closed discussion** is conducted for the benefit of the participants themselves. It is a discussion among three or more people in which there is no audience present. There are many types of closed discussions, of which the most common is the round-table discussion in which a group picks or is given a topic, does research, prepares an agenda, and then meets to discuss the topic. For example, a group of data-processing technicians may have a round-table discussion to decide what series of programs to use for a new accounting system.

Round-Table Discussions

The **round-table discussion** requires that a group be given or allowed to select a topic, prepare an **agenda**—a sequence for the discussion—and then meet to discuss the topic. The most typical use of the round-table format is the periodic formal meeting of an organization. A group of data-processing technicians, for instance, may participate in a round-table discussion to decide what series of programs to utilize in instituting a new accounting system.

Brainstorming Sessions

A special form of closed discussion, one in which no agenda is planned, is the **brainstorming session,** a technique frequently used in business and industry. A brainstorming session is designed to reveal all possible solutions to a problem. In this type of discussion, each member is asked to cite as many solutions as possible without considering the relevance or practicality of these solutions. The group does not analyze the solutions in a brainstorming session; instead, its sole function is to enumerate as many solutions as possible, to creatively generate ideas for solving the problem facing the group or the organization. This list of solutions can later be assessed by a committee and, if appropriate, implemented. Or

When a group is too large to use small-group discussion techniques successfully, it can be broken down into smaller units of five to seven people to conduct a buzz session.

the brainstorming group itself may later consider the suggestions and make some decisions as to which are the most workable, practical, and desirable for the organization.

A corporation that needs a new approach to evaluating the job performance of its employees may call its middle-management officials together to brainstorm. In the session, each manager contributes as many ideas as possible, but the group does not evaluate the suggestions. Instead, the list of ideas is referred to a subcommittee for evaluation and possible recommendation to higher management.

Buzz Sessions   Another special form of closed discussion is the **buzz session,** in which a large group of people (such as a classroom group of students) is broken down into small groups of five to seven people to spend a designated amount of time discussing a predetermined topic. Each smaller group is asked to appoint a recorder, who reports the results of the small-group discussion to the larger group. Buzz sessions are especially effective when a group is too large to use small-group discussion techniques successfully.

Quality Circles   The value of groups in the American work force has been recognized as corporations attempt to increase productivity through Japanese man-

The quality circle brings together a group of employees to analyze a work-related problem and to determine solutions.

agement techniques. For example, many American industries have adopted the quality circle concept in an effort to involve workers much more directly in the decision-making process. The **quality circle** brings together a group of employees to analyze a work-related problem and then determine solutions to pass on to upper management. General Electric, General Motors, Ford, Kaiser Aluminum, Exxon, and Westinghouse are only a few of the corporations that have instituted quality circles.[6]

The implementation of quality circles requires considerable commitment on the part of management because time must be set aside for the group to work on the recommended solutions. A commitment of time and money is also needed to train the employees in the nature and the process of quality circle techniques. Unfortunately, some organizations skip this crucial step and thus are disappointed in their overall results. Just putting a group of employees in a room and telling them to generate and solve problems is not usually very productive because most people are unfamiliar with how groups operate, how the leadership role should be managed, how to go about investigating problems systematically, and how to select workable, desirable, and practical solutions.

Furthermore, although the quality circle group process is widely hailed in American industry as a means for involving workers, not all group efforts are necessarily productive. Participation in the decision-making process can, of course, lead a person to have greater commitment to his or her work—but in some cases group membership leads people to work less than they may individually. "When the individual thinks his or her own contribution to the group cannot be measured," noted one source, "his or her output tends to slacken. This notion we call **social loafing.**"[7]

Work Teams   A variation on the quality circle concept is the **work team,** in which groups of workers are organized into small teams of twelve to fifteen people to encourage participation, group decision making, and ownership of results among all members. Organizations such as Honeywell have found that the concept leads to improved employee morale, greater responsiveness to and flexibility in meeting customer needs, and increased quality.[8]

The work team is typically set up so that all members have total responsibility for all of the functions of the unit. All the members report directly to the team leader so that layers of management are eliminated and each person can have a direct influence on the activities of the group. Team leaders evaluate their workers, who in turn evaluate their leaders. All team members must necessarily be taught to be proficient in group techniques as well as being cross-trained to do all of the jobs in the unit.

A successful application of this group system was instigated at Herman Miller Incorporated, a *Fortune* 500 manufacturer of office furniture. The company's profits had slumped, the corporation instituted work teams, and the result was a more productive working environment and increased profits.[9]

Teleconferences   A modification on the traditional closed business meeting is the **teleconference,** the use of long distance audio and/or video telephone systems to conduct meetings.[10] The format has the advantage of connecting organizational members so they can conduct their business without the costs and time demands of long distance travel. This technique is being used to conduct meetings by educational, industrial, governmental, health, and similar associations.

Although conference time via telephone lines is expensive, the costs can be much less than those required to fly in members of a marketing staff, for instance, and put them up in hotel rooms to have a sales meeting. In education, money and time are saved because classes do not have to be called off as instructors travel to conferences.

A teleconference requires careful planning. The time and place must be set, an agenda established and distributed in advance of the meeting, and all necessary materials arranged for.

The conducting of a teleconference necessitates special considerations. If the meeting is conducted by telephone, each person should identify himself or herself before speaking, and attention should be paid to the adjustments that must be made for the lack of nonverbal clues.

If the teleconference is conducted via a videophone or television system, planners must recognize that people may not feel comfortable being on camera. In addition, visual aids must be prepared that lend themselves to being photographed, plans must be made to display the aids, and enough cameras and other equipment must be assembled to enable efficient use of the technology.

Corporations such as Marriott, Bank of America, Aetna Life Insurance Corporation, and the United Steelworkers of America make regular use of teleconferences. Many universities and hotels have built teleconferencing centers in their facilities for their own as well as public use. Recognized as the fastest growing segment of the telecommunications industry, teleconferencing has become a $150-million-a-year business.[11]

Nominal Group Technique

Another group format used in organizations is the **nominal group technique,** in which members individually generate ideas, pool them, clarify them, rank-order them, and then discuss them. The nominal group technique, which was developed to avoid group conflicts,[12] includes generation of the ideas in writing, round-robin recording of the ideas, discussion and clarification of each idea, and a preliminary vote on the importance of each idea.[13] The system has the advantage of ensuring equal participation from all members. As a result, some organizations make use of this nominal group technique as an alternative to the more traditional brainstorming discussion.

Committees

One of the most familiar types of closed-discussion groups is the committee. A **committee** consists of a group of people who come together for a specific purpose within an organization. The purpose is usually to study an issue and make decisions and recommendations on how to handle it. Unfortunately, because many committees are poorly organized and unproductive, the phrase *refer that to committee* has come to suggest the "kiss of death" for issues in many organizations. The key to effective functioning in a committee is to clarify the objectives, organize the work, manage the time, and communicate openly for a productive end.

Focus Groups

A special type of group that is growing in popularity in many industries is the focus group. The **focus group** is designed to bring together a representative number of consumers of a particular industry's products to react, through discussion, to the quality and use of the company's products, new marketing plans, and new or revised product lines.

The focus group is usually led by a professional moderator who follows a careful agenda to ensure that all viewpoints are aired in the discussion. The consumers may receive a small fee for their participation in what typically is a two- to four-hour session. The results are used by the industry's researchers to supplement data from surveys, product tests, and sales records for planning future ad campaigns, modifying existing product lines, or creating new products. Even though some experts argue that a focus group can never be truly representative of all consumers, corporations that use focus groups for research have found this approach to be a creative way to get direct input from users or potential users.

Support Groups   A support group is an important system that allows people to interact with others who share similar goals or problems. "The purpose of a **support group** is to increase people's knowledge of themselves and others, assist people to clarify the changes they most want to make in their life, and give people some of the tools necessary to make these changes."[14]

It is estimated that nearly 1 million special types of support groups known as growth groups have been established in the past few years and that "people are coming together in record numbers both to cope with affliction and to deal with normal processes in life."[15] Growth groups deal with meeting preventive and remedial aims (such as Alcoholics Anonymous); helping people develop positive attitudes and better interpersonal skills (Attitudes in Awareness); working toward personality change, stress management, assertion training, and treatment of eating disorders (Weight Watchers); learning coping skills (Adult Children of Alcoholics); managing relationships (Marriage Encounter); overcoming perfectionism; offering support for grieving (Mended Hearts); and making family adjustments (Parents Without Partners).

In the counseling setting, some therapists believe that support groups may be more effective than individual counseling because they can provide the empathy and knowledge of people who have gone through similar experiences and can share their thoughts and feelings.[16] Support groups are considered an effective device for those persons working through trauma caused by rape, incest, physical abuse, battering, and phobias. The life spans of these groups may be long or short, depending on the needs of the members.

A newspaper advice columnist encouraged the use of support groups when she told a troubled correspondent, "I can't say enough about the groups that operate on the theory that people who share the same problem can get strength from one another. If you are having a problem with children, parents, family, friends, or with yourself, there is probably a self-help group for you."[17] Even the medical field has become a supporter of support groups. One study indicated that women with advanced breast cancer who had group therapy in addition to medical treatment lived twice as long as women who were given medical treatment alone.[18]

Study Groups   Students are increasingly participating in **study groups** to manage the information required in a particular course or to prepare for licensing examinations in such areas as nursing, psychology, law, physical therapy, and medicine. These groups enable members to share responsibility for the information and offer various points of view regarding interpretation of concepts. In addition, working in a group can offer motivation to study.

To be productive, a study group should follow some basic principles:

1. Do not limit the group to friends or participants who will not help in the learning process.
2. Meet on a regular basis in a location that lends itself to studying and not to socializing or interruptions.
3. Insist that all members of the group attend and participate.
4. Require that each member be prepared for sessions.
5. Work out the answers to the questions as a group, allowing each member to take a turn in leading the group and in providing explanations.
6. Ask each person to bring in a set of possible questions.
7. Review old course exams or study guides as part of the learning process.[19]

Study groups are increasingly important in education as alternate teaching methods are explored. The approach known as *cooperative learning,* which is prevalent in elementary and secondary schools, is based on placing students in small heterogeneous groups to work on academic tasks. Students are encouraged to share ideas and help each other learn. Small-group cooperative learning has been found to have considerable benefit in the classroom because student learning improves, their problem-solving skills are enhanced, social relationships improve, and they have a more positive attitude toward school.[20]

Informal Meetings   Not all groups organize themselves by establishing a formal structure. In **informal groups,** the members assemble with no direct purpose or plan of action. An informal group is probably best characterized as one that offers participants unstructured sharing time. A group of working mothers, for example, may meet in the executive cafeteria on an occasional basis to have lunch and talk about the problems of balancing careers and families. Such a group can serve a highly useful purpose in providing support to its individual members without any structured meeting time, agenda, or program.

If, however, you are a member of such a group and you want to make it function more effectively, try to observe the components of the group's action: the decision-making process, the role of leadership, the role of the participants, and the setting. If the group seems to be making no progress and you observe that no one has emerged to guide it, you can assume a leadership role by making a comment about how you think the group should proceed. Conversely, if one person appears to be dominating the activities or is using controlling techniques to accomplish personal purposes at the expense of the group, you can temper that person through tactful suggestions. If there is a powerful struggle among several strong individuals for the leadership role, you can point out how the conflict of these members is hindering the group's progress.

In an informal group, all members should be involved. If some do not participate, you may be able to draw them into the discussion through questions. Nevertheless, every member has the right—and at times the need—to abstain from making comments in an informal group. So it is wise not to badger or intimidate the quiet members in such a group.

An effective participant in an informal group should stick to the subject under discussion, should support his or her points of view, and should encourage a cooperative atmosphere. This cooperative atmosphere is fostered by everyone listening actively throughout the discussion.

A participant can also aid the group by being alert to such factors as the physical setting. For example, if the group is not operating effectively, a change in the seating arrangements may help. The time of the meeting, the length of the session, poor lighting, and the room temperature can also affect group members. An early morning meeting that drags on, for instance, may fray some of the members' nerves.

Because of time limitations, groups are sometimes forced into hasty decisions. A group that has one hour to reach a conclusion but uses fifty-five minutes for nonproductive activities is forced to make a hurried, five-minute decision or reach no decision at all. To avoid this situation, one person can keep track of the time as the meeting proceeds and inform the group of the time that remains.

Informal groups are a major part of almost any work organization. They also serve a major role in most social and family environments. Thus attention to the communication effectiveness of these groups can enhance the quality of life for all.

Public Discussions   A **public discussion** is conducted for the benefit of both participants and observers; it thus tends to be somewhat formal. Usually participants are given a schedule for the discussion, and much of the preliminary

Public discussions are conducted for the benefit of both participants and observers.

work concerning the arrangements and agenda is accomplished in planning sessions before the presentation.

Panel Discussions   One type of public discussion, the **panel discussion,** is characterized by interaction among group members. The number of participants may vary, but it is a good idea to restrict the group to no more than six or seven people. Otherwise, meaningful interaction may become difficult. Although the audience must see and hear the participants, the panel members do not need to focus their interaction on the audience. Rather, they should talk with each other, and let the moderator attend to the flow of the agenda.

Symposiums   The panel is sometimes confused with a much more formal type of discussion, the **symposium,** which consists of three to seven prepared speeches or reports connected by introductions and transitions, which are usually delivered by a moderator or chairperson. A good symposium may be followed by a panel discussion in which the participants discuss issues related to their speeches. A true symposium format, however, provides little or no opportunity for the members of the group to interact with each other.

Forums   Any public discussion in which the audience members participate with questions and comments is known as a **forum.** This generally follows a panel, symposium, or speech. For example, in a symposium-forum on the occult, experts may present ten-minute speeches on aspects of their individual research. After the speeches (the symposium section), a forum can be held, with the chair opening the program to the audience for questions and comments. The forum offers an excellent vehicle for involving the listeners and clarifying or further developing any points or issues. In addition to panel discussions, symposiums, and forums, there are two special types of public discussions: small- and large-group conferences.

Small-Group Conferences

In a **small-group conference,** people share detailed information about some technical issue or problem. The health care field provides a good example of the small-group conference. In this kind of gathering, nurses and physicians in a clinic or a hospital ward meet on a regular basis to discuss a specific patient's progress. The group follows a rather tight agenda because time is usually quite limited.

An interesting development in communication technology has made it possible for organizations of all types to set up group meetings via teleconferences. In a teleconference, by means of connecting telephone systems, persons throughout a wide geographic area can discuss issues with each other while avoiding the high cost of traveling to a central location. Much of the development in this area has stemmed from the use of audio-conferencing devices such as the telephone speaker-phone. With this device, a telephone receiver can be amplified throughout a large office or a conference room so that the participants can speak conversationally and their voices can be picked up through the receiving device. Telephone companies have also developed interactive video systems through which people can see as well as hear each other over long distances.

Large-Group Conferences

A **large-group conference** provides an opportunity for participants to conduct small-group discussions over a period of two to three days. The purposes here are to share information, deliberate policy, and determine value. Such a conference requires extensive planning and may combine several forms of discussions. Some conferences, for example, begin with a symposium or with one guest speaker who presents a keynote speech. This opening presentation sets the stage for a series of smaller meetings in which issues are discussed in some depth.

Large-group conferences vary in format depending on their purposes and on the time available. An example illustrates the flexibility that such a conference may have. At a Washington conference on careers in communication, the meeting opened with a speech on career education presented by an official from the U.S. Department of Education. This speech was followed by two days of small-group discussions among conference participants on a variety of career areas. Specialists from such fields as public relations, speech writing, organizational communication, and telecommunications met with the groups and discussed the communication competencies necessary for success in their fields. These sessions were followed by a summary session of the entire group in which the chairpersons of the small-group meetings gave reports on the proceedings. These proceedings were later summarized and published for others in the communication field.

Conferences of various sizes have become a popular way for many organizations to bring together management and/or marketing people and motivate them to increase the productivity of the organization. Many organizations today have employed meeting managers to arrange conferences and all their physical details (transportation, hotel accommodations, food functions, special events). Many meeting managers work as consultants to larger organizations, planning all the meetings for the contracting group. Indeed, meeting management has become such big business that there are special associations for meeting management professionals that sponsor their own conferences on running effective meetings and publish journals such as *Successful Meetings* and *Meeting Management*.

The popularity of conferences for bringing together a sales staff or a management staff from an organization's installations throughout a region or even the world is reflected in estimates that as much as $2 billion a year is spent on motivational meetings for managers.[21] Despite spending this phenomenal amount on conferences, most organizations have made no systematic analyses to determine if the meetings have any real effect! It can be assumed, however, that the opportunity to come together and interact with other professionals in an organization can be productive to any group wishing to share information, deliberate policy, or determine value.

The Family as a Group

A **family** is a group of people who declare themselves to be a family. Typical kinds of families include natural families (a married couple with or without children), blended families (families created by divorce and remarriage or death and remarriage), single-parent families (one parent with a child or children), extended families (a cluster of relatives which may also include friends), and self-declared families (heterosexuals living together, homosexuals, communal groups).

Families are groups operating as a system by the very nature of their purposes and functions—decision making, interpersonal relationships, and mutual dependency. The family group has a connectedness and a history that lead to shared meanings, problems, and decision making.

There is no best way for a family to operate. There are functioning families whose members learn to operate under stress and chaos. There are functioning families that have open channels of communication and operate in varying degrees of cooperative harmony. Obviously, the chances for successful intragroup communication and effective decision making seem to center on the family that operates with mutual connectedness and concern for each other.

"We are each born into a family. We are socialized and encultured within a family. We mature from a family. If we create a family we use information and behaviors learned from a family. And, when we die, we diminish a family. Families surround us, shape us, contribute to our destiny."[22]

Most family communication follows a structure that resembles a mobile. The parts (the family members) are segments of the same unit, and any reverberation of a problem goes through the system and throws off the mobile's balance. How well the family functions depends on the members' abilities to communicate with each other and balance the varying parts of the system.

Family discussions center on answers to some basic communication questions. What are members allowed to talk about (e.g., death, alcohol use, sex, money)? What words can be used to talk about certain subjects (e.g., death—"passed on"; alcohol—"Daddy is sick")? Where can members talk (e.g., in the kitchen, at the table while eating, in the bedroom, in the car, "only in our own house—this is nobody else's business")? Who can talk about it (e.g., mother and father only, father talks—others listen)?

Despite what seems like a plan, most families typically enforce rules randomly and lack consistency in their methods of operation. In some families, pure lines and rules of communication are established and upheld at all costs, sometimes resulting in abuse, punishment, banning, and/or threats.

Although it is not common in most households, the family unit may at times operate with a formal format. Some families use a technique called the **family powwow,** a structural discussion format used to reveal what is going on in the family members' lives. A device designed by counselors to be used by both healthy and troubled families, the powwow starts with compliments all around and goes on to a review of the previous week. A checkup for the upcoming week follows, problems are talked out, and other matters affecting the family are discussed. The phone is usually taken off the hook, and rules—such as no eating, no playing around, and mandatory attendance—are enforced. It is common for a different family member to be in charge of each meeting, which is normally held weekly. Majority voting is not generally used as it forces the losers to be subordinate to the winners, which is counter to the whole concept of the family powwow.[23]

The Functions of a Group

Effective communication in a small group requires sensitivity to the types of groups, the purposes of groups, and the dynamics of the group process. The functions of almost any group may therefore be classified in two ways: according to the group's **task,** or purpose, and according to the group's **maintenance,** or how it meets the interpersonal needs of its members. Often a person's communication within a group is a result of her or his decision to work in a group. Consequently, it is helpful to recognize the advantages and disadvantages of this arrangement.

The group process offers an opportunity for input from many people who have different points of view. A group can also provide the opportunity for a person to participate because some people feel less threatened in a small group than they do when taking responsibility solely for themselves. In addition, taking part in group action can lead to greater commitment among participants to the decisions reached by the group. Workers involved in discussing new procedures, for instance, may approach their tasks with more enthusiasm because they helped to develop those procedures. And because many people take part in the decision-making process and many points of view and ideas are presented, a better decision is likely to be reached than if one person worked alone.

Although the group process does offer these important advantages, it also has some disadvantages. For example, group discussion takes much longer than individual decision making because it involves many people with diverse points of view. It also requires participants to give up some individuality for the purpose of compromising with other group members.

Yet another disadvantage of the group process may surface when people blindly commit themselves to group cohesion to the exclusion of careful analysis. This phenomenon is called **groupthink** and is defined as "the mode of thinking that persons engage in when concurrence seeking becomes so dominant in a cohesive in-group that it tends to override realistic appraisal of alternative courses of action."[24] The disastrous Bay of Pigs invasion in 1961 may have resulted from groupthink among President Kennedy's group of advisers. And the tragic explosion of the space shuttle *Challenger* was the result of groupthink among NASA's engineers, scientists, and contractors. Indeed, the presidential commission reviewing the *Challenger* disaster recommended that NASA incorporate a "plan for improved communications [along] with [one] for management restructure."[25]

The dramatic results of groupthink stem from the pressure to conform to group norms. Research in group communication has revealed what is known as the **risky shift phenomenon,** which holds that decisions reached after discussion by the group are filled with more experimentation, are less conservative, and contain more risk than decisions reached by people working alone before the discussion is held.[26] A group of managers who have come together to solve a problem of worker morale, for instance, may be likely to adopt a more radical strategy (even confrontation) than any of the managers acting alone. This holds true because a manager by himself or herself is apt to be more careful and assume less risk in dealing with almost any issue.

Group Task Functions

The task functions of a group require the establishment of a structure that facilitates accomplishment of the group's objectives. To do so, a group has to assemble, establish its purpose, and set a plan of action.

Formulating a Discussion Question

After the group has assembled and has established its purpose, the group is wise to word the goal as a **discussion question.** For example, if the purpose of the group is to decide what type of grading system should be used on campus, the question can be "What should be done to solve the problem of inconsistent grading policies on campus?"

The following general principles are useful for wording a discussion question:

1. Be sure the purpose is put in question form (otherwise, it cannot be discussed).
2. Keep the question short and simple (so that it can be easily understood).
3. Word the question so that it does not show bias (you cannot honestly discuss a question that states the expected conclusion).
4. Word the question so that it cannot be answered with a yes or a no (you need to allow for other alternatives).

Formulating an Agenda

A good strategy for group members is to spend time at the beginning of their deliberations determining the most useful sequence for the discussion. This is much like drawing up a categorical checklist of questions for an interview.

No matter what the purpose of the discussion, the group will probably want to have an outline, or agenda, to follow. The agenda allows the group to cover the topic systematically and thus accomplish the task in the most efficient way possible. The agenda should be used like a road map: it should contain just enough detail to allow the group to travel the path to the task but should not be so rigid that it does not allow for any detours. In structuring an agenda, group members should be careful not to discuss the topic in detail—this sort of interaction should take place later during the group discussion. One way to plan an agenda is for each member to do research on the subject and prepare his or her own agenda in advance. Then the group can meet for a short time (possibly fifteen minutes) to share individual outlines and draw up a group one. No discussion of the issues should take place while the agenda is being put together; this phase only lists possible topics. Of course, the formulation of an agenda varies according to the specific type of discussion being planned.

Information-Sharing Discussions.   In an **information-sharing discussion,** the participants use a series of questions to probe for factual information. The typical wording of such questions is "What is (are) . . . ?" For example, a question formulated by a corporate group may be "What are the current theories of management training?"

A plan for an information-sharing discussion can have an agenda similar to the following one. To devise this outline, the group selected a subject and broke it down into topics. After deciding on these topics, the group drew up a set of questions about them. The resulting agenda was used by all the participants in the discussion.

Agenda for a Specific Information-Sharing Discussion

A group of administrators from different personnel departments are meeting to share information on practices in the training of managers.

Question: What are the current theories of management training?

   I.   What terms should be defined?
       A. Management?
       B. Training?
       C. Education and development?
  II.   What are the approaches to traditional personnel training?
       A. How are employees trained prior to their assumption of a management position?
       B. What are some techniques for classroom training?
       C. What are some strategies for on-the-job training?
 III.   What is the performance-analysis training model?
       A. What are the strategies for determining our needs?
       B. How do we assess the value of needs in the organization?
       C. What approaches can be used to develop the training program?
           1. For acquisition of management skills?
           2. For maintenance of management skills?
  IV.   What is the human-resource-development approach?
       A. What is the role of the classroom trainer?
       B. What is the role of the administrator?
       C. What is the role of the consultant?
       D. How is the human-resource-development approach implemented?

V. How does the manager serve as a trainer?
   A. What is the role of the manager in training?
   B. How does the manager conduct training sessions and manage the group at the same time?
   C. What are the reasons for putting training in the hands of the manager?
   D. What is the role of the training professional?
VI. Conclusion

Value Discussions.   A group may have as its task going beyond the sharing of information to determine the value of a specific question. Thus **value discussions** deal with determining the worth of the status quo. In a value discussion, a group may interact about a question of significance through a process of analysis-synthesis. In this process, the group breaks the topic into parts to look at functions, relationships, and so on (the **analysis phase**). The group then combines the parts for the ultimate evaluation (the **synthesis phase**). The following agenda is an example of a format a group can use in attempting to determine the value of something:

Agenda for a Value Discussion

I. What are the purposes of the issue or item being evaluated?
II. To what extent has each purpose been achieved?
III. What features or qualities have helped to achieve each purpose?
IV. What flaws or defects have prevented each purpose from being achieved?
V. Are the purposes worth achieving?

All steps in the agenda should be phrased as questions to remind the group that the topics are to be discussed rather than assumed as statements of fact. Alterations can sometimes be made in this basic format. For example, a group may want to combine steps III and IV and discuss qualities and flaws at the same time. The following proceedings of a group of law enforcement officials illustrate the value agenda:

Agenda for a Specific Value Discussion

Question: What is the value of undercover police work in the criminal justice system?

I. What purposes does undercover work achieve?
   A. Why are police placed undercover?
   B. What kinds of crime is undercover work geared to combat?
   C. What kinds of criminals are undercover police attempting to apprehend?

II. To what extent has each purpose been achieved?
    A. Does the public feel safer with the knowledge that there are undercover agents at work?
    B. Is there a decrease in the crimes that have been targeted?

III. What features or qualities have helped to achieve each purpose?
    A. What types of training do undercover agents have?
        1. Is street knowledge a useful tool?
        2. Is textbook knowledge a useful tool?
    B. How does undercover work assist the business and industrial communities?
    C. Do the media have an effect on the public's view of undercover agents?
    D. Why is undercover work better than uniform patrol work?
    E. Can an undercover agent infiltrate organized crime?

IV. What flaws or defects have prevented each purpose from being achieved?
    A. Is there corruption in the undercover program?
    B. What are the risks to the officers involved?
    C. How much more does undercover work cost than uniform patrol work?

V. Are the purposes worth achieving?
    A. Will any crimes be deterred as a result of undercover work?
    B. Are the crimes affected by undercover work worth the risk to the officers?
    C. Is the cost worth the effects achieved?

Problem-Solving Discussions. A more complex and probably more frequent task of groups is a **problem-solving discussion,** a situation in which a group of people get together to resolve a problem. Because the problem-solving discussion is a good technique for gaining input from a variety of sources, many companies prefer this approach to problem solving. These companies profess that workers who participate in making policy decisions are more productive in the long run because they have a greater commitment to implementing their own decisions. After all, once people have spent time and effort working on a plan of action, they are more likely to abide by that plan. Colleges and universities have found that the inclusion of faculty members on committees to select the institution's administrators, for example, can lead to better supervisor-worker relationships.

In a problem-solving discussion, a question of policy may be worded in several ways. For example, "What should be done to solve the problem of poverty in the United States?" or "What should be the federal government's policy on tax reform?"

Like an interview, an effective problem-solving discussion by a group requires a structured format. For this reason, many groups have adapted educational philosopher John **Dewey's critical-thinking sequence** for individual problem solving in the group process. In this sequence, a group first looks systematically at a problem and then at possible solutions to it.[27] Thus an agenda based on Dewey's ideas includes the following steps:

Dewey's Critical-Thinking Sequence for Problem-Solving Model

    I.   What is the problem?
   II.   What are the causes of the problem?
  III.   What are the possible solutions?
  IV.   What are the advantages and disadvantages of each solution?
   V.   What is (are) the best solution(s)?
  VI.   How can the best solution(s) be put into effect?

As in any suggested agenda, flexibility is appropriate in this format as well. A group in a problem-solving discussion should always feel free to adjust the format, as long as the analysis-solution sequence remains. For instance, the group may want to ask what criteria the solutions must meet before it begins to discuss those solutions. To illustrate this flexibility, the following agenda shows how Dewey's sequence can be adapted to a problem-solving discussion by combining steps III and IV and then steps V and VI:

Agenda for a Specific Problem-Solving Discussion

Question: What can be done to solve the problem of computer hardware and software incompatibility?

    I.   What is the problem?
       A. What terms do we need to know so as to deal with the problem?
          1. What is computer hardware?
          2. What is computer software?
          3. What is meant by "computer hardware and software incompatibility"?
          4. Is the incompatibility of hardware and software always a problem?
       B. How does this problem concern us?
          1. As professionals?
          2. As consumers?
          3. As businesses?

II.   What are the causes of the problem?
    A.   Is the desire for profits the cause of computer hardware and software incompatibility?
        1.   Is competition among leading companies a cause of incompatibility?
        2.   Is the purposeful creation of new, more marketable, more profitable products a cause of incompatibility?
    B.   Does computer design cause incompatibility?
        1.   Does the swiftly growing and changing nature of computer design cause incompatibility?
    C.   Does a lack of standards contribute to incompatibility?
        1.   Does a lack of effort by groups enforcing standards contribute to incompatibility?
        2.   Does a lack of government standards contribute to incompatibility?

III.   What are the possible solutions and their advantages and disadvantages?
    A.   Would government guidelines bring about greater compatibility?
        1.   Would a government standards group help?
        2.   Would regulation of competition help?
        3.   Would a patent system help?
    B.   Would public encouragement of hardware and software compatibility solve the problem?
    C.   Would forming a group of manufacturers bring about greater compatibility?
    D.   Could groups dedicated to enforcing standards solve the problem?
        1.   Would improvements in existing groups help?
        2.   Would more consumer-oriented groups help?

IV.   What is the best solution?
    A.   What is the best solution for buyers?
        1.   For the business consumer?
        2.   For the public consumer?
    B.   Would compatibility help or hurt research?
    C.   How can this solution be implemented?

Voting   In addition to detailing a system for arriving at results, the group has responsibilities for determining how decisions will be made and accepted by all members within the group. A voting process can serve a useful purpose in providing a system for arriving at final decisions. The members of a group must agree on how decisions are to be made when the purpose of the group is to decide on a course of action. Most groups

Voting is a procedure in which each member is given the opportunity to indicate agreement or disagreement.

go through a procedure—voting—in which each member is given the opportunity to indicate agreement or disagreement on an idea or a candidate. Voting can ensure that the members of the group agree on the outcome of the discussion. There are four common voting methods: consensus, majority, plurality, and part of the whole. It is imperative that the method of voting be agreed on before the group starts working toward the final solution, for any alteration in the method can affect the outcome of the group's action.

Consensus refers to "all."[28] In a consensus decision, every member of the group must agree on a proposal before it can be put into action. This is often the method used for decisions in which dire consequences can result from the outcome of the action. For example, most juries operate by consensus.

In contrast, in a **majority** vote the winner must receive more than half of the votes, excluding those who do not vote or who abstain (that is, those who do not want to vote).[29] For example, if there are ten people in a group and all vote, it will take six votes for a majority to rule. If, however, one of the people does not vote, then it will take five votes for passage according to the majority method.

Plurality means "most."[30] Often when there are more than two options available, a group may turn to plurality voting. If, for example, three candidates are running for an office, in plurality voting the one getting the most votes is declared the winner. In the same way, if five ideas have been proposed as solutions to a problem, the solution selected will be the one receiving the greatest number of votes.

Part-of-the-whole voting occurs when a specific number or a specific percentage of those who are eligible to vote is all that is required to bring about some action. For example, some constitutions (the rules of operation of an organization) can be changed only if 75 percent of those eligible to vote agree to the change. A group has the right to set any number or percentage it wishes so as to allow action to take place. Group members are encouraged to decide on these numbers before starting the decision-making process. The method selected for evaluating the voting can have a profound effect on the outcome of a proposed action. For example, the proposed federal Equal Rights Amendment was not enacted as a U.S. constitutional change, even though more than a majority of the states approved its inclusion, because the part-of-the-whole method was used. In this case, a two-thirds vote was needed but was not obtained. If a majority voting system had been used, the amendment would have been enacted.

Criteria

An additional group function is to decide on the criteria for selecting and evaluating the outcome of an action-centered discussion. To do this, the **criteria,** the guidelines for selection, must be clear and agreeable to all the group's members. In business and industrial settings, for example, criteria must be set for decisions on operational procedures, plant locations, budgeting, and evaluation of job candidates. In social settings, such matters as the budget and time and space restraints must be agreed on before a party or a reception can be planned.

To assist groups in discussing criteria, business consultants have devised a popular method to work through the criteria phase of any discussion. Members of the group are encouraged to separate what the group must have from what the group wants—to identify required elements and desired elements—to give the discussion of criteria and the subsequent solutions greater focus.[31]

Procedures

Still another task for any group is the setting up of the **procedures** (rules of operation) to be followed in reaching a decision. Formal organizations usually develop a constitution and bylaws that clearly spell out these procedures. A set of parliamentary guidelines such as *Robert's Rules of Order* is usually adopted as a framework for handling procedural disagreements.[32] Less formal organizations may allow the leader of the group to determine the operational procedures. Whatever method is used, however, it should be agreed on before any formal work of the group is undertaken.

*One advantage of group dis-
cussion is that it allows minority opinions to be voiced
and considered.*

Group Maintenance Functions

Accomplishment of the group's task is greatly affected by the personal interactions of its members. Within any group, the development of these interpersonal relationships can be charted through four stages, which constitute the **group maintenance functions:** formation, cohesion, reinforcement, and ending. These functions allow the group to proceed from formation to disbandment in a series of sequential, organized steps.

Group Formation

The formation of a group represents the first stage in group maintenance. Much as in an interview, the establishment of understanding and rapport among the members of the group should characterize initial interactions. Obviously, it will be difficult for a small group to communicate well unless its members get to know each other and begin to feel comfortable with each other. Thus work on specific tasks should not begin until rapport has been established and all members have begun to feel as if they belong to the group.

Group Cohesion

After a group has been formed, it must develop mechanisms by which conflicts that arise can be dealt with. This can be managed if the members are willing to give opposing viewpoints a fair hearing. One important benefit of group discussion is that it allows minority opinions to be voiced. Once group members have listened to and understood their opponent's point, their response to it should reflect as much and indicate the source of and reason for agreement or disagreement.

The resolution of conflict within a group may require compromise. If people plan to accomplish tasks as a group, they may have to investigate opposing positions before reaching a solution.

Resolution of conflict represents one significant aspect of group maintenance, but **group cohesion**—the common bond among group members—is an equally significant concern. If a group's operation is characterized by adherence to goals and norms (both verbal and nonverbal) and a generally positive orientation toward the group itself, with each member sharing responsibility, then the group is more likely to accomplish its task than if time is taken up by personality clashes and petty bickering.

Of course, some members of a group may disagree with each other and even dislike or distrust each other. Disagreement and other problems, interestingly enough, can be healthy for the development of group cohesion if the members recognize that effective realization of goals can occur in the context of varying opinions and personalities.

Nevertheless, some group members may be hard pressed to acknowledge that accomplishing the task is more important than proving who is right. There is no magic formula for getting others to give up personal ego and work toward group goals. But honesty, a focus on the issues rather than on the people, and a willingness to occupy the middle ground between winning all arguments and giving in all the time for the sake of peace help smooth the way. Realistically, this path of action is often easier to theorize about than to accomplish, but being aware of the very nature of group process often helps.

Cohesion can spring from the positive dynamics among group members. Sometimes people relate well to each other from the very beginning because they have common interests, mutual ideas, or past acquaintanceship. Under such positive conditions, little work is needed to establish group cohesion. Sometimes, however, group members may have a **hidden agenda**—an objective or purpose for joining the group that goes beyond the purpose of the group as a whole. When individual members work for their own unstated ends rather than for the group's objectives, the result is counterproductive. A hidden agenda is apparent, for example, when a department manager discussing budget allocations promises to support any plan that divides the resources equitably but then opposes all the plans that are presented. In this case, the manager has a hidden agenda; he or she wants most of the funds for his or her department and thinks a delay will tire the participants and lead to a decision that favors that department. Thus the manager is trying to manipulate the group toward a personal goal.

Sometimes cohesion comes from manipulation of the group through creation of a common enemy. In a business, for instance, one member of the work force may attempt to rally employees against the boss. Unless justified, it can only be hoped that group members will recognize and reject attempts to manipulate the group to achieve cohesion.

Group Reinforcement

Another dimension of group maintenance is reinforcement. For once a group has established cohesion, it is capable of **reinforcement,** support of each other's needs, both expressed and unexpressed. If a group member who is usually reluctant to contribute makes a comment about an issue, for example, other members can reinforce that person for her or his contribution, thereby encouraging passive members to participate more often. Through attention to both verbal and nonverbal cues, members can be alert to each other's needs and can provide appropriate reinforcement.

These group functions may also serve to reward individual group members. If, for example, one member approaches another after a meeting and applauds her or his suggestions for financing a new program, that person will probably feel rewarded. Through reward, recognition, and praise, individual members find satisfaction in group participation.

Group Ending

The cohesion and reinforcement a person gets from participation in a group makes it difficult, at times, to disengage from that group. Such a step is often necessary, however, once tasks are accomplished or when individual needs change or organizations require different configurations of groups. Thus we are wise to consider positive ways to disband a group but still continue its positive results.

Just as in disengagement from a personal, dyadic relationship, ending a group can be difficult. Because we become attached to the members and to the goals of a particular group, it becomes a safe, comfortable support system in career and social settings. The breakup of American Telephone & Telegraph illustrated some of the difficulties people had in disengaging from particular work groups and finding themselves placed with new work units and people. Because the personal support system had disappeared with the breakup, the company had to consciously build both formal and informal work groups for employees. Some employees likened the breakup to divorce and required some time to readjust to different group structures.

Listening in the Group

Researchers have identified some major communication problems that must be controlled to maximize the flow of information within a group.

Factors that inhibit good communication in a group include unfocused discussion, interruptions, poor listening, individual domination, constraining communication climate, premature evaluation, information overload (dealing with too many ideas at once), inadequate structuring of ideas (not relating ideas to one another), and premature focus on finding a solution.[33] Effective group communicators work to overcome these problems, especially through improved listening skills.

Both group leaders and group participants must be effective listeners. Indeed, the majority of your time in any particular group should be spent listening to others so that any contributions you make will be meaningful, responsive, and pertinent to the topic at hand. Consequently, as a listener, you should strive to concentrate, listen carefully to understand the speaker's message, accurately decode the message to reflect the original intent of the speaker, respond to the speaker with meaningful feedback, and actively listen throughout the discussion.

A good listener is sensitive to verbal and nonverbal cues. If you observe that a group member is anxious, for instance, you may want to allay his or her fears by such comments as "That idea is really worth thinking about," or "I'm glad you brought that up." If you observe that a participant has not contributed to the discussion and appears nervous, you can say, "It's important that we get your opinion because everyone's ideas are relevant." Or you can ask the person specifically to react: "Barbara, will you please give us your reactions to the proposal that the Employee Management Association donate $50 to the United Way campaign?"

Good listening skills are also crucial to the accomplishment of the group's tasks. After all, to respond to others and to build on their ideas, you must listen carefully to what they say. Because the purpose of group communication is often to explore a topic thoroughly from various viewpoints, each member is smart to keep an open, receptive mind. Of course, total open-mindedness cannot be expected from every group member, nor can the abandonment of beliefs and points of view. But minority opinions should nevertheless be given a hearing, and each person's attitudes should be considered so that the full value of the ideas expressed can be gained. In short, all participants should be committed to the principles of good listening while participating in any group discussion. Such active engagement in communication benefits individuals and groups alike.

Roles of Group Members

Participants in small groups function in a variety of roles. It is helpful to recognize these roles and maintain some consistency while functioning in them. The following descriptions explain the roles group members may assume in their task and maintenance functions within groups:[34]

Task Roles

- *Initiator-contributor*—presenting new ideas or new perspectives
- *Information seeker*—asking for facts and clarifications
- *Opinion seeker*—asking for opinions to get at some of the values of the group
- *Information giver*—presenting facts and opinions
- *Opinion giver*—presenting values and opinions
- *Elaborator*—providing examples and solutions and building on the contributions of others
- *Coordinator*—identifying relationships among the ideas presented in the discussion
- *Orienter*—clarifying ideas for the group through summaries and identification of the group's direction
- *Evaluator-critic*—analyzing the group's decisions
- *Energizer*—stimulating the group to greater productivity
- *Procedural technician*—handling mechanical tasks such as paper distribution and seating arrangements
- *Recorder*—recording the transactions of the group
- *Encourager*—supplying positive reinforcement to the group members
- *Harmonizer*—mediating various differences among group members
- *Compromiser*—attempting to resolve conflicts within the group
- *Gatekeeper-expediter*—keeping the channels of communication open by encouraging the members
- *Standard setter*—establishing group norms and patterns of behavior
- *Follower*—passively accepting the ideas of others

In addition to performing roles that facilitate the group process, persons may consciously or unconsciously assume roles that can be counterproductive to the group's efforts. It is wise for participants to be able to recognize these roles as well and, if possible, to avoid falling into such patterns themselves. It is just as important, of course, not to allow others to assume these roles either.

Counterproductive Roles

- *Aggressor*—attacking the group or the problem under discussion
- *Blocker*—providing negative feedback and opposition

- *Recognition seeker*—attempting to focus attention on oneself
- *Self-confessor*—expressing one's own feelings and perspectives rather than focusing on the group
- *Playboy or playgirl*—playing around with little or no regard for the group process
- *Dominator*—attempting to take over the group
- *Help seeker*—expressing insecurity and self-deprecation to gain sympathy
- *Special-interest pleader*—disregarding group goals and arguing the case of some special, specific group

Responsibilities of Group Members

All participants should remember that the entire group is responsible and accountable for final decisions. Thus being a member of the silent majority—those who say nothing during the decision-making process—does not release you from accountability for that decision. For example, if the group decides that each member should pay $5 more in dues, you must pay the extra fee, even though you may not have said anything during the discussion and may not have even voted on the issue. Despite your lack of participation, if you expect to remain a member of the group, you cannot announce, "I didn't say anything and I didn't vote, so I don't have to pay!"

Group members should also be knowledgeable. After all, any discussion will progress more satisfactorily and be more interesting if it can be conducted beyond the level of personal opinion. Though personal beliefs are important, facts and expert opinion will reveal what authorities believe and what testing has proven. In other words, the use of supporting evidence ensures that your conclusions will have substance. Good research techniques come into use here, enabling you to locate and develop adequate support for your positions. Consider how you can apply evidence such as statistics, testimony, and illustrations to your discussions. Your participation will be enhanced if you use this research to support your comments clearly and concisely.

Some groups are plagued by people who insist on dominating the discussion and the decision-making process. Indeed, these people may well be destroying the entire group. Discussion should not be a solo performance by one group member; each participant should respect the rights of the others. A person who dominates a discussion group does not allow varying points of view to be presented, and therefore the purpose of the discussion and the basis for group action—an interchange of information and ideas—are impossible to achieve.

A further responsibility of discussion participants is to respond to each other with pertinent, meaningful comments and questions. Group members should assume an active role in communicating with each other so that the entire group can benefit. Response patterns in small-group discussions are like those in interviews. It is appropriate to give responses and to react to both verbal and nonverbal messages from other members. As in an interview, honest, supportive, relevant responses are essential for continued progress toward the group's goals.

Participants in a group discussion, much like therapeutic listeners, must also try to set aside their own prejudices and beliefs so as to listen and respond to what others have to say. This ability to suspend judgment is difficult, but it is the only way to cut down group conflict so that progress can be made toward the group's goals. Try to resolve any conflicts by adopting an openness to compromise and conciliation and by trying to work out differences of opinion systematically. Rather than trying to win arguments, you are wise to recognize and, if possible, adapt to the viewpoints of others. The results may be a stronger collective approach to the issue. Do not, however, allow a verbal bully to force you into a compromise or adopt a solution that you feel is not in the best interests of the group. Sometimes a compromise, because the plan of action is so watered down that little is accomplished, is not a very good solution.

Despite the encouragement given each member of the group to be a participant, you always have the right, if you so desire, to be a passive member. But your decision to be passive should be made because you decide to take that action, not because you have been intimidated by a verbal bully or feel that your point of view is not worthwhile. At times, we all have a need to sit back and observe. Or we may not be enthusiastic about the task, may lack knowledge of the task, or may be unprepared, and that is all right. Nevertheless, keep in mind that as a member of a group, you are responsible for whatever final decision is reached.

Leaders and Leadership

The strength of a group is found not only in effective participation but also in meaningful leadership. The **leader** of a group is the person who is recognized as being responsible for guiding the group through its tasks (see Figure 10.1). The leader may be elected, may be appointed by an outside source (by the manager, for instance), may volunteer, or may emerge by taking control of the proceedings (for example, a father in a family). A group may also have more than one leader. For instance, a group may have several chairpersons. Furthermore, in some groups the recognized leader may not be the only one who is guiding the group; other members may share this function either by being appointed or by assuming such responsibility.

Figure 10.1

Berko-Wolvin-Wolvin Model of the Leader/Leadership Relationship
The leader is the group's guide. Leadership is the ability to influence, which can be used either positively or coercively. Both leader and leadership functions can be carried out by (a) the same persons(s) or (b) separate persons.

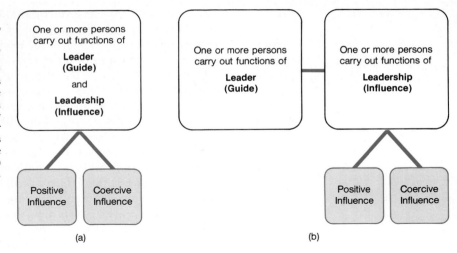

One or more persons carry out functions of
Leader (Guide)
and
Leadership (Influence)

Positive Influence   Coercive Influence

(a)

One or more persons carry out functions of
Leader (Guide)

One or more persons carry out functions of
Leadership (Influence)

Positive Influence   Coercive Influence

(b)

The leader of a group is the person who is recognized as being responsible for guiding the group through its tasks.

The ability to influence others' opinions and actions is known as **leadership.** It can be demonstrated by one or more people in a group, and the use of the power that derives from leadership can be viewed in two ways. First, power can be defined as enforcing obedience through the ability to withhold benefits or to inflict punishment. In this sense, power is coercive. **Coercion** usually centers on offering a selection of choices, all of which are undesirable. For example, in a meeting of nurses to discuss whether shifts should be rotated, many of the nurses may not want this action to be taken. But if the head nurse is in favor of rotating the shifts, then the power of the position may come into play. He or she may say, "It's my responsibility to determine staff assignments, and anyone who cannot accept this idea can request a transfer to another department." Thus the decision has been made through coercive power because the options offered may not be desirable to the members of the nursing staff. Or in a family situation, a father can control the members by stating, "As long as you are living in my house, you will do as you are told or get out."

Second, power can be defined as the ability to influence others to perform or produce results. This kind of power does not use force or coercion. With this type of power, the influence of the person, rather than the authority of the position, is paramount. For example, in a meeting of nurses, the head nurse may see conflict within the group and may suggest a solution whereby those nurses who want to be on a rotating shift may do so and those who do not may select a permanent shift. The head nurse presents reasons for this solution and asks the others for suggestions. Eventually, the group accepts the head nurse's suggestion with or without changes because it was explained well and because the head nurse was willing to accept alterations and had a record of being flexible in such situations. This influence through positive leadership in a group is a productive way to use power for the benefit of the entire group.

The tendency of certain people in leadership positions to act coercively has given rise to an examination of alternate leadership styles. One of these styles is **transformational leadership,** in which the person takes on the role of transforming agent. A transforming agent is one who can change both the behavior and the outlook of his or her followers. This person keeps the interest of the group and its goals in mind, rather than forcing her or his will on the group. Therefore she or he gives up the command and control model of leadership.[35]

Another style is **superleadership,** in which people are led to lead themselves and thereby release the self-leadership energy within each person.[36] Such an approach is especially appropriate to today's downscaled organizations, where all qualified employees will not have the opportunity to move up the corporate ladder into management and/

or executive positions. Consequently, each person can and should be encouraged to develop his or her own leadership skills to stay at a productive level within changing organizations.

Types of Leaders

As people use their power to influence the outcome of any group effort, they exhibit characteristics by which their style of leadership can be categorized. There are three basic types of leaders.[37]

- An **authoritarian leader** dominates and directs a group according to personal goals and objectives, regardless of how consistent these goals are with the group members' goals.
- A **democratic leader** directs a group according to the goals of its members and allows them to form their own conclusions.
- A **laissez-faire leader** lets group members "do their own thing."

No one type of leader is best for the operation of all groups. The needs and orientation of the group will determine whether a specific type of leader will be successful. Thus, if group members are very task oriented, they may be productive while working with a laissez-faire leader. The laissez-faire style may be disastrous, however, if group members are unable to function productively on their own. In contrast, a democratic leader will work well with a group that requires minimal supervision. If group members cannot accomplish their tasks because they lack self-discipline, an authoritarian leader may be needed to direct their activities and assign specific responsibilities. Research on leadership style suggests that the power position of the leader, the task at hand, and the needs of the group should determine how and when a leader must adapt his or her style to any given group.[38]

Responsibilities of Leaders

Regardless of his or her style, a group leader has the responsibility for guiding the group toward accomplishing its task and for maintaining it as a functioning unit. For this reason, the leader should be as knowledgeable in the group's particular area of concern as all the group members are so that concern is treated thoroughly and objectively. Many groups prefer their leaders to serve primarily as organizing agents who lead the discussion (more as a moderator) rather than as active participants. Such practices stem from a fear that a leader who participates by citing personal views and evidence may run the risk of dominating a discussion. This does not suggest, however, that a leader cannot or should not participate; it only implies that care should be taken to allow and encourage all members of the group to participate.

A leader also has unique responsibilities in a discussion because he or she opens the discussion, establishes the topic area, and sets the ground rules. He or she may also have to establish the meeting date and place, arrange the physical facilities, and so forth. If necessary, the leader should introduce group members. As the discussion proceeds, he or she can provide meaningful transitions from one area on the agenda to the next. A good leader also concludes the discussion with a summary that highlights what the group has accomplished and what the next step is to be. Clearly, the leader has many responsibilities for ensuring the successful outcome of any group discussion, and these responsibilities require commitment to the group and its objective.

A key to successful small-group communication is effective leader/ leadership. The leader/leadership can make all the difference in the outcome of the meeting or activity by how she or he sets up the meeting and operates it. Whether in business, the family, or study groups, group members must give consideration to (1) the participants, (2) knowing the purpose of the activity, (3) setting a focus for the discussion, (4) allowing for dissent, (5) developing a plan to encourage participation, and (6) making sure everyone understands what is going on. An effective leader is an effective communicator.

Summary

In this chapter, the small-group communication process was examined. The major ideas presented were:

☐ A small group usually consists of three or more persons but generally not more than twelve; five is considered the ideal number.

☐ Groups are brought together for some common purpose or goal.

☐ One of the major functions of a group is that of decision making.

☐ Closed discussions are conducted for the benefit of the participants themselves.

☐ Types of closed discussions are round-table discussions, brainstorming sessions, buzz sessions, quality circles, work teams, teleconferences, nominal group technique, committees, focus groups, support groups, and study groups.

☐ Informal groups have no set structure of operation.

☐ Public discussions are conducted for the benefit of both participants and observers.

☐ Public discussions include panels, symposiums, forums, and small- and large-group conferences.

☐ The family operates as a group.

☐ The group process offers an opportunity for input from many people who have different points of view, thus providing an opportunity for greater commitment among participants and resulting in stronger decisions.

☐ Groups generally take a longer time to make decisions than individuals do.

☐ Group action often requires compromise by individual members; in addition, the group process may lead to groupthink.

☐ For discussion purposes, the group should develop a discussion question.

☐ An agenda is an outline for the group to follow.

☐ One method for solving problems that is often used by groups is the Dewey critical-thinking sequence for problem-solving model.

☐ Most groups use a direct or indirect voting procedure to assure that members agree on the outcome of the discussion and on any action that may be taken.

☐ The procedures to be followed by the group should be agreed on before starting the decision-making process.

☐ Group maintenance functions include the formation of a group, the development of working relationships, the reinforcement of group members, and the disbandment of the group.

☐ Hidden agendas are objectives or purposes that go beyond the purposes of the group as a whole.

☐ Everyone participating in a group discussion must function as an active listener throughout the discussion.

☐ Participants in small-group communication must assume a variety of roles to accomplish their task and maintenance functions.

☐ Participants should remember that the entire group is responsible and accountable for its decisions.

☐ The leader of a group is the person who is recognized as being responsible for guiding the group through its tasks.

☐ Leadership is the ability to influence others' opinions and actions.

☐ The three types of leaders are authoritarian leaders, democratic leaders, and laissez-faire leaders.

Key Terms

small group
closed discussion
round-table discussion
agenda
brainstorming session
buzz session
quality circle
social loafing

groupthink
risky shift phenomenon
discussion question
information-sharing discussion
value discussions
analysis phase
synthesis phase
problem-solving discussion

work team
teleconference
nominal group technique
committee
focus group
support group
study groups
informal groups
public discussion
panel discussion
symposium
forum
small-group conference
large-group conference
family
family powwow
task
maintenance

Dewey's critical-thinking sequence
consensus
majority
plurality
part-of-the-whole
criteria
procedures
group maintenance functions
group cohesion
hidden agenda
reinforcement
leader
leadership
coercion
transformational leadership
superleadership
authoritarian leader
democratic leader
laissez-faire leader

Learn by Doing

1. Use specific examples to describe situations in which each of the following types of discussion groups would be used:
   a. Information-sharing discussion
   b. Value discussion
   c. Problem-solving discussion

2. Some people would rather work alone than in groups. This chapter explains some advantages and disadvantages of group action and decision making. Be prepared to defend or counter this statement: "The advantages of working in a group outweigh the disadvantages." Go beyond the arguments given in the chapter to use personal or hypothetical examples in developing your answer.

3. Consider a group in which you have worked that was not successful in reaching its goal or that had difficulty in reaching its goal because of the leader. What was the problem? How could the problem have been solved?

4. You are placed in a group in your class. Each group is to take twenty minutes in which to agree on what a time traveler should take into the future, using the following information for these decisions:

   A time machine travels to the year 5847. The world has been destroyed in a nuclear holocaust, and all that remain are a few men and women living a primitive existence and having no record or memory of the past.

The traveler decides to rebuild the future world but can make only one trip back and forth in time. On the trip, which can encompass any years between the dawn of humanity and the present, the traveler may collect such useful items as living things, printed materials, food, toilet paper, and so forth. The only limitation is one of weight: excluding the weight of the time traveler, no more than two hundred additional pounds of material may be carried in time. Problem: what should the time traveler take into the future?[39]

After the small-group discussion, the class meets to discuss the following questions:

a. What effect did the differences in the group members' backgrounds have on the group's decision?

b. What was the role of the leader in the group?

c. What inferences can be drawn from this experience about how groups operate?

d. What was the greatest problem the group encountered in reaching its decision? Could this have been resolved? How?

5. a. The following are statements on which you are required to take a stand. You may thoroughly agree (TA), agree (A), disagree (D), or thoroughly disagree (TD). Mark each statement with the relevant code.

(1) Organized religion is not needed in modern society.

(2) Corporations have an obligation to their stockholders to make profits; this obligation supersedes all others.

(3) We have little control over what we communicate about ourselves to others.

(4) Every member of an organization should be permitted to present views at a meeting, regardless of how long this may take.

(5) The changing moral structure of the present society has led to confusion and breakdown of traditional morality.

(6) Television has had a negative influence on Americans.

(7) Advertising is necessary for the continuation of the free enterprise system.

(8) War is an inevitable result of international conflict.

b. You are assigned to a group when you come to class. The group must reach a consensus (total agreement) on one of the four responses (thoroughly agree through thoroughly disagree). Group members may rewrite any of the statements until they come to agreement on one of the items.

6. Your group, consisting of twenty-five people, is voting on an issue. How many votes will it take to pass a motion affirming the action in each of the following cases?

     a.   All vote: a majority is needed.

     b.   All vote: a consensus is needed.

     c.   All vote: a two-thirds vote is needed.

     d.   Twenty-one vote: a majority is needed.

     e.   A plurality is needed. Candidate A has six votes; B has eight votes; C has eleven votes. Who wins?

     f.   Consensus is needed. Twenty-three vote yes; two do not vote. Does the motion pass?

7. It is frequently said that a call for a consensus vote usually results in some sort of compromise agreement. Why would this be so?

8. Do you think your family:

     a.   Could or would have been successful in holding family powwows?

     b.   Could or would have gained from holding family powwows?

     c.   Could or would have had a different atmosphere if it had operated or would operate on a family powwow system?

9. For your next examination in this class, form a study group. After the exam, a class discussion is held on the value or lack of value of this approach to group action.

Notes

1. Research by Executive Standards for Connecticut General Life Insurance Company, cited in Stewart L. Tubbs, *A Systems Approach to Small Group Interaction* (Reading, Mass.: Addison-Wesley, 1988), p. 8.
2. "Six Secrets to Improve Your Future Business Meetings" (Austin, Tex.: 3M Meeting Management Institute).
3. See Kathleen M. Galvin and Bernard J. Brommel, *Family Communication*, 3rd ed. (Glenview, Ill.: Scott, Foresman, 1991).
4. "Success of Intensive Care Depends on Teamwork," *Washington Post Health*, March 12, 1986, p. 5.
5. Aubrey Fisher and Donald G. Ellis, *Small Group Decision Making*, 3rd ed. (New York: McGraw-Hill, 1990), pp. 153–157.
6. Arnold Kanarick describes the communication benefits of this technique in "The Far Side of Quality Circles," *Management Review*, 70 (October 1981), 16–17.
7. Bibb Latane, Kipling Williams, and Stephen Harkins, "Social Loafing," *Psychology Today*, 13 (October 1979), 104.
8. Ted Rees, Randy Harris, and Harry Lit, "Work Teams That Work," *Manufacturing Systems*, 7 (March 1989), 42–45.
9. Kenneth Labich, "Hot Company, Warm Climate," *Fortune*, 119 (February 27, 1989), 74–78.
10. For a review of teleconferencing as it affects communication, see Andrew D. Wolvin and Carolyn Gwynn Coakley, *Listening*, 3rd ed. (Dubuque, Iowa: William C. Brown, 1988), pp. 348–350.

11. Ron Zemke, "The Rediscovery of Video Teleconferencing," *Training* (September 1986), 46.

12. Gerald L. Wilson and Michael S. Hanna, *Groups in Context* (New York: McGraw-Hill, 1990), pp. 63–65.

13. André L. Delbecq, Andrew H. Van de Hen, and David H. Gustafson, *Group Techniques for Program Planning: A Guide to Nominal Group Techniques and Delphi Process* (Glenview, Ill.: Scott, Foresman, 1975), pp. 7–16.

14. Marianne Schneider Corey and Herald Corey, *Groups, Process and Practice,* 3rd ed. (Monterey, Calif.: Brooks/Cole, 1987), p. 9.

15. Marilyn Elias, "Self-Help Groups," *Denver Post,* July 13, 1980, p. 38.

16. As stated by Susan Forward, media psychologist, Talknet Radio Network, WERE—AM, Cleveland, Ohio.

17. "Ann Landers," *Washington Post,* March 15, 1990, p. B12.

18. "How Cancer Patients Are Talking Their Way to a Longer Life," *Good Housekeeping* (June 1990), 251.

19. William J. Higgins, "Group Study: Strength in Numbers," *Commuter Connection,* 4 (October 1990), 1.

20. Ruth E. Parker, "Small-Group Cooperative Learning," *National Association of Secondary School Principles Bulletin,* 69 (March 1985), 48–57.

21. Berkeley Rice, "Do Management Development Meetings Change Attitudes and Behavior?" *Successful Meetings* (June 1987), 32–35.

22. Judy Goldberg, unpublished syllabus for "Family Communication," Arapahoe Community College. Littleton, Colorado.

23. As discussed in Barbara Burtoff, "Family Pow-Wows," *Elyria Chronicle-Telegram* (Ohio), October 1, 1985, p. B-1. Discussion is based on the ideas of Richard Gilles, dean of the College of Arts and Sciences at the University of Rhode Island in Kingston; Linda Jessup, director of the Parent Encouragement Program, Silver Springs, Maryland; and Michael Popkin, counseling psychologist and creator of the Active Parenting program. The videotape *Active Parenting,* which includes a segment on family meetings, as well as handbooks and workbooks for operating family powwows, is available from Michael Popkin of Atlanta, Georgia.

24. Irving Janis, *Victims of Groupthink* (Boston: Houghton Mifflin, 1972).

25. *Report to the President: Actions to Implement the Recommendations of the Presidential Commission on the Space Shuttle Challenger Accident* (Washington, D.C.: NASA, July 14, 1986), p. 3.

26. J. A. F. Stoner, "Comparison of Individual and Group Decisions Involving Risk," M.A. thesis, Massachusetts Institute of Technology, 1961. It should be noted that Meyers and others dispute the effect of the risky shift, hypothesizing in their research that group discussion strengthens group members' initial positions on issues. For a summary of the research, see David G. Meyers, *Social Psychology* (New York: McGraw-Hill, 1987), pp. 337–346.

27. John Dewey, *How to Think* (Boston: D. C. Heath, 1910), pp. 68–78.

28. In parliamentary procedure, the term *consensus* means "unanimous." In nonparliamentary use, the term is often assumed to mean "generally." For voting purposes, it is synonymous with "all."

29. Sarah Corbin Robert, *Robert's Rules of Order,* rev. ed. (Glenview, Ill.: Scott, Foresman, 1981), p. 339.

30. Ibid., p. 343.

31. Charles H. Kepner and Benjamin B. Tregoe, *The Rational Manager: A Systematic Approach to Problem Solving and Decision Making* (New York: McGraw-Hill, 1965).

32. Robert.

33. Benjamin J. Broome and David B. Keever, "Facilitating Group Communication: The Interactive Management Approach," paper presented at the Speech Communication Association Convention, Chicago, November 1986, pp. 4–5.

34. Kenneth D. Benne and Paul Sheets, "Functional Roles of Group Members," *Journal of Social Issues,* 4 (Spring 1948), 41–49.

35. James MacGregor Burns, *Leadership* (New York: Harper & Row, 1978). For an analysis of leadership by noted social critics and leadership experts, see the March-April 1987 issue of *Liberal Education,* 73. Also see Judy B. Sosener, "Ways Women Lead," *Harvard Business Review* (November-December 1990), 119–125.

36. Charles C. Manz and Henry P. Sims, Jr., *Superleadership* (New York: Prentice-Hall, 1989).

37. Ralph White and Ronald Lippitt, "Leader Behavior and Member Reactions in Three Social Climates," in D. Cartwright and A. Zander, eds., *Group Dynamics* (New York: Harper & Row, 1968), pp. 318–335.

38. See Fred Fielder, *A Theory of Leadership Effectiveness* (New York: McGraw-Hill, 1967).

39. Contributed by Isa Engleberg, Prince George's Community College, Largo, Maryland. Used with permission.

PART THREE

Public Communication

11 *Planning the Message*

Chapter Outline

*Learning
Outcomes*

After reading this chapter, you should be able to:

Define public communication/public speaking

Indicate the similarities between interpersonal and public communication

Explain the role of the participants, setting, and purpose/topic in relation to public communication

Define and explain the roles of prior, process, and postspeech analyses

Clarify the role of the purpose statement as it relates to a public speech

Define and explain the purpose of the goal, topic, and method in relation to developing a speech.

T he act of communication involves a transaction between a communicator/source and a communicator/receiver. Much of our communication is interpersonal, with two people exchanging the roles of the communicator/source and the communicator/receiver. But in other cases, one communicator/source presents a message to several communicator/receivers, who respond with primarily nonverbal feedback. We call this type of transaction **public communication** or **public speaking.**

You may think that public speaking is something you do not need to be concerned about, but this is not the case. In fact, a study entitled "Do Real People Ever Give Speeches?" revealed that "a surprising number of persons . . . do speak to audiences of ten or more people fairly frequently."[1] These people were asked, for example, to give speeches at bowling banquets, to address parents of children in day care, or to talk at driver safety lectures, in classes, and at union meetings.

No matter what their career and social situation, people are often called on to give speeches. Speakers can appear in a variety of roles: speaking to a group to which they belong or at conventions, or testifying before public bodies, or speaking on the radio or on TV. In the work force, people may be asked to be public speakers as they present reports and briefings to smaller groups within the company or to the public. In addition, members of religious groups are often asked to give reports, offer remarks, and make other kinds of presentations to their congregations.

Public speaking can come into play in almost any sphere. For example, researchers conducting a survey of social workers in Michigan discovered that they have to use public communication abilities. The reason for this is that the social worker "is often called upon to chair a meeting, conduct a workshop or make a presentation and the success of many

*In public speaking, one com-
municator/source presents a
message to several communication receivers who send
back non-verbal feedback.*

social service programs is dependent on the professional's ability to present an understandable and persuasive case as he or she seeks community support."[2]

Corporations have recognized the importance of this skill by establishing speakers bureaus to provide representatives who discuss company issues and programs before various audiences. For many of these corporations, public communication is no longer viewed simply as the responsibility of the public relations department. Indeed, many utilities companies now send out a wide range of employees—including meter readers, engineers, chemists, executives, managers, and home economists—to present speeches and slide shows on energy-related topics. The firms train these speakers and assign them to address civic, service, and social organizations based on the needs of these groups.[3]

This sort of program illustrates awareness among corporation executives of the importance of public communication. For this reason, executives now appear on television commercials and schedule important speeches to groups throughout the areas they serve in an effort to maintain public contact.

No matter what your college major or present position, the odds are that you will be doing some type of public speaking in the course of your career. For you and for every other American, public speaking plays a significant part in the communication process.

Similarities Between Interpersonal and Public Communication

In interpersonal and public communication many basic principles are the same. In each, the communicator/source must gain the attention of the communicator/receiver, motivate him or her to listen, clarify terms, use appropriate language, organize ideas clearly, adapt to the needs of the receiver, choose appropriate examples and appeals, use relevant elaborations and explanations, develop a purposeful message, reinforce ideas, and use supplemental aids if needed.

As in all communication, there are at least three factors to consider when planning a public communication.

1. *The participants*—the persons engaged in the communication event
2. *The setting*—the place, time, and emotional climate of the event
3. *The purpose and topic of the communication*—what the communicator is trying to accomplish (answer a question, bid for attention, change a point of view, or influence others to take an action) and what the subject of the presentation is

Getting Started

The first questions asked by someone who is going to present a speech are "How do I get started?" and "Then what do I do?" When preparing a speech, first decide on a topic and formulate a purpose statement. Next do any necessary research to collect material that develops the purpose statement. After this preliminary work, construct an introduction that will get the audience's attention and give listeners the necessary background material so they will be ready to hear the details of the subject. When these details have been provided, move on to the statement of the central idea, which tells the audience what the speech is all about. The body of the presentation is then formulated so that the purpose is accomplished. The conclusion summarizes the points and wraps up the presentation. Though not all speakers follow this exact order, it will assure the presenter of a well-constructed speech.

Components of Analysis Any act of communication is based on three parameters: the participants, the setting, and the purpose of the communication. In a presentational speaking context, these three parameters may affect the topic selected, the language used, the types of examples and illustrations chosen, and the supplementary aids needed to support and/or clarify ideas.

The **participants** include the speaker and the members of the audience. The **setting** includes where the speech is being given, what the time limit is, and when the presentation is being made. The **purpose** centers on the speaker's expected outcomes for the presentation.

To give effective speeches, analyze the three parameters. Such an investigation is done in three stages: prior analysis, process analysis, and postspeech analysis. Though the majority of the work takes place during the **prior analysis,** which occurs before the speech is given, watching the audience for feedback—the **process analysis**—and paying attention to the reactions after the speech—**postspeech analysis**—are also important.

Prior Analysis

In some instances, you are given a topic and told who is going to be in attendance and how long you are to speak. At other times, you may be left on your own to figure out what you are going to do with the time you have before the audience.

Topic Selection

If you are given total freedom to choose a topic, examine yourself first. What are you interested in speaking about? What do you know about that would be of interest to others? What subject would you feel most comfortable with and most knowledgeable about? Do you think you could develop an interesting and successful presentation on this subject?

You are your best resource. This does not mean you have to know everything about the topic at the start. You can read, do interviews, and investigate the topic beyond your present level of knowledge. Most people do their best job of speaking when they choose something they are interested in talking about.

Though it may seem ideal, being given a totally open choice of topic may be a scary proposition. One of the major stumbling blocks of inexperienced speakers centers on "What should I speak about?" In searching for a topic, you may want to consider your speaking inventory—your life experiences and interests. Consider such areas as your hobbies and special skills, your work, places you have traveled, things you know about (sports, machinery you can operate, games), jobs you have held, your experiences (accidents, special events), funny things that have happened to you, books you have read, movies you have seen, interesting people you know, people you admire, your college major, class topics that you found interesting, social and political views you hold, or your religious or ethnic background. Do not assume that because you are not the world's greatest authority on something or that because you have had limited experiences in certain areas, you have nothing to talk about. You do! We all have an inventory of possible ideas to share. To find your speaker's inventory, do this chapter's "Learn by Doing," activity 1.

There are various ways that a speaker can adapt to feedback received from an audience.

If you are giving the speech for a class assignment, you may want to see which of the areas in your speaking inventory fit the requirements. Once you have selected a topic from your inventory, continue your search by examining the people to whom you are going to speak. This investigation is called **audience analysis.**

If you are preparing a speech for a class or work situation, look around at the people in the room. Try to figure out who they are. If you are going to speak to a group of strangers, ask the person who engaged you for some information about the group: "Why are these people gathered together?" "What types of presentations have they liked in the past?" Also, think about topics they have heard and read about frequently. People tend to tune out material that is trite, overused, uninteresting, and not significant to them.

Some of your questions and observations can center on audience factors: age, sex, religion, cultural background, intellectual level, occupation, ethnic background, political affiliation, and social and economic background. By finding out this demographic information, you can decide which topic from your inventory may fit this particular group.

Age.   A person near the age of retirement may be interested in discussing the present structure of the Social Security system, but it is highly doubtful that a six-year-old will be equally attentive. This is just one example of the importance of analyzing your audience in terms of age.

Sex.   A self-help group for women who have children with learning disabilities will obviously have particular needs that should be recognized and addressed by any invited speaker. In a similar fashion, a group of single fathers will reflect interests and concerns that a speaker should relate to.

Furthermore, be aware that making sexist statements often brings problems. For example, former president Reagan found himself in trouble when he addressed a female group and said, " 'If it wasn't for women, us men would still be walking around in skin suits carrying clubs!' "[4] This statement was intended to acknowledge the contributions of women to American society and came just after the resignation of a member of his staff who had accused him of not offering equal opportunities for women in his administration. Unfortunately, because of the way in which the statement was worded, it was taken as demeaning and as encouraging the stereotyped view that a woman's primary role is to nurture others.

Religion.   A speaker can establish or destroy a common bond with specific religious groups through his or her selection of a topic. It seems unwise, for example, to propose before a Catholic audience that Catholicism has been responsible for the destruction of such civilizations as those of the Mayas and the Incas.

The same holds true for politicians, as a candidate for the presidential nomination discovered when he referred to Jews as "Hymies" and New York as "Hymietown" during a primary campaign.[5] That slip of the tongue cost him many votes.

Cultural Background.   An audience's cultural background is often as important as its religious affiliation. Speaking about Polish food or customs to a group that happens to be of Polish extraction seems plausible, but telling stories that ridicule or make fun of Poles is not wise.

Intellectual Level.   An analysis of the audience's intellectual level, educational background, and training in a particular subject can help you select a topic. Remember that people can feel threatened if what you are talking about is beyond their understanding. Some people may be alienated, for example, if a communication expert begins a speech by saying, "There appears to be a definite anthropological basis, as developed through the works of Hall, for the proxemic behavior of all people." Instead, the speaker is better off discussing an elementary aspect of nonverbal communication with any group that does not include specialists in the field. Proxemic behavior, because it is unfamiliar to most people, is probably a poor choice.

Occupation. It is an excellent idea to form a common bond with an audience by using occupational interests and experiences as the basis for your communication. This is comparatively simple because we all do it daily—students discuss their school activities with each other; factory workers discuss problems; doctors and nurses complain about hospital procedures. A problem arises when a speaker fails to realize that her or his occupational concerns may be of little or no interest to the audience or are of interest to only a select group.

Ethnic Background. Along with religious affiliation and cultural background, the ethnic make-up of the audience is a prime consideration. For example, a film producer will show an understanding of audience analysis by choosing "the changing role of blacks in films" as the topic for a speech to a predominantly black audience.

Political Affiliation. The speaker rose from his seat, crossed to a position behind the lectern, looked at his audience, and said, "The changing role of politics in America indicates that the Democratic Party is out of touch with the mainstream and should be considered a dead institution." He then went on to develop the reasons for his stand, ending his presentation with the statement, "There will be no Democratic Party beyond the next five years." When he was finished, there was a stony silence in the room. After a few moments, the members of the audience rose from their seats and began to talk, ignoring him completely. The setting? A Democratic women's club meeting in a small midwestern town. The speaker obviously did not consider the audience's political beliefs.

Social and Economic Levels. In selecting a topic, you should analyze the social and economic levels of the group. For example, in addressing a gathering of patrons of the arts, you may well remark on a recent symphony performance made possible by the contributions of such a group. But if you try the same approach with a group of less wealthy people, the results may be disastrous.

Communication among members of different social strata may be awkward or uncomfortable. This is developed beautifully in the musical comedy *My Fair Lady,* based on George Bernard Shaw's *Pygmalion,* in which Eliza, a lower-class flower girl, is a failure with upper-class Londoners because of differences in language, attitudes, and interests until she learns their vocabulary, pronunciation patterns, and conversational topics.

Language Selection Like the topic, the language selected for use during a speech must also be adapted to the audience. Clearly, the average thirteen-year-old's vocabulary is not the same as an adult's. By the same token, certain terms that are common to a specific religious or cultural group may be unknown to a person who is not a member of that group. And a person who is well versed in a specific topic can easily forget that the audience may not have the same knowledge or know the same terms. For example, a mental health clinician who talks about "closing the case at intake so as to maximize rehabilitative procedures" is using a specialized vocabulary that will not be understood by someone who is not in the mental health field.

The effect of poor audience analysis was clearly brought out when the Secretary of the Interior spoke without considering the wrath of the American people regarding slurs on minorities and persons with handicaps. In explaining the make-up of his advisory committee, the secretary stated that it was composed of " 'three Democrats, two Republicans, every kind of mix you can have. I have a black, a woman, two Jews, and a cripple. And we have talent.' "[6] Political experts agree that this statement dealt the final blow to his tenure in office.

A crucial factor in effective communication is the adaptation of your vocabulary to the level of your audience. Of course, this does not mean that you have to talk down to the level of your least-informed listener, but at the same time you must be aware that the audience may not be able to understand you.

In selecting your terminology, you may ask, "What words didn't I know before I became the 'expert' I am now?" Whatever words you come up with should be clarified for the audience. Before you read this book, for example, the words *kinesics* and *proxemics* may have been unknown to you. Thus in giving a speech about the information in this book to an audience of people who have not read it, you are wise to define these terms as they are mentioned. Remember that your nonverbal vocabulary can also be misconstrued. A person holding up an index finger and a middle finger in a V may be trying to indicate victory (as British Prime Minister Winston Churchill did during World War II). But depending on the age and background of the audience, the sign may be interpreted to mean "peace" (as it was during the campus unrest of the late 1960s, early 1970s, and again in the 1990s), "I have to go to the lavatory" (as used by a child who was told by the teacher to signal in times of physical necessity), or the number two. You must be aware that different groups use signs in different ways. If you assume that your usage is universally accepted, you may be misunderstood.

Process Analysis In the second stage of analysis, process analysis, you analyze the feedback you are receiving during the speech itself. Nonverbal cues of atten-

The setting for public communication may be affected by its emotional climate—the psychological state of the participants.

tiveness, boredom, agreement, and hostility can all be conveyed through posture and facial expression. Some speakers and theater performers are sensitive to what they term a "cough meter." If you have lost your audience, you will hear the results as the people clear their throats, cough, and become restless.

Effective process analysis requires that you interpret cues accurately and then adapt to them. Be careful not to assume, for instance, that a hostile response from one or two people represents the response of most of your listeners. The more experience you have in reading and adapting to feedback, the more accurate your process analysis will be.

There are various ways to adapt to the feedback you receive. For example, if you feel the audience does not understand a point, add an illustration, clarify your terms, or restate the idea. If you sense that the audience is not attentive, change the volume of your voice, use a pause, move forward, ask a direct question, or insert an interesting or humorous anecdote.

Postspeech Analysis

A postspeech analysis enables you to determine how the speech affected the audience. After all, this information can be useful in preparing and presenting future speeches. One very direct way to conduct a postspeech analysis is to have a question-and-answer session—the questions your audience asks may reveal just how clear your presentation really was. The tone of the questions may also reflect the general mood of the listeners, telling you how positively or negatively they have received you and your message. Informal conversations with members of the audience after the speech will also reveal a good deal.

Other postspeech techniques include opinion ballots, tests, questionnaires, and follow-up interviews. Some researchers even use electronic devices to measure such physical characteristics as pupil dilation, heart rate, and perspiration level of the listeners' palms. Nevertheless, these electronic techniques are usually appropriate only in laboratory settings and are of little practical value to public speakers.

Setting   Just as you analyze your audience, so, too, should you analyze the setting in which you find it. For instance, a speaker who is called on to address the local Jaycees at their monthly dinner meeting should be aware that

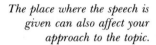

The place where the speech is given can also affect your approach to the topic.

the setting calls for a light, short speech after the meal has been served. At the same time, the place, time limit, time of day, and emotional climate are all important factors in public speaking.

Place   The effect of a place on the tone and topic of a speech is sometimes fairly obvious. For example, a detailed description of a dissection lecture originally given in a biology class may not be suitable for an after-dinner speech.

The way you give a speech also varies with the setting, with the same topic being approached differently in different settings. Suppose, for example, the subject is the changing sex roles in American society. In a sociology class, a speaker may consider the history of male and female roles in the United States, the differences in sex roles in various cultures, and the factors that have brought about changing attitudes toward male and female roles. In contrast, at a women's rights meeting, the speaker, realizing the participants have already accepted the idea that society looks down on and discriminates against women, may focus on a particular aspect of this issue by discussing a strategy for obtaining new legislation to ensure equal opportunities for women.

Such factors as the size of a room, the temperature, the lighting, the arrangement of the furniture, and the physical comfort or discomfort of the audience all affect your communication. For example, we tend to speak in proportion to the size of a room, with a large, crowded one leading to larger gestures and louder speech and close, intimate conditions lending themselves to quiet tones. Physical proximity cuts down the broadness of gestures. A brightly lit room fosters louder sounds than a dimly lit one, and a furniture arrangement that encourages people to sit in clusters produces more intimate transactions than one that requires members of the audience to spread out.

Time   Both the time limit and the time of day affect a speaker's performance. Time limits are set for various reasons. For example, the room may have to be vacated by a particular hour, or audience members may have other commitments. The time limit may also be dictated by a radio or television commitment. The speaker may impose certain restrictions. For example, the length of a speech may be planned on the basis of past observations of how long a particular group was capable of paying attention. Or a speaker may set a time limit because audience members can dedicate only a particular segment of their meeting to the presentation.

Whatever the reason for the time limit, a speaker has an obligation to stay within the prescribed boundaries. This requires careful narrowing of a topic and careful structuring of its presentation.

Speakers should also be aware that the time of day can affect an audience. The early morning and the late night hours, for example, often are difficult times to hold the attention of an audience. At times like these, careful consideration should be given to using humorous or dramatic devices that will wake up the audience and keep it alert. Presentations immediately after lunches and dinners may be affected by the drowsiness that typically follows a meal. In these cases, special care should be taken to select unusual, dramatic, or humorous material to hold the audience's attention.

Emotional Climate   The setting for public communication may also be affected by its **emotional climate**—the overriding psychological state of the participants. A community recently devastated by a tornado, for example, certainly would have a special emotional climate. Thus a speaker called on to present a speech in such a setting would have to adapt his or her message to the tragedy and deal with the fears, bitterness, and trauma experienced by the audience. Similarly, a speaker invited to address a civic organization in a community that had just been named "outstanding community of the year" would want to adjust the message to reflect the pride and satisfaction felt by the participants. Special occasions like this often create an emotional climate and provide a framework for selection of both materials and language.

Purpose

In developing a message, a speaker should know specifically what she or he wants to communicate. Thus before they even start to develop their presentations, many public speakers write a **purpose statement** in which they define their subject and develop the criteria by which they will evaluate material that may be included in the speech.

Speakers who cannot write a purpose statement often do not have a clear idea of what they are trying to say. They usually make a broad statement such as "I'm going to talk about income taxes." Unfortunately, this sort of statement is so vague that it allows the speaker to wander in both preparation and presentation. In this case, the speaker may be asked what specifically about income tax she or he plans to address—the history? the regulations? the penalty system? Though developing a clear purpose statement may take time, in the long run it usually saves frustration and time by making the speaker select a narrow, specific area and stick to it. The purpose statement typically consists of three parts: the goal of the speech, the statement of the topic, and the method or process to be used to develop the speech.

Goal The **goal** of a speech is expressed in terms of its expected outcome: **to inform** (imparting new information and securing understanding or reinforcing information and understandings that were accumulated in the past) or **to persuade** (attempting to get the listener to take some action, accept a belief, or change a point of view).

Topic The **topic,** the subject of your speech, should be stated as specifically as possible. If you are not specific, you may find yourself mentally wandering around, unable to find and narrow your material. There is a difference between talking about "my trip to New Zealand" and "the art of natural wool weaving as done by New Zealand artists" or listing your topic as "education" when, in fact, you will be speaking about "why I believe that assessment tests should be given for placement of all college freshmen into communication classes." If you are not specific in your topic choice, your listeners may never get your point.

Make sure you keep your audience analysis in mind when wording the subject. A topic that fits you quite well may not fit the audience at all. The way you approach a subject may determine whether an audience

The topic of a speech should be stated as specifically as possible.

becomes interested. Examine the topic from the audience's standpoint. If you were listening to someone else speak on this topic, what approach would interest you? For example, if you are knowledgeable about word processing, telling the audience what you do as a word processor may not fascinate them. If, however, you are speaking to college students, describing how they can use a word processor to improve their grades will be a better approach. To go even further, if the group consists of other word-processing personnel, you can share with them "five tricks I've learned that have made it easier for me to save time while operating word-processing equipment."

Remember, you are only one of the participants. You must also take the audience into consideration. People tend to listen to topics that they perceive have some effect on them. If given the opportunity, select and narrow a topic that gives you a fighting chance to grab and hold the audience's attention. To do so, keep these points in mind. First, you have only a certain amount of time. Make sure you can adequately cover the topic you have decided on in the time allowed. Also, do not be egotistical in believing that the audience will listen just because you are speaking. For example, if you are typical, you mentally pick up your books and leave class the instant the class period is supposed to be over, no matter how much the instructor believes that she or he has time for "just one more idea." Audiences do about the same thing to a long-winded speaker who exceeds their expectations for the time limit.

Second, decide how to approach the presentation. If the topic requires an in-depth study of one factor, then present a **vertical development,** a single issue in great detail. If, however, the topic requires a complete survey of surface-level ideas, present a **horizontal development.** Either approach can be successful, depending on the subject and your purpose. If, for example, you are going to share with the audience the topic of a play production, you may narrow the topic so that you cover only how a play is cast and go into specific detail about each phase of choosing the actors and actresses (vertical development). In contrast, you can use the same amount of time to discuss the process used for staging a play. In this case, you tell just a little about casting, blocking stage movements, and conducting rehearsals (horizontal development). In the former speech the audience becomes very knowledgeable about one phase of staging a play, whereas in the latter speech the audience has a general idea of the entire process. Be careful, however, of using the horizontal approach. Do not spread the ideas so thin that there is little idea development.

Third, analyze your audience and satisfy its needs. As in making any decision about a speech, you are wise to ask yourself what phase of your topic the audience will be interested in hearing about and how to get the idea(s) across. Narrow your topic from broad to specific by deciding how to best approach your listeners. For example, how much background will they need? If the topic is complex, devote time to definitions and background information. The more complex your subject is, the more specific you have to be. Also, repeat your major concepts in various ways to ensure that the audience understands. Think of a class in which you had difficulty grasping ideas—if the instructor had broken the topic down into segments and approached each segment from several perspectives, so that if you did not grasp the material one way, you could another way, you would probably have had an easier time.

Similarly, be aware of how to approach and narrow a topic. For instance, a speaker has decided to share with a class of nonmedia majors his knowledge about how a television show is produced, believing that because they are media consumers they should be curious about how their favorite TV shows get from script to screen. After analyzing the audience, the speaker realizes that the vocabulary of TV production is complex. A typical beginning production class vocabulary list contains about 250 terms. An understanding of many of these words is necessary to grasp even the most elementary phases of TV production. Obviously, the speaker cannot impart all these terms and cover all the phases of TV production. If he narrows the subject to the role of the director, and then narrows it further to how a director plans what pictures will appear on the screen and in what order, the task becomes manageable. By explaining what a "storyboard," "script," and "calls" are, the speaker has laid the necessary foundation. Then he can go into an explanation of the seven steps for getting the shots on the TV screen. If he uses visual displays and accompanies the explanation with a videotape of a show in production, he has narrowed the subject and selected the process by which he can achieve his goal.

Method   When you write out a purpose statement, use key words to indicate the **method,** or process, you are going to employ in developing your goal. In an informative speech, for example, key words can include:

"By analyzing"
"By demonstrating"
"By explaining"
"By summarizing"
"By comparing"
"By contrasting"
"By describing"
"By discussing"

"By listing"

"By showing."

Examples of informative purpose statements are:

To inform the audience why competency testing is being used as a determination for high school graduation by discussing the three major reasons for its use.

To inform the audience how to make a cut-glass sun hanger by listing the supplies needed and the step-by-step construction procedure.

To inform the audience that vitamin C protects against the common cold by examining four scientific studies that provide evidence for this viewpoint.

To inform the audience why I believe that the Beatles had an important effect on modern music by showing the changes in music before and after the Beatles' era.

To inform the audience why I believe that the theory of color therapy is valid by examining the research and findings by color therapy investigators.

In a persuasive speech, you can use these key words in your purpose statement:

"To accept that"

"To attend"

"To join"

"To participate in"

"To support"

"To agree with"

"To contribute to"

"To lend"

"To serve"

"To volunteer to"

"To aid in"

"To defend"

"To offer to"

"To share"

"To vote for"

Examples of persuasive purpose statements are:

To persuade the audience to accept the belief that Columbus discovered America by investigating four different viewpoints concerning the discovery and showing why the Columbus version is correct.

To persuade the audience that video games have no adverse physical and psychological effects on children by presenting the research that proves the lack of effect.

To persuade the audience to fill out and sign living wills by listing five reasons for them to take the action.

To persuade the audience to accept the concept that getting help from a mental health professional can be a positive act by examining the five most common reasons people seek help and the statistics showing the success rate of treatment for those problems.

By keeping these three factors—goal, topic, and method—in mind you can avoid some of the major pitfalls of neophyte speakers. These pitfalls include not finishing the speech in the time limit, not accomplishing the speech's purpose, and not allowing the audience to gain the information.

Summary

This chapter examined the planning of a public communication. The major ideas presented were:

- ☐ Public communication, or public speaking, involves one communicator/source presenting a message to several communicator/receivers, who respond with primarily nonverbal feedback.

- ☐ Three factors should be considered when planning a public communication: the participants, the setting, and the purpose or topic of the communication.

- ☐ Prior analysis of the audience takes place before the speech is given.

- ☐ Potential audience members are analyzed in terms of such relevant factors as age, sex, religion, cultural background, intellectual level, occupation, ethnic background, political affiliation, and social and economic levels.

- ☐ Analysis of the feedback a speaker receives during the speech is called process analysis.

- ☐ After the presentation, postspeech analysis helps to determine the effectiveness of the speaker's efforts.

- ☐ The place in which a speech occurs has an effect on the topic, tone, and way the speech is given.

- ☐ Both the time limit and the time of day may affect a speaker's performance and the audience's reception.

- ☐ A setting for a speech may also be affected by the emotional climate of the participants.

- ☐ In developing a message, a speaker should know specifically what he or she wants to communicate.
- ☐ A purpose statement defines the subject and develops criteria by which material to be included in a speech can be evaluated.
- ☐ The purpose statement consists of three parts: the goal of the speech (which states its purpose), the statement of the topic, and the method or process for developing the speech.

Key Terms

public communication	emotional climate
public speaking	purpose statement
participants	goal
setting	to inform
purpose	to persuade
prior analysis	topic
process analysis	vertical development
postspeech analysis	horizontal development
audience analysis	method

Learn by Doing

1. One of the keys to giving an effective oral presentation is to choose a subject in which you are interested and about which you have some knowledge. Fill out this "My Speaking Inventory":
   a. Hobbies and special interests
   b. Places traveled
   c. Things I know how to do (sports I can play, skills I have)
   d. Jobs I have had
   e. Experiences (accidents, special events)
   f. Funny things that have happened to me
   g. Books I have read and liked
   h. Movies and plays I have seen and liked
   i. Interesting people I have known
   j. People I admire
   k. Religious and nationality customs of my family
   l. Talents I have (musical instruments played, athletics)

2. A student is selected, blindfolded, handed ten pennies, and told that a wastebasket (preferably a metal one) is placed somewhere in the room. It is the student's task to throw the pennies, one at a time, into the wastebasket. The student is spun around several times to

become disoriented. The class is not to make any sounds while the experiment is going on. After the student tosses all the pennies, he or she is given the opportunity to repeat the activity, but this time everyone in the class is to give directions simultaneously. Then the experiment is run a third time, but now the student is to select one person who will give directions. After the three attempts, discuss the value of audience feedback, what happens when there is too much or not enough feedback, and how feedback can be used during public communication.

3. Use a topic related to your academic major to develop a purpose statement for both an informative and a persuasive speech to be given to a group of classmates. Then prepare another informative purpose statement for the same general topic but for a different audience. Do the same thing for an additional persuasive speech. Notice how the outcome of the speech varies according to the nature of the purpose statement.

4. Select a topic that you would feel comfortable speaking about to a group of people. Indicate how you would develop a speech on this topic for each of the following audiences:
   a. A high school assembly
   b. Your speech class
   c. Senior citizens
   d. A female audience
   e. A male audience

   Did you alter the presentation depending on the audience? Why or why not?

5. What questions would you ask a person who has invited you to give a speech to a club or organization? Why did you pick these questions?

6. Name some specific situations in which as a speaker you might alter your presentation because of the attitude of the prospective audience.

7. Select a general topic (The Iraqi-U.N. war, cubist painting, the U.S. presidency, abortion, and so on). Prepare a purpose statement for a speech of thirty minutes, fifteen minutes, and five minutes. Go back and analyze each of the purpose statements you wrote. What changes did you make? Why did you alter the statements?

Notes

1. Kathleen Kendall, "Do Real People Ever Give Speeches?" *Central States Speech Journal,* 25 (Fall 1974), 235.
2. "Interdepartmental Study Looks at Public Communication Skills," *Communication Research Bulletin,* 3 (Winter 1981), 1.

3. Dan H. Swenson, "Relative Importance of Business Communication Skills for the Next Ten Years," *Journal of Business Communication,* 17 (Winter 1980), 47.

4. *Time,* September 12, 1983, p. 53.

5. Bill Peterson, "Jackson Strong Showings Bring Respect to His Candidacy," *Washington Post,* April 4, 1984, p. A-8.

6. *Facts on File* (1983), 741.

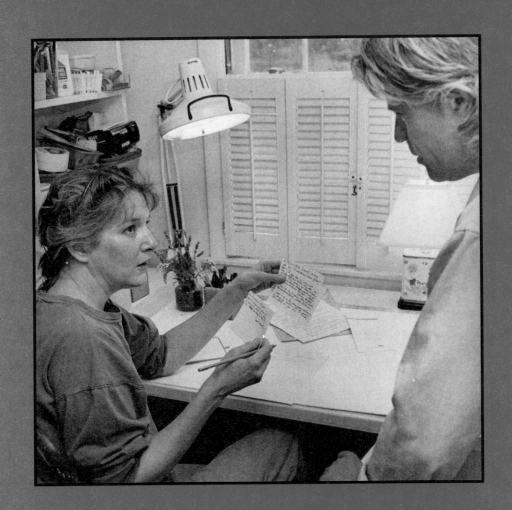

12 Developing the Message

Chapter Outline

Learning Outcomes

After reading this chapter, you should be able to:

Identify the sources used to develop public speaking messages

Detail basic reference sources used for obtaining overviews, concepts, data, and other types of information necessary for the development of public speeches

Illustrate the value of using and the method for finding books, magazines, newspapers, journals, indexes, government publications, special-interest-group publications, and nonprint media

Record research information

Identify the types of and explain the role of support material in the development of a speech

Identify and illustrate means of presenting and focusing supporting material

Clarify the role of attention in public speeches.

I t is important to remember that a good relationship between the speaker and the listener is best achieved when the listener clearly understands the intent of the message. It is important that the speaker develops the message by defining terms, offering clarifying examples, explaining abstract concepts, presenting proving statistics, restating ideas, and illustrating thoughts with supplementary aids.

Sources of Information

Most of the information we use to develop messages is based on personal experiences, personal observations, or learning acquired through sources such as school, the media, and reading. As we are exposed to information, we retain a certain amount of it. This knowledge forms the core of our communication. We select words and examples from this storehouse, and we use it to organize messages.

Sometimes, however, to develop a message, we need information that is not in this core. In such cases, we must find outside sources to aid us. As a research chemist, for example, you could probably answer someone who asked you what your company's major products were. But what would you do if you were asked to describe the company's budget in detail or relate a complete history of the organization? Most speakers would find such topics difficult to handle.

Figure 12.1

Quick Guide to Basic Reference Tools

Overviews and Concepts

Encyclopedias—use for historical, conceptual, and factual information written by experts and for bibliographies (at the ends of articles) of works by important authors.

Handbooks—use for more detailed overviews of subjects, usually in single volumes devoted to narrow fields, with articles written by experts, often with bibliographies at the ends of sections. (To locate in the card catalogue, look under *handbooks, manuals,* or the specific title of the handbook or manual.)

Dictionaries—use for definitions of terms you do not understand and for synonyms of terms for key words. Many dictionaries specialize in one subject only. (To locate in the card catalogue, look under *dictionaries,* then a specific title such as "education.")

Annual Reviews—use for recent overviews of significant developments in a subject field, usually with bibliographic information included. (To locate in the card catalog, look under *yearbooks.*)

Data

Fact Books—use for hard information on names, places, and dates in a concise format. (Listed as *almanacs* in the card catalogue. Examples: *Facts on File, Information Please Almanac.*)

Statistical Sources—use for statistical support and documentation of your ideas. (Listed in the card catalog under *statistics* and then the subject heading: for example, "Statistics—Labor Supply.")

Biographical Sources—use to verify the credentials of authors, to get information about people. (To locate in the card catalogue, consult personal names in subject headings or the name of the occupational group of the person.)

Springboards to More Information

Bibliographies—use to identify other books, parts of books, films, and magazine articles on a subject. (To locate in the card catalogue, consult the subject headings followed by the words *bibliography, biobibliography, discography,* or *film catalogue.*)

Indexes—use to locate more information; usually but not always limited to periodicals. Indexing is done for research reports, government publications, and parts of books, plays, poetry, or songs. (To locate in the card catalogue, consult subject headings by *indexes, abstracts,* or *bibliography.*)

In addition to personal knowledge, other sources of information are available to communicators who have the time and need to seek out additional material (see Figure 12.1). These sources include books, magazines, newspapers, special journals, indexes, government publications, and the publications of special-interest groups. Additional sources include nonprint materials such as tape recordings, records, films, videotapes, charts, and models as well as interviews or correspondence with knowledgeable people in a particular field.

*Sources of information avail-
able in libraries include
books, magazines, journals,
indexes, and publications.*

In addition to locating information, a speaker must assess its validity. All sources of information reflect certain perceptions and biases. Consequently, it is wise to try to determine the bias of a source and to interpret its information accordingly.[1] Thus, when doing research for a presentation, it is a good idea to find several agreeing authoritative sources so that your supporting details will be credible to your listeners.

Books Personal, academic, and public libraries can be the sources of much information; nevertheless, you must know how to find the materials you need. In academic and public libraries, books are shelved according to a numerical system and can be located by looking in the card catalog under the title, the author's name, or the general subject. The code number on each card indicates where the volume is shelved.

In many libraries, computer output microfiche (COM) or electronic catalogues accessed through on-line computers have replaced traditional card catalogues. Because of the wide use of computers, the COM may be accessed from places outside the library. Besides COM, some libraries

*Many libraries are using
computers as well as card
catalogues.*

have their catalogues on magnetic tape that requires a computer terminal for access.

Unfortunately, not all subjects are easy to locate. For example, an
average library's card catalogue or COM would reveal no information if
you looked under the title "Arapesh." Thus to learn which books contain
material about this subject, you would need some additional information. By looking in the encyclopedia, you would discover that the Arapesh are a primitive mountain-dwelling people of New Guinea whose
society was investigated by anthropologist Margaret Mead and discussed
in her book *Sex and Temperament in Three Primitive Societies*. Based on this
information, you could look in the COM or card catalogue under such
subjects as anthropology, Margaret Mead, New Guinea, and *Sex and
Temperament in Three Primitive Societies*. You could then check the indexes
of the books listed for references to needed facts.

Books are of great value in supplying information, but they can
quickly become out of date. It generally takes at least a year for an
average book to move from the author's final draft through the printing
process and onto the shelves of a library. In addition, the author has
taken a period of time to write the book, which also dates the information. Some subjects change little, and in these areas books are a good

research source. But for quickly changing subjects, more up-to-date sources are needed for a thorough investigation.

Magazines

Most magazines are designed to print recent information quickly. Sources such as *Time, Newsweek,* and *U.S. News & World Report* are published weekly, so their information is current. Researchers must be aware, however, that because these sources gather their data so quickly, some inaccuracies may occur. In addition, the editorial staffs of magazines—like the authors of books—sometimes have political and ideological biases that may temper what they write or influence what subjects they include.

To find information in magazines, start with the *Readers' Guide to Periodical Literature,* a publication that indexes magazine articles by subject, title, and author. Remember, however, that not all magazines are listed in this guide. Check inside the cover of the bound volumes to see which magazines are listed. Many libraries also indicate which magazines they subscribe to so that researchers can narrow their choices to those publications.

Further periodical listings may also be found in the *International Index* or in indexes to special magazines that report on particular areas, such as computers, nursing, or dental care. Business information can be found in *Business Periodicals Index* and educational concepts in *Education Index;* the arts are covered in the *Humanities Index,* and psychology and sociology are in the *Social Sciences Index.*

Newspapers

Newspapers, like magazines, contain current information that is published daily, weekly, or biweekly. Again, as is the case with magazines, because of the speed with which newspapers are written and printed, you must be aware of the possibility of error. Many libraries do not keep past issues of newspapers, but some store newspaper information on microfilm. In addition, some newspapers, such as the *New York Times,* have indexes similar in format to the *Readers' Guide to Periodical Literature.*

Journals

Professional organizations often publish journals reporting research and theories in their specific fields. The Speech Communication Association, for example, publishes such journals as *Communication Education,* the *Quarterly Journal of Speech, Communication Monographs,* and *Critical Studies in Mass Communication.* Thus students interested in finding out about some area of speech communication can refer to these journals. Similarly, students of law enforcement can find topics directly related to their field in such publications as *The Training Key,* a brochure circulated by the International Association of Chiefs of Police, and the *Journal of Law and Criminology.*

Indexes   Encyclopedias, atlases, and bibliographical guides are all indexes that provide descriptive information in certain categories. In trying to find bibliographical material about the author Carl Sandburg, for instance, you are wise to consult *Who's Who Among North American Authors. Who's Who in America,* another index, is also a possible source for this information.

Remember that an index gives you a minimal amount of information. Thus, if you want in-depth material about Carl Sandburg, a more fruitful approach is to search the subject index of the card catalogue or COM to locate such sources as *Carl Sandburg* by G. W. Allen and *Carl Sandburg, Lincoln of Our Literature* by N. Callahan.

When using encyclopedias, you do well to recognize that many of them are expensive to produce and therefore are not totally reprinted each year. As a result, some material in encyclopedias may be out of date as well as limited.

Government Publications   The U.S. government publishes pamphlets, available at minimal cost, on a variety of subjects. These can be found at bookstores inside federal buildings in many major cities of the United States. But if there is none in your area, write to the Superintendent of Documents, U.S. Government Printing Office in Washington, D.C., and ask for information about the specific topics you wish to research. Because it takes time for the information to be processed, plan ahead if you want to use this source. Also be aware that many libraries have government pamphlets in their research sections.

Special-Interest-Group Publications   Special-interest groups such as the American Cancer Society, the Coalition for Rural Development, the American Chemical Society, and the American Society for Training and Development publish information regarding their research and programs. A telephone call or a letter to such an organization often brings a prompt response with the requested materials. Information about these groups can be located in the telephone book or in *Gale's Encyclopedia of Associations.*

Nonprint Media   Much information is also available from nonprint media. In fact, libraries and audiovisual departments of colleges and universities often have tape recordings, records, films, filmstrips, and videotapes from commercially and locally prepared sources covering a variety of topics. These sources are usually catalogued in a manner similar to that used for books and periodicals. Some nonprint materials are available for general circulation, but others must be used on the premises.

Interviews   Interviews can be used to find information that is not available from written or audiovisual sources or to supplement other types of research. After all, what better way is there to find out, for example, how the budget of your college is developed than by talking to the treasurer or the budget director? Such interviews can be conducted in a variety of ways. If someone is not available for a face-to-face or a telephone session, you can submit a series of questions to be answered either through writing or tape recording.

Interviews can be used to find information that is not available from written or audiovisual sources or to supplement other types of research.

Computer Searches   Normally, a researcher gets information by going to a library and look-ing in a card catalogue or a reader's guide or asking the reference librar-ian what sources are available. No matter how thorough this method of search is, many references are usually missed. Until fairly recently, little could be done about this situation. Now many libraries and educational institutions have developed a way to tap into formerly unavailable sources. The development of the computer and of systems for the library computer search has changed the nature of information gathering in many libraries and on college campuses.

The computer search is a computer-based retrieval system that allows the researcher to compile a bibliography or a set of facts relevant to a specific topic. Searches may be used for a variety of purposes, including gathering research or references, compiling a reading list, acquiring sta-tistical information, or simply keeping abreast of developments in a field.

Naturally, a major advantage to this method is the time saved, as a computer retrieves in minutes information that otherwise takes much longer to compile. The search is also quite comprehensive and can locate references that the most careful conventional searches may not. Another feature is the timeliness of the material; these databases are frequently updated. Database searching is done by the use of BRS Information Technologies, DIALOG, or Lockheed Corp. services. These three com-mercial vendors of computer services are often tied into long distance services (TYME, TYMNET, or Telenet Communications Corporation) that allow people who subscribe to the service and have special equip-ment, usually a modem, to search for and store information. These databases can be accessed from classrooms, dorms, homes, or faculty offices. A charge is made by the minute for the use of the service.[2]

Recording Your Research

When you do research, keep a record of where your information came from so you can refer to the source to find additional information, answer questions about a source, or give oral footnotes during a speech. When you write a term paper, footnote **quotations** (material written or spoken by a person in the exact words in which it was presented) or **paraphrases** (someone else's ideas put into your own words). Do the same in public speaking, except orally. For example, in a speech concerning male-female communication, this **oral footnote** is appropriate: "Deborah Tannen, in her book, *You Just Don't Understand,* stated, 'Habitual ways of talking are hard to change. Learning to respect others' ways of talking may be a bit easier. Men should accept that many women regard exchanging details about personal lives as a basic ingredient of intimacy, and women should accept that many men do not share this view.' "[3]

In some instances, you may also feel that it is necessary to establish the quoted author as an authority. In this case, your oral footnote may say, "Deborah Tannen, an internationally recognized scholar, has received grants from the National Endowment for the Humanities and the National Science Foundation and is a professor of linguistics at Georgetown University."

There are many ways to record both the bibliographical information and the notes that result from your research. One method is to use a running bibliography that lists the names of the authors, the sources used, and the places, publishers, and dates of the materials' publication. The list is numbered so that it can be used in taking notes. An example is shown here:

BIBLIOGRAPHY
1. Lewis, Garland. *Nurse-Patient Communication,* 3rd ed. Dubuque, Iowa: William C. Brown, 1978, p. 4.
2. Russell, Mary. "Career Planning in a Blue-Collar Company," *Training and Development Journal,* 38 (January 1984), 87–88.
3. Interview with Mr. Allen Meyers, White House speech writer, Washington, D.C., April 26, 1984.

As you do your research and record your information, you can refer to the source by number, thus eliminating the necessity of continually writing out the bibliographical material. You can refer to the male-female quotation, for example, as 1-122 (source 1 on the bibliography, page 122). Because the material is directly quoted, put quotation marks around it. If it is paraphrased, the use of quotation marks is not necessary, but be aware that the material is not original to you, but from another source.

Notes can be taken on three-by-five-inch or four-by-six-inch cards or on sheets of paper. If cards are used, a footnote reference looks like the following:

Topic	The Role of Communication in Nursing
Source	1–4
Information	"Communication is a vital part of the nurse's work whether it involves direct contact with patients or other nursing personnel."

If you use sheets of paper, you can identify the source in the left-hand margin and later cut the paper into strips when you begin to organize your speech. The form looks like this:

Source 1–4   "Communication is a vital part of the nurse's work whether it involves direct contact with patients or other nursing personnel."

Supporting Material

When gathering material to develop a speech, you are wise to keep in mind how that material can be used to support the main points within the body of the speech. **Supporting material** gathered through research should clarify your point or offer proof—that is, it should demonstrate that the point has some probability of being true. Some forms of support are more useful for clarity, whereas others are more useful for proof.

No matter what type of supporting material you use, choose the most accurate. The forms of support you select depend on your purposes, but the most common are illustrations, specific instances, expositions, statistics, analogies, and testimony.

To make a statement and prove it, begin with a **statement of declaration**; give the necessary exposition (stating the major contentions of the speech), such as clarifying necessary terms; and then develop the idea with illustrations, specific instances, statistics, analogies, and testimony. Without such clarification and development, the audience will often not understand the idea and will have little reason to accept your contentions. For example, a speech on bulimia included these statements:

Statement of declaration: "Bulimia is an eating disorder that involves binging and purging."
Exposition—definition of term: "Binging is when the bulimic takes in as much food as possible, as much as 20,000 calories at a time."
Statistics: "This would be like eating 210 brownies or 5½ layer cakes or 18 dozen cookies."
Exposition—definition of term: "Purging is the evacuation of the food."
Specific instances: "The ways they do this are by self-induced vomiting, use of laxatives (as many as 100 at a time), or ingestion of diet pills."

Illustrations   Examples that explain a subject through the use of detailed stories are called **illustrations.** They are intended to clarify a point, not offer proof. They may be hypothetical or factual.

If the illustrations are hypothetical, the speaker should make this clear to listeners by saying, for example, "Suppose you were . . ." or "Let us all imagine that . . ." Hypothetical illustrations can be used, for instance, by a medical technician taking a listener on a theoretical trip through the circulatory system. The following example uses a hypothetical illustration to support the point that laws are necessary:

> Suppose that America were a land without laws. People would then have no restraints. They would be free to murder their neighbors, steal from shopping centers, drive as they wished, and destroy the property of others. Chaos would reign, and human beings would soon be forced to return to a situation in which only the fittest would survive. This might lead to the establishment of laws so that individuals could live in harmony with their neighbors.

In contrast, a factual illustration is a real or actual story. It can be introduced by statements such as "When I came to school this morning . . . " or "President Truman used to reminisce . . ." A factual illustration can be used by a mother relating her personal experience during delivery or by a rape survivor who tells the story of the assault. One speaker developed a speech on safety codes with this factual illustration:

> Where Memorial School stands today, Jefferson School once stood. One day a devastating fire struck Jefferson School. Many students and teachers struggled frantically to escape the ravaging flames, but the fire quickly burned out of control. Eighty students and four teachers lost their lives in that tragic fire, and hundreds of others were seriously injured; they carry their scarring and crippling wounds to this day. The new Memorial School can never eradicate the memories of those who died during the tragic fire.

A speaker must select illustrations carefully so they will be relevant to his or her listeners. For example, a funny story about Uncle Henry that does not relate directly to the point is best saved for another time. To be interesting, illustrations should be presented concisely. In addition, if the story goes on and on, listeners will have difficulty following or remembering the point the speaker is trying to develop.

Think back to some of the more memorable speakers you have heard. They probably used a number of relevant, interesting stories to support their points. This technique offers listeners something to identify with and have feelings about. As a result, they can better understand the points being made.

Specific Instances

Condensed examples that are used to clarify or prove a point are called **specific instances.** Because they are not developed in depth, you can say a great deal quickly by using them and can provide listeners with evidence they can relate to your point.

If you want to develop the idea that speech communication is an interesting major for college students, you can support your point with specific instances of careers that employ communication majors: speech writing, teaching, research and training in business and industrial communication, political campaigning, health communication, and public relations. These are all careers that should be familiar to your listeners. If, however, you add an unfamiliar example such as human cybernetic processing, you run the risk of losing your listeners while they try to figure out what you mean. Thus be sure to use specific instances that will be understood by your listeners.

Exposition   An **exposition** gives the necessary background information to listeners so they can understand the material being presented. Sometimes, for example, the speaker will want to define specific terms, give historical information, explain the relationship between herself or himself and the topic, or explain the process that will be used during the presentation. In using exposition, the speaker must also attempt to anticipate or alter a message to provide listeners with the background information they need for understanding the transaction.

The speaker, realizing an obligation to aid the audience in understanding the message, may feel a need to define terms and ideas that will be used in the presentation. For example, a speaker who wants to explain the advertising campaign to be used in marketing a product may find it necessary—during introductory remarks or within the message—to clarify such terms and phrases as "bandwagoning," "plus-and-minus factor of surveying," and "Nielsen average rating."

An audience may need historical information as well. For listeners to understand the outcome of the Watergate investigation, for instance, they may need to know the specific events that led to the decision to launch the investigation. Similarly, in discussing the plays of Tennessee Williams, the speaker is wise to give a biographical history because many of Williams's plays draw on his personal life.

Listeners may also need a bridge between the speaker and the topic to understand why the speaker is discussing the subject or to establish the speaker's expertise. For example, a student nurse who is explaining the nursing program she recently completed should share her educational background with the audience. A woman who has undergone surgery for breast cancer will want to make that fact clear to a group of X-ray technicians when explaining the emotional impact that X-ray treatment can have on a patient. A person who has known and worked with someone intimately seems a credible source to discuss her or him. For instance, composer Richard Rodgers described the working style of Oscar Hammerstein II, his collaborator on such musicals as *South Pacific*, *Oklahoma*, and *Carousel*.

In addition, indicating the process to be followed during a presentation or the results the speaker wants to achieve may also be helpful to listeners. An outline of the major points to be made can be distributed or displayed, or the speaker can explain what she or he will be doing and will want the audience to do as the speech proceeds.

A speaker discussing the organizational structure of the U.S. Information Agency might provide this exposition:

> The United States Information Agency is designed to tell America's story to people in other countries. The agency is made up of special offices that serve this purpose through their work in film, production, radio and television support, publications, and Voice of America broadcasting. Their effort is reinforced through the Overseas U.S. Information Services posts in prime locations throughout the world. The effectiveness of these services is assessed through an office of research. The key to the success of the various branches of the agency rests with the people who work in the services. They are committed to telling America's story professionally.

Statistics

Any collection of numerical information arranged to indicate representations, trends, or theories is an example of **statistics.** Statistics are used by communicators to provide a measurement ("The upper limit of hearing by the human ear is 20,000 Hz per second"); to compare ("The normal intelligible outdoor range of the male human voice in still air is 200 yards, while female screams register higher readings on decibel meters than male bellows");[4] and to demonstrate amounts ("The most recent census indicates the population of Ecuador is 8,053,280 people").[5]

Nevertheless, before accepting statistics as proof, the wise speaker follows the advice found in the book *How to Lie with Statistics* and asks herself or himself the following questions:

1. Who says so?
2. How does he or she know?
3. What is missing?
4. Did somebody change the subject?
5. Does it make sense?[6]

When statistics are accurately collected, have been properly interpreted, and are not out of date, their use is a valid aid in reaching conclusions. Unfortunately, not all statistical studies are accurately done, properly interpreted, or current.

Statistical Surveying

Statisticians have developed methods for collecting data that can be used with some degree of assurance that the resulting information will be correct.[7] Ideally, to find out everyone's opinion on a particular issue, everyone should be asked, but, of course, this is usually impossible for large groups of people. Thus to make educated guesses, statisticians have devised methods of random sampling that allow less than the entire population to be surveyed. These methods recognize the probability of error, and a speaker should so indicate when given the statistical results of a survey.

Be leery of studies in which people are allowed to call in to a radio or television station because in this sort of survey the population cannot be controlled; that is, the same people may call in over and over, or they may not be representative of the entire population. Also be suspicious if the number of people questioned is very small. Asking ten people at your college or university a question and then publishing the results as representing the entire school do not constitute a valid survey.

Proper Interpretation of Data   If a particular group or person is trying to get a specific result, that tester may keep testing until she or he gets the desired conclusion or may ignore results that do not agree with the goal. For this reason, be wary of statistics that are taken out of context, that are incomplete, or that do not specify the method used to collect the data.

Currency of Data   Studies and surveys done in the past may have been perfectly accurate at the time they were conducted. This does not mean, however, that they are accurate now. It is important that you use or receive the latest data and not allow yourself to be influenced by information that is not up to date. When you give statistical information, always note when it was collected. When you receive it, be sure to ask for such information if you have any doubts. As a communicator/receiver, it is your responsibility to make sure that your conclusion is based on accurate information.

In using statistics, you are wise to remember that a person can retain only a limited amount of information. Thus long lists, complicated numerical combinations, and extended digits may well be lost if you do not help listeners by simplification or visualization. For example, a long list—such as the figures representing the cost of each material used to produce a piece of machinery—can be written on a blackboard or poster or can be projected on a screen. In this way, listeners view as well as hear, and they can refer to the numbers as needed.

Complicated numerical combinations can be treated in the same manner as long lists. Consider, for example, the difficulty of learning geometry, algebra, or accounting without supplemental aids that assist the oral presentation. A number such as $1,243,724,863 is difficult to comprehend, but the phrase "approximately $1.25 billion" is within the grasp of an audience. Speakers should remember that although they may be familiar with the numbers and have them written down for reference, listeners are not so fortunate and must be helped to retain the message. If statistics are important enough to be included in a presentation, they are important enough to be clarified. Technical subjects in particular require visualization. Speakers are responsible for determining the best way to convey the message to listeners. Here is an example of how statistics can be used effectively to support the thesis that there is a great deal of illegal immigration into the United States from Mexico: "The Immigration and Naturalization Service reported more than 1 million arrests for illegal crossings of the Mexican border in the fiscal year that began last October 1—a 40 percent rise over the same period a year earlier."[8]

Misuse of Information

The use of statistics can be questionable, however. Sometimes information is misused (accidentally or intentionally) or not all facts are given, sometimes facts are misinterpreted, and sometimes figures are used to prove something other than their original intent. Consider the following statements: "There were 51,000 rapes in the United States in a given year." "Two children die each day in the United States as a result of child beating." "College expenses will rise around 8 percent for resident students and 6 percent for commuting students next year." These are all numbers, statistics. But are they valid? How should we interpret these statistics?

There may have been 51,000 rapes reported to the police departments in the United States in a year, but was that the total number? Were all rape cases reported to the police? Who determined the number of children's deaths? On what basis can we predict rising college expenses? These numbers may be statistics, but there is good reason to question their accuracy and therefore their value. Such statistics should be accompanied by their sources and by an explanation of how they were compiled.

Analogies

A speaker often uses an **analogy** to clarify a concept for listeners—that is, the speaker compares an unfamiliar concept to a familiar one. For example, in the section of this book dealing with the processing capacity of the human cortex, an analogy was drawn between a cybernetic process and a computer process. This comparison was not intended to indicate that the cortex and the computer are one and the same but to show that if a reader understands the functioning of a computer, he or she may also understand the basic operation of the cortex. A supervisor, for example, may compare the purpose of a team conference to that of a football team. Each group has important members functioning in specific capacities; each wishes to contribute to the final product—success.

Analogies often take the form of comparisons and contrasts. A comparison attempts to show the specific similarity between two or more subjects, whereas a contrast highlights specific differences. Thus in comparing oranges and limes, a speaker can point out that both are citrus fruits, have rinds, produce juice when squeezed, and are grown in tropical or subtropical climates. In contrasting them, a speaker can mention differences in color (orange versus green), shape (round versus oval), and taste (sweet versus tart).

Remember, however, that an analogy is effective only if the listeners are familiar with the object, idea, or theory being used as the basis for the analogy. Comparing one unfamiliar idea to another unfamiliar idea does little except further confuse an audience. Contrasting a patient on an operating table to stars in the sky may confuse listeners unfamiliar with either astrology or surgical techniques.

A speaker should also be careful not to overextend the comparison or contrast. A college president once developed an inaugural speech by comparing the school to a football team. The analogy compared faculty members to team players, students to spectators, the president to the coach, and on and on and on. After a while, the listeners became confused and stopped paying attention, and the intended effect was lost.

A speaker also has to exercise care in selecting analogies; those that cannot be substantiated may prove counterproductive. Historians, for instance, are reluctant to draw historical analogies because the social, political, and economic forces of one era cannot be duplicated in another. Thus the crises and upheaval in the world today and those during the decline and fall of Rome may not be analogous.

Testimony

A direct quotation (an actual statement) or a paraphrase (a reworded idea) from an authority is known as **testimony.** Speakers provide testimony in communication to clarify ideas, back up contentions, and reinforce concepts. Thus a speaker may turn to this type of supporting material when he or she believes that an authority is more knowledgeable about the topic being discussed. The speaker may also believe that the opinion of an authority will make listeners more receptive to a particular idea.

An **expert** is a person who through knowledge or skill in a specific field gains respect for his or her opinions or expertise. We turn to lawyers, mechanics, economists, architects, and laboratory technicians to answer questions and give advice about their areas of expertise. We trust their opinions because their knowledge has been acquired through personal experience, education, training, research, and observation. We also respect people who have academic degrees, are licensed, have received accreditation, or are recognized by peers as leaders in their fields. For example, Neil Armstrong, the first man on the moon, can obviously offer expert testimony regarding the appearance of the lunar surface. By the same token, Dr. Michael Gottlieb, the noted AIDS virus researcher, is an expert on the effects of AIDS on the immune system.

In an effort to present precisely the views of experts, a speaker should be careful to quote accurately, indicate the time and circumstances under which the information was presented, and provide the source of the material. In addition, the testimony should be relevant and no longer than necessary. Listeners have difficulty handling lengthy readings of testimony and tend to tune them out rather quickly.

The selected quotations should be true to the source's original intention. Testimony taken out of context is not only misleading and confusing; it is also dishonest. Before you accept testimony as support, assess it by asking some basic questions.

1. *Is the material quoted accurately?* Advertisers for plays or movies are sometimes guilty of using only those lines or parts of lines that offer praise. For example, a statement that originally read, "The movie was effective if you like a weakly developed plot, poor acting, and confusing dialogue" could become "The movie was effective. . . ." Those little dots make all the difference; they indicate that something has been omitted, and, in this case, the omission totally changes the meaning. For the same reason, be alert to phrases such as "in part," "seemed to indicate," and "implied." These, too, are signs that not all the evidence is being presented.

2. *Is the source biased because of position, employment, or affiliation?* A quotation by the chairperson of the board of directors of a major tobacco company that cigarette smoking may not lead to cancer should be suspect because of the speaker's biased position. As listeners we must be careful not to blindly accept sources that serve the speaker's points of view. Debaters, politicians, researchers, speakers, and journalists are often guilty of manipulating listeners through this practice.

3. *Is the information relevant to the issue being discussed?* For example, in attempting to prove that vitamin C is not beneficial in protecting against the common cold, a speaker may say, "Vitamin C, as contained in oranges, can cause more harm than good. Take a dozen oranges, peel them, and crush them into a pulp. They will be in exactly the same state as they would be if you swallowed them. Pour the juice into a goldfish bowl, and place the fish in the bowl. Within minutes the acid in the juice may cause the goldfish to die." This statement has no relevance to the issue being discussed.

4. *Is the source competent in the field being discussed?* For example, what qualifies an actor to recommend changes in college administration procedures? And what makes an athlete competent to recommend cars, insurance, credit cards, or soft drinks? Unless we can show that

these people are qualified in these subjects, quotations from them should not be accepted as authoritative.

5. *Is the information current, if currency is important?* An advertisement for a musical production at a university theater raved: "*Gypsy*, the best damn musical I've seen in years." Yes, a drama critic in a major newspaper did write that in reviewing the play. Unfortunately, unsuspecting readers may not realize that the statement described the original New York production of *Gypsy*, not the performance being staged by the university students.

Vehicles for Presenting Supporting Material

Three means of presenting and focusing supporting material are restatement, forecasting, and the use of supplementary aids.

Restatement   Have you ever been on the receiving end of a message and found yourself totally confused because of the amount of material it involved? Speakers often forget that listeners may not be able to sift through the information as it is presented. Therefore to avoid confusion, summarize each segment of a presentation by **restatement** before proceeding to the next one. Effective restatement is accomplished by rewording key points so that major ideas stand out for the listeners without becoming boring or repetitious. Internal summaries are not always necessary; but if material is complicated, a speaker is wise to use this method of clarification. For example, a speaker can restate the sentence "The United States should adopt a more aggressive foreign policy" with "Our nation, then, needs to pursue a more vigorous, definitive approach to its international relations." Care should be taken, however, not to use too many restatements because they can easily lose their impact.

Forecasting   To get the audience ready to focus on the next idea to be presented, speakers use forecasts. A **forecast** is a statement that alerts the audience to ideas that are coming. Forecast statements include "Let's now examine the three examples of how bulimics purge food" and "By understanding the definition of bulimic, you can gain insight into why this is a psychological, not a biological, illness."

The Use of
Supplementary Aids   Many speakers find the use of **supplementary aids**—visual, audio, and audiovisual—valuable in supplementing the oral segments of their presentations. Nevertheless, a speaker should ask two questions before de-

At times it is impossible to bring real objects to the speaking environment.

ciding to use such aids: Is the aid relevant to the presentation? Will listeners better understand the material through the use of an aid? Aids are intended to facilitate listener understanding, not function as decorative touches.

Aids are used not only in formal presentations but also in informal settings. For example, showing someone a picture of your house while describing its architectural style, sketching its floor plan, and displaying samples of the wallpaper or furniture involves the use of a visual aid. Similarly, in discussing your favorite musical group, you may play a record or a cassette tape to illustrate its sound.

In a public speech, statistical differences can be greatly enhanced by the use of charts. In the classroom, supplementary aids can be used to teach particular techniques. For example, nurses sometimes insert needles into grapefruits so they can learn how to give shots; firefighters study methods of ladder placement on film; and a tape recording of an interrogation can supplement a discussion of methodology for law enforcement students. All these aids are intended to supplement the speaker's voice.

Visual Aids   **Visual aids** appeal to our sense of sight. They can include real objects; models; photographs, pictures, and diagrams; charts; cutaways; and mockups.

When it is possible to use real objects they can greatly enhance a point or illustrate a concept.

Real Objects.   To demonstrate the process of swinging a hammer, why not use a real hammer? An actual form to show how a traffic ticket is filled out? Or the specific chemicals that are mixed to produce a particular product? All these are examples of using real objects as visual aids.

Models.   At times, it is impossible to use real objects. In such cases, a scale model (in exact proportion to the dimensions of the real object) or a synthetic model (not in proportion but nevertheless representational) may be used. For example, although a Boeing 747 jet cannot be brought into an aviation classroom, a scale model certainly can be.

Photographs, Pictures, and Diagrams.   A photograph of a death scene and the victim can be shown to a jury in a murder trial because the actual scene or victim cannot be produced during the trial.

Charts.   A **chart** is a visual representation of statistical data that gives information in tabular or diagrammatic form. For example, by showing increases and decreases in sales in a visual manner, a speaker can discuss a general trend as a total unit instead of as a series of fragmented ideas. By the same token, a series of columns representing the number of doctors available to a hospital compared with the number needed presents a visual image of the problem.

Cutaways.   It often is difficult to look inside certain objects. A **cutaway** allows us to see what we normally would have to imagine, thus enabling us to understand the object better. To show the seating plan of an airplane, for instance, a segment of the body is peeled away to reveal the interior. To show the layers of materials used to construct a house, a wall is cut in half so that we see the aluminum siding, the insulation, the studding, the wallboard, and the wallpaper.

Mockups.   A **mockup** is used to show the building up or the tearing down of an article. For example, a biology textbook may show an outline drawing of the human body on a page that has a series of clear plastic sheets attached to it. Each plastic overlay shows a specific drawing, and as it is flipped onto the original sketch, an additional aspect of human anatomy is revealed. Thus one sheet illustrates the bone structure, another adds the heart and circulatory system, and a third reveals the nervous system.

Audio Aids   **Audio aids** appeal to our sense of hearing. Such devices as records, tape recordings, and duplications of sounds may be the only way to demonstrate particular sensations accurately for listeners. For example, a discussion of composer Stephen Schwartz's music in the plays *Godspell,* *Pippin,* and *The Magic Show* can be enhanced by allowing the audience to hear excerpts. And playing a recording of Martin Luther King's famous "I Have a Dream" speech is an excellent way to demonstrate his style of oral presentation.

Audiovisual Aids   **Audiovisual aids** such as films, videotapes, and tape-slide presentations combine the dimensions of sight and sound. Thus a film of John F. Kennedy's "I Am a Berliner" speech allows the audience not only to hear his performance but also to see the reaction of the West Germans standing before the wall that separated East and West Berlin. In the same way, a videotape of an executive's speech is an excellent way to illustrate that person's vocal and physical mannerisms. And a tape-slide presentation in which the pictures are synchronized with a prerecorded oral text makes the step-by-step procedure a nurse uses in preparing a patient for surgery much more vivid.

Attention Devices

Attention results from focusing on one stimulus over all others in the environment at any given time. When you consider the amount of stimuli that are continually bombarding us, it is no wonder that speakers have difficulty gaining and maintaining the attention of their listeners. The keeping of attention is made even more difficult by the fact that listening involves a process of tuning in and tuning out throughout the message. Some research suggests that our attention span may be no more than five seconds.[9]

Because we can attend to any one stimulus for only a short period of time, a speech must be sufficiently compelling to ensure that listeners will tune back in to the speech during the tuning-in/tuning-out process. To accomplish this, try to choose concrete, specific supporting materials rather than general or abstract ones.

Abstractions are usually not interesting to listeners. Thus the speaker who explains the process of lunar landings to a nontechnical audience will probably find that an abstract discussion of the principles of velocity and stress will not hold his or her listeners' attention. Instead, the speaker should use illustrations from past Apollo landings because they are more concrete and will be more interesting to the audience.

The material you choose ought to be familiar to your listeners. For example, the familiarity most audience members have with inflation can provide an economist with interesting material for a speech describing a new economic program. Thus the use of familiar examples helps to serve as a means of enabling listeners to comprehend concepts that may be newer and more complex.

To be a compelling speaker, you must work to be vivid in your presentation. Lively descriptions, a colorful choice of language, and a vigorous style can all encourage listeners to pay attention to your message. For example, a speaker addressing a group of potential airline flight attendants can stress the importance of cabin safety with some vivid descriptions of past accidents.

Humor is another useful strategy. If relevant and in good taste, humor can gain and keep the listeners' attention. It may also allow them to relax. Humor was creatively used by a minister who was asked how long a good sermon should be: "I use one rule," he said. "The mind can only absorb what the seat can endure."

In trying to keep your audience's attention, you may also wish to use the device of novelty—treating a subject in a unique fashion. One speaker, for instance, used novelty when he started a speech by saying, "I'm much like you in many ways. I have two arms, two legs, two hands, two eyes, and two ears. I wear clothes, go to school, and enjoy good food. I'm different from you, however, because I'm on methadone. You see, I'm a heroin addict."

Another device is suspense. Here a spokesperson may use a series of questions: "What has three professional theaters under one roof? What contains expensive Italian marble, Scandinavian crystal chandeliers, and gifts from throughout the world? What is designed to be a living memo-

Lively descriptions, colorful language, and a vigorous style can all encourage students to pay attention to your message.

rial to a great American president? The Kennedy Center in Washington, D.C." ·

You may also want to use material that contains conflict as an attention device. For example, a speaker can use conflict to interest listeners in a local political issue: "We have to decide today whether we are going to use our tax revenues to hire more teachers or more police officers. Both alternatives have advantages and disadvantages. Let me explain each of them to you."

Above all, a speaker should be careful to use a variety of devices that are relevant to the subject of the speech and to the listeners. Effective speakers seek out materials that contain such devices to capture and maintain the attention of their listeners.

Summary

This chapter dealt with the process of developing a public communication message. The major ideas presented were:

- [ ] The sources of information available to a speaker are personal experiences, personal observations, and accumulated learning, plus information derived from research and interviews.

- [ ] Research information may be found in books, magazines, newspapers, journals, indexes, government publications, and publications from special-interest groups. Additional information can be found in nonprint media and interviews.

☐ The computer search is a retrieval system used to compile a bibliography or information about a topic via an electronic system.

☐ When doing research, you should keep a record of where the information came from.

☐ An oral footnote indicates the source of the information included in a speech.

☐ A quotation is material written or spoken by a person in the exact words in which it was originally presented.

☐ To paraphrase is to put someone else's ideas into your own words.

☐ Supporting material is used in a speech to clarify the speaker's point or to demonstrate that the point has some probability of being true.

☐ Supporting material can include illustrations, specific instances, expositions, statistics, analogies, and testimony.

☐ Care should be taken in using statistics and testimony to ensure the accuracy and validity of the information.

☐ Three means for presenting and focusing supporting material are restatement, forecasting, and the use of supplementary aids.

☐ Restatement summarizes each segment of a presentation before proceeding to the next one.

☐ A forecast statement alerts the audience to ideas that are coming.

☐ The use of visual, audio, and audiovisual aids is often a valuable way to help the listener understand the message.

☐ Visual aids can include real objects; models; photographs, pictures, and diagrams; charts; cutaways; and mockups.

☐ In choosing attention devices, you are wise to select those that are concrete, familiar, compelling, humorous, novel, suspenseful, or conflicting.

Key Terms

quotations	expert
paraphrases	restatement
oral footnote	forecast
supporting material	supplementary aids
statement of declaration	visual aids
illustrations	chart
specific instances	cutaway
exposition	mockup
statistics	audio aids
analogy	audiovisual aids
testimony	attention

Learn by Doing

1. Each student selects a controversial subject area (abortion, mercy killing, legalization of marijuana, and so forth) and identifies a person who is an authority on the subject. The student then interviews that person and gives an oral presentation to the class on the result of the interview. The student should clearly state the interviewed person's stand concerning the issue and the reasons for the stand. After all the presentations have been made, a class discussion is held on the value of the interview as a means of collecting relevant data for a speech.

2. Use the information collected from the interview in activity 1 to research the same topic. Look for the views of other authorities on the subject. Then give a speech approximately five minutes long comparing the results of the interview with the results of the research.

3. Each student is to make a presentation to the class in which a supplementary aid is absolutely necessary for the audience's comprehension of the message (examples: a description of Van Gogh's style of brush stroke, the musical sound of the Rolling Stones versus the sound of the Beach Boys, the architectural styles of the Mayans of the Yucatan). The speech is to be approximately three minutes long.

4. Find the following:
    a. The name of one book in your college library that contains information about the life of Woodrow Wilson, with a list of some of the information using the bibliographical form explained in this chapter
    b. A magazine article about nuclear-waste disposal
    c. The longitude and latitude of Elyria, Ohio
    d. Three encyclopedia notations about the White House
    e. The definition of the word *cacophony,* citing a dictionary
    f. The name of a journal published by the Speech Communication Association
    g. The population of the United States according to the 1950 census
    h. The birthplace of Carl Sandburg
    i. The name of a government pamphlet
    j. The gross national product of the United States in 1979
    k. The name of the person who wrote the musical *Miss Saigon*

5. Use the format explained in the chapter to make three note cards for a speech with the purpose statement "to inform the class about the effects of the Salk polio vaccine." Two are to be quotations; one, a paraphrase. No more than one card can come from a book.

6. Find or create a hypothetical illustration or a factual illustration that could be used for the speech described in activity 5.

7. What expository materials do you think would be needed by members of your class if you were to present the speech explained in activity 5?

8. Locate and footnote three sources of testimony concerning the effects of smoking on human beings.

9. Find a humorous story that you could use as an introduction for a speech about the educational system of the United States, women's rights, or sports.

Notes

1. *In Evidence* (Boston: Houghton Mifflin, 1969), Robert Newman and Dale Newman provide insight into the types of bias present in many different sources of information.

2. For a discussion of computer searches, see Carolyn Wolfe and Richard Wolfe, *Basic Library Skills,* 2nd ed. (Jefferson, N.C.: McFarland, 1986), pp. 113–118.

3. Deborah Tannen, *You Just Don't Understand* (New York: William Morrow, 1990), 122.

4. Norris McWhirter, *Guinness 1984 Book of World Records* (New York: Sterling, 1984), p. 28.

5. Rob Rachowiecki, *Ecuador* (Berkeley, Calif.: Lonely Planet Publications, 1986), p. 13.

6. Darrell Huff, *How to Lie with Statistics* (New York: Norton, 1954), pp. 123–142.

7. Two excellent sources on statistics are Herbert Arkin and Henry Hill, *Sampling in Auditing: A Simplified Guide and Statistical Table* (Price Waterhouse and Company, n.d.); and D. A. Johnson and W. H. Glenn, *The World of Statistics* (St. Louis: Webster, 1961).

8. "Haul of Illegals Hits All-Time High," *U.S. News & World Report,* October 3, 1983, p. 11.

9. D. A. Norman, "Memory While Shadowing," *Quarterly Journal of Experimental Psychology,* 21 (February 1969), 85–93.

13 *Structuring the Message*

Chapter Outline

After reading this chapter, you should be able to:

Explain why it is important to carefully structure speeches

Structure a speech to meet the needs of the listeners

Define and explain what makes an effective introduction, central idea, body, and conclusion for a speech

List and give examples of introduction attention getters for a speech

Identify the purpose of orienting material and the various types of orienting materials

Explain the purpose of the central idea of a speech

List and give examples of the methods of issue arrangement for the body of a speech

List and give examples of the methods for concluding a speech

Identify and illustrate the types of overall organization of a speech.

*L*isteners have limited attention spans, so they are always tuning in and tuning out on speakers' messages. Consequently, it is important to present a carefully structured message that facilitates the listener getting back "on track" at the point that he or she tunes back in on the speech.

If a speech is well ordered, the chance of its being successful increases. In addition, the most effective approach to enhancing listener comprehension of a message is through the development of well-supported points.[1] Speakers who can build in **redundancy,** repetition of their points, probably foster listening comprehension of their messages. Television commercials use the technique of redundancy by repeating extensively to reinforce the message in the viewer's mind. A careful plan for putting together a speech is a major part of the process of preparing presentations and developing effective speeches.[2]

The Basic Elements of a Speech

A public communication message is usually divided into four parts: introduction, central idea, body, and conclusion. This structure may be outlined as follows:

I. *Introduction* (attention-gaining and -orienting material)

II. *Central idea* (the purpose of the presentation and a specific statement of its main idea)

III. *Body* (the major points to be expressed in the presentation) The body of the speech may be expanded into subdivisions as necessary to develop the major points of the message.

IV. *Conclusion* (a summarizing and a motivating statement)

The Introduction   The purpose of the **introduction** is to gain the listeners' attention and orient them to the material that will be presented.

Attention Material   Many types of introductory devices can be used to gain the audience's attention, including personal references, humorous stories, illustrations, references to the occasion or setting, rhetorical questions, action questions, unusual or dramatic devices, quotations related to the theme, and statements of the theme.

Personal References.   Introductions containing personal references give a speaker's reasons for undertaking a presentation on a specific topic. For example, a patient may relate the personal experience of receiving aid from the Muscular Dystrophy Association to introduce a presentation that appeals for funds. Or a heart specialist may share his or her medical background and training with the audience before making statements about the hazards of being overweight.

The purpose of the introduction is to gain the listeners' attention.

Humorous Stories.   Humorous stories are often an effective way to start a presentation. Nevertheless, the humor should fit the audience and the occasion, be relevant to the material that follows, and set the desired tone. A story or joke that is quite funny in one setting may be totally inappropriate in others. For example, an athlete's humor may be received positively in a locker room and negatively in a formal social setting.

Remember, too, that humor may be intended in one way but received in quite a different way. Because the purpose of the introduction is to gain an audience's attention and provide a bridge into the body of the speech, an audience is likely to believe that the topic will be aligned with the humorous story told in the introduction and may become confused if the rest of the speech is not related to the story. A speaker could begin a presentation with a humorous anecdote: "A railroad agent in Africa had been bawled out for doing things without orders from headquarters. One day headquarters received a telegram from the agent which read, 'Tiger on platform eating conductor. Wire instructions.'"[3] From this story an audience can logically expect the speech to be about following directions, making creative decisions, or working as a railroad agent, but not about computer programming or fashion design.

Humor sets a tone. Thus when a presentation is to be serious, it may be difficult to attain a somber tone if the introduction has led the audience to anticipate something lighter. And telling a series of jokes at the start of a speech may give an audience the impression that the presentation will contain only humor.

Illustrations.   Illustrations such as stories, pictures, and slides help to make ideas more vivid for listeners because they create a visualization or an image of the topic to be discussed. For example, showing pictures of the results of a new skin-grafting process for burn victims clearly illustrates the topic to be discussed. Similarly, a speaker who is going to talk about the need for well-equipped police cars can begin a speech by saying, "Picture yourself on a dark road some night with car trouble or maybe even an injury that prevents you from driving. Suddenly you see the headlights of a car. It could belong to almost anyone. But wouldn't you feel better if it turned out to be a police officer with all the equipment you needed?"

References to the Occasion or Setting.   In referring to the occasion or the setting, a speaker is trying to make the audience feel a strong bond, an alliance, an empathy, with her or him. When this is accomplished, audience members will be responsive because they regard themselves as substitute participants. Such references can be to mutual experiences, common beliefs, or mutual needs. For example, in addressing an

Independence Day company picnic, a speaker may refer to the founding of the nation and how both the speaker and the audience have benefited from the acts of our forefathers.

Rhetorical Questions.   Questions for which no outward response is expected are called rhetorical questions. For example, a speaker may say to an audience, "Have you ever asked yourself what you would do if someone tried to rob you?" In this case, the speaker does not intend to count how many have or have not asked themselves the question. Instead, his or her purpose is to have the audience members ask themselves the question so as to build their curiosity.

Although sometimes overused, rhetorical questions can still be an effective method of getting the audience to ponder a topic. Many times a speaker asks a second rhetorical question if she or he feels that one question will not gain enough attention.

Action Questions.   Action questions are presented as a means of getting the audience involved in the speech and making the listeners think and respond. For example, a speaker once started a presentation by asking, "How many of you have ever been involved in an auto accident? Will you please raise your hands?" After the hands went up, the speaker said, "For those of you with your hands up, do you remember that instant when you knew the accident was going to happen and you couldn't do anything about it?" After a pause, the speaker went on. "For those of you who haven't experienced that feeling, it's one of total helplessness." Thus in a few brief sentences the speaker had involved the audience in a constructive way and was able to move easily into the next segment of the speech.

Unusual or Dramatic Devices.   Unusual or dramatic devices get the attention of the audience because of their curiosity or shock value. In one dramatic opening, a medical lab technician set up equipment and drew blood from a student volunteer to show how blood is analyzed. Another speaker, in presenting a speech to illustrate the influence of predetermined assumption, asked for a volunteer who felt knowledgeable about rock music groups. The speaker wrote the names of three rock groups on the board and played short cuts from three songs. The volunteer identified which song was by which group. He was wrong in all three cases. The speaker stressed that she had selected pieces that were not typical of the groups, and therefore the "expert" was misled by his predetermined assumptions.

Quotations Related to the Theme.   Speakers sometimes begin by quoting the words of a famous person, reading an account of a specific event,

Illustrations help make ideas more vivid for listeners because they create a visualization or an image of the topic to be discussed.

reciting a section of a poem or play, or reading a newspaper editorial. In presenting the topic of student unrest during the late 1960s and early 1970s, for example, a speaker may read a section of James Michener's book *Kent State* that tells of the students killed at Kent State University. This will get the audience involved in picturing the events that took place there.

Such quotations must be relevant to the subject. But even when they are relevant, quoted ideas become meaningless if they are not presented effectively. The greatest mistakes most speakers make in providing quotations is to read them too quickly, without stressing the appropriate words. Quotations are most effective when read meaningfully, slowly, and loudly enough to be heard.

Statements of the Theme.   This type of introduction is used to indicate to the audience exactly what the speaker is going to talk about. Unfortunately, many untrained speakers start out their presentations by saying, "Today I am going to tell you about. . ." Obviously, this is not a particularly effective opener.

A more creative theme statement is likely to hold the audience's attention. For example, a mechanic, in speaking to a group of women at a YWCA, started his presentation by saying, "I don't like changing tires, and you probably don't either. However, if you get stuck some night on a lonely road and there's no way to call the auto club, and no one else around to change your tire, you'll probably thank me for spending the next couple of minutes telling you the five steps that can make tire changing easy."

Orienting Material

Orienting material is designed to give the audience the background necessary to understand the basic material of the speech. It is designed to tie the material to the central idea, provide necessary information, establish personal credibility for the speaker, and make the subject important to the listeners. Orienting material usually includes historical background, definition of terms, personal history and/or a tie to the topic, and the importance to listeners.

Historical Background.   Often a speaker has to explain what led up to present occurrences. For example, a speech intended to persuade the audience to vote for a renewal of a school levy ought to include the facts that illustrate the history of the levy.

Definition of Terms.   If a term or terms are going to be used during the entire speech or as the basis for the speech, the time to define the term is in the orienting section. In a speech about agoraphobia, for example, the definition of this emotional illness, the fear of being out in public, should be given as orienting material so the audience understands it early in the presentation. This does not preclude defining other terms later. Only those terms that are universal to the speech have to be included in the orienting segment.

Personal History and/or Tie to the Topic.   A speaker gains credibility if she or he has some personal tie to or experience related to the topic. A speaker intending to demonstrate the steps in mouth-to-mouth resuscitation is well advised to include her or his Red Cross training and background as a lifeguard. This documentation establishes the speaker's authority to speak about the subject. If such material is included before the presentation via a speech of introduction, then inclusion of the speaker's personal connection with the topic is probably not necessary; if not, a speaker who wishes to establish credibility with the audience includes his or her background, if one exists, as it relates to the topic.

Importance to the Listeners.   The most critical part of the orienting material is the tying of the subject to the listeners in some way. Listeners pay attention to ideas and issues that are relevant to them, so it is imperative that the speaker make that link at the outset. One good strategy is to show the importance of the topic based on the interests of the audience: "Look around you; many of you have just filed your income tax forms and wonder whether you will be audited." It may also be useful to connect the topic to a larger segment of the population to illustrate how the subject has importance to both the immediate listeners and to the general public: "The Internal Revenue Service reported that 106,853,000 income tax forms were filed in 1991. Your tax form was probably one of these."

The Central Idea   The purpose statement, which is designed to help the speaker to prepare a speech, can also serve as the basis for developing a **central idea**—the overall point of the speech. This central idea gives the point of the speech explicitly; at the same time it implies what type of response the speaker wants from listeners.

If, for example, the purpose statement of a speech is "to inform the audience of the complex process employed in compiling information for *The Guinness Book of World Records*," then the central idea is that "the process of collecting information for *The Guinness Book of World Records* is complex." If the purpose statement is "to persuade listeners that they should vote for the school-bond issue on November 2," then the central idea is that "we should all vote for the school-bond issue on November 2."

The importance of actually stating the central idea in a speech cannot be overemphasized. The audience that is not given the central idea will be frustrated and may never be sure what the exact point of the speech really is.

The central idea should be presented as a statement because a speaker who uses a question ("Should the federal government provide financial aid to private educational institutions?") is not indicating to the listeners what the main point really is. A speaker who presents the point as a statement ("The federal government should provide financial aid to private educational institutions") is clarifying which persuasive stand will be advocated. Notice also that the statement is concise and contains only one overall idea.

The Body   The **body** of a message develops the major points of the speech as well as any subpoints that pertain to the speaker's central idea. In this way, the speaker can communicate effectively by organizing the issues in the body of the presentation in such a way that the listeners have little or no difficulty understanding the message.

When a speech lacks this sort of organization, listeners may become so confused they simply give up trying to understand it. Perhaps, for example, you had a history instructor who started a lecture by talking

If a speaker is not organized, the members of an audience may get so confused that they stop listening.

about the causes of World War I, then inexplicably wandered into a discussion of the marriage customs of Greece, and then commented on the Equal Rights Amendment. By the end of the class, you were no doubt confused and came away without a complete message or a well-defined idea. To avoid such problems, the subpoints of the body of a speech can be organized in a variety of ways. These methods of sequencing are called **issue arrangement.**

Methods of Issue Arrangement

Issue arrangement can take one of six forms: spatial arrangement, chronological or time arrangement, topical arrangement, causal arrangement, comparison-contrast arrangement, or problem-solution arrangement.

Spatial Arrangement. Many people organize information automatically, even though they are not aware of it. Suppose some friends of yours are visiting you at your college. They have never been on campus before, and ask you to tell them about the institution. You start by describing the building located on the south end of the campus and then proceed to talk about all the other buildings, citing their locations from the south to the north. You have organized your presentation according to **spatial arrangement.** In other words, from a set point of reference (the southernmost building), you proceeded to explain each building in terms of its geographical location. This is a common method for giving directions, for routing merchandise in a store or factory, or for talking about where you went on your vacation.

In using spatial arrangement, a speaker sets a point of reference at some specific location. He or she then proceeds to give directions starting from the established reference point. Thus the organization is based on keeping the places in a set order following a pattern: left to right, north to south, from the center to the outside.

To illustrate this process, we can see how spatial arrangement can be used for the body of a speech with the purpose statement "to inform the audience of the financial tax base of Ohio by examining the state from north to south." Accordingly, the body section of the speech's outline may look something like this:

III.   Financial tax base of the state of Ohio
    A. Northern Ohio
        1. Toledo
        2. Lorain/Elyria
        3. Cleveland
        4. Youngstown
    B. Central Ohio
        1. Mansfield
        2. Akron
        3. Canton
    C. Southern Ohio
        1. Dayton
        2. Cincinnati
        3. Columbus

The major headings in the body of this speech are developed in a north-to-south pattern, and each of the subdivisions is developed from west to east.

In using any of the methods of organization, the speaker does not have to organize the subdivisions in the same way as the major headings. In this case, however, ease of understanding was derived from using the same method for the major headings as for the subdivisions. An alternate method would have been to use spatial order for the major headings and chronological order for the subdivisions by going from the city with the highest per capita tax to that with the lowest per capita tax within each part of the state.

Chronological or Time Arrangement.   Another method of organization is **chronological or time arrangement,** which orders information from a beginning point to an ending one, with all the steps developed in numerical or time sequence. For instance, recipes are often treated in time sequence, as are reports of chemistry experiments or the charts of patients in a hospital. By telling what happened—or should happen—first, second, and so on, the speaker presents a pattern that allows the audience to understand the ideas being presented.

For example, chronological arrangement can be used to develop the body of the speech with the purpose statement "to inform the audience of the major accomplishments of the Reagan administration by identifying those accomplishments from 1981 through 1988." In this case, the outline may read:

III. Accomplishments of the Reagan administration
    A. Accomplishments of the first term
        1. 1981
        2. 1982
        3. 1983
        4. 1984
    B. Accomplishments of the second term
        1. 1985
        2. 1986
        3. 1987
        4. 1988

Topical Arrangement.   Ideas can also be organized on the basis of their similarities. Thus in using a **topical arrangement,** a speaker explains an idea in terms of its component parts. For example, in speaking about dogs, a speaker may discuss cocker spaniels, poodles, and then collies, developing ideas about each breed (the component part) completely before going on to the next one. The speaker can also organize the presentation of ideas by talking about the temperament of each breed, then about the size of each breed, and finally about the coloring of each breed. In this way, the speaker is organizing the ideas by classifying the animals according to specific identifiable characteristics (the component parts) and by developing each subsection into identifiable patterns of information.

Topical arrangement lends itself to certain situations—for example, explaining to a future operating-room technologist the instruments to be used, the procedures to be followed, and the responsibilities of each member of the team. A speaker discusses all aspects of one component before proceeding to the next.

To illustrate this process, we can construct an outline of the main headings and subheadings of the body of a speech whose purpose statement is "to inform the audience about Siamese cats by discussing their coloring, vocal characteristics, and behavior patterns."

III.   Characteristics of Siamese cats
    A. Coloring patterns
        1. Seal point
        2. Chocolate point
        3. Blue point
        4. Lilac point
    B. Vocal characteristics
        1. Does not meow
        2. Sounds like a baby crying
        3. Talks back
    C. Behavior patterns
        1. Crawls into any opening
        2. Plays with small objects
        3. Jumps onto high surfaces
        4. Likes warm surfaces
        5. Is extremely curious

Causal Arrangement.   In developing an accident report, a police officer uses a method called **causal arrangement.** This is the process of showing how two events or objects are connected in such a way that if one occurs, the other will necessarily follow. In other words, if one incident happened, it caused the second incident to happen (cause to effect). Thus the officer determines what series of events took place (the cause) and then demonstrates how these led to a particular result (the effect). She may say, for example, that "car X was proceeding south on Main Street and failed to stop at the corner of Main and Canal streets for the red traffic light. Car X proceeded into the intersection and . . ." The officer can also start from the standpoint of what resulted to what happened (effect to cause, or the accident to its details). This is a good method to use when there is a specific observable result that can be understood by determining what happened.

For example, the following outline was developed for the body of a speech whose purpose statement was "to inform the audience, by listing and discussing the events, that a series of identifiable events results in a disabling fear known as agoraphobia":

III.   Series of events resulting in agoraphobia
    A. Sequence of events
        1. First event
            a. Physical symptoms such as heart palpitations, trembling, sweating, breathlessness, dizziness
            b. No apparent cause for the physical symptoms

>   2. Second event
>   a. Duplication of physical symptoms in a place similar to the site of the first event
>   b. Increasing awareness of fear of going to certain places
>   3. Third event
>   a. Symptoms occurring when there is a thought of going to a place similar to the site of the first event
>   b. Feeling of being out of control when thinking of leaving the safety site (usually the person's home)
>   B. Result—agoraphobia
>   1. Personality changes
>   a. Frequent anxiety
>   b. Depression
>   c. Loss of individual character
>   2. Emotional changes
>   a. Impassiveness
>   b. High degree of dependence on others
>   c. Constant alertness

Note that the events leading up to the final result are listed, with the final result discussed last. An alternative form would have been to give the final result first and then list the events leading up to it. The former method is called cause(s) to effect; the latter, effect from cause(s).

Comparison-Contrast Arrangement.   Suppose you are asked by a friend to explain the similarities between a community college and a four-year institution. Your explanation will probably follow the **comparison method** of organization, in which a speaker tells how two or more examples are alike. In the case of the colleges, you will talk about the similarities in curriculum, staff, facilities, activity programs, and costs. If, however, you are asked to tell the differences between the two, you will use the **contrast method,** developing the ideas by giving specific examples of differences between the two types of institutions. By combining these two methods into the **comparison-contrast arrangement,** you can tell about both the similarities and the differences.

To illustrate this process, you can set up the body of a speech with the purpose statement "to inform the audience of some of the similarities and differences between state-sponsored two- and four-year colleges in Ohio" in the following way:

> III. Similarities and differences between two- and four-year state-supported Ohio colleges
>   A. Similarities
>   1. Are governed by the Board of Regents

    2. Receive state funding
    3. Offer general studies courses
    4. Must receive permission to add new curricula
    5. Are governed by a board of trustees appointed in part by
        the governor
 B. Differences
    1. Two-year colleges: funded in part by their local communi-
        ties; four-year colleges, not funded by communities
    2. Two-year colleges: offer associate degrees; four-year col-
        leges, bachelor's and advanced degrees
    3. Two-year colleges: have certificate and two-year terminal
        programs; four-year schools, no certificates or terminal pro-
        grams
    4. Two-year colleges: less expensive

Problem-Solution Arrangement.   The **problem-solution arrangement** is
commonly used when a person is attempting to identify what is wrong
and to determine how to cure it or make a recommendation for its cure.
This method can be used to think through a problem and then structure
a speech. A person dealing with the problem of child abuse, for instance,
may wish to begin by analyzing the problem: the influence of family
history, the lack of parental control and/or knowledge, and the different
types—physical, sexual, mental—of child abuse. Such an analysis may
then lead to a consideration of various solutions, such as stricter legislation mandating penalties for child abuse, stronger enforcement of child
abuse laws, improved reporting procedures, and greater availability of
social services to parents and children alike. The key to effective
problem-solution arrangement is to deal with solutions that will be workable, desirable, and practical for those who are going to implement them.

    An alternative form of the problem-solution method is the **see-blame-
cure-cost method.** In this technique, the evil or problem that exists is
examined (see), what has caused the problem is determined (blame),
solutions are investigated (cure), and the most practical solution is selected (cost).

    When you develop a problem-solution message, always clearly state
the problem, its cause, the possible solutions, and the selected solution.
This allows your listeners to share a complete picture of your reasoning
process. If the message is well developed, listeners will know why the
selected solution is best, how it will work to solve the problem, what it
will or will not do, what the costs will be, how long it will take to work,
and what is needed to implement it.

    The problem-solution method can be used to decide among treat-
ments or procedures, products to buy, or machines to employ, as the

problems of life, business, industry, and government are confronted and solutions found. As an example of this process, consider the following outline for the body of a speech with the purpose statement "to inform the audience why I believe that the solution to the acid rain problem is to require coal-burning companies and smelting plants to build taller smokestacks, use scrubbers, and wash their coal before using it":

III.   Solution to acid rain problem
   A. Problem
      1. Acid rain is caused by substances such as sulfur oxides and nitrogen oxides.
      2. Acid rain falls anywhere that is downwind of urban or industrial pollution.
      3. Acid rain has significant negative effects.
         a. It decreases the fertility and productivity of soils.
         b. It causes freshwater lakes and streams to become barren of fish, amphibians, invertebrates, and plankton.
         c. It deteriorates such materials as stone, marble, and copper.
         d. It affects human health through the contamination of the water we drink and the fish and wildlife we eat.
   B. Solution
      1. Coal-burning companies and smelting plants should be required to build taller smokestacks to disperse the pollution.
      2. Scrubbers—traps in smokestacks that can catch up to 90 percent or more of the sulfur oxides emitted—should be required for all industrial users of smokestacks.
      3. All coal burned by industrial users should be washed before it is used.

A more detailed presentation of the speech can include discussions of the testing of each element of the solution. This can be accomplished by including subdivisions under each of the statements of solution to explore whether it is workable (developing why the suggestion will solve or help solve the problem), desirable (explaining why the suggestion will not cause greater problems), and practical (indicating how the suggestion can be put into practice).

Here is an outline to a problem-solution speech with the purpose statement "to explain why, by listing my reasons, I believe the use of a waterbed can aid in overcoming common sleeping problems."

III.   Solution to several common sleeping problems
   A. Problems
      1. Insomnia (difficulty in falling asleep)
      2. Chronic backaches

     3. Sleeping discomforts caused by pregnancy
     4. Concerns for unborn child
     5. Bedsores caused by confinement to bed
B. Solution—use of a waterbed
     1. It increases ease in falling asleep because of flotation feeling.
     2. It has the same soothing effect as sleep-inducing drugs without the medicinal side effects.
     3. It provides longer periods of sleep with less movement.
     4. It eliminates sore muscles and swollen joints, thus reducing stiffness.
     5. Its heat reduces tension, which reduces stress.
     6. It increases comfort during pregnancy by allowing the user to lie in a stomach-down position.
     7. Its flotation and heat act like a second uterus for the unborn child.
     8. Even body distribution on the surface of the mattress reduces bedsores.

Major and Internal Methods of Arrangement. For each speech, the speaker usually decides on one major method of development, always keeping in mind that other methods may be used as necessary to present the subdivision of the complete idea. For instance, in developing a presentation on the causes of World War II, a speaker may decide to use a chronological arrangement as the major method of development and a spatial method for some of the internal segments of the presentation. Thus he or she may talk about what was happening in 1935 in England, France, Germany, Russia, and Japan; then proceed to tell about events in 1936 in these countries; then discuss happenings in 1937; and so on. In this way, the audience can develop a listening pattern that allows for clarity.

No matter which pattern you select to develop a message, use that pattern consistently throughout your presentation. Otherwise your audience will be confused by sudden changes or shifts or by a failure to follow a sequence through.

The Conclusion   Depending on the purpose of a speech, the **conclusion** can be used to summarize, pull thoughts together, or motivate listeners to take a prescribed action. Whatever the purpose, a good summary should restate the major points of the speech so that the listener can recap what has been covered. Some introductory techniques may also be used as methods for concluding.

The clincher wraps up the speech.

The Clincher   Some communication theorists believe that all speeches should end with a summary of the major points, followed by one of the concluding devices, which is called a **clincher.** The conclusion section of the speech thus has two major parts and looks like this in an outline:

IV.   Conclusion
    A. Summary (restatement of issues and restatement of the central idea)
    B. Clincher (concluding method)

    The advantage of following this procedure is that it gives the speaker one more chance to reinforce the major ideas she or he has presented and then wraps up the presentation with a clinching message. Because the central idea must remain with listeners after the presentation, the conclusion section is a vital part of the message and must be developed carefully to attain the best possible results. Clincher techniques include personal references, humorous stories, illustrations, rhetorical questions, action questions, unusual or dramatic devices, or quotations.

    In using a *personal reference* technique, a heart specialist who established expertise at the start of the speech may want to reestablish his or her authority in the conclusion. In the case of *humor* as a technique, a speaker may find it appropriate to end the presentation with a humorous story that summarizes his or her ideas. As in the introduction, humorous stories should be appropriate to the central idea of the speech. As for *illustrations,* a young person who had become dependent on drugs can end a speech with an illustration of how difficult it is to turn away from the drug scene. A speaker who posed *rhetorical questions* at the beginning of a presentation can conclude by answering them. For example, the speaker who asked audience members what they would do if they were robbery victims can restate the major alternatives presented in the message.

The speaker who asked the audience members to raise their hands if they had ever been involved in an auto accident can summarize the feelings of helplessness that a person has when he or she cannot be in control of a car. This summary answers the *action question* and restates the major ideas of the presentation.

One speaker concluded a speech about the necessity for proper dental hygiene by passing out a small cup of disclosing solution and a small mirror to each member of the audience. She then asked them to rinse out their mouths with the solution, which turned plaque and other substances on or between the teeth bright red. The results of this activity effectively illustrated the importance of proper brushing and the value of *unusual or dramatic devices.*

Quotations that restate the major theme of a presentation can be used in ending it. For example, a speaker can summarize a speech against the death penalty by reading the vivid description of an execution presented in Truman Capote's book *In Cold Blood.*

The Overall Organization of a Speech

In organizing a speech, you must make decisions about the type of introduction, the preparation of the statement of your central idea, the various methods of arranging the material in the body of your speech, and the various techniques you can use to conclude. These four parts of a speech are arranged in sequence and are tied together so that the entire presentation has an overall organizational structure.

The three basic approaches to overall speech organization are the partitioning, unfolding, and case methods. Whatever type of overall organization you choose, you should realize that to remember a message, listeners require effective repetition of key points. They do not have a chance to run through the message a second time to grasp points that were not clear originally. A reader can reread a passage, but a listener cannot relisten unless the speech has been recorded (and even then, it may not be played back immediately). Consequently, you need to be obvious in stating your main points—the central idea and the issues in the body—and in providing transitions and internal summaries that assist listeners in following the sequence of your speech.

The Partitioning Method

The **partitioning method** of organization depends on a great deal of repetition and is the most direct order for listeners to follow. The sequence requires you to adhere to this outline:

I. Introduction
    A. Attention material
    B. Orienting material
II. Central idea
    A. Statement of central idea
    B. Restatement of central idea
    C. Division (listing of issues by some method of issue arrangement)
        1. First main issue
        2. Second main issue
        3. Third main issue (and so on)
III. Body (Transition: forecast of the first issue)
    A. First main issue
        1. Discussion of first main issue through examples, illustrations, and explanations
        2. Discussion of first main issue through examples, illustrations, and explanations (and so on)
    (Transition: restatement of first main issue and forecast of second issue)
    B. Second main issue
        1. Discussion of second main issue
        2. Discussion of second main issue (and so on)
    (Transition: restatement of second main issue and forecast of third issue)
    C. Third main issue
        1. Discussion of third main issue
        2. Discussion of third main issue (and so on)
IV. Conclusion
    A. Summary (restatement of issues and central idea)
    B. Clincher

When using this type of organization as a speaker, you start with the introduction and lead into your central idea. Then you state the central idea, restate it, and divide it by listing the main issues you will cover in the order in which you will cover them. This restatement and division constitute what is called the **partitioning step** or **initial summary.** For example, a speaker whose central idea is that "there are several problems with the use of radiation therapy" may use this partitioning step: "To understand these radiological difficulties, we will look at the harmful effects of radiation therapy and the poor quality of radiation facilities in hospitals."

From the partitioning step, you move into the first issue of the body of the speech by using a transition that forecasts the first issue. For example, the speaker just mentioned may say, "Turning, then, to our first point, let us consider the harmful effect that radiation therapy has had." But if a direct statement may be unacceptable to listeners because of opposition to the idea, an indirect forecast can be used: "We can begin with a look at the effects of radiation therapy." This forecast should lead into a discussion of the issue in which the main points are covered through the use of attention devices and clarity tools. Restatement is also important, for as new material is added, the speaker should hold the audience's attention and clarify his or her points by repeating those points in different words. This enables listeners to remember the main point rather than getting lost in supporting illustrations.

In moving from one issue to the next in the body of the speech, a speaker is wise to use clear bridges between ideas. These bridges, called **transitions,** provide the listener with a connection between the points. Thus a good transition consists of two parts: the restatement of the previous issue and the forecast of the next one. For example, a speaker presenting a talk on marine biology provided a transition between two issues by stating, "From the evidence presented, it appears that the problems of water pollution are massive. How, then, can we tackle these problems?"

Use of the partitioning sequence requires a careful transition containing a summary and a forecast between each issue. Note, however, that a speaker ought to have only a small number of issues in the body of the speech. The more issues that must be developed, the longer the speech will be—and a long speech may strain the listening process.

Once the last issue in a partitioned speech has been discussed, the presentation is concluded with a summary that again restates the central idea and the main issues. This summary gives listeners a chance to review in their own minds the points that have been discussed.

Successful partitioning organization requires the repetition of major points. Indeed, it follows the format I tell the audience what I'm going to tell them, then I tell them, and then I tell them what I've told them.

The following outline develops a speech according to the partitioning method of organization:

Purpose statement: To inform the audience of the alternatives an intake counselor has by listing and discussing the options.

   I.   Introduction

      A. Attention material: each of us probably makes hundreds of decisions every day. We decide what to eat, what to wear, what television program to watch, what time to go to bed.

      B. Orienting material: in my work as an intake counselor with the Department of Juvenile Services, I must make decisions that can seriously affect a child's life. An intake counselor gets the police report when a juvenile commits a crime, calls in the parents and the child to decide what actions should be taken, and counsels them. An investigation of such work can help you to understand some of the procedures that local governments use to combat the problems of juvenile delinquency.

  II. Statement of central idea

      A. Let us consider the alternatives an intake counselor has.

      B. The counselor can make three major decisions.

      C. These decisions are:

          1. Send the case to court.

          2. Close the case at intake.

          3. Place the child on informal supervision for forty-five days.

 III. Body

(One decision that a counselor may make is to send the case to court.)

      A. The law states that you must send the case to court if:

          1. The charge is denied.

          2. The juvenile has a prior record.

          3. You notice signs of trouble with the family.

          4. The case is like Tommy's. Tommy had been picked up for breaking and entering. . . . (Thus a case may be sent to court. A counselor may also decide to close a case at intake.)

      B. There are several reasons for closing the case at intake:

          1. The child admits guilt.

          2. The incident was a first offense.

          3. The parents are supportive and the home life is stable.

          4. An example of a case closed at intake was Henrietta's. . . . (As a result, a case may be closed at intake. A counselor may also decide to put a juvenile under informal supervision.)

      C. Supervision for forty-five days is warranted if:

          1. The child or the family is in need of short-term counseling.

          2. The procedure is not used often.

          3. The court has never ordered this in the past.

4. The case is like Lynn's. Lynn . . .
(Through informal supervision, some children can be helped.)
IV. Conclusion
    A. Summary: the basic decision is to arrange court appearances, stop the action at the beginning, or supervise the client.
    B. Clincher: The goal of the whole intake process is to provide whatever is best for the child so that the child will have proper care, treatment, and supervision.

Even though partitioning organization can be used for a speech with any purpose, it is especially well suited to informative speaking and informative briefing. Because the aim of such a speech is to increase the listener's comprehension of a particular body of information, a clear structure and a repetition of the major points are warranted.

The Unfolding Method

The **unfolding method** of organization can be used for a speech with any purpose; but if you want to persuade your listeners of something, you will find this format the most useful. Unfolding organization differs from partitioning organization in one important way: it does not restate the central idea or include the division step. Here is one possible sequence for an unfolding format:

I. Introduction
    A. Attention material
    B. Orienting material
II. Statement of central idea
III. Body (organized by some method of issue arrangement)
    (Transition)
    A. First issue
        1. Discussion of first issue through examples, illustrations, and explanations
        2. Discussion of first issue through examples, illustrations, and explanations (and so on)
    (Transition)
    B. Second issue
        1. Discussion of second issue through examples, illustrations, and explanations
        2. Discussion of second issue through examples, illustrations, and explanations (and so on)
    (Transition)
IV. Conclusion
    A. Restatement
    B. Clincher

This unfolding format may be appropriate for an audience that initially agrees with the central idea and issue that the speaker plans to develop. At other times, however, a speaker may want to use variations of this format. For example, if audience analysis leads you to conclude that you are going to face a hostile audience, a group unsympathetic to your purpose statement, you will want to approach your listeners more subtly, moving from particular facts to a general conclusion. Thus you will use a variation of the unfolding format.

If members of the audience oppose your stand, it does not make sense to alienate them by stating your central idea early in the presentation. Instead, lead them through the main points, moving from areas of shared agreement into areas of controversy. If you arrange the main issues subtly and word them carefully, you may be able to establish acceptance of your purpose statement just before you reach the conclusion. In proceeding, follow this variation of the unfolding format:

I. Introduction
   A. Attention material
   B. Orienting material
   (Transition)

II. Body (organized by some method of issue arrangement)
   A. Discussion of first issue
      1. Examples and illustrations
      2. Examples and illustrations (and so on)
   B. Statement of first issue
   (Transition)
   C. Discussion of second issue
      1. Examples and illustrations
      2. Examples and illustrations (and so on)
   (Transition)

III. Statement of central idea
   (Transition)

IV. Conclusion
   A. Restatement
   B. Clincher

For instance, if you are trying to persuade a group of people to vote for a candidate and you know the audience is not committed to that candidate, you are wise to develop your position by stating the issues, stands, and actions of the candidate; stressing the positive aspects of your candidate; and building strong support for him or her. After establishing this argument, you then reveal the voting action you want from the audience. Some members of the audience may be swayed.

The unfolding method of organization is more flexible than the partitioning method because it lends itself to a variety of formats. For example, in the unfolding method of organization, you can move the statement of the central idea anywhere in the speech as long as it comes before the conclusion. And your transitions do not have to restate and forecast issues; they simply have to establish clear connections. Furthermore, in this method you do not have to restate all the issues and the central idea in the conclusion. Remember, however, that a good conclusion should summarize and conclude your presentation.

As a speaker, you want to maintain a clear framework for your listeners so that the speech moves forward sequentially. Remember that the speech is of no value if at the conclusion the audience does not clearly understand your central idea.

The following outline develops a speech according to the unfolding method of organization:

Purpose statement: To persuade each member of the audience by listing and discussing the reasons for donation that he or she should donate his or her body to science.

  I. Introduction
     A. Attention material: picture a three-year-old girl attached to a kidney machine once a week for the rest of her life—or for as long as the kidney machine is available. Picture a little boy whose world is blackness or a father who is confined to his bed because he has a weak heart.
     B. Orienting material: such pictures are not very pleasant. But you can do something about them.
 II. Statement of central idea: you should donate your body to science.
III. Body
     A. Scientists need organs so that others may function normally.
         1. List of organs that can be donated.
         2. The need for speed in transplanting organs. (Thus specific organs can be used.)
     B. Your body can be used as an instrument for medical education.
         1. Who can donate and how.
         2. The need to eliminate shortages.
        (As a result, your entire body can continue to serve a useful purpose.)
IV. Conclusion
     A. Summary
         1. Organs are needed so that others can function normally.
         2. Your body can be used for medical education.
     B. Clincher
         1. I am a benevolent person who believes that everyone is born with a benevolent nature. I know that you and I will help those less fortunate than we are. I am a potential organ and

cadaver donor through a will. A donor's card can be obtained through any medical foundation. I cannot overemphasize the need for body and organ donations.
2. Don't, as the proverb states, wait for "George to do it." You do it! Take immediate action to become an organ and cadaver donor.

The Case Method   In some respects, the **case method** of organization is less complex than the partitioning and unfolding methods because here the speaker discusses the central idea without breaking it into subpoints. As a result, this format is especially suitable for speeches designed to amuse, entertain, or present a single issue. If, for example, your central idea is that "kids say the funniest things," then the body of a speech you organize using this method includes a series of examples of children's clever sayings connected by clear transitions. Here is the format for a speech developed by case organization:

I. Introduction
    A. Attention material
    B. Orienting material
    (Transition)
II. Central idea
    (Transition)
III. Body
    (Organized in a sequence)
    A. Example (a case)
    (Transition)
    B. Example (a case)
    (Transition)
    C. Example (a case; and so on)
    (Transition)
IV. Conclusion
    A. Summary
    B. Clincher

When you use case organization, be careful not to develop subpoints in the body of the speech so that they become main points in themselves. The danger of subdividing is that you may not develop each subdivided point fully, and your listeners may become confused. If, for example, your central idea is that "kids say the funniest things" and you say in one of the transitions, "Kids say funny things at school and at camp," you have subdivided your central idea into two issues.

The following outline develops a speech according to the case method of organization:

Purpose statement: To inform the audience of some ways in which left handers are discriminated against by listing some examples.

  I. Introduction
      A. Attention material: have you ever pondered the design of a butter knife or the structure of a gravy ladle?
      B. Orienting material: these structural problems are important to all of us who are afflicted with a key social problem—left-handedness. (Those of us who are left-handed believe that . . .)
 II. Statement of central idea
      A. Left-handers are discriminated against.
      B. Let's look at some examples.
III. Body
      A. Example: tell a story of the difficulties encountered when using scissors.
          (Transition: another experience I've had . . .)
      B. Example: tell a story of the problems with school desks designed for right-handed people.
          (Transition: this experience points out another one. . . .)
      C. Example: tell a story of the problems with words such as "gauche" and "southpaw."
          (Transition: so you see . . .)
 IV. Conclusion
      A. Summary: left-handers are discriminated against all the way from the design of scissors to the names they are called.
      B. Clincher: to add insult to injury, recent research suggests that left-handedness may result from brain damage at birth. But then we're in good company. Eleven presidents of the United States have been left-handed!

Summary

In this chapter the principles of structuring a message were investigated. The major ideas presented were:

- [ ] A public communication message is usually divided into four parts: introduction, central idea, body, and conclusion.
- [ ] The introduction contains the attention and orienting material.
- [ ] The central idea describes the purpose of the presentation and gives a specific statement of its main theme.
- [ ] The body develops the major points of the presentation.
- [ ] The conclusion summarizes the presentation and may also contain a motivating statement.
- [ ] Attention material can include personal references, humorous stories, illustrations, references to the occasion or setting, rhetorical

questions, action questions, unusual or dramatic devices, quotations related to the theme, and statements of the theme.

☐ Orienting material gives an audience the background necessary to understand the basic material of the speech.

☐ Orienting material includes historical background, definition of terms, personal history and/or tie to topic, and importance to the listeners.

☐ The central idea should be presented as a statement.

☐ The methods of ordering the subpoints of the body of a speech are called issue arrangements.

☐ Issue arrangement takes one of six forms: spatial arrangement, chronological or time arrangement, topical arrangement, causal arrangement, comparison-contrast arrangement, or problem-solution arrangement.

☐ A summary restates the major points of the speech.

☐ Clinchers can include personal references, humorous stories, illustrations, rhetorical questions, action questions, unusual or dramatic devices, and quotations.

☐ The basic approaches to overall speech organization are the partitioning, unfolding, and case methods.

Key Terms

redundancy	comparison-contrast arrangement
introduction	problem-solution arrangement
orienting material	see-blame-cure-cost method
central idea	conclusion
body	summary
issue arrangement	clincher
spatial arrangement	partitioning method
chronological or time arrangement	partitioning step
topical arrangement	initial summary
causal arrangement	transitions
comparison method	unfolding method
contrast method	case method

Learn by Doing

1. Your instructor asks for a volunteer and gives that volunteer a card that has a drawing on it. Each member of the class has a sheet of paper and a pencil. The volunteer tells the class how to draw the diagram exactly as it appears on the card. No one is allowed to ask any questions. When the volunteer has finished giving directions, the members of the class compare their drawings with the original. After the activity, the class discusses the following questions:

    a.   If he or she did not do so, would it have helped if the volunteer had given a general overview of what to draw before beginning to give directions? Discuss this question in relation to your reading about the purpose of an introduction.

    b.   Did the instructions have a conclusion? How could a conclusion restating the major points have helped you?

    c.   Were there any words used in the directions that caused noise to enter into the communication? What were they? How did they cause problems?

    d.   Was the structure of the directions clear?

    e.   Do you think a question-and-answer session following the instructions would have been valuable? Why or why not?

2.   Do activity 1 again. This time, the next volunteer builds on the positive things the first volunteer did and makes improvements based on the discussion. This time the activity is followed by a question-and-answer session. Note how many people altered their drawings during the question-and-answer session. Draw some conclusions about the value of the question-and-answer session.

3.   A series of statements follows, each of which describes an action or feeling you may have experienced. Select one of the statements and prepare a short presentation (approximately two minutes) that explains the action or feeling. Be sure that the presentation has a clear structure, as explained in the chapter.

    a.   "Something happened to me that made me sad."

    b.   "Something happened that was both good and bad for me."

    c.   "Something happened that made me glad."

    d.   "I got very angry at myself."

    e.   "I made a promise and kept it."

    f.   "I knew the truth, but I lied anyway."

    g.   "Down with . . ."

    h.   "Hurrah for . . .

    i.   "Why does it always happen that . . . ?"

    j.   "Don't parents (you may substitute 'bosses,' 'professors,' 'children,' or 'politicians') realize that . . . ?"

4.   A speaker informs the class about an unusual topic—something the audience has no knowledge of. Sample topics are the language of bees, the Christmas customs of Puerto Rico, rafting on the Colorado River, or organic architecture. Be sure the speech has a clear structure and lasts no more than five minutes.

5.   Select a subject that you are expert in, and present a speech to your classmates in such a way that when you finish, they, too, have an understanding of the topic. Clearly structure the speech, and take no more than six minutes to deliver it.

6. Prepare a speech of no more than five minutes informing the class about a controversial theory. Sample topics are, "The Loch Ness monster exists"; "Vitamin C prevents and cures the common cold"; "Rational emotive therapy can alter behavior"; and "Alcoholism is an inherited disease." Explain the theory and the various arguments concerning the theory. Do not include your views in the presentation. Be sure the speech is clearly structured.

7. You are going to give a speech about your education (elementary, high school, college). Prepare an introduction for the presentation that represents each of the following introductory devices:
    a. Personal reference
    b. Humorous story
    c. Rhetorical question
    d. Unusual or dramatic device

Notes

1. Charles Petrie, "Informative Speaking: A Summary and Bibliography of Related Research," *Speech Monographs,* 30 (June 1963), 79–91.
2. Richard A. Lindeborg, "A Quick and Easy Strategy for Organizing a Speech," *IEEE Transactions on Professional Communication,* 33 (September 1990), 133–134.
3. Morris Mandel, *Stories for Speakers* (New York: Jonathan David, 1964).

14 *Presenting the Message*

Chapter Outline

Modes of Presentation

The Impromptu or Ad Lib Mode

The Extemporaneous Mode

The Manuscript Mode
Preparing the Manuscript
Reading from the Manuscript

The Memorized Mode

Oral and Physical Presentation

Vocal Delivery

Pronunciation

Physical Elements
Gestures
Movement
Posture
Eye Contact
The Use of Visual Aids

Speaker Anxiety

Learning
Outcomes

After reading this chapter, you should be able to:

Identify the four modes of speech presentation

Detail how to develop an impromptu or ad lib presentation

Define and explain the advantages and disadvantages of an extemporaneous presentation

Define and explain the advantages and disadvantages of a manuscript presentation

List some factors that make for an effective manuscript presentation

Detail pointers on preparing an oral style manuscript

Clarify how to read from a manuscript

Explain the advantages and disadvantages of the memorized mode of presentation

Identify some oral and physical factors that lead to an effective presentation

Clarify how to use visual aids in a presentation

Define "speechophobia," and identify some do's and don'ts for dealing with it.

*I*n preparing for a speech, you should be aware that there are several basic means of channeling a message. These include both the oral and physical elements of the presentation. You should also be aware that these elements are sometimes affected by the use of such devices as notes, outlines, manuscripts, and visual aids.

Modes of Presentation

There are four basic modes of presentation: impromptu or ad lib, extemporaneous, manuscript, and memorized.

The Impromptu
or Ad Lib Mode

Sometimes a speaker uses information acquired from past experiences, speaks with little or no preparation, and organizes ideas while he or she is communicating. This approach is referred to as **impromptu speaking.** Some speech theorists separate this from **ad lib speaking,** in which a speaker has no time to organize ideas and responds immediately when answering a question, volunteering an opinion, or interacting during an interpersonal experience. The impromptu mode gives the speaker a

The ad-lib format allows the speaker to be natural and spontaneous and tends to represent the speaker's real feelings.

short period of time to decide what to say; therefore the speaker does not communicate quite as spontaneously as he or she does when ad libbing. For example, when a teacher asks a question in class and gives the students a minute or so to think of the answer, students use the impromptu mode when answering.

Nevertheless, the impromptu and the ad lib modes are both identified by the short period of time used to prepare an answer and by the lack or minimal use of notes. They offer the advantage of being natural and spontaneous and tend to represent a speaker's real feelings because so little time is available to develop defenses.

Both these modes are weakened, however, by the lack of time the speaker has to develop organized and well-analyzed statements. Another drawback, which derives from the elimination of research time, is the speaker's lack of opportunity to use statistics, examples, or illustrations to explain his or her ideas clearly. Still another liability is the speaker's tendency to ramble or use unnecessary phrases such as "you know" and "stuff like that" to gain thinking time or gloss over nonspecific information. Finally, the lack of preparation can also result in uncertainty.

Putting together an impromptu speech requires quick work and immediate decisions. The process is the same as preparing for any other type of speech, except that there is less time to organize the material.

Unless you know in advance that you are going to be asked to speak, you are not going to have the opportunity to do any research. Therefore, everything to be included must come from your own personal knowledge. As you try to organize your thoughts, keep the following in mind:

1. Ask yourself what topic you wish to present.
2. Word a purpose statement that represents the topic.
3. List the major headings that develop the purpose statement. (If paper is available, jot them down. Write these in the vertical middle of the sheet of paper so you have time to add the introduction and the statement of the central idea later. Skip spaces in between each of the major headings so that if you have time available for developing subpoints, you will be able to write them in.)
4. Arrange the major headings according to one of the methods of organization (spatial, chronological, topical, causal, comparison-contrast, or problem-solution). Use the list you developed for step 3 to jot down the order of each heading next to the item.
5. Decide on an introduction. Most ad lib speakers tend to use a rhetorical question or a reference to the theme, but often you can think of a story (an illustration), a dramatic device, or another introductory device. Because you probably will not have time to write out the whole introduction, jot down several key words so you will remember what you want to say.
6. Formulation of the statement of the central idea, because it parallels your purpose statement, should be no problem.
7. The easiest form of conclusion is simply to restate the major points you made. If you can think of a clincher, all the better. (Below the list of major headings, write down several words that will remind you of the planned conclusion.)
8. If you have time, go back to see if you can think of any examples that back up the major ideas you want to present. If you have examples, write them in at the appropriate place. If not, try to think of some as you speak, making sure that you clarify or define any words that may be unfamiliar to your listeners.

The Extemporaneous Mode

People who have more time to prepare for their presentations most often use the **extemporaneous mode** of speaking, developing a set of aids, such as notes or outlines, to assist them in presenting their ideas. In this situation, the speaker knows in advance that she or he will be giving a speech and can therefore prepare by doing research. Teachers and clergy, for example, are frequently extemporaneous speakers.

The extemporaneous mode offers these significant advantages:

enough time to structure the presentation and find the information needed to develop the central idea; the security of having notes or an outline to refer to throughout the speech; the use of quotations, illustrations, and statistics in written form for backing up ideas; less dependency on reading than in the manuscript mode; and a more spontaneous and natural oral presentation and physical presentation than are likely in the manuscript or memorized mode.

Unfortunately, the extemporaneous mode of delivery has some disadvantages as well. For example, if a speaker does not allow sufficient time for preparation and rehearsal, he or she may get mentally lost during the presentation. Furthermore, if a speaker refers to materials too frequently during the speech or has too many notes, she or he may fail to interact with the audience. And because extemporaneous material is never written out word for word, a speaker will not have a permanent record of the speech.

To avoid having an excessive number of notes, you should limit the quantity to those needed for security, without being overdependent on them. In determining just what is essential, you are wise to consider the following analogy. The first time you drive to a particular site, you may need an in-depth set of directions, complete with route numbers, road markers, and indications of the exact mileage. On your second trip you need less information, and by the third trip you need almost none. So it is with your use of notes and outlines. You should have enough information to feel comfortable and free to navigate through the presentation with no fear of getting lost. The only way to discover the extent of your readiness is to take several test drives through your speech to ascertain how much prepared information you really need to have with you in the form of notes.

The Manuscript Mode

In the **manuscript mode** of delivery, the material is written out and delivered word for word. This method offers the advantages of providing accurate language and solid organization. In addition, it gives the speaker a permanent written record of the speech.

But the manuscript mode also has some disadvantages. Because the manuscript provides a word-for-word written record of the speech, the speaker cannot adapt it to suit the audience during the presentation. As a result, the speaker is very dependent on prior audience analysis.

Another problem with the manuscript mode of delivery is that it requires the ability to read effectively from the written page. A good manuscript speech should be conversational and animated, and the speaker should use extensive eye contact, vocal inflections, and physical actions to maintain rapport with those who are listening.

One method for establishing eye contact with the audience while fol-

Speakers using a manuscript have to be careful to look at the audience frequently.

lowing the manuscript in an unobtrusive way is called **eye span.** This involves training your eyes to glance down quickly, allowing you to pick out a meaningful phrase and deliver it to the audience. As you reach the end of the phrase but before you have finished saying it, glance down and grasp the next phrase to be spoken. (It is helpful in using eye span to underline key words and mark off phrases.) Television newscasters who do not have a teleprompter available often use this system to maintain contact with viewers by looking into the camera as they speak.

Effective manuscript presentation also requires an effective oral style. Remember that writing a speech for the listening ear is quite different from writing an essay for the reading eye. Because your listeners will hear your words only once, your choice of language, materials, and structure must be designed to achieve instant understanding. To illustrate this process, take an essay that you wrote in English class and read it aloud. You will probably find that it sounds unnatural because of its complex sentences, impersonal references, and written language style. For example, in writing, a phrase such as "as seen above" may be perfectly acceptable, but in a speaking situation it can cause the audience to look at the ceiling. Thus the need for an effective oral style is apparent.

Usually speakers adopt the extemporaneous mode rather than the manuscript mode because it allows them to interact more freely with the audience and adapt better to feedback. There are times, however, when we find it necessary to prepare an exact word-for-word presentation. For example, the manuscript mode must be used when we are going to be quoted, when we must meet specific requirements, or when we have a need for exact word selection. A business executive who makes a statement for the company, a police officer who reports about an arrest that is of importance to the community, and a nurse who is responsible for reporting the condition of an important hospital patient all must be sure that their statements are exact.

Some people find it necessary to hand out copies of their statements to the newspaper, radio, and television media for reproduction after the oral presentation. This is true of political candidates as well as labor representatives and the officers of boards of education. In all these cases, the quoted material of these speakers must be presented in a manuscript mode. In a similar fashion, people who appear on radio and television write down their remarks so they can fit their presentation into exact time slots. And speakers who have been asked to talk for only a predetermined time at a meeting or conference also find it useful to script their information.

Preparing the Manuscript

Even though written language and spoken language are meant to develop the same ideas and to accomplish similar communication objectives, there are some distinct differences between the uses of the language and the form in which the language is presented. Therefore in preparing a speech in which you are going to use a manuscript, you must be sure to prepare the material as spoken, rather than written, language. One is meant for the ear and the other for the eye.

Effective oral language is designed for instant intelligibility by the listener. Unlike the reader who has the opportunity to reread a passage, the listener has only one opportunity to receive, understand, and interpret the oral message unless he or she has used an audio- or videotape recorder and can replay passages for review.

When composing something that will be heard, rather than read, you must write as though you are speaking, not reading. To do this, write as you would talk, say the material aloud as you are writing, and practice reading the material aloud. In addition, be aware of these pointers.[1]

1. *Use the active, not the passive, voice.* ("The manager wrote the report" rather than "The report was written by the manager.")
2. *Keep sentences short.* The reading eye cannot comprehend a sentence much more than seventeen to twenty words. The listening ear has an even shorter span for comprehension, so write for that shortened attention span.

3. *Do not describe; amplify.* Long descriptions are boring to listeners; instead, show them your point in a short verbal and even a visual segment. Use supplementary aids if they are appropriate.

4. *Use short, simple words.* Remember that while readers have the privilege of going over your material again, listeners do not have that option.

5. *Use repetition.* Memorable speakers are those who repeat words and phrases stylistically. They have realized that it sometimes takes more than one hearing for the receiver to grasp their meaning.

6. *Write to reflect your audience's personality.* Adapt the word choice and even the style to your listeners.

7. *Write for one member of the audience.* A good way to personalize your manuscript is to think about one person as you put it together.

8. *Do not climb too far up the ladder of abstraction.* Keep your language concrete and clear. Avoid using doublespeak and technical terms that the audience may not understand.

9. *Avoid referent problems.* Be careful not to use "they" to refer to one person. Also be very specific as to the referent. If you use a person's name and then another person's name, avoid "he" to refer to one or the other person if both are men. The audience will not know which one you are referring to.

10. *Watch the context of your sentence.* Planned humor is an excellent device to get and hold attention, but unplanned humor that emerges from the way sentences are worded can be embarrassing.

11. *When you are finished, stop.* A short, to-the-point presentation often has the greatest impact. The classic example of this is Lincoln's "Gettysburg Address."

12. *Avoid using "you" when referring to yourself.* If a member of the audience is expected to apply the material to himself or herself, then "you" is appropriate, but if the reference is to an experience you, the speaker had, or something you are going to do, then use "I."

13. *The word "we" is more involving than the word "you."* "We" gives the audience the idea that you are including yourself, thus establishing a common bond between you and your listeners.

14. *Unless it is absolutely necessary, round off any numbers you use.* It is difficult to comprehend a number such as $1,124,569.68. Referring to "a little more than $1 million" is much easier to grasp.

15. *Avoid using words and phrases not intended for listening, including phony fancies and verbs turned into nouns. Phony fancies* are fuzzy words or expressions a person uses to sound important, impressive, or knowledgeable. A few examples include "for the purpose of finding" rather than "to find"; "in reference to," "of the order of magnitude,"

or "pertaining to" instead of "about"; "prior to" in place of "before"; and "procure" rather than "get." Some expressions that start out as verbs in our heads end up as nouns when written or spoken. Examples include "he tends," which becomes "he exhibits a tendency to"; "I appreciate," which is expressed as "allow me to express my appreciation"; and "let us consider," which becomes "let us take into consideration."

16. *Be appropriate.* To do so, language must be adapted to the components of communication—the speaker, audience, topic, and occasion. Use language with which you are comfortable. The purpose of language is to convey a message, not impress the audience. The use of "big" words, technical terms, and acronyms to represent ideas may give the impression that you are well versed in the subject, but if the audience fails to understand the message, the end goal of the presentation—understanding—is lost. Your strategy in word selection centers on analyzing the components of the speaking situation and selecting the oral words that best convey the message.

17. *Be clear.* Clarity is based on the selection of simple, specific expressions—words that allow for understanding because they are aimed at the audience's level of knowledge. Commonly, this requires substituting little words for big ones. To achieve clarity, do not speak down to the audience, but use language the audience understands. Compare the ease of understanding between each of these first and second statements.

    1a. A joyful feeling of contentment is not a commodity that can be obtained through the normal channels of currency exchange.

    1b. Money can't buy happiness.

    2a. A basic writing implement, used judiciously, has the potential for greater impact than an ancient, double-edged weapon.

    2b. The pen is mightier than the sword.

    In addition, clarity is achieved through the use of a grammatical style that does not confuse. What was really meant by each of the following church-pulpit announcements?

    "This being Easter Sunday, we will ask Mrs. Johnson to come forward and lay an egg on the altar."

    "This afternoon there will be a meeting in the north and south ends of the church, and children will be baptized at both ends."

18. *Use phrases easily remembered.* Many memorable phrases are clear ideas with profound meanings that were expressed with simplicity. Two examples of such messages are Franklin Delano Roosevelt's

appeal for national unity against the depression of the 1930s when he said, "We have nothing to fear but fear itself," and John F. Kennedy's inaugural call for a national referendum of dedication when he said, "Ask not what your country can do for you; ask what you can do for your country." Many bumper stickers and highway advertising signs express ideas in specific terms by employing clear ideas in a few well-chosen words. Examples include "Born to Shop," "Save the Whales," and "If You Can Read This, Thank a Teacher."

19. *Be vivid.* Vividness is based on the use of words that express forceful ideas and ideas that create emotional or sensory allusions for the listener. Advertisements that stress "lemon scents," "fluffy softness," and "bone chilling cold" create vivid sensory images. Vividness allows the audience to become involved in the ideas being expressed. Selecting words or images that incite strong emotions such as fear allows for the development of vividness. For example, a commercial against drug use showing a dead body in a morgue, an identification tag hanging from one toe, followed by a voice stating, "Drugs kill!" creates a vivid message. When you select words, use oral language that communicates vividness.

It takes considerable experience to retrain your writing style so you can produce a speech that is appropriate for the listening ear. Just because you are a great writer does not mean you can prepare a great speech. Indeed, great prose writers do not often make great speech writers because, as one expert noted, "public speaking must be recognized as a separate art. . . . The words may be the same, but the grammar, rhetoric and phrasing are different. It is a different mode of expression—a different language."[2]

Reading from the Manuscript

Using a manuscript can be difficult because you must look at the audience at the same time that you are trying to read your material with animation and naturalness. To do this, you will have to work out some system of following the script in an unobtrusive way so you can look at the audience without losing your place. Be careful not to move or flip the manuscript pages unnecessarily because this draws attention away from you and toward the manuscript. Also, try to avoid falling into a flat-sounding reading style. Instead, read according to the meaning by stressing important words and ideas, and vary your tone of voice so that you are speaking naturally. Some speakers run the index finger of their left hand down the side of the manuscript so they are continually pointing to the start of the next printed line that they will be reading. This way, when they look up, they can find their place when they return to the manuscript.

It also helps to arrange the script in a manner that keeps you from getting lost. Double or triple space the information; do not divide sentences by starting them on one page and finishing them on another; and do not write or type on the back of the pages. If useful, place virgules and underscores in the script so that you remember when to pause and what words to stress.

Virgules are slash marks that are used to indicate a pause or a stop. Usually, a / is used for a short pause, / / for a longer pause, and / / / for a full stop, **Underscores** are used to indicate that a word or phrase is to be stressed. The word *now* is to be stressed in the sentence: Do it now. Notice that the entire meaning of the sentence changes if the underscoring becomes: Do it now. If you feel that such underscoring will help you to present the material in a meaningful way, be sure to use it. Usually a single underscore indicates a minor stress and a double a stronger stress; a triple underscore increases both the volume and the power with which you stress the word or phrase.

The Memorized Mode

In the **memorized mode,** a speech is written out word for word and is then committed to memory. Fortunately, public speakers seldom use this mode of communication because it is potentially disastrous. After all, because the speaker commits the information to memory, forgetting any one idea can lead to forgetting everything. Whereas speakers who use the extemporaneous or the manuscript mode can refer to information, those who use the memorized mode have nothing available for reference. Memorizers may be so concerned about getting the exact word in exactly the right place that the meaning of the words becomes secondary.

The few advantages of the memorized mode include the ability to select exact wording and examples, look at the audience during the entire speaking process, and time the presentation exactly. For this reason, some speakers like to memorize their openings and closings to ensure that they can comfortably get started and finished. But the manuscript mode provides these same advantages and is less fraught with danger. Thus the disadvantages of memorized speaking usually so overshadow its advantages that few people choose to use this mode.

Oral and Physical Presentation

People who have captured their listeners' attention are apt to share certain qualities. These include confidence and ease, authority, conviction, credibility, sincerity, warmth, animation, enthusiasm, vitality, intensity, concern, and empathy. They also make effective use of eye contact, conversational tone, variety of pitch, pacing, projection, and phrasing.[3]

For example, regardless of whether they approved of his politics, speech analysts generally agreed that early in his administration Ronald Reagan established himself as an effective communicator, a skill that helped get some of his programs passed against great odds. As one critic observed, "He has a style that doesn't interfere with the content, and he seems to be able to make his listeners sit up and take notice."[4]

Vocal Delivery   Audience members often have to be enticed to actively participate in a speech. They will tend to listen with attention when the speaker is dynamic and enthusiastic. A well-prepared speech can be enhanced by effective vocal and physical delivery. The vocal elements of communication are pitch, volume, rate, quality, animation, and pause. **Pitch** is the tone of sounds, ranging from high (or shrill) tones of soprano to low (or deep) tones of bass. **Volume** is the fullness or power of the sound, ranging from loud to soft, and **rate** is the speed at which words are spoken. (Most people speak about 150 words per minute, the equivalent of one-half to two-thirds of a double-spaced, typewritten page.) **Quality** is the characteristic tone of a speaking voice, and **animation** has to do with the liveliness of the presentation. A **pause** is a temporary stop or hesitation. All these elements set the vocal level of speech.

A speech can be enhanced or diminished by the vocal level of the presentation. Someone who speaks in a monotone—a flat, boring sound resulting from constant pitch, volume, and rate—or with a shrill pitch (much like fingernails dragged across a blackboard) will eventually cause the audience to tune out. Another distracting vocal trait is speaking at so rapid a rate that receivers cannot follow the ideas. So is nasal-toned speech, which sounds as if the speaker has a cold. In addition, the extremes of constant whispering or shouting may interfere with communication. Some people have physical problems that prevent them from articulating words correctly, and others have extremely high or low vocal pitches or unpleasant tonal qualities. These problems can all be dealt with by a speech therapist. In contrast, the concerns of the communication classroom are those difficulties that students can deal with on their own.

For example, if your vocal presentation lacks pitch variation, try to raise and lower those levels as you speak. You can do this by tape-recording a presentation several times, each with a different pitch. You can follow the same procedure to correct too fast or too slow rates of speech. Even if you do not think you have any problems, tape-recording is an excellent way to observe your vocal delivery. Remember, however, that sitting down with a recorder and speaking into it will not give you as accurate a tool for assessment as using the recorder in a natural setting. Once you have an accurate recording, ask yourself if you would like to listen to you. If the answer is yes, go right on fascinating people

Effective speakers are confident and enthusiastic.

with your dynamic animation. If the answer is no, identify your exact problems and concentrate on making changes to correct them. If you feel incapable of adjusting or altering on your own, seek advice from your speech instructor.[5]

Pronunciation   "To **pronounce** means to form speech sounds by moving the articulators of speech—chiefly the jaw, tongue and lips. There are many different and acceptable ways of pronouncing American English, because our language is spoken differently in various parts of the United States and Canada."[6] **General American speech,** defined as that spoken by well-educated Americans and Canadians of the Mideast, Midwest, and Far West, tends to be the most acceptable of the regional dialects. Nevertheless,

> Speech in general and pronunciation in particular are appropriate if they are consistent with the objectives of the speaker in his/her role of communicator of of ideas. The listeners, the occasion, and the speaker as a personality are some of the factors that determine appropriateness. Speech becomes substandard

if the pronunciations are such that they violate the judgments and tastes of the listeners.[7]

Because you will be evaluated not only on the basis of what you say but on how you say it, you should be aware of some common pronunciation problems and their causes. Then you can work toward making your use of oral English representative of the type of image you would like to portray. There are several common types and causes of pronunciation problems.[8]

1. *Sloppy or incorrect articulation.* If you say "air" for "error" and "dint" for "didn't," you are mispronouncing because of laziness in the use of articulators. As you practice a speech you have prepared, be aware of the words that you are mispronouncing. Be conscious of dropping the "g" sound at the end of words ending in "ing," such as "going," "doing," and "watching." Also be aware of slurring words together. "Alls-ya-godado" is not an understandable substitute for "all you have to do." "Jaknow?" is not as clear as "Did you know?"

2. *Affectation.* In New England and southern speech, saying "eye-thuh" for "either" is generally acceptable, but in the Far West or Midwest it sounds out of place. To sound "classy," some people pick up a "British" sound. If used inconsistently, such overdone pronunciation sounds affected and can be distracting. As you prepare to speak to an audience, notice when you put on an arrogant act or overdo the pronunciation of words such as "envelope," "tomato," and "ask."

3. *Ignorance of correct pronunciation.* Most of us have reading vocabularies that are far greater than our speaking vocabularies. Sometimes, when reading aloud, we come across a word that is out of our speaking vocabulary and is known to us only through our eyes. Other times, we encounter a technical term or a name to which we have not been previously exposed. In preparing a public speech, you may want to look up in a dictionary any word whose pronunciation you are not entirely sure of. It is very difficult to fake your way through a word that is beyond your pronunciation abilities, and incorrect pronunciation tells the audience you have not prepared properly.

4. *Vowel distortion.* Some of us have grown up in environments in which words are mispronounced because of vowel substitutions. "Milk" may have been pronounced "melk," "secretary" may have been "sekatury," "many" may have been "miny," "just"—"jist," "Washington"—"Warshington," "pumpkin"—"punkin," and "get"—"git." In all these instances, there is no easy cure for the distortion problem. In some cases, you may need the help of a speech pathologist to correct the problem. Being aware of the distortions allows some people to begin monitoring their own pronunciations and correcting themselves.

5. *Pronunciation outside the normal pattern.* If we assume that general American speech is the norm, certain pronunciations are generally not considered acceptable in the marketplace of business, education, and the professions. "Asked" is not "axt," "something" is not "sumptin," "many" is not "miny," and "picture" and "pitcher" are not the same word.

Physical Elements

The physical elements of communication include personal elements such as gestures, movement, posture, and eye contact. The use of visual aids is another physical element.

Gestures

Gestures involve the use of hands, body movements, and facial expressions. Interestingly enough, researchers have determined that people who use hand movements when they talk appear freer, more open, and more honest to an audience.[9]

Each person uses his or her own gesture pattern while communicating. Because of this, some people use a great number of gestures, whereas others use only a few. Gesture patterns result from environmental influences and are often tied to the emotional involvement we portray while we are speaking. Emotional involvement also affects our vocal delivery in the form of alterations in pitch, volume, and rate. Because each of us acts as a total organism in making physical movements, broad gestures are usually accompanied by loud volume and strong pitch changes. Nonemotional involvement ordinarily results in fewer gestures.

Students in speech communication classes sometimes ask their instructors to teach them how to gesture. Unfortunately, it is impossible to do so because gesturing is the result of the speaker's degree of involvement, excitement, and dynamism. False enthusiasm and the gestures that accompany it, which can be taught, only distract the audience.

To be effective, gestures have to be completely natural. That is why you should not worry about what to do with your hands; forget them and they will take care of themselves. Your hands will be active when your body calls for this movement—unless you are gripping the lectern so tightly that you cannot let go or have your hands jammed inside your pockets and cannot get them out or are playing with keys, money, jewelry, or the buttons on your clothing.

Movement

Movement (such as walking in front of an audience) is influenced by the emotional distance a speaker wants to establish, the amount of emotional energy within the speaker, and the speaker's need to stay near the lectern to refer to notes or use a microphone. A person who wants intimate interaction with audience members will move or lean toward them. But if the desire is to create a more formal feeling, the speaker will remain stationed behind the lectern, using it as a barrier.

Most movements before an audience are natural, but to avoid distracting their listeners, some speakers consciously limit the size of the area they cover so that their movements do not become more interesting than their speaking. Of course, if a microphone is anchored to the lectern, the speaker must remain there. A speaker's use of notes or manuscript may also limit his or her freedom to leave the speaker's stand. In addition, the arrangement of the audience may confine the speaker's space. Under these conditions, a speaker has little flexibility regarding movement.

It is usually a good idea for a speaker to employ opening and closing pauses in the presentation. Because it takes an audience a while to settle down to listening, a speaker is wise to assume a comfortable position before the audience and pause for several seconds before starting the presentation. At the end of the speech, the speaker usually presents the last sentence emphatically—by raising or lowering the voice—to indicate that the presentation is over. The speaker should then pause again for several seconds before leaving the lectern.

Posture   The effective speaker devotes some attention to **posture,** for a forceful stance adds to the dynamic image that a speaker can convey through these nonverbal, physical dimensions. The speaker's posture should not distract from the speech itself. Speakers must be careful not to lean to one side or to shift their weight back and forth. Listeners can also be distracted by the speaker who puts one foot across the other or leans on the lectern.

Eye Contact   Establishing **eye contact** by looking into the eyes of your audience as you speak is another key to effective speaking. Members of an audience will feel involved in the presentation if you look at them. Maintaining eye contact also helps you receive the feedback so you can adjust the presentation accordingly. To use eye contact effectively, look directly at the listeners, not over their heads. Also shift your focus so that you are not maintaining contact with just one section of the audience, and be especially careful not to overlook those in the front or back rows.

The Use of Visual Aids   Keep the following basic suggestions in mind when you use visual aids in a presentation:

- *Do not stand between the visual aid and the audience because you will block the view.* If an aid is important enough to use, it is important that the audience see it.
- *Speak toward the audience, not toward the visual aid.* Focus your attention on the aid only when you want the audience to look at it.

A speaker who wants intimate interaction with audience members will move or lean toward them.

- *Know the visual aid well enough so that you do not have to study it while you talk.*
- *Point to the particular place on the aid that you are discussing.* If, for example, you are speaking about the Yucatan peninsula and you have displayed a map, point specifically to this area of Mexico with your finger, a pencil, or a pointer. You know where the Yucatan is, but your listeners may not.
- *Use the aid at the point in your presentation where it will have the greatest impact.* Also prepare the listeners for the aid by explaining what they are going to see. (For example, "We are going to look at a chart that will demonstrate what has been happening to one business in this country during the last five years.") Then clarify what the aid is illustrating. ("This chart shows the decline that has taken place in shoe production in the last five years. As you will note, the production in 1970 was . . . , whereas the chart shows a decrease in 1990 to. . . . ") Finally, pull the ideas together. ("Thus a look at one industry, the shoe industry, can help us to see. . . .")
- *If you do not need the aid for part of the speech, put it down, cover it up, or turn it over.* An exposed visual aid can distract listeners' attention. Indeed, it may become so interesting that they will not pay attention to your presentation. If you are going to refer to the visual aid

throughout the presentation, keep it exposed; but once its purpose is completed, dismiss it.

Speaker Anxiety

Very few speakers escape the "butterflies." There is no cure for them except to realize that they are beneficial, rather than harmful, and certainly never fatal. Actually, the tension usually means that the speaker, because he or she is keyed up, will do a better job. Edward R. Murrow, considered by many to have been the finest television news commentator, called stage fright "the seat of perfection," and Mark Twain once comforted a fright-frozen friend about to give a speech with, "Just remember they don't expect much."[10]

Even normally brave people are frightened by public speaking, a condition known as **speechophobia.** "Ms. [Sally] Ride (the first U.S. woman in space) has been giving an average of one speech a day, traveling across the country and Europe. . . . In a question-and-answer period after her speech to the American Bar Association, a woman asked, 'Were you afraid?' 'I was a lot more scared getting up to give this speech,' she replied."[11]

Yet even with all these assurances that your anxiety is normal, you are probably still saying to yourself, "I don't want to get up. My knees knock, my stomach churns, my legs shake, and my mouth gets dry." So in lieu of a cure, here are some suggestions for dealing with speaking anxiety.

Do not avoid the experience of giving a presentation. The more you speak, the more comfortable you will get. Though the nervousness may not go away completely, it should let up as you get more practice.

Do not fail to prepare, assuming that the longer you avoid confronting the situation, the less time there will be to build up anxiety. If you are not prepared, the panic will probably be greater than it would be if you had the material to get you by.

Do not take drugs or alcohol because you think they will relax you. All they will do is dull your reflexes and increase your chances of forgetting and making a total fool of yourself.

When it comes to relaxation,[12] speakers find it helpful before beginning to take several deep breaths and expel all the air from their lungs. Others like to shake their hands at the wrists to "get out the nervousness." Some people favor grabbing the seat of their chair with both hands, pushing down and holding the position for about five seconds, repeating this movement about five times. This tightens and then loosens the muscles, which cause a decrease in physical tension.

Though traditionally many speakers try to shake off their anxiety, Gestalt therapy has suggested a different approach, which advocates that speakers get in touch with their feelings. Rather than shaking your anxi-

One of the best ways to relax during a speech is to be ready for it. So prepare and practice!

ety off, it recommends that you let it go as far as it can. What will happen, if you are typical, is that it will reach a peak and then subside. If you are dubious, try the following experiment: sit in a chair, and place your hands one inside the other with the palm of one hand resting on the palm of the other hand and the fingers of one hand wrapped around the back of the other. Force your hands together and keep forcing them. Do not let them move. Even though the force will make your hands start to shake, keep on forcing them together. Soon your whole body will probably start to shake. You will then reach a point where the shaking will stop and relaxation will set in.

There are two ways you can use this exercise in speaking. If, immediately before you get up, you perform the hand-in-hand activity, you will probably be physically relaxed by the time you get up. Or think of the experience of getting up before the audience and feel the anxiety. Let it stay in your mind, imagining that you are going through the experience. Let yourself be as nervous as you can; psychologically push it as far as you can. Some people report that by imagining the upcoming experience in its worst way, the actual experience becomes much easier.[13]

Another technique is to change your expectation level. We all tend to perform the way we expect to perform, so **expectancy restructuring** is based on the idea that if you expect to do well, then you will do well. Thus if you have negative expectations, you must change them to positive expectations. If you are afraid to get up and give a speech, assuming that the experience will be negative, you may experience some or all of the negative side effect of that fear—sweating palms, quivering voice, and so forth. To overcome this, prepare a well-structured and documented speech so that you have confidence that the material will be well received. Then go through the process of visualizing the actual setting in which you are going to give the speech. Picture yourself getting out of your chair, walking to the front of the room, arranging your materials on the podium, looking at the audience, and giving the speech. As you see yourself presenting the material, look at various people. They are nodding their heads in agreement; they are interested and are listening attentively. You complete the speech and return to your chair, feeling good about yourself. The more you visualize this positive experience, the more your expectation level of success will increase. Soon you will be expecting success, not failure.

One of the best ways to relax is to be ready for the speech. This means starting to prepare far enough in advance so that you have enough material, the speech is well structured and well organized, and you have a chance to practice it. Some speakers try to convince themselves that they will do better if they just get up and talk, with little or no thought as to what they will be saying. This is a fool's contention; it is usually the message of a procrastinator or a person who is not properly aware of his or her responsibility to audience and self. Yes, some speakers can get up and "wing it," but the normal mortal cannot. So prepare and practice!

There is no one best way to rehearse. For most people, sitting at a desk and going over the material by mumbling through the outline or notes are the starting point. This will alert you to ideas that do not seem to make sense, words you cannot pronounce, places where you go blank because you need more notes, and/or areas that need more or fewer examples. Make the changes, and continue to orally review your notes until you are satisfied with the material.

Once you are satisfied with the material, try to duplicate the setting in which you are going to speak. In most instances, you will probably be standing behind a lectern. If so, practice with a lectern, put a box on a desk, use your computer printer stand on a table, or place a piece of cardboard over the bathroom sink. Stand and speak. This will get you comfortable with moving pages and looking up from the notes or manuscript; you will also find out whether your typing or writing is going to cause you reading problems.

Duplicate as closely as possible what you are going to do. If you are going to use visual aids, use them. If you are going to demonstrate some object, demonstrate it. The more familiar you become with exactly what you are going to do, the more likely it is you will be comfortable doing it. Indeed, you practice typing at a typewriter, you practice driving behind the wheel of a car, and you practice athletics by duplicating game or competitive settings, so do the same thing with your speech.

Stop practicing when you are comfortable with your material and have worked out the problems related to using notes and supplementary aids. Do not overpractice. You can never become "perfect." You are striving to become as comfortable as you can in what is a stressful situation for almost all of us.

During the speech, place yourself in a balanced and comfortable stance. Do not lock your knees as this makes the whole body rigid, causes difficulties in breathing, and often results in shaking, a dry mouth, and vocal quivering. Try not to lean on the lectern because this will cut off your gestures and discourage any natural movements.

When you begin, put into practice what many speakers have found to be the best stress reliever—the triangle stance. In the **triangle stance** (Figure 14.1), you place one foot—foot A—at a slight angle and foot B at about a forty-five-degree angle, as if it were coming out of the arch of foot A. Keep your feet about six inches apart. Shuffle your feet slightly until you feel comfortable and balanced. Place your weight on foot A. You will feel the leg of foot B relax. You may also find that it helps if you slightly extend the hip of the foot A side of your body. This process allows you to breathe and gesture easier. As you proceed through the

Figure 14.1

Foot Placement to Aid in the Relief of Speaker Anxiety

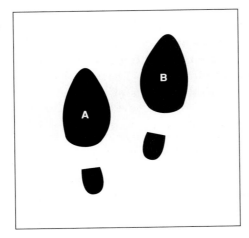

speech, you can alter the stance by altering the foot A and B positions, always remembering to put your body weight on the foot that is farthest back.

Look at the people in the audience who are alert during the presentation, nodding their heads as you speak. Concentrate on your material. Try to relax and do as well as you can . . . no one can ask for anything more!! And if all else fails, remember that there have been no reported deaths from the shock of giving a speech.

Summary

This chapter examined the oral and physical elements of delivering a speech. The major ideas presented were:

☐ The speaker can use four basic modes of presentation: impromptu or ad lib, extemporaneous, manuscript, and memorized.

☐ Impromptu speaking requires you to present your ideas with little or no preparation.

☐ Ad lib speaking allows you no time to prepare.

☐ In the extemporaneous mode of speaking, you develop a set of speech aids, such as notes or an outline, to assist during the presentation.

☐ In the manuscript mode of delivery, you write the material out and deliver it word for word.

☐ In the memorized mode, you write the speech out word for word and then commit it to memory.

☐ The vocal elements of communication are pitch, volume, rate, quality, animation, and pause.

☐ To pronounce means to form speech sounds by moving the articulators of speech.

☐ There are many different and acceptable ways of pronouncing American English.

☐ The physical elements of communication include gestures, physical movements, posture, eye contact, and the use of visual aids.

☐ Speechophobia is the fear associated with giving a speech.

Key Terms

impromptu speaking	animation
ad lib speaking	pause
extremporaneous mode	pronounce
manuscript mode	general American speech

eye span   gestures
virgules   movement
underscores   posture
memorized mode   eye contact
pitch   speechophobia
volume   expectancy restructuring
rate   triangle stance
quality

Learn by Doing

1. The class sits in a circle. The instructor throws a ball to someone in the circle and passes an envelope to that person. The person selects one of the statements from the envelope, takes several minutes to prepare, and gives a one-minute presentation on the topic. But before speaking, the first person tosses the ball to someone else, who will be the second speaker. While the first person is speaking, the second person selects a topic and prepares a speech. Each speaker, in turn, tosses the ball to the next speaker. This process continues until all members of the class have spoken.

    The envelope may contain these statements:
    a. "I did something that I was proud of."
    b. "I made a promise and I kept it."
    c. "I believe that college is necessary."
    d. "The thing I like best about my job is . . ."
    e. "The thing I like least about my job is . . ."
    f. "The person I respect most is . . ."
    g. "The place I visited that I like most was _____ because . . ."
    h. "If I had $1 million, I would . . ."
    i. "If I had three wishes, they would be . . ."

2. On a three-by-five-inch card, list three topics you think you could speak about for a minimum of two minutes. Your instructor selects one of these for you to give an impromptu speech about. You have two minutes to get ready. You may use any notes you can prepare within that time.

3. Prepare a speech of three to five minutes using the extemporaneous mode. Choose a subject about which you have a great deal of feeling. (A pet peeve, a belief that someone holds that you cannot accept, and a speech for or against a political candidate are all possible topics.) All students present their speeches on the same day. On the prescribed day, the class is divided into groups of three to six. Present your speech to the other members of your group. After all the presentations, each student makes two positive comments about the

first speaker's presentation and suggests one improvement. The second speaker's presentation is then discussed, and so on. After this practice day, you present your speeches to the class as a whole. Before the class presentation, you adjust your presentation according to the analysis given by your group members.

4.   The instructor brings to class a shopping bag filled with miscellaneous articles (a comb, an eraser, a panda bear, a feather, a ball, a block, and so on). Students are seated in a circle, and the bag is handed to one student, who reaches into the bag without looking and pulls out an article. The instructor reads one of the following statements, and the student gives a speech of at least one minute:

a.   "I would like to be a (name of the object removed) because . . ."

b.   "I would not like to be a (name of the object removed) because . . ."

c.   "(Name of the object) reminds me of a time in my life when I found myself . . ."

d.   Compare and contrast the object you removed from the bag with another object by stating all their similarities and differences.

5.   Some of the most commonly mispronounced words in general American speech are listed here. Look up each word in a dictionary or pronunciation guide. During a class session, you are asked to pronounce these words and use them in sentences: *across, acts, actually, all, ambulance, any, asked, because, catch, doing, familiar, fifth, genuine, going, horror, hundred, introduce, just, library, next, nuclear, particular, picture, prescription, probably, pumpkin, recognized, sandwich, secretary, Washington, with.*

Notes

1. Judson Smith, "Writing for the Eye and Ear," *Training* (March 1981), 67–68.

2. Louis P. Nizer, as quoted in Jerry Tarver, *Professional Speech Writing* (Richmond, Va.: Effective Speech Writing Institute, 1982), p. 100.

3. Dorothy Sarnoff, "Self Esteem," *New Woman*, 13 (July 1983), 76.

4. "How to Speak Better in Public: An Interview with Sandy Linver," *U.S. News & World Report*, April 6, 1981, pp. 60–61.

5. Try to view this exercise constructively. Some research suggests that the experience of hearing your own voice for the first time can be shocking, even frightening, if you are not prepared for it. See Phillip S. Holzman, "On Hearing One's Own Voice," *Psychology Today*, 5 (November 1971), 66–69, 98.

6. Stuart W. Hyde, *Television and Radio Announcing*, 4th ed. (Boston: Houghton Mifflin, 1983), p. 130.

7. Jon Eisenson, *Voice and Diction: A Program for Improvement* (New York: Macmillan, 1974), pp. 158–159.

8. Hyde, pp. 131–132.

9. M. L. Clark, E. A. Erway, and L. Beltzer, *The Learning Encounter* (New York: Random House, 1971), pp. 52–65.

10. George Plimpton, "How to Make a Speech," *Psychology Today,* 15 (October 1981), 58–59.

11. "Ms. Ride Yearns for an End to Her Speaking Schedule," *Norfolk Virginian Pilot,* August 3, 1983, p. A-2.

12. There is no definitive research available to prove that any of these activities work for everyone, but they have been used successfully by some people. These activities, and references to additional means such as chemicals and physical conditioning, were summarized in a presentation by Martin Freedman at the Eastern Communication Association Convention, Ocean City, Maryland, May 1980.

13. This discussion is based on information shared by Les Wyman at a workshop at the Gestalt Institute, Cleveland, Ohio, 1982.

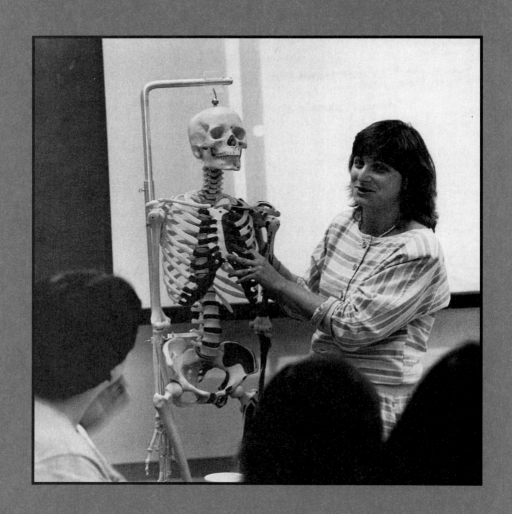

15 Informative Speaking

Chapter Outline

After reading this chapter, you should be able to:

Define informative speaking

Discuss the need for informative speaking in the information age

List and explain the classifications of informative speeches

Detail how to develop the informative speech

List and explain the steps a successful informative speaker takes in developing a speech.

We live in an information age. Because we live in such an advanced technological society, we can handle a vast amount of information through computerized information systems. But those very systems are responsible, then, for creating so much more information that we must be able to process. "At least 80 percent of what you were taught in school will be proved wrong. Knowledge is doubling at the rate of 100 percent every 20 months."[1] Because we have to handle so much information, many of us have experienced "information anxiety," an inability to cope with all this data.[2] It appears this anxiety will not diminish. One social critic suggested that the need for people who can retrieve and explain information is going to greatly increase in the future.[3]

The Role of Informative Speaking

Because time has become a precious commodity to most of us, we have to rely more directly on informative speakers in all sorts of settings to provide us with the information we need. Complex, technical users manuals, for instance, require more reading time than many of us are willing to or can take, so we turn to the salesperson for information on how to operate the new VCR, fax machine, or satellite dish, or we turn to companies that offer special training in operating the computer. Job training is based on a great deal of oral instruction, and the classroom lecturer delivers most of the material necessary to master the content of many courses.

Businesses have recognized this need for information disseminators. For example, The Boeing Company employs an information specialist to assist employees to better present information. According to one specialist, "A factor vital to the health of any corporation is the constant exchange of accurate information. Although traditional, written forms of business communication remain important, the oral exchange of information occupies an increasingly important role in the functioning of today's companies."[4] Organizations are even hiring consultants to do information training and to train employees to be trainers as the quick upgrading and changing of equipment and job needs take place.

The Concept of Informative Speaking

If we accept that disseminating information is important and is done in business and industry, the question arises, Do real people give speeches? A survey of the speaking habits of adults revealed that between 55 and 63 percent of the respondents gave at least one speech every two years to ten or more people, with 71 percent of these speakers giving at least four speeches during that time. People are more likely to give job-related speeches of the informative than of the persuasive type. Also, people with more education and income give speeches most frequently. Knowing this, a person who wants a high-income job is wise to get a solid education and prepare to become an effective speaker.[5]

Traditionally, **informative speaking** has been defined as discourse that imparts new information, secures understanding, or reinforces accumulated information. At present, however, controversies persist among communication theorists in regard to this definition. For instance, some theorists wonder whether all speaking is persuasive in nature; that is, whether the traditional distinction between informative speaking and persuasive speaking is simply a matter of theoretical degree.

This text assumes that all communication contains elements of persuasion. After all, the audience in the traditional informative speaking format must be persuaded to accept the information presented by the speaker. (Indeed, even the act of using materials to gain attention is persuasive because the speaker is asking listeners to pay attention to the speaker rather than to any other competing stimuli.) If there are distinguishing elements between an informative and a persuasive speech, they center on the structure of the message and the appeals used in the persuasive format.

Characteristics of Informative Speaking

As in any other type of speaking, the development of an informative presentation is dependent on analysis of the audience. Consideration must be given to the audience's present knowledge about the subject, the concepts known by the audience that can function as foundation, and the extent to which definitions, understandable analogies, examples, and clarifiers need to be used. The speaker must also determine the appropriate language level, the attention devices to be used, and the structure of the message that will best fit the group. Research suggests that the speaker, as the information source, may think his or her listeners lack the necessary information, whereas the listeners themselves may not feel the same way.[6] Because of this discrepancy, the astute speaker determines the listeners' real needs and uses that information to develop the speech.

In an informative presentation, the speaker must always keep the purpose of the presentation in mind. In this connection, a clear purpose statement of the speech is essential. Consider these examples: "to inform by defining what the drug Rho-Gam is and to explain the reasons it has eliminated the need to give blood transfusions to some newborn children who have a problematic factor in their blood composition"; "to inform the audience of what the Heimlich maneuver is, how it was developed, and how this technique can prevent people from choking to death"; "to inform the audience of what the Heimlich maneuver is and to teach them the steps necessary to do the maneuver by demonstrating each phase." Note that in the last two examples, although the subject is the same, the goal is different. The former explains the maneuver and its value. The latter explains the maneuver and then teaches the steps for performing it.

These purpose statements may sound rather formal, but they are stated in a manner that narrows the subject and indicates specifically what will be included in the speech. Thus the purpose statement serves as a fence around the territory to be covered in a presentation and indicates how to "corral" the information. If you do not set up these sorts of boundaries, you may find yourself discussing many things but not achieving your desired outcome.

Classifications of Informative Speaking

There is no universally accepted classification of informative speeches. One classification system examines presentations about objects, processes, events, and concepts. At the same time, this system accepts that there are specific types of informative speeches that can be identified by the setting in which they are used or by their uniqueness. Examples include informative briefings, technical reports, lectures, question-and-answer sessions, and speeches of introduction.

Speeches About Objects

Speeches about objects describe a particular thing in detail. The object may be a person, a place, an animal, a structure, a machine—anything that can be touched or seen. The object is identified, and then the details concerning some specific attribute of the object are discussed.

Here are examples of purpose statements for informative speeches about an object: "to inform the audience about the renovation of Blair House, the nation's guesthouse for visiting diplomats, during the

Speeches about objects describe something in detail.

Reagan presidency"; "to inform the audience what a compact disc (CD) player is and to cite some specific factors to consider when purchasing a CD"; "to inform the audience why a dolphin is classified as a mammal and to describe some of the experimental work on identifying the language capabilities of this unique creature."

As with any speech, consideration must be given to the time limit of the presentation, which will determine how to narrow the topic. Each of the purpose statements is appropriate for a five-minute speech.

Speeches About Processes

Speeches about processes instruct the audience about how something works, is made, or is done so that the listeners can apply the skills. The end purpose may be either to gain understanding of the process or to be able to do something. This technique is used in training a group to operate a piece of equipment or in explaining a manufacturing process. Purpose statements for informative speeches about processes include "to inform the audience of the step-by-step process of using the move feature of the WordPerfect word-processing program"; "to inform the audience of the step-by-step process employed by the Chrysler Corporation in developing a design for an aerodynamic automobile"; "to inform the audience, through a demonstration, of the process that should be used to fill out the income tax short form."

Speeches about processes often lend themselves to development according to a chronological method of organization. In this method, the speaker describes the first step of the process, then the second, then the third, and so on.

Speeches
About Events

Speeches about events inform the audience about something that has happened, is happening, or is expected to happen. This type of presentation can be developed in many ways, but it tends to work well in a chronological, comparison-contrast, or spatial arrangement. Here are several purpose statements for informative speeches about events: "to inform the audience of the spread of the AIDS virus through a statistical examination for the years 1980–1991 in the United States" (time sequence arrangement); "to inform the audience of the similarities and differences in the American and Russian revolutions based on their economic causes" (comparison-contrast arrangement); "to inform the audience of the pioneer western migration in the United States by tracing the major stages of the movement from the East Coast to the West Coast" (spatial arrangement).

Speeches
About Concepts

Speeches about concepts examine theories, beliefs, ideas, philosophies, or schools of thought. Much of the formal educational process deals with speeches about concepts.[7] Concept topics include explanations and investigations of business theories, philosophical movements, psychological concepts, and political theories.

Because many of the ideas relating to concepts are abstract, a speaker must be sure to use precise language, define terms, give historical background, avoid undefined slang and jargon, and use appropriate clarifying support materials such as audio, visual, and audiovisual aids. Examples of purpose statements for informative speeches about concepts are "to inform the audience of the existential movement in philosophy through a statement of Jean-Paul Sartre's definition and his application of it in the play *No Exit*"; "to inform the audience about the theory that abused children grow up to be child abusers through an examination of three classic research studies"; "to inform the audience of the theory that musical theater composers Alan Jay Lerner and Frederick Loewe used the theme of the search for a perfect time, a perfect place, and a perfect love story as the basis for their musicals."

Informative
Briefings

Most business, organizational, and technical communicators gain current knowledge in their fields as a result of **informative briefings.** The fundamental objective of an informative briefing is to share data and insights among people with common interests. The briefing usually involves delivery of information to the audience, followed by the exchange of data, ideas, and questions among participants.[8] This common internal-communication device is used to explain organizational policies, procedures, and issues. Examples of informative briefings are the sales

Much of the formal educational process deals with speeches about concepts. Topics include business theories, philosophical movements, psychological concepts, and political theories.

manager of an automobile agency informing her staff about the new models, the head of a nursing unit explaining to his staff the procedures that must be followed when treating new patients, or the military commander explaining the implications of an aerial attack plan to the press.

As with any other kind of speech, preparation for an informative briefing requires careful analysis of the audience to determine what background and definitions will be needed to ensure audience comprehension. It is not uncommon, given the nature of when and how briefings are used, for the audience to be more knowledgeable about the subject than a traditional assemblage. If the audience has considerable knowledge, the speaker does not have to cover the background material in as much depth as he or she would for uninformed listeners.

Technical Reports

A **technical report** is a concise, clear statement explaining a process, detailing a technique, or discussing new elements either to people within a business or industry or to people outside it. Unfortunately, a majority of executives in corporate America are convinced that recent college and university graduates cannot give technical reports effectively. Executives surveyed said that fewer than 20 percent of the people they worked with were capable of giving a concise, clear oral report and that they had far greater difficulty training people to do this than to write a clear letter.[9]

One of the major factors in the development of a technical report is determining the proper format. The first rule of giving a report is to ask those who requested the report what form they would like it to take. Find out how much time is going to be allowed and how much detail will be required.[10]

In giving a technical report, the speaker must know who will be in the audience. If the report is to be given to nontechnical people, all technical words must be defined, and analogies familiar to the audience should be included to clarify the ideas presented. This does not mean the speaker has to water down the material so that it is invalidated. Instead, the speaker should be sure to define words, give examples, and present ideas in a variety of ways to make sure that the audience understands the concepts being set forth.

If your presentation includes technical drawings or a number of statistics, use handouts so that everyone can examine the materials. If the group is small, consider allowing audience members to ask questions as you develop your ideas so that they have the opportunity for immediate clarification where necessary. Be careful, however, to maintain control of the structure and the material as you answer questions dealing with your presentation.

When you structure a technical report that involves a recommendation, start with a statement of the proposal unless there is a compelling reason not to do so. (You may want to hold the recommendation until the end if you know the audience will be hostile to the proposal or if you want to lead up to the recommendation by giving total background before revealing your solution or recommendation.) After you have proposed the idea, explain how you arrived at the conclusions or recommendations. Give just enough background to clarify but not so much as to make the presentation dull.[11]

Lectures   Probably the most familiar type of informative speaking with which all of us have experience is the **lecture,** the formal presentation of material to facilitate learning. Lectures are an integral part of academic life, serving as the main vehicle for the presentation of information in almost all subject fields. In addition, lectures are used in other settings—the guest speaker at Parent-Teacher Association, Kiwanis, fraternity, or sorority meetings; invited lecturers for lunch- or dinnertime seminars in corporate headquarters; public lectures by distinguished authorities as part of a museum, an arts, a religious, or an academic setting.

To be effective informative presentations, lectures should conform to the same characteristics we expect in other forms of informative speaking. A good lecture should be carefully adapted to the intended audience so that the speaker does not make inaccurate assumptions about the level of knowledge and vocabulary that the listeners share. An effective lecture should be clearly organized with easy-to-follow transitions so that the listeners can stay "on track" with the lecturer's flow of information. A memorable lecture should also be well developed, with the speaker using supporting details to elaborate each of the points. Like all informative speaking, lectures often tend to be top-heavy with explanations and consequently are considered to be dry. A variety of supporting materials (stories, statistics, analogies) enhance the explanatory details and involve the listeners more readily. The insertion of humor is also a way of getting and holding attention. So is the use of interaction; here the speaker involves the listeners by asking them questions, probing for information, and inviting inquiries during the presentation instead of waiting until the question-and-answer session.

The timing of a lecture is another key to success. Lecturers should be aware of the time frame. The audience expects a lecturer to stay within the framework of the assigned time (such as a class period) or within the boundaries of what the audience can comfortably absorb.

The lecture should be clearly structured. Terms that are alien to the audience and thus cause organizational and semantic interference should be avoided. Supplemental aids can be used to facilitate the listeners' understanding and keep them interested in the presentation.

Question-and-Answer Sessions

The **question-and-answer session** that follows many speeches is a type of informative speech itself.[12] It is an on-the-spot test of unrehearsed answers that measures the speaker's knowledge, alerts the speaker to areas in the speech that were unclear or needed more development, and gives the listeners a chance to probe for ideas.

In some instances, the question-and-answer session allows the receivers to point out the weakness of the speaker's arguments or present alternative views. This occurs more frequently after persuasive speeches than after informative presentations. Indeed, some communication analysts wonder whether the proposal of alternative concepts is really an acceptable role of the questioning session. If confronted by a hostile questioner, the speaker will have to determine whether she or he wants to deal with the issue or remind the prober that the purpose of this part of the speech is to ask questions, not give a counterspeech or engage in debate.

When you enter into a question-and-answer session, set the ground rules. Ask the program chairperson about the process to be used and the time limit, and give him or her any restrictions you wish to place on this segment of the speech. Some speakers like to call on the participants. Others prefer to allow the chairperson to entertain the questions. Some presenters want all questions written out beforehand and want to select the questions they will answer. If you have any restrictions, let the chairperson know of them before you give the speech, and inform the audience of the rules.

The most difficult part of many question-and-answer sessions is to get the first question asked. Once this hurdle is overcome, questions seem to flow naturally. To overcome the "Who will ask the first question?" trauma, you may want to have someone in the audience prepared to ask a question. Another technique is to ask a question yourself. This can be accomplished by stating, "I've often been asked my views concerning . . ." and then proceeding to indicate your views.

Here are some additional suggestions for carrying on the question-and-answer session:

- *Before you answer a question, restate it so that everyone hears the inquiry.* If the question is complicated, simplify it in the restatement.
- *Do not speak just to the questioner; speak to the whole audience.*
- *Be patient.* If you have to repeat material you have already covered, do so briefly.
- *If a question goes on and on, prompt the asker to summarize the question.*
- *Keep your answers short.* Restate the question, give your response, clarify any vocabulary if necessary, give an example if appropriate, and then stop. Following the response, some speakers ask the questioner whether the answer was satisfactory.
- *Back up your responses with examples, statistics, and quotations.*
- *If the question is overly complicated or of interest only to the asker, suggest a discussion with the questioner after the speech or via correspondence.*

- *If the question is irrelevant, indicate that it is interesting or thought provoking but does not seem appropriate to the presentation.* Do not get sidetracked from the purpose of the speech or pulled into a private debate with the questioner.

- *If you do not know an answer, say so.* You can offer to find out the answer and report back accordingly.

- *Limit the discussion to one question per person, and avoid getting caught in a dialogue with one person.* Others who have questions will become frustrated, and those who do not will get bored.

- *Be willing to be corrected or at least to recognize another's viewpoint.* Thank the person for his or her clarification or acknowledge that more than one point of view is possible ("That's an interesting idea," or "The idea can be viewed that way"). You may win the battle of words by putting down or insulting the questioner, but you will lose the respect of the listeners in the process. Indeed, it is futile to get involved in a battle of words with a heckler or a person with a preconceived attitude or bias. In the 1988 presidential campaign, Vice President George Bush and newscaster Dan Rather became involved in a battle of words. The result was a debate by the electorate on who was the winner of the conflict and a seeming loss of respect for both men.

- *Know when to end the session.* Do not wait until interest has waned or people begin leaving. You can lose the positive effect of a speech by having an overextended question-and-answer session.

Speeches of Introduction

The purpose of a speech of introduction is to identify the person who will be speaking to the audience and give any other information that may spark the listeners' interest in the speaker. Too often, speeches of introduction are ineffective because the presenter has not carefully prepared remarks appropriate to the listeners' needs. When you introduce a speaker, clearly identify who the speaker is by whatever name, title, and identification he or she wants used; you can also talk about where the speaker is from as well as the speaker's accomplishments and when they took place. Establish the credibility of the speaker by highlighting significant aspects of his or her credentials and background that indicate knowledge or expertise in the subject. Present the speaker as a person in whom the listeners will be interested. You can offer comments on the importance or relevance of the topic and the significance of the speaker.

A speech of introduction should be short and to the point. Remember, the listeners have come to hear the speaker, not the person making the introduction. Some cautions for the speech of introduction include:

- *Do not overpraise the speaker.* Indicating that he or she is the best speaker the audience will ever hear sets the presenter with an almost impossible goal.

- *Avoid using phrases such as "It is an honor and a privilege" or "This speaker needs no introduction."* These are overused and meaningless.

- *Set the proper tone for the speech.* If, for example, you know that the speech is going to be humorous, try to fit humor into the introduction.

- *Be sure you can pronounce the speaker's name as he or she wants it pronounced.*

- *Get the information you need from the speaker as far in advance as possible so that you have time to work on the presentation.*

- *If possible, ask what he or she wishes to have highlighted.*

Developing the Informative Speech

Every informative speaker has a challenge—to get the audience to understand and retain the information presented. When we consider that the typical listener remembers only about 10 percent of an oral presentation three days after hearing it, we recognize how great the challenge is.[13]

Learning-theory specialists stress that the basis for retention and understanding is the establishment of relationships (associations and connections) with physical or mental activities. We can learn through repetition (by hearing the ideas over and over again). We can learn through experiencing (doing a task to see what it is).[14] We are more likely to remember things that have relevance to us. We remember information we are exposed to that will somehow make our life easier, that helps us to know something we did not know before, or that we will be rewarded for knowing. In other words, we will remember when we see a reason to do so. We also remember because something makes sense to us—the order in which it is presented makes the idea(s) easy to understand, or the examples and other developing materials make the idea clear.

When you plan an informative speech, consider using supplementary aids to help your listeners remember your message. Understanding how we learn can be of assistance in determining the approach you will take. It is estimated that we learn 1 percent through taste, 1.5 percent through touch, 3.5 percent through smell, 11 percent through hearing, and an astonishing 83 percent through sight.[15] Once you know this, you realize that your best chance of getting people to remember is to have them hear and see the content of your presentation. Such devices as slides, charts, illustrations, pictures, and models help to reinforce and/or clarify what you say. There are several pointers to keep in mind when developing an informative speech.[16]

1. *Order your ideas clearly.* Select a method of organization that aids your audience in following the step-by-step development of the speech.

2. *Use a chronological method of delivery if the speech lends itself to a first, second, and third progression or is date oriented (years or ages).* Sample subject: explaining a science experiment that requires a specific progression.

3. *Use a spatial method of delivery if the speech has some type of geographical basis that lends itself to go from east to west, or top to bottom, or inside out.* Sample subject: tracing the voyage of Christopher Columbus from Spain to the New World.

4. *Use a topical method of delivery if the subject divides into specific parts of a broad area.* Sample subject: describing the life cycle, characteristics, and dangers of the gypsy moth.

5. *Use comparison-contrast when the topic centers on illustrating similarities and differences.* Sample subject: comparing Nebraska's unicameral (one-house) legislature with the two-house legislative system of all other states.

6. *Use the familiar to explain the new.* If a person does not understand something, present an analogy based on something already familiar. For example, you can explain how an FM radio signal travels by comparing it to the way a bow and an arrow work. The arrow goes as far as the bow projects it and then drops. If something gets in its way, however, the arrow stops moving. Similarly, the FM signal goes as far as its thrusting signal power allows it to move unless something gets in its way and stops it. The analogy is one of the most impressive clarifying devices available to an informative speaker.

7. *Use vivid illustrations.* Descriptions, stories, comparisons, contrasts, and verbal pictures add to the possibility of gaining and holding the audience's attention. An audience member who can visualize something is likely to remember it.

8. *Avoid being too technical.* If you have ever tried to follow directions for using a computer program when you knew nothing about computer language, or if you have ever tried to repair a piece of electrical equipment using a technician's manual, you know the difficulty of understanding materials that may be fine for an expert but are not geared to the layperson. If your subject is at all technical, evaluate the vocabulary level of audience members. Based on their backgrounds and experiences, choose terms that are not likely to confuse, or clarify the technical terms you do use. Remember, the purpose of the speech is not to impress the audience with your vast vocabulary; the purpose is to accomplish the informative objective of the speech. Select words that will help, rather than hinder, your task.

9. *Personalize your message.* Audiences are more attracted to real, human-element examples, rather than fictional or hypothetical ex-

amples. If at all possible, use illustrations that allow your audience to identify with the plight of a victim, understand the joy of what happened to someone who mastered the process you are teaching, or learn how someone's life was altered by the historical event you are sharing.

10. *Do not speak down to your audience, but do not overestimate audience knowledge.* There is no clear guideline for evaluating an audience's knowledge level other than to learn as much as you can about what the audience knows specifically and generally. It is senseless to draw an analogy to the familiar if it is not familiar. For example, professors brought up during the John F. Kennedy era often forget that many present-day college students were not even born during JFK's presidency. Drawing comparisons of today to that time, for example, may be beyond the conceptual level of a freshman political science class.

11. *Use as much clarification and detail as you feel are necessary to ensure listener understanding.* If anything, err on the side of overexplanation. Most audience members appreciate a speaker who makes an effort to communicate clearly.

Use clarification and detail to ensure audience understanding.

The Informative Process in Action

It is helpful to study the process of speech preparation by investigating the steps a successful speaker took in developing a speech. Consider the presentation outlined in Figure 15.1, in which the speaker is describing what is involved in establishing and running a small business. The speaker owns a jewelry boutique in Denver that specializes in unique, individually designed pieces. The speaker is well known to her listeners as a successful businessperson.

Informative speaking occupies a prominent place in today's information age. Because listeners must turn to information sources in increasing numbers, informative speakers must present information in a clear, meaningful, interesting way so that the message is understood and the audience wants to listen.

Figure 15.1

Sample Speech Outline

Purpose statement: To inform the audience that effective management is the key to success in business by examining what it takes to own, start, and manage a business as well as by examining the sources of assistance available for small-business owners.

	I. Introduction
Attention material using quotation to interest listener	A. Attention material: small-business expert Oliver Galbraith of San Diego State University has commented, "One of the great opportunities every United States citizen has is the chance to start a business. This opportunity, which is denied in many other nations, has sometimes been referred to as the American Dream. Unfortunately, this dream, after becoming a reality, can all too easily become a nightmare."
Orienting material demonstrating how listeners can be affected	B. Orienting material: You may have the dream of owning your own business. Historically, business starts rise by 16.4 percent, while business failures rise by 9.6 percent. Let me share my experience with you to help you decide if you want to own your own business.
Topic of speech	II. Statement of the central idea: effective management is the key to owning your own business.
	III. Body
Statement of first issue	A. What it takes to own your own business
	1. You the manager
Personal examples of speaker	a. Drive
	b. Thinking ability
	c. Competence in human relations
	d. Communication skills
	e. Technical knowledge
Tie to audience	2. Your business
	a. Compatibility with your needs and interests

	b. Compatibility with your customers
	c. Profitability
Statistics—use of visual	(1) Profitability table from Price Waterhouse
Transition	(As you can see, it takes a great deal to own your own business. There are procedures you can follow to get your business started.)
Statement of second issue	B. Procedures for starting your own business
Discussion of effective cash planning	1. Cash planning
Example	a. The Conference Board, *A Guide to Consumer Markets,* estimates of sales volume
	b. Capital requirements
	c. Dealing with lenders
Discussion of good business plan	2. Devising a business plan
Example for reinforcement	a. *Wall Street Journal* cites business plans as the key to success of such companies as Federal Express
Description using visual aid	b. Format of a plan

Format of a plan:

(1) Executive summary
(2) The business
(3) Products/services
(4) Industry analysis
(5) Market analysis
(6) Marketing strategy
(7) Management and organization
(8) Implementation plan
(9) Potential risks and pitfalls
(10) Financial statements and projections
(11) Sensitivity analysis

Discussion of what form to choose	3. Deciding on form of ownership
	a. Sole proprietorship
	b. Partnership
	c. Corporation
Details on location selection	4. Selecting a location
	a. Potential market
	b. Availability of employees
	c. Number of competitive businesses
	d. Chamber of Commerce assistance
Transition	(Once you get your business started, you will need some strategies for managing that business.)
Statement of third issue	C. Managing your business
Discussion of effective management	1. Establishing your goals
	2. Buying and pricing
	3. Selling
Details on record keeping	4. Record keeping
	a. Federal, state, and local laws and regulations
	b. Inventory
	c. Sales, cash, and credit
	d. Employees
	e. Fixtures, equipment, and property
	f. Bookkeeping
Description of handling personnel	5. Handling personnel
	a. Selection
	b. Training
	c. Supervision
	d. Motivation

Transition	(Although managing your own business is not easy, there are sources of assistance you can turn to.)
Statement of fourth issue	D. Sources of assistance

        1. Small Business Administration
           a. Documents
               (1) *Starting and Managing a Small Business of Your Own*
        2. State and local sources
           a. State economic development offices
           b. County small-business clinics and individual counseling programs

IV. Conclusion

Reiteration of main issues	A. Summary

        1. It takes a great deal to own your own business.
        2. Several procedures are useful in starting a business.
        3. Once you get the business started, you will need some strategies for managing that business.
        4. There are sources to assist you in business management.

Quotation for inspiration	B. Clincher: Former president Ronald Reagan has noted that "few experiences are more unique to the American character than going into business for oneself."

Summary

In this chapter on informative speaking, the key ideas presented were:

☐ Informative speaking imparts new information, secures understanding, or reinforces accumulated information.

☐ Informative presentations are dependent on the analysis of the audience.

☐ Types of informative speaking include presentations about objects, processes, events, and concepts.

☐ Informative speeches, when classified by setting or uniqueness, include informative briefings, technical reports, lectures, question-and-answer sessions, and speeches of introduction.

☐ The challenge for an informative speaker is to get the audience to understand and retain the information presented.

☐ To develop an informative speech, order ideas clearly, use the familiar to explain the new, use vivid illustrations, avoid being too technical, personalize the message, and do not speak down to the audience.

Key Terms

informative speaking   lecture
informative briefings   question-and-answer session
technical report

Learn by Doing

1. As a homework assignment, list two topics each that you are interested in speaking about for an informative presentation on objects, processes, events, and concepts. In class, your instructor matches you with a partner. With the assistance of your partner, select a topic for a speech based on audience analysis (your class), setting (your classroom), and purpose (an informative speech of three to five minutes). After you have both selected your topics, meet with another group. Present a short informative speech indicating what topic you have selected and why this subject suits you, the audience, the setting, and the purpose. The speech should use a structure that includes an introduction, statement of central idea, body, and conclusion.

2. Bring to class an object or piece of machinery (e.g., a camera, food processor, or microscope) that you feel members of your class cannot operate or that you have a different approach to operating. Be prepared to teach someone else how to use the equipment. In class you are placed in a group with four of your classmates. Decide the order in which you will present the material. After this is done, the first speaker gives a two- to four-minute presentation on how the object works. Then the second speaker demonstrates how the object operates. So does the third speaker, and so forth. Your success as a speaker is based on whether the person following you can operate the object.

3. Before a series of speeches to be given by class members, your instructor assigns you the name of a person in your class whom you will later be introducing. Interview that person, and collect all the information you will need to prepare a speech of introduction (topic of the speech, some background information on the speaker, why the subject was chosen, the qualifications of the speaker to present a speech on this topic, and so on). On the day of your partner's speech, introduce her or him.

4. What analogy could you use to explain each of the following?
    a. The growth cycle of a plant
    b. A tornado
    c. Living with a cat or a dog
    d. Attending a university or community college

5. You are going to give a "what-if" speech. On each of three 3-by-5-inch notecards, indicate something that could go wrong immediately before, during, or after a speech (e.g., you drop your speech outline in a puddle of water just outside your classroom building; the bulb goes out in the projector halfway through your slide presentation; an audience member challenges your statistics during the question-and-answer period). The instructor collects the cards, shuffles them, and hands them out one by one. When you get your card, immediately give a presentation that includes as restatement of the occur-

rence and a contingency plan for dealing with the situation.[17] (This assignment may take place when a short amount of time remains at the end of any class period.)

6. All students present one-minute speeches in which they state something that bothers them in everyday life. They should tell what the peeve is, why it is a peeve, and what they would like to see done about it, if anything.

7. Use your vocational preference, or an occupation you may be interested in, to investigate some phase of the career and present an informative speech on it. The presentation must include the use of a supplementary aid. Sample speech topics: a future audiologist explains the differences among several brands of hearing aids; an accounting major illustrates how a balance sheet is prepared; an aspiring musician demonstrates how music is scored.

Notes

1. Connie Koenenn, "The Future Is Now," *Washington Post,* February 3, 1989, p. B5.
2. Richard Wurman, *Information Anxiety* (Garden City, N.Y.: Doubleday, 1989).
3. Ibid.
4. Michael F. Warlum, "Improving Oral Marketing Presentations in the Technology-Based Company," *IEEE Transactions on Professional Communication,* 31 (June 1988), 84.
5. Kathleen Kendall, "Do Real People Ever Give Speeches?" *ERIC ED* 255 974 (1985), 11 and *Central States Speech Journal,* 25(Fall 1974), 233–235.
6. Richard Hoehn, *The Art and Practice of Public Speaking* (New York: McGraw-Hill, 1988).
7. These categories are based on those reported in James H. Byrns, *Speak for Yourself: An Introduction to Public Speaking* (New York: Random House, 1981), Chapters 14–17.
8. H. Lloyd Goodall and Christopher L. Waagen, *The Persuasive Presentation* (New York: Harper & Row, 1986), p. 105.
9. John T. Molloy, "Making Your Point, Not Burying It," *Self* (April 1981), 92.
10. Ibid.
11. The suggestions for structuring a technical report are based on Richard Weigand, *Business Horizons,* School of Business, Indiana University, Bloomington, as reported in *Communication Briefings* (January 1986).
12. This discussion is adapted from Maureen Haningan, "Master the Game of Q&A," *Working Woman* (December 1984), 34–35.
13. Hoehn.
14. G. H. Jamieson, *Communication and Persuasion* (London: Croom Helm, 1985), pp. 5–16.
15. Hoehn.
16. Ibid.
17. This activity is based on John Alfred Jones, "Preparing Contingency Plans for Public Speaking Situations," *Communication Education,* 30 (1981), 423–424.

16 *Persuasive Speaking*

Chapter Outline

Learning Outcomes

After reading this chapter, you should be able to:

Explain how people are influenced by persuasive messages

Explain how people are influenced by coercive messages

Illustrate how speaker credibility, logical arguments, and psychological appeals can affect listeners

List and explain how speaker credibility, logical arguments, and psychological appeals can be used in the preparation of a persuasive speech

Analyze a persuasive speech to ascertain its potential effectiveness based on logical arguments and psychological appeals

Prepare a persuasive speech using credibility, logical arguments, and psychological appeals.

E very day as listeners we are bombarded with messages intended to convince us to take some action, reinforce some commitment, accept some belief, or change some point of view. And almost every day we knowingly or unknowingly attempt to bring about these changes as speakers. The process of influencing and decision making has traditionally been defined as a persuasive one; as such, it is complex and involves many communication variables.

Persuasion is an important process. Through it, we affect others and they affect us. **Persuasion** can be defined as "the process by means of which one party purposefully secures a change of behavior, mental and/ or physical, on the part of another party by employing appeals to both feelings and intellect."[1]

The Process of Persuasion

The basic process of persuasion requires that you make a claim and then back it up with what appear to be good reasons and emotional appeals that will make the listeners accept that claim. To do this, you must plan your presentation thoroughly, analyzing the audience and presenting arguments that will appeal to that particular person or group. The **theory of field-related standards** establishes that not all people reach conclusions in the same way and thus may react differently to the same evidence or psychological material. Therefore in establishing your arguments, you may want to include as many appeals as you can to cover the various thought processes of the members of your audience. For example, in establishing arguments for why your listeners should vote for a particular candidate, you can list several of that candidate's positions, rather than just one.

In addition, **group standards,** the habits of thinking or the norms of a particular group, may be used as a guide for developing your arguments. For example, if you are speaking to a group of labor union members, you can assume that on labor-related issues, they will have views that favor the union rather than management. Thus if you are going to propose a change in the present style of plant operation, show how it will be good for the union.

Individual standards, the thinking of those people within a group who have influence over the group's members, also have to be included in the criteria for persuasion. If these influential members can be persuaded to go along with the proposal, then the entire group will probably go along. But who are the leaders? Who holds the most influence? Who really pulls the strings? If possible, try to find out and appeal to that person or group. For example, if the labor leaders go along, the union membership probably will also. If the president of the club agrees, the rest of the group may well follow.

As you develop a persuasive speech, organize your material to assure your chances of success. There are many ways to do so. An understanding of two methods—critical reasoning and comparative advantage reasoning—can give you a basis for developing an effective persuasive message.

Through **critical reasoning,** you establish criteria and then match the solutions with the criteria. For example, if you are proposing a plan of action for solving a club's financial problems, you can set criteria that include not having to raise the members' dues and planning an activity that can raise money quickly without extensive planning. You may then propose that the club stage a lottery and sell raffle tickets, establishing how the lottery fulfills the established criteria.

In contrast, when you are using **comparative advantage reasoning,** you begin by stating the possible solutions, including the status quo (the present mode of operation). You then demonstrate how the proposal you are presenting is the most workable (how it can solve the problem), the most desirable (why it does not cause any greater problems), and the most practical (how it can be put into operation). You also establish that this particular proposal has fewer disadvantages than any other.

Again, take the example of the need to raise funds. To achieve this goal by means of the comparative advantage reasoning process, you propose that a lottery be set up. You then explain why this is a workable plan by indicating that other organizations have used the process and by presenting precise statistics on the amounts of money raised by other groups in similar circumstances. You then indicate that the lottery is desirable because it will not cost the members of the organization a great

Group standards are the habits of thinking or the norms of a particular group.

deal of money, it is not illegal, the risk of losing money is not great, and a lottery does not place a heavy burden on any one member of the organization. Next, you show that the proposal is practical because a local printer can have the tickets ready by the next week and the finance committee of the club has already worked out a plan for distributing the tickets and handling the money. Finally, you explain why this system is better than raising dues, dissolving the organization, continuing the status quo, or having a bake sale.

Influencing Through Persuasion

The purpose of the persuasive process is to influence. The persuasive process, for example, occurs when salespersons from different data-processing corporations present speeches in an attempt to secure the sale of their system to the purchasing agents of a company. Based on the presentations, the purchasing agents decide to buy products from salesperson A because of her arguments stressing her product's lower cost and ease of operation. Thus salesperson A presented the more effective persuasive message based on the analyzed needs of the purchasers.

Another form of influencing takes place when we are not given a voluntary choice. If, for example, a robber shoved a gun in your back

Persuasion is the process by which one party purposefully secures a voluntary change of behavior on the part of another.

and said, "Give me your money or I'll kill you," you would not voluntarily choose either alternative; yet you must choose. This attempt to change behavior relies on force and is known as **coercion.**

Coercion differs from persuasion because it leaves no desirable alternative to the person who is being influenced to make a change of mental or physical behavior. For example, a supervisor who tells a group of workers, "You have a choice—work nights or quit," is using coercion. This technique may be effective in bringing about change, but it usually leads to resentment, discouragement, and lack of respect and trust on the part of the person who has been coerced. For this reason, parents, teachers, managers, and others who hold influencing positions usually find that more cooperation and more positive feeling appear when they use constructive persuasive techniques rather than coercive tactics.

Despite the negative aspects of coercion, it is sometimes used when other persuasive methods fail, and the person using it accepts that negative backlash may occur. Former president Richard Nixon's wage and price regulations of the early 1970s are a case in point. In an effort to bolster and stabilize a sagging economy, Nixon announced that industries should freeze wages and prices on most consumer products and that corporations should voluntarily adopt wage-price guidelines appropriate to their particular products. When this persuasive approach did not work, Nixon set up a wage-price control board to force compliance with the guidelines. But the public reaction was strong and negative: union workers protested, big business objected, and the stock market faltered. Indeed, the reaction was so strong that some economists believe that the inflation and recession of the mid-1970s were a direct result of a negative backlash from these coercive economic policies.

Even influence that is not coercive can sometimes be dangerous because such influence can make believers do what they may not want to do or endorse what they may not agree with. One of the best defenses against persuasive manipulation is to recognize that the process has the potential to be unethical or distort the truth. Persuasive communication strategies are essentially amoral—neither good nor bad. It is only how the strategies are used, and to what ends, that gives communication a dimension of morality. By knowing this and by being equipped to recognize manipulative and coercive methods, you may be able to protect yourself from being "taken." Likewise, persuasive speakers have a responsibility to their listeners to not manipulate the listeners' motivations to unethical ends.

In addition, psychological appeals aimed at fear, hatred, social pressure, and shock often dull our senses to the point that we perform acts we may not consider if we stepped outside the situation and objectively evaluated the potential consequences. A particularly horrifying example of manipulation can be found in Adolf Hitler's use of appeals focused on building a "master race." Unfortunately, many people responded to these appeals, participated in the destruction of other human beings as a result, and later came to regret their actions.

Persuasion may be accomplished by repeated exposure to messages. Seldom does one short persuasive message result in any real change on the part of the receiver. As a result, massive amounts of money are spent waging persuasive campaigns for all sorts of consumer products, social causes, international efforts, and government projects. This approach relies on systematic, repeated exposure to persuasive messages with the objective of enhancing the retention of the basic thesis of the persuasive message.

Components of the Persuasive Message

The classical Greek philosopher/rhetorician Artistotle first described Western culture's system of persuasion as based on the use of three components.[2] In today's terms, these three components can be identified as speaker credibility (**ethos**), logical arguments (**logos**), and psychological appeals (**pathos**). Though Artistotle wrote more than two thousand years ago, his theories still characterize the development of an effective persuasive message.

Persuasion can be accomplished on the basis of repeated exposure to messages.

As we examine these three elements, consider how important each of them is in affecting your ability to persuade others or the ability of others to persuade you. Also consider how the three elements must interrelate for a persuasive message to be as effective as it can be. Note, however, that listeners responding to a persuasive message do not necessarily separate (may not be able to separate) the logical arguments from the psychological appeals. Research has illustrated that listeners rarely distinguish the rational from the emotional.[3] Indeed, because people may respond on an emotional level to a well-reasoned argument, each person will have different interpretations of and reactions to the persuasive techniques used in various presentations.

Speaker Credibility   The reputation, prestige, and authority of a speaker as perceived by the listeners all contribute to **speaker credibility.** In most persuasive situations, listeners need to accept the speaker before they will accept his or her message. Thus a speaker's credibility is related to the impact of the message and may in fact be the most potent of all his or her means of persuasion. If you as a listener dislike, mistrust, or question the honesty of a person, she or he will have a difficult time persuading you to accept her or his beliefs.

Have you ever gone into a store to purchase an item and then not bought it because you felt that the salesperson was not being honest with you or that you could not trust what she or he said? Do you avoid some stores or refuse to make purchases from certain people because you do not trust them, either because of personal experience or because of negative reactions from people you respect? Former president Richard Nixon encountered this with the Watergate disclosures. His trustworthiness in the eyes of the American people—indeed, the world—took such a nose dive that he was ultimately forced to resign from office.

As a speaker, you must realize that credibility or lack of it may exist even before you speak. A person's prior reputation with an audience can help or hinder his or her persuasive ability. For example, if Dr. Albert Bruce Sabin, developer of the polio vaccine, had addressed the American Medical Association about the need for a national immunization program for communicable diseases, he would have had initial credibility, and his ideas would probably have been accepted. But an unknown or negatively perceived speaker would have had a much more difficult persuasive task.

If you are unknown in a public speaking situation, your credibility can be built by advance publicity or by the introduction to you and your speech. Try to determine what your listeners know about you before preparing your speech. After all, you must be aware of whether your credibility is nonexistent, positive, or negative.

If you have no reputation with the audience, establish your credibility through the chairperson's introduction and through the quality of your presentation. If you are positively perceived, build on that advantage by developing a well-documented and logical presentation, thus reinforcing your positive image. If you are negatively perceived, compensate for it. Try to alter your listeners' beliefs by emphasizing qualities about yourself they may respond to positively. For example, a former convict, when speaking to an audience about the need for altering prison procedures, started his presentation with these comments:

> I am a paroled convict. Knowing this, some of you may immediately say to yourself, "Why should I listen to anything that an ex-jailbird has to say?" Well, it is because I was in prison, and because I know what prison can do to a person, and because I know what negative influences jail can have on a person, that I want to speak to you tonight.[4]

If you know that you are negatively perceived by your listeners, make a special effort to develop a well-documented speech, one that takes on the issues of disagreement and asks the audience to give you a fair chance to be heard. A Democratic candidate, speaking before a predominantly Republican audience, can state:

> I realize that I am a Democrat and you are Republicans. I also realize that we are both after the same thing—a city in which we can live without fear for

our lives, a city in which the services such as trash and snow removal are efficient, and a city in which taxes are held in check. You, the Republicans, and I, the Democrat, do have common goals. I'd appreciate your considering how I propose to help all of us achieve our joint objectives.

Factors of Credibility   Several factors contribute to a speaker's credibility: occupation, education, clothes, personal looks, personality, respect for others, sensitivity to trends, knowledge of the problem being discussed, ability to verbalize, vitality, trustworthiness, and general expertise.[5] Some of these factors, such as clothing and personal appearance, may surprise you. Nevertheless, noncontent stimuli such as dress, voice, and manners do affect the attitude of the audience toward the speaker. And because the persuasive act is a cumulative act in which many factors are compressed by the listeners to aid them in reaching conclusions, each factor in the process must be considered.

Politicians—knowing that physical appearance, clothing, and hair style create images—pay close attention to these factors. After the Kennedy-Nixon television debates during the 1960 presidential campaign, for example, one of the most prevalent comments centered on how terrible Nixon appeared physically. Kennedy, in contrast, looked vigorous and healthy (aided by a suntan and an appropriately colored suit!). Since then, critics have determined that proper make-up and attire could have improved Nixon's image significantly.[6] This important historical event has guided political consultants ever since in carefully tailoring a candidate's image to appeal to voters.

Trustworthiness also affects credibility because listeners appear to be more accepting of changes when they perceive the speaker to be a trustworthy source. The professional position a person holds, for example, may make it easier or more difficult for him or her to gain the respect of an audience. In a poll taken by the Gallup organization, interviewers asked a sample of Americans how they would rate the honesty and ethical standards of people in different fields. The results of this poll (see Figure 16.1) reflected the credibility ratings of the various occupations studied.

Establishing Credibility   An unknown speaker has little initial credibility. Therefore she or he is wise to consider some techniques for gaining personal acceptance. Above all, a speaker should demonstrate that she or he is trustworthy, competent, and dynamic. These three factors operate as dimensions of a speaker's credibility during a speech.

As we have seen, **trustworthiness** follows from a person's integrity. Thus you want to convince your audience that you are honest, reliable, and sincere. For example, if you are attempting to persuade your listeners to sign pledge cards to donate their eyes to an eye bank and you can show a card that certifies you as a potential donor, you can enhance

Figure 16.1

*Honesty and Ethical
Standards*

	Standards (%)				
Profession	*Very high*	*High*	*Avg*	*Low/Very Low*	*No opinion*
Druggists/pharmacists	12	50	31	5	2
Clergy	12	43	35	7	3
Medical doctors	9	43	38	9	1
Dentists	8	44	41	4	3
College teachers	8	43	36	5	8
Engineers	8	42	36	4	10
Police officers	9	40	41	9	1
Funeral directors	6	29	44	11	10
Bankers	4	28	52	13	3
TV reporters/commentators	4	28	46	20	2
Journalists	4	26	51	15	4
Business executives	3	22	55	14	6
Newspaper reporters	2	22	54	18	4
Senators	4	20	52	20	4
Lawyers	4	18	43	31	4
Local officeholders	2	19	56	20	3
Building contractors	3	17	50	21	9
Congressmen	3	17	52	24	4
State officeholders	2	15	55	24	4
Real estate agents	2	14	54	25	5
Labor union leaders	2	13	37	39	9
Stockbrokers	2	12	50	22	14
Insurance salespeople	2	11	47	36	4
Ad practitioners	1	11	48	31	9
Car salespeople	1	5	36	53	5

From Graham Hueber, "Clergy, Pharmacists Again Rated Highest for Honesty and Ethical Standards" (Princeton, N.J.: The Gallup Poll, February 28, 1990). Reprinted by permission.

your credibility as a sincere person. In other words, if your personal experiences show that you follow the recommendations you are making, the audience is more likely to accept your advice as reliable than if you are seen to be hypothesizing.

Competence, another component of credibility, refers to the wisdom, authority, and knowledge a speaker demonstrates. Thus you must prepare yourself to be an expert on your topic so that listeners will have confidence in what you are saying. You can demonstrate competence by including up-to-date research findings, documenting sources of information, and connecting yourself to the topic.

You can also strengthen your position by quoting recognized experts in the field. In this way, listeners draw the conclusion that if experts agree with your stand, then your stand must have merit. In addition, quotations from experts let your audience know that you have taken the time to probe the attitudes and findings of others in the field before reaching conclusions.

For this reason, when you use supporting material, be certain to document your sources. Tell the audience the source and date of your material as well as the identities of the people responsible for creating or developing the information. If the sources are unfamiliar to your listeners, establish their credentials. For example, if you are attempting to persuade your listeners that there are advantages to living in this age of change and uncertainty, you can quote an expert:

> Dr. Rollo May, a practicing psychotherapist and professor at Harvard, in his book *Love and Will*, supports my contentions when he writes, "One of the values of living in a transitional age—an age of therapy—is that it forces upon us the opportunity, even as we try to resolve our individual problems, to uncover new meaning in perennial man and to see more deeply into those qualities which constitute the human being as a man [person]."[7]

If possible, associate yourself with the topic. For example, if you are proposing a plan of action concerning safety regulations, and if you have had experience on a construction crew and refer to this experience, your listeners will more readily accept your point that the construction industry needs more stringent safety regulations than if you did not have the personal experience.

Although you will want to reinforce your qualifications and your research while developing your presentation, your audience may react negatively if you begin a presentation with a lengthy review of your research, experiences, and/or general qualifications. Your expertise should have been highlighted in your introduction by the program chairperson. So let your credibility emerge directly throughout the speech: "It has been my experience that . . . "; "I have observed that . . ."; "My research indicates that . . . ." Remember that specifics that are documented by time, place, and description are usually perceived to be more valid than personal opinion, especially if the presenter is inexperienced in the field.

Another characteristic of credibility is **dynamism,** the projection of vigorous, concerned, powerful image. One of the most dynamic contemporary American presidents was John F. Kennedy. In his famous speech in Berlin at the height of the cold war between communist and Western nations, for example, Kennedy created good will and a common bond with his audience by saying "I am a Berliner" in German. In a similar incident, Kennedy's wife spoke in Spanish to a crowd of people on a tour through South America; she promoted positive feelings, as did

1988 Democratic presidential nominee Michael Dukakis when, early in the campaign, he spoke to a largely Hispanic audience in fluent Spanish. By showing dynamism and concern for people and by demonstrating common bonds with them, a speaker can create positive credibility.

In addition to demonstrating good will, a speaker can reflect dynamism through the image he or she projects. Energy, enthusiasm, sincerity, and authority can all be communicated through a speaker's appearance and delivery. Nonverbal aspects of vocal tone, gestures, posture, eye contact, and dress convey an impression to listeners. Here again, the televised Nixon-Kennedy debates of 1960 revealed the importance of a dynamic image because the winner, Kennedy, projected such an image through his physical appearance (a dark suit, a tan, and careful attention to camera shots) and through his energy, vitality, and attentiveness.[8] Because of the importance of this image, communication experts work extensively with government and corporate executives and with diplomats and politicians to improve their delivery and image on television and radio interview shows, press conferences, and public speeches—all to ensure acceptance of their messages through dynamic presentations.

By demonstrating trustworthiness, competence, and dynamism throughout your speech, you can help listeners to accept you as a person of credibility and possibly move them toward accepting your message. Calculate carefully—on the basis of your audience analysis—what will most enhance your trustworthiness, prestige, and authoritativeness with your listeners, and use these factors to build your message.

Logical Arguments

Logical, well-reasoned arguments are the foundation on which to build a persuasive message. Thus on the basis of audience analysis, you determine your listeners' beliefs concerning your central idea and build your arguments accordingly. Remember that, although your listeners may be swayed by credibility or by emotional appeals, over a long period of time they may forget the immediate impact of these techniques and remember only your basic premises. Consequently, you must make certain that your arguments are well substantiated.

Although there is some evidence in communication research to suggest that listeners cannot distinguish sound arguments and evidence,[9] listeners, especially when they are dealing with information about which they know little or are skeptical, probably look for logical connections in the messages they are receiving.[10] Communication analysts have suggested that a well-reasoned message can have a decided impact on the speaker's credibility. As one source noted, "When listeners want reasons spelled out, they mercilessly put down as stupid or too sloppy to be trusted communicators who do not reason or who do it badly. It is easy to show that general absence of clarity, consistency, completeness, and

Energy, enthusiasm, sincerity, and authority can be communicated through a speaker's appearance and delivery.

consecutiveness in discourse is, in the world's eye, the mark of the fool."[11]

Remember that all factors in the persuasive situation ought to be centered on the audience and that an audience is influenced by clarity of ideas, vividness of language, examples, and specifics that illuminate the reasons for the chosen solution. Consequently, organize and package your materials in such a way that your contentions lead to the belief that only one conclusion can be reached—the conclusion you are proposing.

The Structure of Logical Arguments

To lead your listeners to the conclusion you wish them to share with you, structure your arguments carefully. Based on your audience analysis, structure the message according to an inductive or a deductive system.

Inductive Arguments. An **inductive argument** is based on probability—what is expected or believed from the available evidence. Thus the more specific instances you can draw on in an inductive argument, the more probable your conclusion will be. Inductive argument can take one of two forms: the generalization conclusion or the hypothesis conclusion.

In a **generalization conclusion,** a number of specific instances are examined. From these, you attempt to predict some future occurrence or explain a whole category of instances. Underlying all of this is the assumption that what holds true for specific instances will hold true for all instances in a given category.

Speaking in Atlanta to the National Conference on Corporate Community Involvement, the vice president of the American Association of Retired Persons described the "graying" of America. He developed an inductive argument by a series of claims:

> Because of better medical care, nutrition and activity, more people are gliding into their 60s and beyond in good physical shape. . . . Mental ability does not diminish merely because of age, according to researchers. In fact, it may improve. . . . The economic health of today's older generation has improved to the point where advertisers are already targeting the "Maturity Market."

Using evidence to support each of the claims, he drew an inductive conclusion: "The upshot of all this change in better physical, psychological and economic well-being is that we are looking at a new breed of older person vastly different from former negative stereotypes."[12]

In the **hypothesis conclusion,** a hypothesis is used to explain all the available evidence. For the argument to have substance, however, the hypothesis must provide the best explanation for that evidence. Reviewing a number of cases in which terrorists had been tried and convicted throughout the world, the U.S. Department of State ambassador-at-large for counterterrorism argued that "the rule of law is working against terrorists and fewer terrorists are being released without trial" in an effort to convince his audience that "we, the people of the world's democracies, will ultimately prevail over those who would through terror take from us the fruits of two centuries of political progress."[13]

Deductive Arguments.   The **deductive argument** is based on logical necessity. If you accept the premise of the deductive argument—the proposition that is the basis of the argument—then you must also accept its conclusion.

One type of deductive argument is the **categorical syllogism,** an argument that contains two premises and a conclusion. For instance, you can argue:

All "A" students study hard (premise).

You are an "A" student (premise).

Therefore you study hard (conclusion).

If your listeners accept the two premises of this argument, then they must accept the conclusion because it is the only one that can be drawn from the premises that have been set forth.

As communicators, we typically use a special form of syllogism called the **enthymeme,** which is a rhetorical syllogism in which one premise is not directly stated. The omitted premise is shared by the communicators and therefore does not need to be reiterated.[14] Speaking in Atlantic City to those attending the Fifth Annual Conference on Writing Assessment, the president of The College Board concluded, "If we can teach our children, from all backgrounds, to write with joy, originality, clarity and control, then I don't think we have much else to worry about," a conclusion based on the premise shared by his listeners that children today should be taught effective writing skills.[15]

A second type of deductive argument is the **disjunctive argument,** an either/or argument in which true alternatives must be established. For example, a U.S. senator argued in a speech to the National Security Information Center in Washington that either the United States builds antimissile defenses—"and fast"—or "we will be inviting war, or, by being unable to conduct it, lose all diplomatic and conventional ability to respond."[16]

A third form of deductive argument is the **conditional argument,** which sets up an if/then proposition. In this form, there are two conditions, one of which necessarily follows from the other. The chief executive officer of Arthur Andersen & Company proposed that the federal government adopt a new accrual accounting system so that the public and Congress could monitor the federal budget. He argued that "if citizens were to demand the financial information to which they are clearly entitled, incentives would be created for sound fiscal management—and, perhaps, for more enlightened political leadership. We could then expect to see better-informed decision making—less fiscal recklessness—and a reduction in the risks caused by the misallocation of capital."[17]

To be effective, then, the premises and the terms in deductive arguments must be agreed on by the speaker and listeners before any of the speaker's conclusions can be accepted. But the astute speaker makes sure that, if the common premise is not actually spelled out, it is shared by all the listeners. Unfortunately, speakers sometimes assume a premise that their listeners do not share. Former president Jimmy Carter, for instance, used to take to the airwaves to describe the measures that Americans should adopt to conserve energy, such as turning down thermostats and installing solar heating devices. Carter assumed that because he gave these messages, Americans were concerned about the energy crisis, believed in its existence, and wanted to do their share to help out. Public opinion polls at the time indicated that Americans did not believe in the energy crisis; they perceived it to be a ploy by the oil companies to inflate prices artificially. Consequently, Carter's appeals to the American conscience probably had little effect because his listeners did not share his basic premise.

Persuasive Evidence   The persuasive speaker must not only structure the persuasive argument to meet the listeners' needs but must also support these contentions persuasively. The most persuasive form of supporting material—**evidence**—includes testimony from experts, statistics, and specific instances. If you can offer solid data to support your contentions, they will serve to strengthen your perceived credibility and at the same time lend substance to the argument you have presented. For example, a speaker who attempts to persuade listeners that the U.S. Food and Drug Administration (FDA) needs more funds to hire inspectors can cite specific instances from the agency's files. Real cases are on record of potatoes that were contaminated with insecticide, turkey stuffing that contained glass particles, and ginger ale that contained mold—all of which were sold to consumers. For additional support, the speaker can cite statistics from congressional budget hearings on the FDA indicating that only five hundred FDA inspectors are available to monitor sixty thousand food-processing plants in the United States.

Essentially, the evidence should support the central idea, connecting it, if possible, with the listeners' previously held beliefs. Persuasive evidence should be carefully tied to the argument at hand and accurately reported from authoritative, reliable sources. For example, the speaker who argues for additional FDA inspectors can connect evidence from FDA files and the budget hearings to the generally held belief that uncontaminated food is necessary for public health and welfare. In this instance, it seems fairly safe to assume that most of the audience agrees with the need for uncontaminated food. But not all speaking situations are this clear-cut. Before trying to build a persuasive case on such assumptions, the speaker has to ascertain through audience analysis that her or his assumptions are consistent with those held by the audience.

Reasoning Fallacies   In addition to presenting carefully structured and supported arguments, you should ensure the validity of your arguments so that your listeners can reasonably draw the conclusions you consider desirable. To accomplish validity of argument, you must avoid some of the more common forms of reasoning fallacies.

One reasoning fallacy that can trip up persuasive communicators is the hasty generalization. A speaker who makes a **hasty generalization** reaches unwarranted, general conclusions from an insufficient number of instances. For example, a speaker making a hasty generalization may argue that gun control legislation is necessary and demonstrate this argument with some instances of freeway shootings in Los Angeles, thus limiting the scope and numbers of possible cases that support the need for gun control. Limited instances may not provide the listener with enough of a foundation on which to base an all-inclusive conclusion.

Another reasoning fallacy that limits the persuasiveness of a message is **faulty analogical reasoning.** No analogy is ever totally "pure" because no two cases are ever identical. Speakers use faulty analogies when they assume that the shared elements will continue indefinitely and/or that they are similar in all aspects relevant to the case under consideration. The speaker who, for example, argues that the current AIDS crisis is analogous to the bubonic plague that ravaged Europe in an earlier era overlooks the medical advances that make the AIDS crisis very different (although no less serious).

A further reasoning fallacy is **faulty causal reasoning.** Faulty causal reasoning occurs when a speaker claims without qualification that something caused something else. If the claim overstates the case, faulty reasoning has been used. Rather than saying "a common cause" or "a probable cause," the speaker can argue, for example, that the Iran-contra affair during the Reagan administration resulted from a permissive attitude and lack of moral accountability on the part of public officials that had pervaded the White House ever since Nixon's Watergate scandal.

An entire set of reasoning fallacies can result from **ignoring the issue.** By ignoring the issue, the speaker uses irrelevant arguments to obscure the real issue. The **ad hominem argument**—attacks on the personal character of a source—is one example. For instance, Gary Hart, a Democratic front-runner in the 1988 presidential race, was forced to abandon his campaign because of the media portrayal and the public perception of him as a "womanizer." At the time, some commentators questioned how the issue related to Hart's ability to be president of the United States.

The **ad populum argument**—an appeal to people in terms of their prejudices and passions rather than a focus on the issue at hand—is another characteristic of ignoring the issue. For example, despite the vast amount of publicity resulting from the Jim and Tammy Bakker PTL affair in the spring of 1987, the religious devotees of the PTL continued to contribute millions of dollars to keep the religious organization going, stirred by passionate appeals from the PTL leaders.

Yet another example of the fallacy of ignoring the issue is the **ad ignorantiam argument**—an attempt to prove a statement is true because it cannot be disproved. For example, proponents of pit bull terriers argue that pit bulls are not dangerous pets because dog-bite statistics show that pit bulls rank ninth in number of bites—after poodles and cocker spaniels.

All reasoning fallacies can interfere with the persuasiveness of a message and can diminish the total impact of the speech. A discerning audience member can see through such a smoke screen. Therefore analyze your arguments to make sure that the structure and supporting evidence lead to valid conclusions that your listeners can accept.

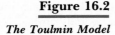
Figure 16.2

The Toulmin Model

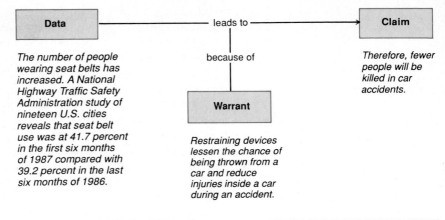

The Toulmin Model of the Reasoning Process

To further understand the structure of arguments, scholars in the field of communication have turned to a model of the reasoning process devised by Stephen Toulmin, a mathematical philosopher.[18] The **Toulmin model of the reasoning process** combines inductive and deductive arguments in an inferential sequence. According to Toulmin, communicators build, or infer, arguments from **data** (evidence such as statistics, examples, and personal testimony or beliefs based on fact or opinion) that they then communicate through a **warrant** (a general proposition held by the listener that bridges the line of argument, explaining the relationship between the data and the conclusion) to a **claim** (the conclusion). The Toulmin model is illustrated schematically in Figure 16.2. Here the warrant is the foundation of the argument and enables the communicator to draw the conclusion (the claim) from the available evidence (the data).

Most arguments, however, are not so concise. Other elements in the reasoning process, most notably qualifiers, often provide exceptions to the claim and stem from reservations that can reduce or even rule out the acceptance of the claim. In response, the speaker has to use further evidence or argument to support the warrant itself and make it more acceptable to the listener. The Toulmin model, expanded in this way, is illustrated in Figure 16.3.

Professional speakers and speech writers sometimes diagram their speech arguments according to the Toulmin model to verify that the lines of argument will hold up when received by their intended listeners. In turn, listeners who receive difficult but seemingly persuasive messages use the model to determine just how acceptable those arguments really are.

Figure 16.3

Expanded Toulmin Model

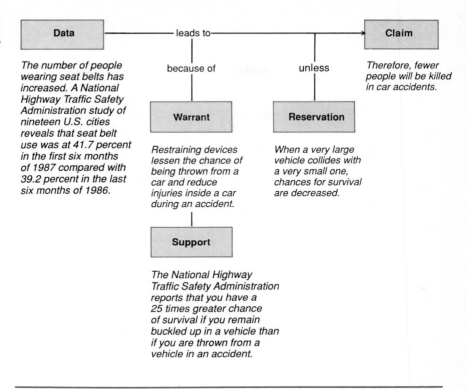

Data

leads to

Claim

The number of people wearing seat belts has increased. A National Highway Traffic Safety Administration study of nineteen U.S. cities reveals that seat belt use was at 41.7 percent in the first six months of 1987 compared with 39.2 percent in the last six months of 1986.

because of

unless

Therefore, fewer people will be killed in car accidents.

Warrant

Reservation

Restraining devices lessen the chance of being thrown from a car and reduce injuries inside a car during an accident.

When a very large vehicle collides with a very small one, chances for survival are decreased.

Support

The National Highway Traffic Safety Administration reports that you have a 25 times greater chance of survival if you remain buckled up in a vehicle than if you are thrown from a vehicle in an accident.

The Structure of the Persuasive Message

When structuring a persuasive speech, the speaker has to consider where to position the arguments. Two possibilities are available to speakers. Some studies support the idea that the strongest argument should come first so that it will have the greatest impact on listeners at the outset. Other studies, however, support the idea that the strongest argument should come last to ensure that listeners retain it.[19]

Yet another consideration is whether to develop both sides of the argument (and thus refute opposing arguments) or to present only your own stand. One potential problem in developing both sides of the argument is that you may raise issues and present ideas your listeners had not previously considered. If you are unable to refute these issues effectively, you may give your listeners a solution other than the one you intended—one they might not have considered if you had never mentioned it!

Because various researchers have offered different answers to the placement and development of the issues, deciding which position to take is often difficult. It is safe to assume, however, that the order of your arguments must be based on careful audience analysis. If you feel that the audience is on your side, state your arguments first, and allow your listeners to believe along with you for the rest of your presentation (a deductive mode of reasoning). But if you perceive your audience to be hostile to your position, build the background, and then present the arguments when you feel that your listeners are ready for them (a more inductive line of reasoning). This strategy requires a thorough audience analysis before you prepare your speech as well as a process analysis during your presentation so that you can make any necessary adaptations based on listeners' responses.

Speakers should be aware of the **inoculation strategy,** which suggests that just as a person can be protected from disease through immunization, so, too, can a listener be inhibited from accepting subsequent counterarguments if he or she is armed with the means to refute them.[20] Thus if you were going to hearings favoring rezoning a residential area in your neighborhood, your local citizens association that opposes the changes should bombard you with arguments against changing the neighborhood before you go to the hearings. Then you will be prepared to recognize the weaknesses in the opposing arguments and, ideally, be strengthened in the support of your own stand.[21]

Another factor to consider in presenting your arguments is **cognitive dissonance,** the mental discomfort that occurs when we accept an action or an idea that does not concide with our previously held attitudes.[22] So if you are trying to persuade a group to purchase stock in a mutual fund, give reasons that reinforce the benefits of mutual funds, allay any fears about such funds, and diminish the attractiveness of alternative investment procedures. Your persuasive task will be especially challenging if your listeners have seen a decline in the value of mutual funds. If you present strong arguments, your listeners will have a stronger commitment to the decision to purchase the mutual fund after they leave your influence and begin to reassess their decisions.

Here again, careful analysis can help you determine what persuasive strategies will be most reinforcing. If the potential buyers have young children, then your argument can center on the long-term proven profit increase of mutual funds over savings accounts, increased profits that can be used for the children's college educations. You can appeal to persons of limited finances by demonstrating that with investment in one share of a mutual fund instead of stocks, the investor purchases stocks in many companies. Then emphasize that the purchase of one share of stock in a company permits ownership in only one company, whereas the multicorporation purchase through a mutual fund broadens the opportunity for profits and lessens the possibility of financial loss because clients are spreading their investments over more than one source of income.

Psychological Appeals

The third component of the persuasive message, **psychological appeals,** enlists listeners' emotions as motivation for accepting your arguments. Just as you must select your arguments and enhance your credibility on the basis of what you know about your listeners, so must you select psychological appeals on the basis of what you think will stir their emotions. The purpose of incorporating some emotional appeals in your speech is to keep your listeners involved with you as you spell out your persuasive plan, even though they probably do not discern the emotional from the rational in your presentation.[23]

Maslow's Hierarchy of Individual Needs

Abraham Maslow, the psychologist noted for developing the concept of self-actualization, proposed a hierarchy of human needs (Figure 16.4) that can help a speaker to analyze the emotional needs of an audience. To use this system, a speaker must determine the level of need of a particular group of listeners and then select appeals aimed at that level.[24] Although Maslow's theory is hierarchical, these need levels can function at the same time. Therefore a speaker need not deal with only one level at a time.

Maslow suggested that all human beings have five levels of need. At the first, or most basic, level are **physiological needs**—hunger, sleep, sex, and thirst. These needs must normally all be satisfied before a person can be motivated by appeals to other levels of need. For example,

Figure 16.4

Maslow's Hierarchy of Needs

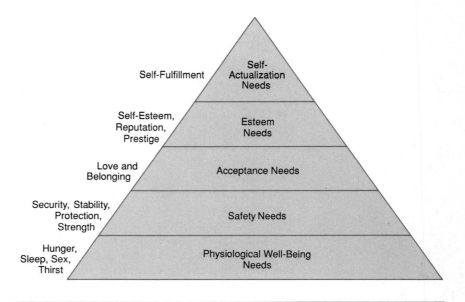

the U.S. Agency for International Development offers aid to developing nations as a means of persuading them through appeals to physiological needs that the democratic form of government offers self-government, free elections, and food and medical care.

The second level of human need, **safety needs,** encompasses security, stability, protection, and strength. Organizations that have had to reduce their work forces and lay off employees have found it persuasive to offer seminars on job searches, resume preparation, and other career skills. Employees concerned about the security of their positions are quick to sign up for such offerings.

The third level consists of **acceptance needs**—the needs for love and belonging. Americans are highly motivated by the need to belong, as evidenced by their affiliations with many groups. Organizations use persuasive appeals to encourage employees to feel a strong sense of identity with the business, and colleges and universities use this need to motivate alumni to contribute to endowment funds.

Esteem needs form the fourth level identified by Maslow. Human needs at this level involve both self-esteem (desire for achievement and mastery) and esteem by others (desire for reputation and prestige). Coaches appeal to this level in persuading team members to do their best during the season.

Finally, Maslow identified **self-actualization needs,** the desire for self-fulfillment or achieving one's greatest potential, as the fifth level in the hierarchy. Although human beings may strive for this level, they rarely satisfy this need. Recruiters attempting to influence top scientists to come aboard the National Security Agency, for example, may present persuasive appeals to a group by stressing how the agency can facilitate their scientific research and development.

Group Needs For any speaker, the needs of audience members may be strongly influenced by the needs of the groups to which they belong. Many Americans have gone through the 1970s "me" decade of self-indulgence and the 1980s "no" decade in the wake of the dangerous health effects of smoking, drunken driving, and AIDS and are now into the 1990s "back to basics" decade of a simpler life style.[25] Adapting to group needs thus becomes a challenge for the persuasive speaker. And the desire to motivate may legitimately be the primary objective of the speech itself. Organizations are booking motivational speakers for meetings and conventions in record numbers, speakers whose main message is to inspire self- and/or financial improvement in salespeople, marketing personnel, and other staff groups. An official of the Washington Speakers Bureau observed that "the thousands of motivational speakers currently in the circuit make up the largest segment of the speaking industry."[26]

The need to motivate others may be the primary objective of the persuasive speech.

Appeals to Motivate Listeners

Once you have determined your listeners' need level (perhaps using Maslow's hierarchy), you can then build into your speech the psychological appeals that will most persuade your audience to accept your point of view. A considerable variety of motivational appeals are available. The following alphabetical discussion of the most typical appeals can assist you in determining which ones will best match the need level of your listeners.[27]

A speaker can appeal to a need for *acquisition* and *saving* by stressing how the proposal can save the listener money or time. In today's economy, people respond to bargains, so advertisers focus many of their ads on possible savings: "Save," "20 Percent Off," "More Free Time." Likewise, many people are motivated to acquire possessions. Collectors of antiques, coins, and stamps are usually strongly motivated by acquisition appeals.

The appeal to *adventure* is another alternative. Here the speaker stresses the listener's desire to explore new worlds, see exciting places, take part in unusual experiences, or participate in different events. The travel industry thrives on the motivation for adventure, and the military services have often used this appeal in recruitment efforts—"Join the Navy and see the world."

Companionship taps our desire to be with other people. Knowing that we are motivated by this need, many advertisers try to depict their products with groups of people, with family and friends found as the theme in many ads. Not being alone, having caring and sharing people in your life, is a powerful appeal. Computer dating services use direct appeals to companionship as their major motivator.

Appealing to a sense of *deference*—to the respect for a wiser, more experienced, higher authority—can also be a successful strategy. A speaker on international issues may defer to the Foreign Service career officer's assessment of a thorny situation. Such deference can make a listener feel comfortable that the speaker is in touch with key people who do make a difference.

The appeal to *dependability and endurance* is particularly effective when a speaker wants to show the reliability of the product she or he is selling. Maytag Corporation stresses this sense in its advertising depicting the lonely repairman who never gets a call to repair a Maytag washer.

The *fear* appeal is used to raise apprehension in a listener. These fears are threatening to the listener or to some of the listener's values, and the threats can motivate him or her to take action to overcome a potential danger. The fear appeal is present in the campaign for safe sex to control the outbreak of AIDS as well as in the food industry's approach to nonsalt and low cholesterol products to reduce the threat of heart attacks. Some persuaders have found it successful to direct the threat at valued others (family members, for instance) rather than at the particular listener. Dangers to family and home can motivate someone to install smoke detectors for the safety of "loved ones," for example. The American Cancer Society's antismoking campaign includes information stressing not only the negative effects of smoking but also the long-term positive benefits of breaking the habit for the smoker and for those who love and live with the smoker.

Though the fear appeal can be powerful, research shows that a speaker must be careful not to overdo its use. A listener can become too frightened to accept the proposed action because the situation is perceived as impossible or hopeless, or the listener may become desensitized because of oversell. This is the case of some cigarette smokers who are so thoroughly convinced that they have been smoking for so long it just does not matter anymore because they have already committed physical suicide. Or some people have decided that because almost daily warnings come out about one food product or the other being harmful, there is no sense in being concerned about what one eats.[28]

Another strong motivator that has emerged in today's society is *guilt*. People may feel guilty for not doing something, so it can be a persuasive appeal. Working parents are bombarded with appeals to guilt for not having or not taking the time to be with their children and are urged to compensate for this loss of time with material goods. Kraft cheese has been sold to American mothers, for example, with a visual of a little girl and the message "Could you look into those big blue eyes and skimp on her?"[29]

Humor is yet another motivator. The speaker who appeals to the listeners' sense of humor illustrates that she or he does not take self or subject overseriously, so everyone can relax a bit.[30] Timing and topics are critical to the effective use of humor; a speaker can use too much or too little humor and lose impact. Humorous touches in television commercials heighten product awareness and certainly command attention. Alka-Seltzer was sold with the phrase "I can't believe I ate the whole thing!"

Although social motivators such as guilt, imitation, and companionship are strong, conflict may be raised between these needs and our sense of *independence*. We admit wanting to be with others, wanting to be part of a group, but we also do not want to be pressured. We want to make up our own minds. Political activities of the early 1970s stressed individual rights—and responsibilities—to be independent, to set an individual course, to "do one's own thing."

Appeals to *loyalty*—to nation, friends and family, organizations—are important to us. John F. Kennedy's famous inaugural appeal, "Ask not what your country can do for you; ask what you can do for your country," is an appeal to this emotion. We demonstrate loyalty to and defend those things and people of whom we are proud and with whom we identify.[31] Organizations work to build corporate loyalty, and schools promote student loyalty.

At times, speakers appeal to their listeners' sense of *power* and *authority*.[32] People often want to hold positions of power over others, to be the leader, to be in charge. They want to feel that they can get where they want to go when they want to go there. This is demonstrated in the names manufacturers give to lines of automobiles—Cougar, Mustang, Firebird. Corporations give people titles to enhance their power and authority—"executive assistant" rather than "secretary" or "marketing manager" instead of "salesperson." The speaker stressing American military initiatives may well appeal to the power and authority many Americans want to maintain as a world-leading nation.

Another motivating appeal is to tap our sense of *pride*. Research on the decline in productivity in American industry has focused on the need for greater worker participation and commitment to the quality of the product. An important aspect in this analysis is the need to motivate the American worker to take pride in work well done by providing rewards for quality results. One airline, for example, aired a television commercial using the theme "We earn our wings every day," featuring a proud stewardess, a ticket agent, and a mechanic from the company. An auto manufacturer ran a series of ads in which employees spoke of their personal commitment to the quality of the product to the extent that they signed their names to the delivery document that came with the car. A shirt manufacturer has the person who makes each product put a brief note in the garment's pocket reading, "This shirt proudly made by _____."

The appeal to *reverence* or *worship* is yet another motivational source. One aspect of this is manifested in hero worship of sports figures, performers, astronauts, and other prominent figures. Clearly, we tend to have a high level of respect for those who have achieved recognition for talent, daring, or unusual achievement. Another aspect of reverence or worship concerns the religious beliefs of people. Americans participate in organized religious activities so much so that 43 percent of American adults were found to have attended church or synagogue in a typical week in 1990.[33] Responding to this resurgence of religious values, advertisers show us a monk at the Xerox copy machine, a Hebrew National bologna spokesperson looking heavenward, and even Gothic golden arches for McDonald's!

A further motivator is *revulsion*. If used with care, the appeal to disgust can be effective. A speaker, for instance, can illustrate the effects of water pollution by showing the listeners some samples from the Chesapeake Bay in an attempt to motivate them to support legislation to clean up the bay. Astute speakers do not, however, arouse such a strong sense of revulsion that the listeners tune out their message. Antiabortionists and antivivisectionists sometimes overwhelm their listeners with revolting photographs of aborted fetuses and maimed laboratory animals.

Sexual attraction is one of the foremost appeals used by advertisers to motivate purchasers to action. Associating a beautiful young woman with an automobile or a handsome young man with a hair product is commonplace.[34]

The appeal to *sympathy* is also powerful. By showing photographs or films of starving children, impoverished elderly, or the unfortunate poor, a speaker can compel listeners to give time, money, or other resources. A sympathetic bond, often coupled with guilt, is created with those less fortunate.

A speaker has a wide variety of options from which to choose in developing persuasive appeals. And because the speaker's choice must depend on a perception of what will motivate his or her specific listeners, the speaker must analyze the audience to determine need levels, select appeals that will meet these needs, and place the appeals in the content of the speech at points where they will have the greatest persuasive impact.

If you determine that your listeners are operating at the level of acceptance needs, for example, then you select appeals that motivate them at this level. Or if you are addressing an audience of employees of a particular organization and wish to persuade them to form an employees' association, you can show them how the association will satisfy their needs for meeting and interacting with other people and for participating in group decision making. Such appeals to acceptance needs can dramatize the self-satisfying advantages of forming such an organization.

The Persuasive Process in Action

Psychological appeals, coupled with the speaker's credibility and well-reasoned, supported arguments, provide a sound, honest approach to influencing others to change their beliefs or actions. The sample persuasive speech outlined in Figure 16.5 illustrates the interaction of these persuasive elements. The purpose of the speech is to raise listeners' concern for the plight of the homeless in the United States. The speaker, a staff member for a U.S. congressman, has worked as a volunteer at the Community for Creative Nonviolence Shelter for the Homeless in Washington, D.C.

Summary   In this chapter on persuasive speaking, the key ideas presented were:

☐ Persuasion is "the process by means of which one party purposefully secures a voluntary change of behavior, mental and/or physical, on the part of another party by employing appeals to both feelings and intellect."

☐ The basic process of persuasion requires that the speaker make a claim and back it up in such a way that listeners accept the claim.

☐ Successful persuasive strategies center on the use of speaker credibility, logical arguments, and psychological appeals.

☐ A speaker's credibility incorporates trustworthiness, competence, and dynamism.

☐ Effective arguments can be structured inductively or deductively, depending on the listener's prior acceptance of the argument.

☐ A speaker should avoid such reasoning fallacies as hasty generalization, faulty analogical reasoning, faulty causal reasoning, and ignoring of the issue.

☐ The Toulmin model of argument includes the data, warrant, and claim.

☐ In arranging the issues in a persuasive speech, a speaker should take into account the positioning and development of arguments, inoculation strategy, and cognitive dissonance.

Figure 16.5

Sample Speech Outline

Purpose statement: To persuade the audience that specific actions should be taken to help the homeless.

Attention material

Orienting material to relate topic to listeners and establish speaker credibility

Topic of speech

Statement of first issue— the problem

Statistics showing number of homeless

Statistics of where the homeless are found

Statistics of who the homeless are

Discussion and statistics showing growth of problem

Statement of why problem is persistent

Discussion and statistics of the nature of the problem

I. Introduction
 A. Attention material: a hypothetical story about someone in your family who ends up on the street as a homeless person in a metropolitan area.
 B. Orienting material: how the problem of the homeless touches all of us today. My experience as a volunteer at the Community for Creative Nonviolence Shelter for the Homeless.

II. Statement of the cental idea: the homeless need our support.

III. Body
 A. The problem of the homeless in the United States
  1. How many homeless are there?
   a. U.S. Department of Housing and Urban Development estimates 500,000 to 600,000 nationwide.
   b. National Coalition for the Homeless estimates 3.5 million nationwide.
  2. Where are the homeless?
   a. 60 percent are in large cities.
   b. 24 percent are in midsized cities.
   c. 17 percent are not in cities.
  3. Who are the homeless?
   a. The median age is thirty-four years old—not just elderly and teenagers
   b. One-third are now entire families—"the new homeless."
   c. Two-thirds are single men and women.
   d. Three-quarters of these are mentally ill, and two-thirds are drug addicts and alcoholics.
  4. Why there are homeless
   a. Deinstitutionalization movement of state mental hospitals
    (1) 1950s: 560,000 patients
    (2) 1980s: 150,000 patients
   b. The shrinkage of low-income housing over the past twenty years
    (1) Redevelopment
    (2) Rent control
    (3) Decline in SRO motels, board and care homes
   c. Personal crises
    (1) Domestic violence
    (2) Job loss
    (3) Eviction

d. Economic conditions
    (1) Single white female heads of households
    (2) Reduction in public assistance programs
e. Alcoholism and drug addiction

Transition (As you can see, the problem of the homeless in the United States is profound and complex. Currently, there are efforts to deal with this national problem.)

Statement of second issue—steps taken to solve problem

Illustrations of solutions

B. What is being done to solve the problem of the homeless?
  1. Charitable community organizations
  2. Cities and counties, e.g., Phoenix
  3. State efforts—Massachusetts has implemented the most successful program to date
  4. Federal assistance
    a. Federal Emergency Management Agency
    b. Department of Agriculture
    c. National Institute of Mental Health
  5. Private organizations, e.g., Community for Creative Nonviolence

Statement of effectiveness of volunteer efforts

Transition

  6. Volunteers—Pine Street Inn, Boston, one of the most successful examples of using trained volunteers

(While some efforts for dealing with the homeless are working, we clearly need to do more to solve this serious national problem.)

Statement of third issue— how to best solve problem

Illustration of congressional plan for solution

Illustrations of personal efforts

C. What should be done to solve the problem of the homeless?
  1. Government response
    a. Federal Interagency Council on the Homeless coordinates research and reports on the problem and pursues increased federal initiatives and resources to address the problem.
    b. Strengthening support services
      (1) Mental health
      (2) Alcohol abuse
      (3) Drug abuse
      (4) Battered wives
      (5) Day care
      (6) Housing
      (7) Job search

Discussion of how individuals can and must help

  2. Your response
    a. Volunteer
    b. Donate money
    c. Offer clothing, food, bedding
    d. Encourage others to participate

IV. Conclusion

Reiteration of main issues

A. Restatement of issues
  1. The problem of the homeless won't go away
  2. We need strong government help
  3. We need *your* help

Reference to introduction

B. Clincher: Reference to opening hypothetical story

☐ Effective use of psychological appeals requires careful analysis of the need levels of the listeners.

☐ Maslow's hierarchy of needs—physiological, safety, acceptance, esteem, and self-actualization—provides a framework for understanding listeners' needs.

☐ The speaker has a wide variety of psychological appeals from which to choose.

☐ The effective persuasive message combines ethos, logos, and pathos in an honest, straightforward presentation.

Key Terms

persuasion
theory of field-related standards
group standards
individual standards
critical reasoning
comparative advantage reasoning
coercion
ethos
logos
pathos
speaker credibility
trustworthiness
competence
dynamism
inductive argument
generalization conclusion
hypothesis conclusion
deductive argument
categorical syllogism
enthymeme
disjunctive argument
conditional argument

evidence
hasty generalization
faulty analogical reasoning
faulty causal reasoning
ignoring the issue
ad hominem argument
ad populum argument
ad ignorantiam argument
Toulmin model of the reasoning
  process
warrant
data
claim
inoculation strategy
cognitive dissonance
psychological appeals
physiological needs
safety needs
acceptance needs
esteem needs
self-actualization needs

Learn by Doing

1. Prepare a speech on a topic about which you have strong feelings. Propose a change in the present procedure, take a stand on a view concerning the subject, or propose a plan of action. The topic should be one to which your listeners can relate and react so that you can persuade them. A sample central idea for this speech might be "_____ College (University) should not raise tuition."

2. Select a controversial topic and prepare a speech in which you advocate a particular solution to the problem. Your task is to persuade your listeners to accept your solution. A sample central idea for this speech might be "Euthanasia should be a legal option for terminally ill patients."

3. Prepare a speech analyzing the persuasive strategies used by some group in advocating a particular cause (for example, women's rights, gay rights, Native American rights). Select a number of persuasive messages by spokespersons for the group you choose, and use examples from these messages to illustrate your analysis of the persuasive strategies.

4. Find print or radio/television ads illustrating the various psychological appeals described in this chapter. Prepare to describe and analyze the use of the appeals in the ads you select.

5. Consider the persuasive elements—speaker credibility, logical arguments, and psychological appeals—and determine what you perceive to be the most influential persuasive strategies with American listeners today. Why do you think so?

6. What do you perceive to be the difference in preparing persuasive speeches and informative speeches? Do you think these differences are valid?

7. Analyze the "credibility crisis" of any of the recent American presidents or presidential candidates. What do you think an official could or should do to maintain credibility in the eyes of the American public?

8. Attend a persuasive speech by someone in a public forum, or analyze a persuasive manuscript in *Vital Speeches of the Day.* Prepare a descriptive analysis of the use of persuasive strategies by this speaker.

Notes

1. Based on Robert Goyer, class notes, Purdue University, West Lafayette, Indiana, 1965.

2. Aristotle, *The Rhetoric of Aristotle,* trans. by Lane Cooper (New York: Appleton-Century-Crofts, 1932).

3. Stanley F. Paulson, "Social Values and Experimental Research in Speech," *Western Speech Communication,* 26 (Summer 1962), 133–139.

4. This is based on a speech by an inmate from the Grafton Prison Farm, Grafton, Ohio, May 1976.

5. For a discussion of the dimensions of credibility, see James C. McCroskey, *An Introduction to Rhetorical Communication* (Englewood Cliffs, N.J.: Prentice-Hall, 1972), Chapter 4. Also see James C. McCroskey and Thomas J. Young, "Ethos and Credibility: The Construct and Its Measurement After Three Decades," *Central States Speech Journal,* 32 (Spring 1981), 24–34.

6. See, for example, Joe McGinniss, *The Selling of the President, 1968* (New York: Pocket Books, 1970), pp. 27–29.

7. Rollo May, *Love and Will* (New York: Norton, 1969), p. 20.

8. Sidney Kraus, *The Great Debate* (Bloomington: Indiana University Press, 1962). Several of the studies in this work bear on the image of the candidates.

9. Wayne Thompson, *Quantitative Research in Public Address and Communication* (New York: Random House, 1967), pp. 50–53.

10. Carroll Arnold, "What's Reasonable?" *Today's Speech,* 19 (Summer 1971), 19–23.

11. Ibid., p. 22.

12. Robert B. Maxwell, "The 'Graying' of America," *Vital Speeches of the Day,* September 15, 1987, p. 710.

13. Jim Courter, "Step By Step," *Vital Speeches of the Day,* July 15, 1987, p. 581.

14. The role of the enthymeme as a rhetorical syllogism has been reassessed by Thomas M. Conley, "The Enthymeme in Perspective," *Quarterly Journal of Speech,* 70 (May 1984), 168–187.

15. Donald M. Stewart, "Good Writing," *Vital Speeches of the Day,* August 1, 1987, p. 633.

16. Malcolm Wallop, "Offense-Defense Strategic Balance in the 1990s," *Vital Speeches of the Day,* August 1, 1987, p. 613.

17. Duane A. Kullberg, "Accounting and Accountability," *Vital Speeches of the Day,* July 15, 1987, p. 608.

18. Stephen Toulmin, *The Uses of Argument* (Cambridge: Cambridge University Press, 1964). Toulmin developed a different view of the argument structure in his *Knowing and Acting* (New York: Macmillan, 1979) and has elaborated his original model in Stephen Toulmin, Richard Rieke, and Allan Janik, *An Introduction to Reasoning* (New York: Macmillan, 1984).

19. For a discussion of some of these research studies, see Raymond S. Ross, *Persuasion: Communication and Interpersonal Relations* (Englewood Cliffs, N.J.: Prentice-Hall, 1974), pp. 187–193.

20. William J. McGuire, "Inducing Resistance to Persuasion," in Leonard Berkowitz, ed., *Advances in Experimental Social Psychology* (New York: Academic Press, 1964), pp. 196–203. Also see W. Richard Ullman and Edward M. Bodaken, "Inducing Resistance to Persuasive Attack: A Test of Two Strategies of Communication," *Western Speech Communication,* 39 (Fall 1975), 240–248.

21. Thomas B. Harte, "The Effects of Evidence in Persuasive Communication," *Central States Speech Journal,* 27 (Spring 1976), 42–46.

22. Leon Festinger, *A Theory of Cognitive Dissonance* (Stanford, Calif.: Stanford University Press, 1963).

23. Paulson.

24. Abraham Maslow, *Motivation and Personality* (New York: Harper & Row, 1970), pp. 35–58. How Maslow's hierarchy reflects today's societal needs is demonstrated in M. Joseph Sirgy, "A Quality-of-Life Theory Derived from Maslow's Developmental Perspective," *American Journal of Economics and Sociology,* 45 (July 1986), 329–342.

25. Bob Spichen, "New Attitude: AIDS, Crusades Promote Change of Habits," *Norfolk Virginian Pilot,* August 12, 1987, pp. 1, 3; and David M. Gross and

Sophfronia Scott, "Proceeding with Caution," *Time,* July 16, 1990, pp. 56–62.

26. Michael Adams, "Motivational Speaking: Is It Just a Quick Fix?" *Successful Meetings* (June 1987), 40.

27. This discussion is adapted from Douglas Ehninger, Bruce E. Gronbeck, Ray E. McKerrow, and Alan H. Monroe, *Principles and Types of Speech Communication,* 9th ed. (Glenview, Ill.: Scott, Foresman, 1982), Chapter 6, and subsequent editions.

28. A comprehensive summary of research on fear appeals is provided by C. William Colburn, "Fear Arousing Appeals," in Howard Martin and Kenneth Anderson, eds., *Speech Communication: Analysis and Readings* (Boston: Allyn and Bacon, 1968), pp. 214–226. Also see Ronald W. Rogers, "Attitude Change and Information Integration in Fear Appeals," *Psychological Reports,* 56 (February 1985), 179–182.

29. Brad Edmondson, "Read This Article—Or Your Kids Will Be Stupid," *Washington Post,* March 2, 1986, p. C-1. See also Lorne Bozinoff and Morry Ghingold, "Evaluating Guilt-Arousing Marketing Communications," *Journal of Business Research,* 11 (June 1983), 243–255.

30. For a discussion of how humor is healthy, see Victor Cohn, "He Who Laughs Lasts Longer," *Washington Post Health,* August 18, 1987, pp. 10–13.

31. For a discussion of the problem with loyalty in work, see Wayne Sage, "The Discontented Worker," *Human Behavior,* 2 (June 1973), 64–65.

32. For a discussion of power as a motivator, see David C. McClelland, "Love and Power: The Psychological Signals of War," *Psychology Today,* 9 (January 1975), 44–48.

33. George Gallup, Jr., "4 in 10 Adults Attended Church in Typical Week of 1986" (Princeton, N.J.: Gallup Poll, December 28, 1986).

34. Wilson Bryan Key, *Media Sexploitation* (New York: Signet Books, 1976), p. 15. For a critical analysis of Key's work, see Cecil Adams, "The Straight Dope," *City Paper,* July 10, 1987, p. 8.

Parting Thoughts

Throughout this text we have looked at the process of human communication as a transaction in which a communicator/source and a communicator/receiver participate. We have viewed this transaction on three levels—intrapersonal, interpersonal, and public.

We have provided you with just a foundation, a beginning from which you can build your knowledge of and abilities in communication. As communication technology becomes increasingly sophisticated, the challenges facing all of us as communicators will continue. Only a solid foundation of communication skills will enable each of us to cope with these challenges and develop the strategies to communicate effectively in this ever-changing world.

We feel that it is important that you responsibly apply the basic principles and techniques we have presented. Communicator/sources have an obligation to present rational, substantial messages that are appropriate to communicator/receivers. Likewise, communicator/receivers owe it to communicator/sources and to themselves to give these messages fair and complete hearings before forming judgments about them.

Our hope is that responsible communication will ensure a continuation of an essential American freedom—the freedom of speech—and an ever-widening international dialogue dedicated to peace throughout the world. Our social and our career relationships depend on that dialogue.

APPENDIXES

Appendix 1

The Resume

Your resume is a summary of facts about yourself. It should highlight your accomplishments as well as interest the reader. A well-written resume opens employment doors; one poorly written shuts them.

Most experts in the employment field agree that a resume should be sent with the original application letter. However, an outplacement service might advise you not to send a resume with an application. Their argument is that a resume should be prepared, but contrary to advice often promulgated, it should not be used. Resumes lose more jobs than they gain. The reason is that if the resume doesn't say precisely what the employer wants to see, he or she assumes that you aren't the right person for the job. Those who propose this approach suggest that you replace the resume with a letter that includes the highlights you wish to stress based on the want ad you are answering (or that the placement service information be sent) and take the resume to the interview to share with the prospective employer if you are requested to produce a personal summary.

If you decide to prepare a resume, here are some suggestions:

1. *Length.* Although resumes have no standard length, one typed page is usually enough for recent graduates. Include all details necessary to sell yourself for that particular job and then stop.

2. *Attitude.* Focus on things in your past that make you appear to be the best candidate for the job. If your grades are high, mention them; if not, do not refer to them. Stress your strengths, whether they are involvement in specific types of courses, extracurricular activities, or employment history.

3. *Preparation.* Use words and phrases you are familiar with, and be sure that spelling and grammar are correct. Type the material on

good-quality paper with a dark ribbon. If you have a word processor, tailor each resume to fit the job description.

What should be included in a resume? All resumes start with the identification (your name, address, and telephone number), which should be at the top of the page. If you have a school address and a permanent address and phone number, include both.

The facts about yourself are found in the body of the resume. The body usually includes your education, work experience, skills or capabilities, and personal interests. In listing your education, start with your present or most recent educational institution and list other institutions in reverse order. Include the school's name and location, your degree, your major and minor, and the dates you attended.

Your list of work experience should include the job title and responsibilities, the employer's name, and the dates you worked. This is usually presented in reverse order starting with your most recent experience. Your list of talents should include skills such as your ability to operate a computer or other business machines and any special knowledge you have, as well as interests (sports, hobbies, and so on).

You may also include references in the resume. Some people prefer to list references in the cover letter that accompanies the resume or to omit them unless they are requested. You may include a statement indicating your job or career objective, but some question the value of this statement as it could discourage a potential employer if the wording does not exactly fit the job description. If you decide to include a career objective (in which you state what type of position you are seeking), word the statement to parallel the job requirements.

If you are a recent graduate you may want to include extracurricular activities and collegiate honors. Accomplishments and achievements such as membership in honor societies, any awards you were given, special academic honors (for example, dean's list), and organizational offices held can be included. Don't brag: just list your accomplishments. State the facts, avoiding words such as "excellent," "widely acclaimed," and "successful."

The layout and design of a resume are important and should say something about you. Let your resume reflect your personality and your abilities. If you are creative, do a creative layout. If you are traditional, follow a traditional mode of organization. Remember, the bottom line is, "Am I proud of the content and appearance of my resume?"

Sample Resume: Recent Four-Year-Degree University Graduate Seeking Her First Career-Focused Employment

MARCIA RENEE HARLAN

<u>Home Address</u>   <u>Office/School Address</u>
124 Winchester Court   Rm.312 Key Hall
Elyria, Ohio 44035   Ohio University
216-366-8113   Athens, Ohio 45701

OBJECTIVE: To work with speech and hearing-handicapped children

EDUCATION: Ohio University, Athens, Ohio
               Bachelor of Science, May 1991
               Hearing and Speech Sciences and
                  Developmentally Handicapped

               Lorain County Community College
               Special Program in Speech and Language Pathology

HONORS: Dean's List—Fall and Spring, 1990 and 1991
               Mortar Board Honor Society, 1990

EXPERIENCE: Lancaster City Schools, Lancaster, Ohio
               Student Teacher in Speech, Language, and Hearing
                  Therapy

               Elyria Public Schools, Elyria, Ohio
               Field Experience in Speech-Language Therapy

               Ohio University Speech and Hearing Clinic, Athens, Ohio
               Client Practitioner—Hearing Impaired and
                  Language Therapy

               Murray Ridge School and Workshop, Elyria, Ohio
               Speech and Language Therapy Intern for Children
                  and Adults

SKILLS: Audiological Testing
               Auditory Trainer Equipment Operation
               Sign Language (ASL and Traditional)
               Sign Language for the Developmentally Handicapped
               Bliss Symbols
               Augmentative Communication Skills
               Computer Operation
               Typing

Appendix 2

Additional Readings

S tudents often find it both interesting and necessary to learn more about a subject. We encourage those of you who wish to do more research to refer to the footnote references at the end of each chapter. In this section we have added additional annotated references that may be of further help. Although this list is in no way intended to be a complete catalogue of the resources available, it does contain some materials that both students and researchers have found useful. These readings go beyond the academic communication research volumes into the fields of psychology, sociology, as well as self-help and self-awareness materials.

Chapter 1

Berko, Roy M., Andrew Wolvin, and Ray Curtis. *This Business of Communicating,* 4th ed. (Dubuque: William C. Brown, 1990). These authors investigate the communication skills needed by people entering or already working in the world of business. Practical ways to use communication skills are also covered.

Borden, George A. *Cultural Orientation: An Approach to Understanding Intercultural Communication* (Englewood Cliffs, N.J.: Prentice-Hall, 1991). This book explores culture's cognitive structures and processes and the belief systems on which they act.

Bormann, Ernest G. *Communication Theory* (New York: Holt, Rinehart & Winston, 1980). This book describes various approaches to the understanding of human communication. Bormann reviews the philosophy of science as well as humanistic approaches to communication and also analyzes communication styles.

Chesebro, James W., and Bonsall, Donald G. *Computer-Mediated Communication* (Tuscaloosa: University of Alabama Press, 1989). This book examines ways in which people respond to personal computers. The authors argue that computers have changed the nature of human communication and, as a result, the values and ideology of American society.

Copeland, Lennie, and Lewis Griggs. *Going International* (New York: Random

House, 1985). This book, subtitled "How to Make Friends and Deal Effectively in the Global Marketplace," includes an entire chapter (Chapter 5) on communicating effectively in other cultures. Designed for the American traveler, businessperson, or both, the book offers a solid foundation for improving intercultural communication. An excellent videotape series has been produced to accompany this book.

Dance, Frank E. X. *Human Communication Theory* (New York: Harper & Row, 1982). A collection of essays by some notable theorists in the communication field that provides insight into various dimensions of the human communication process.

Devito, Joseph A. *The Communication Handbook: A Dictionary* (New York: Harper & Row, 1986). A listing and discussion of the central terms used in the broad field of communication.

Faber, Adele, and Elaine Mazlish. *How to Talk So Kids Will Listen and Listen So Kids Will Talk* (New York: Avon, 1980). This book, by the authors of *Liberated Parents/Liberated Children,* introduces effective verbal communication skills for parents to use with their children. The verbal messages are designed to help children deal with their feelings, engage cooperation, provide an alternative to punishment, encourage autonomy, extend praise, and free children from playing roles.

Farrell, Warren. *The Liberated Man: Beyond Masculinity, Freeing Men and Their Relationships with Women* (New York: Bantam, 1975). This book is for every man who has ever thought, "A job, a wife and kids—there must be something more." Farrell offers a positive, practical alternative to the economic, emotional, and physical burdens that many men face.

Galvin, Kathleen M., and Bernard J. Brommel. *Family Communication: Cohesion and Change,* 3rd ed. (New York: HarperCollins, 1991). This book offers a detailed look at the dynamics of the family unit from a communication perspective. The authors summarize the extensive research on family communication and offer experiences to exemplify the principles so that the reader can make applications of the research to family situations.

Ginott, Haim. *Parent and Child* (New York: Avon, 1965). Communication is the key to the relationship between parent and child. Ginott's direct, fresh, and easily understood method of getting through to a child is designed to promote responsibility, love, and respect.

Goldhaber, Gerald M. *Organizational Communication,* 5th ed. (Dubuque, Iowa: William C. Brown, 1990). One of the classics in the field, this book offers a thorough description of the process of communication within the organization. Goldhaber develops his description of the communication system from an analysis of organizational behavior, offering strategies for organizational change through effective communication.

Griffin, Em. *A First Look at Communication Theory* (New York: McGraw-Hill, 1991). Aimed at students who have no background in communication theory, this book presents thirty-one specific theories in a way that makes them both interesting and understandable.

Hart, Roderick P., and Ronald L. Applbaum (eds.) *Scott, Foresman PROCOM Series* (Glenview, Ill.: Scott, Foresman, 1984). This series of short books, by different authors, is designed to provide insight into communication in professional fields. The collection includes books for trial attorneys, corporate managers, engineers, office workers, government workers, nurses, physicians, and police officers.

Jamieson, Kathleen Hall, and Karlyn Kohrs Campbell. *The Interplay of Influence,* 2nd ed. (Belmont, Calif.: Wadsworth, 1988). A detailed analysis of mass media and the biases inherent in both news and entertainment programming and advertising. The authors detail strategies for influencing radio and television decision makers as well as strategies for understanding the efforts to influence listeners.

Johnson, William B., and Arnold H. Packer. *Workforce 2000* (Indianapolis: Hudson Institute, 1987). This study identifies six challenges facing American organizations and their changing workforce: stimulating world growth, improving service productivity, dealing with the aging workforce, meeting the needs of women and families, integrating blacks and Hispanics, and improving workers' education and skills.

Kelly, Lynne, Linda C. Lederman, and Gerald M. Phillips. *Communication in the Workplace: A Guide to Business and Professional Speaking* (New York: Harper & Row, 1989). Recognizing the importance of strong communication skills for success on the job, this text helps explain the concepts of effective communication in various business and professional settings.

Littlejohn, Stephen W. *Theories of Human Communication,* 3rd ed. (Belmont, Calif.: Wadsworth, 1989). This book offers a thorough review of the major influences on our understanding of human communication theory. Littlejohn surveys the major theories in symbolic interactionism, general systems theory, language, meaning, information processing, persuasion, interpersonal communication, and mass communication. His chapters offer a complete review for the serious student of communication.

Naisbitt, John, and Patricia Aburdene. *2000* (New York: William Morrow, 1990). Building on their earlier book, *Megatrends,* which examined the trends that were shaping the 1980s, the authors project the influences that will affect society in the 1990s. They treat the globalization of the economy, renaissance of the arts, emergence of free-market socialism, privatization of the welfare state, cultural nationalism, Asian influences, women in leadership, biological advances, religious revival, and individualism as the major forces shaping the 1990s.

Napier, Augustus, and Carl Whitaker. *The Family Crucible* (New York: Bantam, 1980). These authors try to help readers understand troubled marriages, troubled children, and troubled selves by examining family therapy.

Newcomb, Horace. *Television—The Critical View* (New York: Oxford University Press, 1985). This collection of essays examines television in terms of program types, cultural meanings, and definitions of the medium itself. The editor urges all viewers to become more critical in processing television messages.

Ouchi, William. *Theory Z* (Reading, Mass.: Addison-Wesley, 1981). Ouchi analyzes the success of Japanese management and describes the people-oriented management style that is given credit for the high level of Japanese productivity. He also demonstrates how Japanese management techniques can best be adapted to the needs of American industry.

Pascale, Richard T., and Anthony G. Athos. *The Art of Japanese Management* (New York: Warner, 1981). This book describes many management techniques

found in Japanese industry. The authors describe the framework for management effectiveness in Japan, revealing that many of the strategies have to do
with effective communication.

Pearson, Judy. *Communication in the Family: Seeking Satisfaction in Changing
Times* (New York: Harper & Row, 1989). Illustrating concepts with true-life
examples, this book discusses roles in family communication, the developmental
stages of families, and communicative behaviors that promote satisfaction.

Peter, Laurence, and Raymond Hull. *The Peter Principle* (New York: Morrow,
1969). These authors apply the popular theory that an individual rises to the
level at which he or she proves incompetent to problems within institutions
(schools, governments, courts, businesses). This theory has prompted some re-
formulation of the criteria for hiring administrators in such institutions.

Peters, Thomas J., and Robert H. Waterman, Jr. *In Search of Excellence* (New
York: Harper & Row, 1982). This book describes some of America's best-run
companies. In their research, the authors uncovered eight basic principles that
characterize the most effective organizations. Many of these principles stem from
effective communication or have implications for effective communication
within organizations.

Peters, Thomas J., and Nancy Austin. *A Passion for Excellence* (New York:
Warner, 1985). This book, a follow-up to *In Search of Excellence,* details the role
of communication—especially listening—as part of the Management by Wandering Around principle. The book offers many actual examples from corporations to illustrate what makes an organization effective: the key to which is
effective communication.

Peters, Thomas. *Thriving on Chaos* (New York: Knopf, 1988). In this work,
Peters argues that today's organizations are characterized by chaos and uncertainty, and effective leaders are able to respond proactively to the unsettling
nature of the workplace and accomplish a great deal. Peters urges attention to
building a listening environment to enhance communication in the organization.

"Retrospective: Communication 1940–1989," *Time* (1989). This special retrospective edition of *Time* magazine is devoted to the history of the communication
explosion, from Franklin D. Roosevelt's first Fireside Chat on January 6, 1941,
to China's televised crackdown on the prodemocracy movement at Tiananmen
Square.

Samovar, Larry A., and Richard E. Porter. *Intercultural Communication: A
Reader,* 6th ed. (Belmont, Calif.: Wadsworth, 1991). This work examines co-cul-
tures both within the United States and globally. It provides both theoretical
and immediately usable knowledge about the intercultural communication processes by presenting nineteen essays, many of which were prepared specifically
for this volume.

Samovar, Larry A., Richard E. Porter, and Nemi C. Jain. *Understanding Intercultural Communication* (Belmont, Calif.: Wadsworth, 1991). A widely used text
dealing with the principles of intercultural communication.

Sheehy, Gail. *Passages* (New York: Bantam, 1977). This classic book examines
the stages of adult life, offering considerable insight into the crises people are
likely to confront at various times and proposing ways of dealing with these
crises.

Splaine, John. *The Critical Viewing of Television* (South Hamilton, Mass.: Critical